NATIONALISM
AND
COMMUNAL POLITICS IN INDIA,
1916-1928

Nationalism and Communal Politics in India 1916-1928

MUSHIRUL HASAN

First Published 1979
© MUSHIRUL HASAN 1979

ISBN 0-8364-0198-0

Published in the United States of America by
South Asia Books

 South Asia Books

First Published 1979
© MUSHIRUL HASAN 1979

ISBN 0-8364-0198-0

Published in the United States of America by
South Asia Books
Box 502
Columbia, Mo. 65201

By arrangement with
Manohar Publications
2 Ansari Road, Daryaganj
New Delhi-110002

Printed in India
Dhawan Printing Works,
26-A Mayapuri, Phase 1
New Delhi-110064

TO MY FATHER

ACKNOWLEDGEMENTS

This book is a revised version of my Ph.D. thesis presented at Cambridge University in 1977. It could not have been completed without a great deal of help from many people in many places. In particular, I would like to thank Professor Eric Stokes, Dr Francis Robinson, Dr C.A. Bayly, Dr B.R. Tomlinson, Dr Sudhir Chandra, Dr Hari Vasudevan, Dr Zoya Khaliq and Dr Anil Seal. They have seen and commented on various chapters of the book in its earlier stages, and I have attempted to rewrite them in line with their criticisms. None, however, have seen the final form of the work and they are in no sense responsible for the statements and views I express in it.

I am grateful to the Master and Fellows of Trinity College and the Managers of the Smuts Memorial Fund for a research and travel grant which enabled me to work in England during 1974 and 1977.

For most of my materials, I have depended on the following libraries: National Archives of India, the Nehru Memorial Museum and Library, the Jamia Millia Islamia Library, the Uttar Pradesh State Archives, Lucknow, the National Library, Calcutta, the Sir Syed Archives, Aligarh, the Mahmudabad Library, the India Office Library and Records, the Cambridge Centre of South Asian Studies and the Cambridge University Library. I would like to thank the librarians and staff of all these libraries for their kind and courteous help.

My greatest debt of gratitude is to my father, Professor Mohibbul Hasan, and my brother, Mujeebul Hasan, whose constant encouragement and generosity made this book possible.

MUSHIRUL HASAN

Jamia Millia Islamia
15 November 1978

ABBREVIATIONS

AICC	All-India Congress Committee
AMUA	Aligarh Muslim University Archives
BENNR	Report on Native Newspapers in Bengal
BNNR	Report on Native Newspapers in Bombay
CUL	Cambridge University Library
CWG	The Collected Works of M.K. Gandhi
DG	District Gazetteer
EUR	European
FM	Firangi Mahal
FR	Fortnightly Report
GAD	General Administration Department
IESHR	*Indian Economic and Social History Review*
INC	Indian National Congress
IOL	India Office Library, London
JAS	*The Journal of Asian Studies*
JMIL	Jamia Millia Islamia Library, New Delhi
JNML	Jawaharlal Nehru Memorial Museum and Library, New Delhi
MAS	*Modern Asian Studies*
MSS	Manuscript
NAI	National Archives of India
NLC	National Library, Calcutta
Poll.	Political
PSC	Public Service Commission
PUNNR	Report on Native Press in the Punjab
SWJ	Selected Works of J. Nehru
UPNNR	Report on Native Press in the North-West Provinces or the North West Provinces and Oudh or the United Provinces
UPSA	Uttar Pradesh State Archives, Lucknow
WRDCI	Weekly Report of the Director of Central Intelligence

Since it is not for us to create a plan for the future that will hold for all time, all the more surely, what we contemporaries have to do is the uncompromising critical evaluation of all that exists, uncompromising in the sense that our criticism fears neither its own results nor the conflict with the powers that be.

KARL MARX

CONTENTS

LIST OF TABLES

INTRODUCTION

The partition of India in August 1947 set off an acrimonious debate on the question of responsibility. Some Indian writings squarely blame the British government for encouraging and fostering Muslim separatism, arguing that the British introduced separate electorates and granted special concessions to the Muslims in order to widen and exploit the existing cleavages in Indian society, and to disrupt the Indian national movement.[1] Various schools of historians have conveniently, but uncritically, accepted this argument which was also often employed by Indian leaders during the freedom struggle.[2]

Historians in Pakistan have no sympathy with this interpretation. The British, according to them, did not creaet Pakistan. It came into being because the Muslims were a nation, distinct and separate from other communities in India,[3] and their conflict with the Hindus had existed long before the British

---

[1]A. Mehta and A. Patwardhan, *The Communal Triangle in India* (Allahabad, 1942); A.R. Desai, *Social Background of Indian Nationalism* (Bombay, 1976 edn.); H. Kabir, *Muslim Politics* (Calcutta, 1969); I. Prasad and S.K. Subedar, *Hindu-Muslim Relations* (Allahabad, 1974).

[2]'The present seemingly irreconcilable differences between the Hindus and Muslims', observed Rajendra Prasad in 1946, 'are in no small measure the result of a deliberate application of the policy of divide and rule'. R. Prasad, *India Divided* (Bombay, 1946), p. 83; Also, see J. Nehru, *An Autobiography* (London, 1936), p. 136; L. Rai, *Unhappy India* (Calcutta, 1928), 2nd edn., pp. 399-400.

[3]The best formulation of this argument is in I.H. Qureshi, *The Muslim Community of the Indo-Pakistan Subcontinent*, 610-1947 (The Hague, 1962) and K.K. Aziz, *The Making of Pakistan: A Study in Nationalism* (London, 1967), pp. 94-95.

came to India.[4] This formed the basis of the two-nation theory advocated by M.A. Jinnah in the early 1940s and, after 1947, served as an *ipso facto* justification of the partition.

The argument that the Hindus and the Muslims were organised on communal lines and were in a state of perpetual conflict and confrontation[5] exaggerates the role of the divisive forces in Indian society and ignores the more powerful cohesive and unifying elements which so often brought members of various castes, sects, and communities together. There is irrefutable evidence to suggest that the vast majority of Indians lived together without antipathy or bitterness,[6] and separate religious loyalties rarely prevented them from working on a cross-communal network. The reasons are not far to seek. Many Muslims had more in common with the Hindu groups than with their co-religionists; so they had every reason to live in peace and amity and promote their common interests. The Hindu and Muslim landowners, for example, often had common

[4]'The Hindu-Muslim problem', according to K.K. Aziz, 'was imbedded in the historical logic of India. Britain only witnessed it; she did not create or aggravate it'. K.K. Aziz, *Britain and Muslim India: A study of British Public Opinion vis-a-vis the Development of Muslim Nationalism in India, 1857-1947* (London, 1963), pp. 206-207.

[5]'The history of medieval and modern India is to a very considerable extent a history of Hindu-Muslim religio-cultural tensions. . . . The divisive forces have proved much more dynamic than the cohesive ones'. A. Ahmad, *Islamic Culture in the Indian Environment* (Oxford, 1964), p. 74.

[6]There is no doubt that the vast majority of Muslims who were originally converts came to live with the Hindus peacefully and merged with them by economic fusion and inter-marriages. Hindu influences on their beliefs and practices went right to the heart of their everyday life. In the villages, many Muslims retained their Hindu traditions and social forms. The Kamalias of Gujarat, for example, professed Islam but worshipped a Hindu Goddess, Bahacharji, and served as musicians in her temple. The integration between Hindus and Muslims was also evident at the *khanqahs* of the sufis. As institutions of cultural adaptation, the *khanqahs* provided a means of incorporating Hindu religious customs and beliefs into the eclectic fold with an Islamic colouring. The Sufis adopted many practices from the Hindu yogis—extreme ascetic discipline, celibacy and vegetarianism. Many of them also had Hindu disciples. One Hassu Taili in the Punjab, for instance, had a number of Hindu disciples. Bengal evolved a new God called Satyapir—a combination of the Hindu God, Satyanarayan, and Muslim *pir*.

interests and habits of cooperation. Not surprisingly, they gave precedence to their class interests over their communal identity in order to preserve their dominance in rural areas.

To treat Hindus and Muslims as monolithic communities is equally misleading. Even a cursory glance at the census reports reveals the differences which divided the members of each community at various levels, a fact which was evident in their political, economic, and social activities. The historian of modern India would do well to discard the conventional but misleading framework of reference of united homogeneous communities. By doing so, he will be able to explain the emergence of communalism from a fresh standpoint, identify the groups who organised communal politics, and discover their interests and motivations. These aspects, which are discussed in this book, would also help us to understand why communalism in general, and Muslim separatism in particular, became such an important force in Indian politics.

Having rejected the framework of a homogeneous community, the historian is then faced with the task of explaining why some Muslims were able to unite their co-religionists over several issues such as the Kanpur mosque incident, the Khilafat movement, the Sarda Marriage Bill, and the popular demand for a separate Muslim homeland. This study seeks to offer an explanation for this. It also attempts to redefine the nature of the Muslim community. The questions it poses are: What is the environment of an Indian Muslim? Is it a homogeneous community, with one life, identical interests, and common aspirations? Or, does it contain a seething mass of heterogeneous people working and thinking apart from each other?

While seeking answers to these questions, the central concern of this book is to examine the relationship between the Indian National Congress and the various Muslim groups in the 1920s—an aspect which, for the most part, is not adequately studied by the standard accounts of the period. The importance of this theme cannot be denied. After all, the Congress emerged as the most powerful political organisation in the country during this period. It reflected, perhaps for the first time in its history, the hopes and aspirations of a wider spectrum of the Indian people, and served as a main channel for the articulation of their interests. This entailed two things.

First, the Congress leaders had to achieve a degree of consensus on various political issues in order to maintain the all-India status and character of their organisation. Secondly, they had to reconcile their all-India political demands with the narrow sectarian and parochial claims of their clients and supporters in the provinces and the districts. But this was by no means easy to achieve as is evident from the attitude of many Muslims.

Soon after the Congress was established in 1885, some leading Muslims decided either to keep aloof from its activities or demanded a price for their cooperation. The Congress leaders had no choice except to try and secure their support through political agreements, unity conferences, and pacts. In doing so, they made certain assumptions about the Muslim community which largely determined their attitude towards the political and religious claims advanced by the dominant Muslim groups. We propose to examine these assumptions and their implications. We will also endeavour to identify the groups with which the Congress leaders tried to forge an alliance in the 1920s, to study their relationships, and to assess their impact on politics as a whole. All these questions are relevant not only for our understanding of communal politics in the 1920s, but also for the subsequent history of the subcontinent. Many Indians, who were in the forefront of national politics in the 1920s, played a leading role in the thirties as well as in the forties. Similarly, several issues which dominated the all-India stage and embittered Hindu-Muslim relations in the years following the suspension of civil disobedience in 1922 continued to divide Indian politicians in the subsequent decades. The great communal debates of the thirties and the forties can be meaningfully understood only if the 1920s are first put into a clear perspective.

There are several levels at which Congress attitudes can be studied. This work concentrates on the national level because it is only at this level that parts of the communal problem came together into a coherent whole. The analysis which it offers is based mainly on the study of all-India organisations and all-India politicians. Leading Indian politicians such as Mohamed Ali, Mukhtar Ahmad Ansari, Gandhi, Motilal Nehru, Lala Lajpat Rai, Madan Mohan Malaviya, Tej Bahadur Sapru and Mohammad Ali Jinnah operated at the national level because their interests were not confined to provincial and local issues. Increasingly, the government was unable to ignore such men in developing its imperial strategy. Provincial and local leaders of various interest groups had equally to take account of the all-India politicians and often followed their directives when it suited them to do so. They did so, for example, during the Khilafat and Non-cooperation movements. Furthermore, many of the principal events in the 1920s—the signing of the Lucknow Pact, the agitation for the release of Muslim detenus, the Khilafat and Non-cooperation movements, and the making of the Nehru Report—were in fact dominated by politicians whose largest role was on the national arena. By observing their activities, we can uncover many hitherto unknown aspects of communal politics in the 1920s.

This study has not, however, ignored the provinces; for the high politics of the Congress, the Muslim League, and the Khilafat leaders can be fully explained only by investigating their relationships with their supporters in the provinces and the districts. Furthermore, the responses of different Muslim groups to various political issues can be understood only at the provincial level against the background of their economic and educational standing in the region. The reason is obvious. Muslims did not respond either to British policies or to Congress activities with one voice because their interests, as this study will indicate, varied from area to area. For this reason, their reactions to the Lucknow Pact, the Montagu-Chelmsford Reforms, and the Nehru Report are analysed in the context of three provinces: Bengal, Punjab and the United Provinces.[7]

The reasons for selecting and concentrating on only three provinces needs some explanation. In Bengal and the Punjab, Muslims formed a majority—54 and 55.33 per cent respectively—of the population. This fact was of little importance so long as the franchise was limited and representation to the legislative councils and local bodies was confined to men of substance only. But once the franchise was extended (under the Montagu-

---

[7] Until 1902, the province now known as Uttar Pradesh, was called the North-West Provinces and Oudh. Throughout this work, the area will be referred to as the UP.

Chelmsford Reforms) and the power distributed, at least
in some measure, according to population, many influential
Bengali and Punjabi Muslims began to play an increasingly
important role in provincial and national politics.[8] They not
only refused to play second fiddle to Muslim leadership in the
UP, but also saw the advantage of formulating their own
independent political strategy designed to promote their regional
interests. Men like Fazl-i-Husain in the Punjab and Fazlul Haq
in Bengal played no small part in the organisation of Muslim
separatist politics. In the aftermath of the Khilafat movement,
they were deeply involved in the acrimonious communal debates
which dominated the national movement and eventually led to
the partition of the country. With their followers they wrested
the initiative from the UP Muslims who, from 1922 to 1937,
ceased to dominate Muslim politics.

In the UP, though the Muslims were a mere fourteen per
cent of the population, they were more advanced, more prosperous, and more influential than their co-religionists in other
provinces. They were the pioneers of Western education in their
community and the founders of some leading centres of learning which played no mean part in the religious, educational,
and social affairs of the Indian Muslims. The M.A.O. College
at Aligarh, the *Dar al-ulum* at Deoband, the *Nadwat al-ulama*,
and the Firangi Mahal at Lucknow were all located in the UP.

The UP Muslims were also in the forefront of politics, a
position they acquired largely because of their influence in
government service and in the professions.[9] They organised the
Simla Deputation which presented a set of political demands
on 1 October 1906 to the Viceroy; they founded the All-India
Muslim League in December 1906;[10] and in 1911, they initiated
the move towards promoting rapprochement with the Congress
which culminated in the Lucknow Pact of December 1916. And
finally, it was mainly the Muslim men of the UP who led and

[8]For an elaboration of this argument, see D.J.H. Page, 'Prelude to
Partition: All India Muslim Politics, 1909-32' (Unpublished D. Phil.
thesis, Oxford, 1973).

[9]For a detailed and scholarly study of the role of the UP Muslims,
see Francis Robinson, *Separatism Among Indian Muslims: The Politics of
the United Provinces' Muslims 1860-1923* (Cambridge, 1974).

[10]*Ibid.*, pp. 143-44, 148-49.

dominated the Khilafat and the Non-cooperation movements. These included, among others, the Ali Brothers, the volatile Khilafat agitators; Abdul Bari, an *alim* of Firangi Mahal and one of the founders of the *Anjuman-i-Khuddam-i-Kaaba*; Mukhtar Ahmad Ansari, the chief organiser of the All-India Medical Mission to Constantinople and president of the All-India Khilafat Conference held in 1922; M.H. Kidwai, one of the founders of the *Anjuman-i-Khuddam-i-Kaaba*, who was much involved in pan-Islamic activities both in India and abroad; and Hasrat Mohani, poet-politician, who was noted for his pan-Islamic and virulently anti-British views. If these men figure prominently throughout this study, it is because of their leading role in Indian politics in general, and the Khilafat and Non-cooperation movements, in particular.

And lastly, this account concentrates on the years 1916 to 1928, a short but vital period in the history of modern India. These years saw the making and the collapse of an extraordinary alliance between the Congress and some Muslims, particularly those from the UP. In 1916, they reached a political agreement in which the Congress accepted the same privileges for Muslims in future constitutional reforms as the government had agreed to in 1906. This was followed by an unprecedented period of Hindu-Muslim fraternisation culminating in the Khilafat and Non-cooperation movements. Gandhi, who was the moving spirit behind both these movements, rose to power during this period not least by forging an alliance with the *ulama* and some leading Muslim professional men. Oddly enough, Gandhi organised, directed, and led the Khilafat movement from October 1919 onwards. His Muslim allies merely followed his leadership. They had plans of their own, but these could not be pressed without the blessings of the Mahatma.

By the end of 1922, however, the joint Hindu-Muslim front in Indian politics collapsed. Gandhi's alliance with the Khilafatists also crumbled, and there was another spate of communal violence in different parts of the country. Many of his Muslim followers deserted him. They took up communal causes and relentlessly compaigned against Gandhi and the Congress leadership culminating in a massive agitation against the Nehru Report, published in August 1928. The wheel had

turned full circle. The men who had helped to formulate the
Congress-Muslim League scheme in December 1916 were, in
1928, reluctant to come to terms with the Congress. Both dates
are, therefore, crucial in the history of nationalism and communalism. They highlight, apart from other developments, the
vicissitudes in the relationship between the Congress and the
Muslims. This aspect forms one of the principal themes of this
study.

CHAPTER ONE

THE MUSLIMS IN THE PUNJAB, BENGAL AND THE UNITED PROVINCES

In 1921, the Muslims numbered 69 million—one-fifth of the population of India. They were unevenly distributed throughout the country, their population ranging from 91 per cent in the North-West Frontier Province to less than 7 per cent in Madras (see Table 1.1). In absolute numbers they were most numerous in Bengal where they were 25,210,802 or 54 per cent of the population. In Bengal, the great majority of them were peasants, in origin probably low-caste Hindus, and were bunched in the northern, central, and eastern districts of the province. They were almost half, 47.3 per cent, in central Bengal, 59.8 per cent in northern Bengal, 69.9 per cent in eastern Bengal, and a mere 13.4 per cent in the western districts.[1]

In the Punjab, which lies on the route by which successive armies entered India, more than half of the population was Muslim. Migration and conversion created an Islamic community located predominantly in the western half of the province. The region was annexed to the Ghaznavid Empire in the eleventh century. It then fell to the Ghurides and remained under their effective control. The city of Lahore came to be of great strategic importance following the recurring Mongol invasions. Other centres like Multan also developed because of strategic and commercial reasons. Consequently, sufis, traders, scholars, administrators, and soldiers flocked to these cities from all

---

[1] *Census*, 1921, Bengal, Part I, p. 159.

parts of Central Asia. Muslim civilization, which has always and everywhere been urban-based, thus found a convenient foothold in the Punjab.

TABLE 1.1

DISTRIBUTION OF MUSLIM POPULATION, 1921

Province		Percentage of Muslim Population
Madras	2,840,488	6.71
Bombay	3,820,153	19.74
Bengal	25,210,802	54.00
United Provinces	6,481,032	14.28
Punjab	11,444,321	55.33
Bihar and Orissa	3,690,182	10.85
Central Provinces and Berar	563,574	4.05
Assam	2,202,460	28.96
North-West Frontier Province	2,062,786	91.62

Source: *Census*, 1921, India, Part II, p. 43.

The Punjab was also an important centre of Sufi activity which led to the conversion of many Hindus to Islam, particularly in the countryside.[2] The sufis established themselves around important towns and often penetrated deep into the rural areas to gain converts. The Suhrawardy order had its base in Multan; the Qadris established themselves at Uch in 1482; and the Chishti order was founded in the region by Baba Farid in the fourteenth century. He settled at Hansi in Hissar district which was inhabited by backward Hindu tribes, and is said to have converted some sixteen tribes in that area.

[2]The main stream of sufi influence followed into India from the north. Shaikh Ali Hujwairi, the author of the well-known work on sufism and the sufis, *Kashf al-Mahjub*, settled at Lahore and died there some time between 1072 and 1079. Shaikh Muinuddin Chishti, the founder of the Chishti order (*silsilah*) in India, established himself at Ajmer a little after 1192. The Qadri, Suhrawardy and the Naqshbandi were the other three main sufi orders in India.

In contrast with their co-religionists in Bengal and the Punjab, the UP Muslims were numerically in a minority. In 1921, they were just over six million, or 14.3 per cent of the total population of the province. But the UP Muslims had enjoyed a unique position in the political, economic, and cultural life of medieval India. This was largely because the region was the seat of Muslim power and the centre of intellectual activity. Turkish rule was first consolidated in the UP, and led to the growth of new cities such as Agra, Jaunpur, Firozabad and Moradabad. Some of these cities were important commercial and industrial centres; others were centres of government and therefore a rendezvous for the learned and resorts for architects, painters, poets, and historians. Jaunpur, the capital of the Sharqi Kings (1394-1500) was the *Shiraz-i-Hind* or the *Dar-ul-ilm* (abode of learning). Agra, on the other hand, was an important commercial and industrial centre under the Mughals. Founded in 1506, in about two centuries it became one of the world's greatest cities. All land routes in northern India radiated to and from Agra, rendering it 'the heart of the Empire' or the 'navel of the whole realm'. The city of Lucknow also remained the prime city of the province at least until 1856, when the kingdom of Oudh was annexed by the British. In size it was the largest city in the British Empire with the exception of the three presidency towns of Calcutta, Bombay and Madras. In cultural importance it had no rival in the UP. In the nineteenth and twentieth centuries, UP Muslims continued to play a key role in education and politics. They were the pioneers of Western education amongst their co-religionists, the founders of the All-India Muslim League, and the architects of Pakistan.

Although the Muslims were numerically strong, they were by no means a monolithic community. In addition to their economic, social, and cultural differences there were deep ideological conflicts which divided them. The Shias and Sunnis, for example, represent the two main sects in Islam. The Shias hold that Ali, cousin of the Prophet Mohammad and husband of his daughter Fatima, was the first legitimate successor (*khalifa*) of the Prophet. According to them, the office of *Imamat*, or spiritual headship of Muslims is hereditary, and it was bequeathed by the Prophet in favour of Ali, their first

Imam.[3] The Sunnis, on the other hand, maintain that the spiritual headship is neither hereditary nor restricted to the line of Ali. The duties of an *Imam* are to look to the temporal and spiritual weal of the community, and hence his nomination depends entirely upon the choice of the people. The Sunnis, therefore, regard Abu Bakr, Umar, and Usman, the first three *Khalifas* as 'heroes of the faith', while the Shias consider them as 'usurpers' of the claims of Ali and his family.

There were not many Shias in India. They numbered only 2,580 in Bengal, and formed a mere three per cent of the Muslim population in the Punjab and the UP. In the UP they were most numerous and influential in Lucknow, Amroha, Jaunpur, Bilgram, Rampur and Fyzabad. Some of the large landowners, such as the Rajas of Mahmudabad, of Pirpur, and of Salempur were Shias. The ruler of Rampur was converted to Shi'ism under the influence of the Oudh rulers.

Western India was the homeland of the Bohras, Khojas, Memons and other trading communities. The majority of Bohras were of Hindu origin, their ancestors having been converted by Ismaili missionaries, the first of whom is said to have landed in Cambay in 1067. They had both a Sunni and a Shia branch, the former included most of the city traders, the latter the rural agriculturists. A majority of them were, however, traders and merchants and only a few sought a career in government service or the professions.[4] The Khojas, like the Bohras, were also a trading community. They were the descendants of the Lohanas and of other trading castes, and were converted to Islam in the fifteenth century. Over the

---

[3]The list of the twelve Shia *Imams* begins with Ali and ends with the *Imam Mahdi*, who has for the present withdrawn from the world, but, it is believed, will appear again on the Day of Judgement. The religious life of the Shias centres round a body of traditions, beliefs and observances which have their source in Ali, Fatima, and their sons Hasan and Husain, who, with the Prophet, make up the *Panjatan-i-Pak*, the Five Holy Ones.

[4]The only exception was the cosmopolitan family of the Tyabjis. Badruddin Tyabji, who presided over the third Congress at Madras, was the first Muslim to qualify at the London bar; his brother, Camruddin was the first Muslim to be trained as a solicitor in England; his son, Mohsin Badruddin, was the first Muslim to pass the covenanted Civil Service examination.

centuries, they spread out of Sind, Kathiawar, and the Punjab and then from the late nineteenth century, began to settle in Bombay. In 1921, their population in India had reached just over one-hundred and forty-six thousand.[5] Some of the leading Khojas in public life were R.M. Sayani, the president of the Congress in 1896; Ibrahim Rahimtullah, member of the Bombay Legislative Council from 1899 to 1911; and Mohammad Ali Jinnah, the founder of Pakistan and its first Governor-General.

Divisions among Muslims were also reflected in their economic and educational status. The vast majority of Bengali Muslims were peasants. Among the ordinary cultivators, they were almost double the number of Hindus, but among the landlords there were nearly twice as many Hindus as Muslims.[6] The Permanent Settlement resulted in many families, mainly Muslims, losing their lands to a new class of Hindu landlords. The Resumption Proceedings between 1828-1846 not only further impoverished the few Muslim families which had survived the Permanent Settlement, but also destroyed the economic basis of Muslim educational institutions, which were almost entirely maintained by revenue-free grants.[7] By the end of the nineteenth century, most of the land in Bengal was owned by Hindus. In eastern Bengal, where Muslims were most numerous, this was particularly evident. In Bogra district, for example, Muslims formed 80 per cent of the population, but there were only five Muslim zamindars. In Bakargunj district, Muslims were 64.8 per cent of the population but owned less than 10 per cent of the estates and paid less than 9 per cent of the total land revenue.[8]

[5]For details, see J.C. Masselos, 'The Khojas of Bombay. The defining of formal membership during the nineteenth century', Imtiaz Ahmad (ed.), *Caste and Social Stratification among the Muslims* (Delhi, 1973), pp. 1-19.

[6]*Census*, 1921, Bengal, Part I, p. 413.

[7]William Bentinck, Governor-General of India from 1823 to 1853, decided to examine the title deeds of landholders and whoever failed to establish his full title to the grants from the Mughals, lost his landed property. See W.W. Hunter, *The Indian Musalmans* (Calcutta, 1945 edn.), pp. 177-79.

[8]A. Seal, *The Emergence of Indian Nationalism: Competition and Collaboration in the Later Nineteenth Century* (Cambridge, 1968), p. 300.

Furthermore, the revenue, judicial and educational reforms introduced by Warren Hastings and Cornwallis also contributed to the discomfiture of many Bengali Muslims. Such reforms either offended their religious susceptibilities,[9] or led to their displacement from various departments. Muslim revenue collectors, as well as judicial and executive officers, were gradually replaced by British collectors and magistrates. The substitution of English for Persian in 1837 and the introduction of examinations for certain services in the judicial service and the law was a further blow. As the Bengali Muslims generally kept away from English schools and colleges, they were unable to fulfil the educational qualifications required in the judicial service and the law. Table 1.2 indicates that from 1876 to 1886, only a handful of Muslims qualified for the Entrance and B.A. examinations at the University of Calcutta. This educational backwardness of Muslims was further reflected in their representation in government service and the professions. In 1851, there were more Muslim pleaders in the Calcutta High Court than Hindu and Christian pleaders combined. By 1868, however, they numbered only one. In 1869, among the attorneys, proctors, and solicitors there were twenty-seven Hindus, but there was no Muslim.[10] They fared no better in the judicial and executive services where there were only fifty-three, or 9.16 per cent, Muslim officers in 1886-87.[11] However, they were relatively better placed in the executive service where appointments on the whole, were by nomination. In the judicial service, on the other hand, recruitment was by nomination founded on a preliminary test, which led to the gradual exclusion of Muslims because of

[9] Warren Hastings (1754-1826), Cornwallis (1738-1805), and their successors modified or abolished many aspects of the Islamic law. The Madras High Court, for example, declared the law of pre-emption opposed to the principles of justice, equity and good commerce. Similarly, the rules of the *Sharia* regarding evidence was replaced by the Indian Evidence Act of 1872, and the Indian Penal Code, 1860, repealed the criminal law of Islam insofar as it was administered in the country. And finally, laws relating to revenues, land tenures and in part also transfer of property were gradually abandoned and replaced by enactments of legislature.

[10] Hunter, *The Indian Musalmans*, p. 164.

[11] *Proceedings of the Public Service Commission* (he nceforth *PSC*), 1886-87 (Calcutta, 1888), p. 36.

TABLE 1.2

STATEMENT SHOWING THE HINDU AND MUSLIM STUDENTS WHO PASSED THE ENTRANCE AND B.A. EXAMINATIONS AT THE UNIVERSITY OF CALCUTTA, 1876-86.

Entrance Examination

Year	1876	1877	1878	1879	1880	1881	1882	1883	1884	1885-86
Hindu	1,196	980	914	905	1,421	1,170	1,216	1,338	—	1,230
Muslim	66	67	66	59	90	67	92	123	—	91

B.A. Examinations

	1876	1877	1878	1879	1880	1881	1882	1883	1884	1885-86
Hindu	118	53	81	92	146	99	178	189	114	268
Muslim	7	3	—	4	4	1	6	15	3	8

Source: *Public Service Commission, 1886-87, Report* (Calcutta, 1888), pp. 78-79.

the growing importance of educational qualifications. This was one of the reasons why Muslim witnesses before the Hunter Commission of 1882-83 and the Aitchison Commission of 1886-87, favoured recruitment by nomination as opposed to competitive examinations.

From the 1880s, the government encouraged Western education amongst Muslims in the hope that they would then become qualified to compete successfully for the official and professional employment created by the Raj.[12] But its efforts achieved little; by 1911, only 12.6 per cent of the Muslim population in Bengal was literate in English.[13] There was also no significant improvement in Muslim representation in the provincial services. In 1913, Muslims held only 10.6 per cent of the jobs in the executive and judicial services, and 12.2 per cent of the government posts on Rs 200 a month and over.[14] Clearly, the imbalance between the Hindus and Muslims in education and government service had not changed significantly since the mid-nineteenth century. This proved to be one of the fertile sources of communalism in Bengal.

In sharp contrast to their co-religionists in Bengal, Muslims in the UP and Punjab were in many respects more advanced, prosperous, and influential. This was due, in part, to the fact that the British introduced fewer drastic changes in the administrative machinery of northern India, and because there was less insistence on educational attainment for securing government posts. Recruitment was not always on the basis of qualifications obtained at college but on account of family background and tried loyalty to the Raj. In the Punjab, for example, Muslims lagged far behind the Hindus in Western

[12]See, for example, the Resolution of the Government of India on Muslim Education, 13 June 1873, quoted in C.H. Philips (ed.), *The Evolution of India and Pakistan 1858-1947: Select Documents* (London, 1962), pp. 180-83 For an analysis of the factors which led the government to adopt special measures to promote western education among Muslims, see Peter Hardy, *The Muslims of British India* (Cambridge, 1972), pp. 80-82, 85-86, 89-91.

[13]*Census*, 1911, Bengal, Part II, Table VIII B.

[14]*Royal Commission on Public Services in India* (henceforth *RCPS*) (London, 1917), Appendix V.

education.[15] From 1858 to 1878, only 57 out of the 3,155 graduates in the province were Muslims.[16] Again, between 1882 and 1886, only 224 out of the 746 candidates who qualified for the entrance examinations, were Muslims.[17] Yet, in 1886-87, there were 127 Muslim officers in the uncovenanted judicial and executive services of the Punjab, or 41.6 per cent of all Indians in the services.[18] By 1913, the employment of Muslims in the provincial service had increased appreciably. At least 66 per cent of the posts in the judicial service carrying a salary of Rs 1,000 and over, were held by Muslims.[19] Similarly, in the UP, where Urdu remained the medium of Muslim education and the language of administration, Muslims retained their important position in the services. Here they were relatively better placed in government service than were the Hindus.[20]

The Muslim landed aristocracy in the UP and the Punjab was also able to survive the rigours of British rule. In the Punjab, their fortunes improved under the British, for many of them played a vital role in putting down the 'Mutiny', particularly in western Punjab. In return, the government bolstered their interests, and when irrigation schemes led to the reclamation of large areas of western Punjab in the late nineteenth century, the Muslim landlords of that area were among the chief beneficiaries. Likewise, the *taluqdars* of Oudh were brought forward as the 'natural leaders of the people' and as the bulwarks of the Raj. In 1859 they received *sanads* which conferred on them full proprietary rights, titles, and possession of their *taluqas*.

At the beginning of the twentienth century, Muslims held approximately one-fifth of the land in the UP.[21] In parts of

[15]In 1901, Muslim literates in English numbered 15,505, or 18.85 per cent, in the Punjab. *Census* 1901, Punjab, Part 2, Table VIII.

[16]*Report by the Punjab Provincial Committee: Appendix to Education Commission* (Calcutta, 1884), p. 116.

[17]*PSC*, Appendices, pp. 78-79.

[18]*Ibid.*, Report, p. 38.

[19]*RCPS*, Appendix VIII.

[20]See Paul Brass, *Language, Religion and Politics in Northern India* (Cambridge, 1974), Chapter three. For the overall economic position of the UP Muslims, see Robinson, *Separatism*, pp. 14-23.

[21]See Table I in Robinson, *Separatism*, pp. 18-19.

Agra division, they were a major landholding group. In Rohilkhand they were dominant. In Bareilly district, they owned
33.1 per cent of the land. The Pathans, in particular, held
considerable estates. In 1909, they held 135,289 acres or 13.38
per cent of the land, mainly in the Bareilly *tahsil* and in the
north of the districts.[22] In the district of Aligarh, there were
a number of Pathan, Syed and Sheikh landlords who increased their holdings between 1839 and 1909.[23] Similarly, the
taluqdars of Oudh not only maintained their position, but
improved it. The leading Muslim *taluqdar* was the Raja of
Mahmudabad, whose income from his estates in Sitapur,
Lucknow, Barabanki, and Kheri districts amounted to
approximately Rs 339,642.[24] He was active in the educational
and political life of the province. He was a trustee of Aligarh
College, vice-chancellor of Aligarh Muslim University from
1920 to 1923, and a vigorous supporter of the agitational
politics of Mohamed Ali, Wazir Hasan, and Raja Ghulam
Husain.[25]

This brief sketch of the economic and educational standing
of the Muslims would help to explain their reactions to various
political and constitutional developments after the establishment of the Indian National Congress in 1885. Moreover, it
would reveal the uneven development of the Muslims and their
relative standing in different regions. This was reflected in
their representation on the legislative councils and the local
bodies, where power rested with those who commanded wealth
and influence. Until the introduction of the Montagu-

[22]*District Gazetteers of the United Provinces*, Bareilly, Vol. 13,
pp. 100-105.

[23]Some of the leading landlord families in the Aligarh district were
those of the Lalkhani Rajputs, the Sherwani Pathans of Datauli, the
Pathans of Bhikampur and the Syeds of Jalali. *Ibid.*, Aligarh, Vol. 6,
pp. 91-92, 106-12; and W.H. Smith, *Final Report of the Revision of
Settlement in the District of Aligarh* (Allahabad, 1882).

[24]*List of Taluqdars in Oudh: Corrected up to 31st March 1920*
(Lucknow, 1920).

[25]After graduating from Aligarh College, he joined the *Comrade*
in 1911 as a sub-editor. From 1914 to 1916 he edited the Raja of
Mahmudabad's *Indian Daily Telegraph*, and founded his own *New Era* in
Lucknow on the model of *Comrade*. He died in 1917 after being knocked
down by a runaway horse.

Chelmsford Reforms in 1919, the franchise was extremely limited and extended to men of substance only. The legislative councils and the local bodies were dominated by landowners, money-lenders, and rich traders, and the size of a particular community was not necessarily reflected in its political influence.

II

Yet, if material interests divided the Muslim community, religion acted as a strong cohesive force. Despite sectarianism, Muslims were knit together by a monolithic unity of faith. Ideally, Islam is a great unifying force with a definite central figure in a single God, a revealed book, the Quran, and a Prophet in the person of Mohammad. All Muslims, irrespective of their doctrinal differences, believe in the Unity of God, the infallibility of the Quran, and the finality of Mohammad's Prophethood. Similarly, there are certain features of ritual which are common to all — features which are recognisable throughout the Muslim world.[26] The daily prayer in public brings Muslims, irrespective of class, to one common place and gives tangible form to the unity and fraternity of the community.[27] When the believers range themselves in rows behind the *Imam* (prayer leader), no one takes precedence over the other.[28] In the words of Iqbal, who emphasised the social aspect of Islamic prayer to prove the superiority of Islam to all other religions,

ایک ہی صف میں کھڑے ہوگئے محمود و ایاز
نہ کوئی بندہ رہا اور نہ کوئی بندہ نواز

[26]Sir Hamilton Gibb has examined the process by which the Islamic institutions were moulded into a coherent unity and given their specifically Islamic stamp. H.A.R. Gibb, *Studies in the Civilisation of Islam* (London, 1962).

[27]This point has been stressed by the *ulama* in order to demonstrate the unifying powers of religious symbols and institutions in Islam. See A.K. Azad, *Maqalat-i-Al-Hilal* (Lahore, 1960 edn.), pp. 11-32, and M. Zafiruddin, *Islam ka nizam-i-masjid* (Delhi, n.d.).

[28]A.A. Maududi, *Islami Ibadat par ek Nazar* (Lahore, 1958) pp. 56-58.

(King Mahmud, Ayaz the slave, their rank in service was the same).

Moreover, the mosque, where public worship is performed, is the local focus of religious and educational activities. It is a chief place of assembly. Here the faithful share their religious and social experiences. For this reason, Muslim theologians have attached great importance to congregation prayers as opposed to worship in solitude.[29]

No less important has been the role of *Hajj* in unifying the Muslims as a religious community, and in giving impetus to the idea of pan-Islamism.[30] The Kaaba, which is both the focal point of the yearly *Hajj*[31] and the centre of day-to-day devotion, is a symbol of Muslim unity. According to Iqbal, who describes the Kaaba in most vivid colours in his *mathnawi,* 'Rumuz-i-Bekhudi', the rite of pilgrimage engenders a feeling of brotherhood amongst Muslims who meet in Mecca and Medina for a common purpose and in a common worship.[32] The significance of the *Hajj* in Muslim religious life and its importance in giving depth to the Khilafat movement is discussed in chapter five.

[29]A. Kamal, *The Sacred Journey: Being Pilgrimage to Mecca* (New York, 1961), p. 45, and Maududi, *Islami Ibadat par ek Nazar,* p. 51.

[30]According to C. Poenson, a nineteenth century missionary in Central Java, 'Arabia not only constitutes the uniting centre for devoted pilgrims, but politicians and leaders of various Muslim peoples meet there and also discuss their political interests and plans; and the returning pilgrims are supplied with tracts for religious stimulation and conversion . . .' . That is why the Dutch authorities in Indonesia attempted to limit the pilgrimage by taking several restrictive measures. See D. Noer, *The Modernist Muslim Movement in Indonesia 1900-1942* (Oxford, 1973), pp. 25-26.

[31]In India, the number of Muslims who performed the *Hajj* was quite significant. From 1882 to 1893, an average of just over 12,000 pilgrims sailed to Hijaz from Bombay. These figures increased considerably in the first decade of the twentieth century, when the government took measures to alleviate the sufferings experienced by the pilgrims. Various *Hajj* Committees were formed to expedite the travel arrangements. UP Government Records. Poll. 1894, 89, 1913, 142, UPSA.

[32]A Schimmel, *Gabriel's Wing: A study of the Religious Ideas of Sir Muhammad Iqbal* (Leiden, 1963), pp. 195-96.

Pilgrimage (*ziyarat*) to the shrines of the sufis or *pirs* also gave greater cohesion to the social and religious life of the Muslims.[33] The saints, believed to retain effective power after their death, can avert calamity, cure diseases, procure children for the childless, or even improve the circumstances of the dead. That is why the sufi shrines attract thousands of Muslims from all parts of the country. The pilgrim salutes the grave, prostrates himself, kisses it, holds sacrificial feasts, and carries away earth from the shrine to rub on the sick, or a pressed cake of it to place under his forehead, when he prostrates himself in prayer.

The annual congregation (*urs*) provides an occasion for devotees from all strata of society to gather together with single-minded devotion. The *urs* centres round a *pir*, who generally represents one of the many sufi orders (*silsilah*) which exist throughout the Muslim world. These have played a key role in the spiritual as well as the political life of the Muslim community. In medieval Turkey the sufi orders often functioned as opponents of political repression.[34] In north-west Africa and eastern Sudan, some sufis were in the forefront of a fierce military resistance against the penetration of the European colonial powers.[35] In medieval and modern India, while the sufis of the orthodox orders, such as the Chishtis, were all agreed that their primary function was to offer spiritual guidance, there are several instances of their involvement in politics. They often acted as spokesmen of the poor, offering their *dargahs* as sanctuaries for those who sought refuge from the injustices and tyranny of the zamindars or local officials. It is therefore not surprising that each village, town, or district in India has its shrine. This is one of the factors which creates a sense of unity amongst Muslims and is revived annually on the occasion of the *urs*.

It would be rash to deny the importance of these common religious experiences which, on occasions, brought Muslims together and fostered a sense of belonging to a common frater-

[33]There are many sufi shrines throughout India. Some of the well known ones are those of Khwaja Muinuddin Chishti at Ajmer, Nizamuddin Aulia at Delhi, and Shaikh Salim Chishti at Fatehpur Sikri. To these and many other centres come the rich and the poor, men from the town and the villages.

[34]F. Rahman, *Islam* (London, 1966), p. 151.

[35]See I.M. Lewis (ed.), *Islam in Tropical Africa* (Oxford, 1966).

nity of Islam. They encouraged some Muslim groups, particularly the *ulama*, to conceive of Muslims as unique and distinct from other communities, and to maintain their distinctiveness by opposing syncretical practices in the countryside and denouncing innovation in Indian Islam as heresy (*biddat*). Thus, Shaikh Ahmad Sirhindi (1562-1624) reacted sharply against Akbar's tentative moves towards religious syncretism and called for strict conformity (*taqlid*) to the *Sharia* in every detail. Similarly, Shah Waliullah (1703-1762) of Delhi sought to unite the Muslims on the basis of the Quranic teachings, and by purging Indian Islam of Hindu customs and practices.

The appeal for unity is, indeed, the theme which runs through the nineteenth century revivalist movements in India and in other Islamic countries.[36] In north India, the idea of maintaining the unity and religious identity of the Muslims through *jihad* was taken up by Sayyid Ahmad Shahid (1786-1831), born twenty-four years after the death of Waliullah. In Bengal, Shariat Allah (1781-1840) of Faridpur started a movement of 'purification' known as the Faraizi movement. His task was to restore the pristine purity of early Islam in rural Bengal by rejecting the Hindu customs which the Muslims had retained after their conversion. Shariat Allah forbade his disciples to participate in, or subscribe to, the celebration of Hindu festivals which, according to him, violated the Islamic doctrine of the Unity of God (*tauhid*).[37]

[36]A positive attempt to acccomplish the unification of all Muslims under one Islamic Government was made by the remarkable personality of Jamaluddin Afghani (1839-1897), probably a Shia from Persia. As part of his mission, he travelled to Afghanistan, Turkey, Egypt, and India. He was in India from 1879 to 1882 and stayed in Bombay, Hyderabad, Calcutta, and Madras. He made contacts with Mohammad Ali Rogay in Bombay and with Syed Husain Bilgrami, private secretary to the prime minister of Hyderabad. In Calcutta, he is reported to have made an impression as an oral teacher and influenced many young anti-British students. But the greatest influence stemmed from his writings, many of which were first published in India, and in some cases soon translated into Urdu. For the influence of Afghani on his contemporaries, see Albert Hourani, *Arabic Thought in the Liberal Age 1798-1939* (Oxford, 1970); Nikkie R. Keddie, *Jamal ad-Din "al-Afghani"* (University of California Press, 1972).

[37]Moinuddin Ahmad Khan, 'Haji Shariatullah', *Journal of the Pakistan Historical Society*, April 1963, Vol. II.

Although the movements started by Sayyid Ahmad and Shariat Allah dwindled soon after their death, their activities represented the first serious attempt to organise Muslims on purely religious lines. Furthermore, their total rejection of the composite and syncretic trends in Indian Islam not only threatened the process of Hindu-Muslim integration but also promoted separatist tendencies among Muslims. Shariat Allah, for example, aroused in the semi-Hinduised peasantry a sense of belonging to the wider Islamic community (*umma*) and left them more susceptible to communal propaganda. This had important political implications.

In the second half of the nineteenth century, some leading *ulama* carried on the mission of Sayyid Ahmad and Shariat Allah. They had good reasons for doing so. Continued British presence undermined the traditional system of thought and conduct which the *ulama* represented, and steadily reduced their influence in Muslim society. The *ulama* reacted bitterly against the government's encroachment upon Muslim educational institutions and its interference with Islamic personal law. They asserted the preeminent position of the *Sharia* and claimed for themselves the sole right to interpret its meaning for all groups and classes.[38] They also resented government's interference with Muslim religious and educational institutions because in Islam religious beliefs are said to have been revealed by God to Prophet Mohammed.[39] They submitted memoranda and sent deputations to the government on this point.[40] But a far more

[38]Shibli made this point in his Annual Convocation Address at *Nadwa* in 1894. He argued that the Muslim community could not develop unless and until the *ulama* had control over the secular and spiritual aspects of its life. S.M. Ikram, *Mauj-i-Kausar* (Lahore, 1970), p. 233.

[39]See, for example, the reaction of Maulvi Fazl al-Huqq Khayrabadi (1797-1861), quoted in A. Ahmad, *Islamic Modernism in India and Pakistan 1857-1964* (Oxford, 1967), pp. 28-29.

[40]Shibli organised a memorial against the Privy Council decision of 1894 which set aside the law of *wakf-ul-alal-auiad*. The law aimed to prevent, where necessary, the subdivision of property among a succession of heirs. The *wakf* was originally created by Muslims in favour of their families and for religious and educational purposes. For an example of a *wakf* deed executed by one Mohammad Jawwad of Mohan, see *Risala-i-Wakf-Alal-Aulad wa Naql-i-Dastaweez-i-Mohani*, Urdu D. 716, IOL.

positive response was in the form of reorganising the traditional Muslim system of education. This was done in order to
prevent the influx of subversive ideas from the religiously alien
and 'morally inferior' British, and to put a premium on unortho-
dox thought and learning, which was calculated to undermine
the position of the *ulama* in Muslim society. Thus Shibli
Numani declared that the purpose of the *Nadwat al-ulama* was
to defend Islam against 'contemporary times'.[41] The *ulama*
generally believed that through *maktabs* and *madrasas*, they
would be able to maintain uniformity in belief and practice by
determining what was true or desirable in the light of the Quran
and the *Hadith* (Traditions of the Prophet).

Traditionally, the *madrasas* were the basis of Muslim
education.[42] Their curriculum, which remained largely unchanged over the centuries, included the study of Arabic and Persian
languages and literature, logic, philosophy, Islamic Law, the
Hadith, and commentaries on the Quran. Aurangzeb, the last of
the great Mughal emperors, is said to have reprimanded his
former teacher for having taught him Arabic, grammar and
philosophy rather than subjects more practical for a future ruler
of a vast empire.[43] But his eloquent and pungent criticism had

---

[41]*Makatib-i- Shibli* (Azamgarh, 1928), Vol. I, p. 329.

[42]The earliest known *madrasas* were established by Shamsuddin
Iltutmish (1211-1236) and Ghayasuddin Balban (1266-1286) in the
thirteenth century. During the reign of Muhammad bin Tughlaq (1325-
1351), there were a thousand *madrasas* in Delhi alone. There were at
least thirty in Jaunpur, and a sixteenth century English traveller visiting
Thata—now a picturesque ruin near Karachi (Pakistan)—reported 400
large and small *madrasas*.

[43]S.M. Ikram, *Rud-i-Kausar* (Karachi, 1958), pp. 424-26; Syed Ahmad
Khan, the founder of Aligarh College, held that the Muslim schools
of the old sort at Deoband, Kanpur, Delhi, Jaunpur, and Aligarh were
'altogether useless' because their syllabus and books 'deceive and
teach men to veil their meaning. . . to describe things wrongly and in
irrelevant terms. . . to hate their fellow creatures, to have no sympathy
with them, to speak with exaggeration, to leave the history of the past
uncertain, and to relate facts like tales and stories. All these things are
quite unsuited to the present age and to the spirit of the time, and
thus instead of doing good they do much harm to the Muhammadans'.
Quoted in Philips, *The Evolution of India and Pakistan*, p. 179. Also,
see Syed Ahmad Khan to Mohsinul Mulk, 11 February 1872, quoted in
S. Muhammad, *Sir Syed Ahmad Khan: A Political Biography* (Meerut,
1969), p. 59.

little effect. In the eighteenth century, Mulla Nizamuddin Sihalawi introduced the *Dars-i-Nizamia*, which became the standard syllabus and the basis for instruction in many institutions.[44] Regarded as the most comprehensive form of orthodox education, the *Dars-i-Nizamia* was adopted by some of the famous *madrasas* in the eighteenth and nineteenth centuries.[45] As a result, they continued to function essentially as schools of theology and strongholds of orthodoxy where a traditionalist course of studies was planned, to the exclusion of modern sciences. The curriculum was confined to the purely religious sciences (*maqulat*) with a bit of grammar and literature. The purely religious subjects were *hadith*, *fiqh*, *kalam* and *tafsir*, with the Quran being at the heart of the curriculum and its memorisation the highest scholastic attainment.

The *maktabs*, which were usually attached to a mosque, were smaller institutions than the *madrasas*. They were usually of two kinds: the first of a purely religious character in which the rituals and the tenets of Islam were taught, and the second of a more secular type in which some Persian literature was also taught.[46] *Maktabs* were mainly set up by private enterprise or public charity, and were sometimes maintained by *wakfs*. In Bengal, a few were aided by the municipality.[47]

The most important *maktab*, which later developed into a *Dar al-ulum* (an institution of high learning), was established by a group of *ulama* at Deoband soon after 1857. As a conservative

[44]For details about the *Dars-i-Nizamia*, see M. Mujeeb, *Indian Muslims* (London, 1967), pp. 407-408.

[45]Some of the famous *madrasas* in the UP were: *Madrasa* Kalaan in Sandila, *Madrasa* Chashma-i-Rahmat in Ghazipur, and the *Madrasa* of Haji Imam Buksh in Jaunpur. In Bengal, there were some famous *madrasas* in Murshidabad, Birbhum and Burdwan. The famous Jalaliya *madrasa* at Burdwan was established by Munshi Sadruddin of Burdwan. See Maulana Khairuddin Ahmad, *Tazkirat-ul-ulama* (Calcutta, 1934), pp. 13-14.

[46]In the Punjab, besides the Quran and the *Kanzul-i-Mussali* (a book of prayers in verse), a number of books on the rituals and the tenets were also taught. These included the *Rah-i-Najaat*, *Risala-i-Namazaan*, *Nasihat Nama*, *Masail-i-Hindi*, *Subha ka Sitara* and *Masail-i-Subhani*. For the syllabus in both types of *maktabs*, see H.S. Reid, *Report on Indigenous Education and Vernacular Schools* (Agra, 1852).

[47]R. Nathan, *Progress of Education in India 1896-97 to 1901-2* (Calcutta, 1904), Vol. I, p. 375.

theological seminary, this institution aimed at resisting social
and religious changes introduced by the British and maintaining the cultural and religious identity of the Muslim
community.[48] Rashid Ahmad Gangohi, one of its founders,
strongly opposed the introduction of Western education as
advocated by Syed Ahmad Khan of Aligarh, and supported the
Indian National Congress in order to counter the activities of
the Aligarh reformer.[49] Similarly, the *Nadwat al-ulama,* founded in 1894, failed to combine both religious and secular types
of education for which it was originally founded. The institution soon developed conservative contours of its own, and its
products became generally indistinguishable from those of
Deoband in theological and intellectual outlook. Both adhered
to the narrow curriculum drawn up by Nizamuddin in the
eighteenth century.[50]

The establishment of the *Dar al-ulum* and the *Nadwa* signified an attempt to make Muslims aware of their
Islamic identity. It was also a warning to the government that
the *ulama* would brook no intrusion in their special field of
religious interpretation and instruction. Over the years, the
ulama resisted the secularising tendencies in continuing to wear
the medieval attire. Their turbans and flowing gowns made
them stand out as symbols of conservatism in a society that was
becoming less Islamic and more secular. Their stubborn defence
of established traditions explains, in large part, the absence of
any significant educational and social reform movement among
Muslims. Even the efforts of the British to improve the traditional system of Muslim education were of no avail because of
the intransigence of the *ulama* who jealously guarded their
theological schools. As a result, these institutions became out
of tune with a society which was rapidly modernising itself. By
concentrating primarily on religious education, they encouraged
Muslims to see their identity primarily in religious terms. A

[48]Syed Mahbub Rizvi, *Tarikh-i-Deoband* (Deoband, 1972 edn.), pp.
314-15.

[49]Mohammad Miyan, *Ulama-i-Haq aur unke karname* (Delhi, 1946),
pp. 98-100.

[50]For books and subjects prescribed at the *Dar al-ulum,* see Rizvi
Tarikh-i-Deoband, pp. 433-38, and Z.H. Faruqi, *The Deoband School
and the Demand for Pakistan* (Asia Publishing House, 1963), pp. 33-36.

majority of them shut themselves off from the contemporary world in their mosques and medieval *madrasas* denouncing each other and dubbing everyone else as ignorant, irreligious, and atheistic. Only exceptional men such as Azad and Shibli attempted to reconcile tradition and modernity by building bridges between the two. But such men were too few and the results of their labours too limited.

In the twentieth century, the concern for maintaining the unity and identity of the Muslim community was expressed in the opposition to the Sarda Marriage Act, passed in 1929. Many leading Muslims argued that, although child marriage was not enjoined by the Quran, it was not expressly forbidden, and therefore the Sarda Act was an interference with their religious rights.[51] So, they launched an agitation against the Act which was supported by the *ulama*, the professional men, as well as the 'prominent loyal Muhammadans'.[52] Like the Kanpur mosque incident and the Khilafat movement, the Sarda Act also united various Muslim groups—in spite of their social, economic, regional, and linguistic divisions—in defence against what they viewed to be a threat to the *Sharia*.[53] Here again religion acted as a powerful cementing force, transcending all other considerations. 'The Muslims have their internecine quarrels', observed the Governor of Bombay, 'but, these apart, the solidarity of Islam is a hard fact against which it is futile to run one's head.'[54] This was a fair observation. Many Muslims perceived themselves as a monolithic religious community and, more significantly, the British Government was only too willing, for its own reasons, to treat them as a distinct political and religious entity.

[51]See UPNNR, for the weeks ending 21 September, 5 and 19 October, 23 and 30 November, 1929; K.A. Siddiqi to Mohamed Ali, n.d., Mohamed Ali Papers, JMIL.

[52]Nawab of Bahawalpur to Irwin, 28 March 1930; Montmorency to Irwin, 14 April, 1930; Nawab of Chhatari to Irwin, 12 May 1930, Irwin Papers, MSS. EUR. C 152 (24), IOL.

[53]See the list of Muslim members of the Legislative Assembly who submitted a memorandum to the Home Member, Government of India, against the Sarda Act. To Mohamed Ali, 14 November 1929, Mohamed Ali Papers.

[54]Lawrence, Second Marquess of Zetland, *Essayez* (London, 1956), p. 119.

CHAPTER TWO

HISTORICAL BACKGROUND

The emergence of the Indian National Congress, its development and its character has been one of the dominant themes of modern Indian historiography. In recent years, a number of regional studies have emphasised that the Congress did not, as had once been supposed, represent simply the interests of any particular class, caste, or interest group. The old assumption that the Congress was the affair of the English-educated, and of professional men, drawn mainly from the higher literate Hindu castes of the three maritime presidencies, has been successfully challenged.[1] It is increasingly clear that the role of the educated in Congress was that of publicists and spokesmen for a much wider range of interests, and that the Congress was the focus of local support whose social composition and political aims were, in fact, much more heterogeneous than either the British or some historians dominated by the official mind have argued. Moreover, since Congressmen had local roles to play, and were often members of the patron-client groups in their own localities, they had a complex relationship with the elites of Indian society, both urban and rural, and with the peasants and workers whom they claimed to represent.[2]

[1]For example, G. Johnson, *Provincial Politics and Indian Nationalism. Bombay and the Indian National Congress, 1880-1915* (Cambridge, 1972); C.A. Bayly, *The Local Roots of Indian Politics. Allahabad, 1880-1920* (Oxford, 1975).

[2]See D.A. Washbrook, *The Emergence of Provincial Politics*: *The Madras Presidency, 1870-1920* (Cambridge, 1976).

One of the main aims and functions of the Congress was
to present a set of demands, mainly to do with the structure
of governance, to their overlords in London and in Calcutta.
The British had imposed on India a polity which was unitary
in form. The provinces and the districts increasingly felt the
force of centralisation and were subject to the same general
rules. Consequently, there were obvious advantages for Indians,
whatever their local differences, to unite when articulating
political and constitutional demands. There was also a strong
incentive for Congressmen to claim that their organisation
spoke for the whole of India, and was thoroughly representative of the 'entire nation'. They described Congress sessions as
national gatherings and spoke of an 'Indian nation, of national
opinion and national aspirations'.[3] 'It is difficult to conceive',
claimed the *Report of the First Indian National Congress*, 'any
gathering . . . more thoroughly representative of the entire
nation than the Congress.'[4] In 1885, the Congress was a small
body of self-elected men, of less than a hundred members; in
1886 it consisted of 434 delegates; a year later it was a body
of 607 delegates. 'Indeed what in 1885 was little more than an
experiment', the Madras Congress proudly announced, 'in 1887
bore every appearance of becoming a permanent National
Institution.'[5]

Furthermore, the Congress programme was declared as
'catholic' and suited to the varied requirements of the Indian
communities. Above all, it was 'non-sectarian'. Ajudhia Nath
Kunzru, a leading pleader in Allahabad during the 1880s,
articulated this view when he said: 'Congress works not for the
good of this or that class, nor of this or that province, but for
the benefit of the whole nation.'[6] Surendranath Banerjea
stated:

Let it not be said that this is the Congress of one social
party rather than that of another. It is the Congress of

[3]*INC* 1885, p. 9; P. Sitaramayya, *Indian Nationalism* (Masulipatam,
1913), p. 70, India Office Library Tracts (henceforth IOL Tracts): 112.
[4]*Ibid.*, p. 15.
[5]*Ibid.*, 1887, p. 2.
[6]*Tribune*, 23 January 1889; Tyabji to Mahdi Ali, 14 January 1888,
Tyabji Papers, NAI.

United India, of Hindus and Mohammedans, of Christians, of Parsees and of Sikhs. . . . Here we stand upon a common platform—here we have all agreed to bury our differences, and recognise the one common fact that being subjects of the same Sovereign and living under the same Government and the same political institutions, we have common rights and common grievances.[7]

Evidently, the early Congress leaders proceeded on two main assumptions. First, that all Indians had common interests which could be preserved and promoted by a national organisation. This was reflected in the formulation of certain demands. One of the main demands, for instance, was that simultaneous examinations for the Indian Civil Service should be held both in India and in Britain. But witnesses from northern India in their evidence before the Public Service Commission rejected the whole principle of examination, fearing that men from their part of the country would fail and Bengalis would succeed.[8] This was one of the early occasions when the Congress' right to speak on behalf of all Indians was seriously challenged. Secondly, the Congress leaders assumed that they constituted a homogeneous group,[9] ignoring the diverse interests, the incongruous combination of ideologies and the contradictions within their organisation. In relation to the Muslims and other minority groups, this contradiction is clearly noticeable in the proclaimed 'non-sectarian character' of the Congress, on the one hand, and the identification of some of its members with Hindu revivalism, on the other. Leaders like Tilak, Pal, Malaviya and Lajpat Rai openly acknowledged their identification of nationalism with Hinduism. Tilak and his followers in Maharashtra took up the cult of Shivaji, seeing in him the hero *par excellence* of past Hindu struggles against Muslim aggression. Many Hindu Congress-men were also associated with cow-protection societies. In

---

[7]*Speeches and Writings of Surendranath Banerjea* (hereafter *Speeches*) (Madras, n.d.), p. 265.

[8]*PSC*, 1886-7, Vol. 2, p, 44.

[9]See, for example, the speech of Subramania Iyer at the opening meeting of Congress. *INC* 1885, p. 9.

1889, Telang proposed a resolution of sympathy with the cow-protection movement in the Congress session and two years later the *pandal* where the Congress session was held was used for the meeting of the Gauraksha Sabha.[10] 'The advanced wing of the Congress party', observed Lansdowne, the Viceroy, 'has found in this fanatical and popular movement a means of establishing a connection between itself and the great mass of the Hindu population.'[11] The alliance with orthodox Hinduism and revivalism inevitably weakened the Congress claim of being a 'non-sectarian' organisation. Indeed, Muslims continually harped on this fact to justify their aloofness from the Congress and began to search for ways to counter what they perceived as a threat to their religion.

The early Congress turned a blind eye to the actual cleavages in the country and claimed a monopoly of representing all categories of Indians. However, it was unable to resolve some of the ideological contradictions which plagued the party from the outset. As a result, its opponents—British and Indian—found it convenient to criticise it and to challenge its claim of being a national body. In other words, whereas the strength of the Congress lay in attracting a wide variety of followers, its failure to recognise the cleavages in the country as well as within its own organisation proved to be a source of weakness and unpopularity amongst certain groups.

There is, however, one qualification to this hypothesis. The Congress leaders recognised the Muslims as a distinct religious community,[12] which had resolutely maintained its identity since the advent of Islam in India and refused to be merged into the mosaic of Indian culture and religion. They further assumed that Muslims were a homogeneous community

[10]P.C. Ghosh, *The Development of the Indian National Congress, 1892-1909* (Calcutta, 1960), pp. 69-70.

[11]Lansdowne to Kimberley, 22 August 1893, quoted in A. Tripathi, *The Extremist Challenge: India between 1890 and 1910* (Calcutta, 1967), p. 69.

[12]Addressing the Punjab Political Conference in October 1906, Lala Lajpat Rai observed that the 'religious ideals' of Hindus and Muslims were so different 'that it is impossible to expect a complete union of them in the near future'. *Panjabee*, 13 October 1906, quoted in P. Nagar, *Lala Lajpat Rai: The Man and His Ideas* (Delhi, 1977), p. 252.

with common interests and identical aspirations, and that a dominant exclusive Muslim self-consciousness had already grown by the 1880s. This is evident from the arguments put forward to enlist Muslim support for the Congress. 'We must meet the masses of that [Muslim] community', suggested the *Hindu*, 'with all the resources of our organisation in the same way that the masses of the Hindu community have been met.'[13] In a speech at Dacca, Surendranath Banerjea pleaded for the sympathy of Muslims for Congress which, he said, 'flings its portals wide open for the admission of all—it welcomes all. The Mohamedans have absolutely nothing to be afraid of from a Hindu majority.'[14] No doubt, behind these appeals there was the realisation that unless Muslims were won over and their fears about Hindu domination allayed, they would place obstacles in the path of reforms. This was stated succinctly in the following words:

> Considering what power the cooperation of the Muslims will impart to the Congress, the Hindus may even go to the length of offering a promise to respect the scruples that the whole of the Muslim community as represented by their delegates, may entertain.[15]

Indeed, in 1888, the Allahabad Congress assured Muslims that no subject would be discussed to which 'the Hindu or Muslim delegates as a body object, unanimously or nearly unanimously'.[16] In 1900, the Subjects Committee bowed to pressure from the Muslim delegates and dropped the Punjab Alienation Bill discussion from the agenda.[17] The decision was carefully calculated, since the controversy was likely to alienate the

[13]*Hindu*, 16 January 1888.

[14]*Speeches*, p. 265.

[15]*Hindu*, 16 January 1881.

[16]*INC* 1888, p. 88. The *Tribune* observed: 'After this assurance let us hope our Mohamedan friends will no longer hesitate to join their Hindu fellow subjects. Nothing can be a stronger proof of the good faith of the Congress than this resolution . . . , and let us hope that the fears of our more suspicious Muslim brethren have been removed.' *Tribune*, 23 January 1889.

[17]*INC* 1900, p. 10.

Punjabi Muslims.[18] Attempts were also made to establish links with various Muslim regional organisations and to approach their leaders in localities.[19] Surendranath Banerjea was the first to initiate talks to secure the support of the Central National Mahommedan Association, founded in 1878 by Ameer Ali.[20] In the UP, Kunzru involved two of his junior colleagues, Nawab Abdul Majid and Syed Abdul Rauf, in Congress activities, and was successful in enlisting some Muslim support in Lucknow and in Allahabad.[21]

To sum up, it can be argued that the Congress was keen on enlisting Muslim support, because they were clearly the most important religious minority in terms of numbers, influence, and historical importance, and it was realised that, without them, it would not be possible to have a 'National Assembly'. Their adherence to the movement was considered vital to give weight to the constitutional demands, and to impress the government that the Congress demands represented the unanimous opinion of all sections in India. This seemed to be the only answer to the government's view of Congress as a body which represented a 'microscopic minority'.

In its endeavour to gain Muslim support, the Congress evolved a strategy which was based on a series of assumptions regarding the distinctive character of the Muslim community, its homogeneity and its diverse interests. Accordingly, its leaders took steps to win over influential Muslims, such as Ameer Ali, Syed Ahmad Khan, Abdul Latif and Badruddin Tyabji and accepted them as spokesmen of their community. This was regardless of the fact that many of them

[18]For an elaboration of this argument, see N.G. Barrier, *The Punjab Alienation of Land Bill of 1901* (Duke University Monograph and Occasional Papers Series, 1965), pp. 67-68.

[19]Delegates who attended the second Congress session toured different cities of North India and spoke to leading Hindus and Muslims. *Hindu*, 17 January 1888.

[20]*Bengalee*, 25 December 1886; 'We were straining every nerve to secure the cooperation of our Mohamedan fellow-countrymen . . .'. Banerjea, *A Nation in Making*, Reprint of 1925 edition. (Calcutta, 1963), p. 108.

[21]For reports of Kunzru's speeches in which he appealed for Muslim support, see *Tribune*, 21 February 1888, 23 January and 6 February 1889.

had little more than local or regional support. However, once the recognition was accorded to such individuals, they were quick to seize the opportunity of promoting their class or personal interests by acting as spokesmen of their community. This was clearly illustrated by the events which preceded and followed the Simla Deputation of October 1906, when the separate and distinct interests of the Muslims were used as a device to gain concessions for a small group of landlords and professional men. Over the next few years, the government, for its own reasons, institutionalised the divisions between the Hindus and Muslims by introducing the principle of separate electorates.

MUSLIMS AND THE CONGRESS

Muslim responses to the Congress need to be studied in two different phases: 1885-1900 and 1900-1915. In the first phase, Muslims generally kept aloof from the Congress as the delegates' lists of the annual sessions indicate. During the next phase, however, they began to take interest in the movement. This is reflected not only in an increased Muslim participation in Congress sessions but also in serious moves to come to terms with the policies of the organisation. We propose to examine both these phases in the context of Bengal, Punjab, and the UP.

At the outset, it must be stated that in their response to the Congress, Muslims did not act as a monolithic bloc. Their reactions to Congress demands rested, as Tyabji perceptively pointed out, mainly on 'local, special and temporary causes'.[22] The so-called all-India Muslim political consciousness in the last quarter of the nineteenth century, which is so often the favourite theme of historiography in India and Pakistan, was a projection of the fears of certain groups in certain areas. It was by no means an all-India phenomenon. The introduction of representative institutions and of open competition to government posts gave rise to material fears amongst some Muslims, and the persistent Congress demands for representative institutions and competitive examinations aroused their hostility.

[22]*Hindu*, 16 January 1888.

This attitude becomes intelligible if one takes into account the impact of Congress demands on various Muslim groups.

The Muslims of Bengal and the Punjab opposed the demand for competitive examinations because they feared that its acceptance would lead to their gradual exclusion from the administration. Ameer Ali, the founder of the National Mahommedan Association which represented the numerically small Western-educated Muslim elite in Calcutta, pointed out that his co-religionists had not made as much progress in education as other communities and, consequently, it was impossible for them to compete on equal terms with the Hindus who had taken to English education much earlier. So, if competitive examinations were introduced, Muslims would have a limited chance of entering the Civil Service. Ameer Ali, therefore, suggested that the University examination should not be the basis for recruitment.[23] Abdul Latif, the organiser of the Muhammadan Literary and Scientific Society of Calcutta, argued on similar lines. He favoured recruitment— partially by competition and partially by nomination. In his view, 'so long as the Government recognise the desirability of giving a fair proportion of public employment to the Moham- medans, no exclusive system of competition for recruitment is possible, for it is impracticable under present circumstances for the Muslims to compete on equal terms'.[24]

Muslim witnesses from the Punjab voiced similar feelings before the Public Service Commission. Maulvi Inam Ali, representing the *Anjuman-i-Islamia*, Lahore, rejected the com- petitive system altogether.[25] Munshi Muharram Ali Chishti, editor of the *Rafiq-i-Hind*, expressed the fear that his community would be 'utterly ruined' if competition was adopted as the basis for recruitment.[26] Munshi Nizamuddin, president of the Zamindari Reforming Society, Lahore, claim- ed separate representation for Muslims in public appointments on the basis of the experience of 'many respected Muslim families in Punjab' who once dominated the posts of Assistant Com-

[23]*PSC*, Vol. 4, pp. 196, 201.
[24]*Ibid.*, pp. 262-68.
[25]*Ibid.*, Vol. 1, p. 162.
[26]*Ibid.*, p. 204.

missioners, 'but of late years, owing to the system of competition, the supply of members of these families for these posts has fallen off'.[27]

The Bengali and Punjabi Muslims also assailed the Congress demand for representative institutions. They pointed out that they had limited chances of gaining representation on local bodies because the franchise extended only to those who fulfilled certain property, wealth, and educational qualifications.[28] For this reason, they claimed separate representation. Mohammad Yusuf, who represented Bihar in the Bengal Legislative Council, suggested in May 1883 that 'it would be an advantage and a more fit recognition of the claims of the Mohamedan population if provision could be made in the Bill (Local Self-Government) for the election of Mohamedans by reserving a certain number of membership for that community'.[29]

Unlike their co-religionists in Bengal and the Punjab, the UP Muslims were well-represented in government service and in the professions. Here also the Congress faced stern opposition from some Muslims, but not for the same reasons. The UP Muslims formed less than 14 per cent of the provinces' population and they were afraid of being swamped by the Hindu majority in a representative and popular government—an argument supported by pungent local examples.[30] This fear was

[27]*PSC*, Vol. I, p. 164.

[28]In the municipality of the suburbs of Calcutta there were only six Muslims out of the twenty-five Indian members in 1875-76. In the triennial election for the Calcutta Municipality in 1897, only six Muslims were elected as against thirty-seven Hindus. *Administrative Report on the Municipality of the Suburbs of Calcutta, 1875-76* (Calcutta, 1876), p. 6; *Statement Exibiting the Moral and Material Progress of India*, 1897-98, p. 6.

[29]Quoted in B. Majumdar, *History of Indian Social and Political Ideas* (Calcutta, 1967), p. 243.

[30]In 1890, the Muslim candidates were defeated in the municipal board elections held in Kanpur and Meerut. The *Najmul Akhbar* wrote: 'Hence it will be perceived that if the elective system was extended to the Legislative Council, an entire exclusion of Muslims from the Councils would follow.' *Najmul Akhbar* (Etawah), 24 March 1890. On this point, see *Jubilee Paper* (Lucknow), 1 April 1890; *Azad* (Lucknow), 1 April 1890; *Mihir-i-Nimroz* (Bijnor), 7 May 1890, UPNNR 1890.

summed up by Haji Mohammad Ismail, representing largely
the views of Muslim landlords and government servants:

> In a country where the Hindus and Muslims are in a ratio
> of five to one, the Muslims must go to the wall, if any
> elective or representative system of government came to be
> established. This is not an imaginary bugbear presented
> to scare away Muslims from the Congress camp, but a
> stubborn fact as daily illustrated in the proceedings of the
> District and Municipal Boards scattered all over the
> country.[31]

This was a reaffirmation of Syed Ahmad Khan's well-known
arguments against the Congress.

Syed Ahmad Khan, the genius behind the founding of
Aligarh College, was an uncompromising critic of the Congress.
His first assault came in December 1887 when he vehemently
criticised the Congress demand for representative legislative
councils, raised the spectre of Bengali dominance, and warned
his audience at the Muhammadan Educational Conference
against the danger of introducing the elective principle. 'In the
normal case', he declared, 'no single Mohamedan will secure
a seat in the Viceroy's Council. The whole Council will consist
of Babu So-and-so Mitter, Babu So-and-so Ghose, and Babu
So-and-so Chuckerbutty.'[32] This speech, as indeed his subsequent writings in the *Aligarh Institute Gazette*, created a great
stir in Congress circles, forcing its leaders to speak and write
in defence of their organisation. But all this was of no avail.
Syed Ahmad continued his crusade with the same zeal which
marked his educational activities.

---

[31]*Aligarh Institute Gazette*, 12 September 1896; Ghulam Sadiq,
a petty landowner of Moradabad, made the following observation:

Assuming that the non-Muslims would be considerate enough to
vote for Muslim candidates, it would still mean that there would be five
Hindus to every single Muslim in the 'assemblies'. As a result, nobody
would ever pay heed to them.

G.S. Sadiq, *Majlis-i-Mausuma Indian National Congress ki nisbat*
(Amritsar, 1893), p. 11.

[32]S.A. Khan, *On the Present State of Indian Politics* (Allahabad,
1888), pp. 10-15; *Tribune*, 21 January 1888.

The landed aristocracy, a section of the *ulama* and some
disgruntled Muslim professional men joined Syed Ahmad in his
onslaught upon the Congress. But their reasons for doing so
differed. The landed aristocracy, which owed its wealth and
status to the Raj, refused to identify itself with the Congress
for fear of antagonising its British benefactors,[33] while several
religious organisations resented the close association of
Congress leaders with the cow-protection societies which fomented
communal violence in parts of Punjab and the UP.[34] And
finally, the Muslim professional groups feared that the campaign, supported by leading Hindu Congressmen, to develop
the Hindi language and to introduce the Devanagri script in
the courts and government departments, would place them in a
disadvantageous position in government service, in journalism,
and in the legal profession.[35] This explains the initiative of
these groups in establishing the Urdu Defence Association in
1898,[36] and the Muslim Urdu Defence Association in Gorakh-

[33]Thus, Mohammad Amir Hasan Khan, the Raja of Mahmudabad,
presided over an anti-Congress meeting in Lucknow in 1899 and criticised
the 'short-sighted, ill-advised and misconceived propaganda of the
Indian National Congress.' Speech delivered by the Raja of Mahmudabad,
1899, Mahmudabad Library, Mahmudabad.

[34]Bayly, *The Local Roots*, pp. 128-29. In July 1893, there were
widespread riots in Azamgarh, Ballia and Ghazipur districts in UP and
British troops had to be sent to quell them. These riots owed their
origin to cow-protection. Similarly, between 1883 and 1891, there were
fifteen Hindu-Muslim riots in the Punjab, mainly sparked off by
disputes over cow-slaughter. For details, see Rizvi, 'Muslim Politics and
Government Policy', pp. 91-92; N.G. Barrier, 'Muslim Politics in the
Punjab, 1810-1890', *The Punjab Past and Present*, Vol. 6, April 1971,
p. 90.

[35]The question of which language should be utilised in education and
administration stirred communal passions both in the UP and Punjab.
The appointment of the Hunter Commission initiated a debate between
Muslims who wanted to retain Urdu as the language of the lower
educational level as well as of administration, and the Hindus who
strove to replace it by Hindi in the Devanagri script. For the development of the Hindi-Urdu conflict and the campaign for Hindi, see
Robinson, *Separatism*, pp. 69-78; Aziz Ahmad, *Islamic Culture*,
pp. 259-62, and Ram Gopal, *Indian Muslims*, pp. 30-43.

[36]*Aina* (Lucknow), 12 May 1898, UPNNR 1898.

pur two years later.[37] They wrote and spoke in support of Urdu, the promotion of its literature and particularly for its acceptance as the medium of instruction in government schools. This debate over language continued, becoming a permanent aspect of communal politics in the UP.

Thus a combination of religious and, more significantly, material fears led the Aligarh Muslim leaders and their followers to launch a crusade against the Congress. But, as Table 2.1 indicates, their success in weaning away their co-religionists from that body was limited. There were enough Muslims in different provinces who did not join Syed Ahmad's bandwagon and paid no heed to his warnings against the Congress.[38] Even in the UP, where the grand old man of Aligarh is supposed to have been most influential, the Congress captured the support of a group of small zamindars from Daryabad, several journalists, and some Muslim lawyers from Lucknow, Aligarh, and Allahabad. This proved that Syed Ahmad's claim to represent his community was hollow; his arguments against the Congress appealed only to the upper class Muslims: landlords of Aligarh and the neighbouring districts, members of the service families, government servants, and a section of the *ulama*. Admittedly, Syed Ahmad's educational activities attracted a wide spectrum of the Muslim community, but the impact of his political message was distinctly limited.

II

Table 2.1 sets out the details of Muslim representation at the Congress sessions from 1885 to 1901. The total number of Muslims who attended was 1,547. Of these, 596 came from the UP, 115 from Bengal, and the remainder from other provinces. What is however significant is the fact that they represented a wide range of interests, though the evidence on the background of many delegates is limited. From Madras and Oudh, there

[37]*Riazul Akhbar* (Gorakhpur), 29 August 1900, UPNNR 1900.

[38]Notice, for example, the criticism of Syed Ahmad's political views in a section of the Muslim Press. See Prem Narain, *Press and Politics in India, 1885-1905* (Delhi, 1970), pp. 83, 92-94.

came a few from the former royal families.[39] From Bombay came wealthy Khoja and Bohra merchants,[40] and from Bengal and the Punjab came lawyers, pleaders, journalists, and a few landowners.

TABLE 2.1

MUSLIMS AND THE CONGRESS, 1885-1901

Year	Venue	Total no of delegates	No. of Muslim delegates
1885	Bombay	72	2
1886	Calcutta	434	33
1887	Madras	607	79
1888	Allahabad	1,248	222
1889	Bombay	1,913	254
1890	Calcutta	702	116
1891	Nagpur	812	71
1892	Allahabad	625	91
1893	Lahore	867	65
1894	Madras	1,163	23
1895	Poona	1,584	25
1896	Calcutta	784	54
1897	Amraoti	692	57
1898	Madras	614	10
1899	Lucknow	740	313
1900	Lahore	567	56
1901	Calcutta	896	76
	Total	14,320	1,547

Over one-third of the 1,620 delegates from the UP were Muslims. Amongst them, there were 222 zamindars, 107 from the service class, 97 *wasiqadars*, (holders of a bond, or of a government promissory note) 61 lawyers, 59 bankers and traders and

[39]The most prominent Muslim family of Madras was that of Humayun Bahadur and his son, Syed Mohammad, who was president of the Congress in 1914.

[40]The two prominent Khojas involved in Congress were Sayani and Mohammad Ali Bhimji. In 1888, Hume expressed satisfaction at the support of the Khojas to the Congress. Hume to Tyabji, 4 September 1888, Tyabji Papers.

17 from education and journalism.[41] They were mostly drawn from the cities of Lucknow, Allahabad, Benaras, Kanpur, Agra, and Aligarh. Six-tenths of them were residents of Lucknow and were elected by the *Anjuman-i-Muhammadi*,[42] *Rifah-i-Am* Association, *Jalsa-i-Tahzib* and the *Anjuman-i-Islam*.[43] They included *wasiqadars*, lawyers, and some leading Shias led by Raza Husain Khan, secretary of the *Rifah-i-Am* Association and a close friend of Babu Ganga Prasad Verma, editor of the *Hindustani*.[44]

Next to Lucknow, Allahabad elected one-fifth of the Muslim delegates. Here the Muslim delegation largely consisted of a number of small zamindars from Daryabad (who were mostly Shias), poverty-stricken Shia dependents of the old royal house of Oudh, a small but influential group of lawyers and pleaders, and dismissed minor officials who nursed a grievance against the government.[45]

An important element in the local politics of Lucknow and Allahabad was the Shia-Sunni conflict which usually erupted in the month of Muharram, when the Shias took out a procession to mourn the martyrdom of Husain, the youngest grandson of the Prophet Mohammad. The Shias on that occasion often indulged in *tabarra* or condemnation of the first three *Khalifas*. The Sunnis reacted by opposing the *tazia* processions. This often led to sectarian violence. In Allahabad and Lucknow, tension between the two sects assumed serious proportions in the 1880s and 1890s leading to violent clashes.[46] In 1891, the Sunnis of Lucknow urged the provincial government

[41]J.L. Hill, 'Congress and Representative Institutions in the United Provinces, 1886-1901' (Unpublished Ph.D. thesis, Duke University 1969).

[42]The president of the *Anjuman* was Nawab Ali Mohammad who served on the Congress Subjects Committee in 1892 and in 1899.

[43]The *Anjuman* deputed thirty Muslims to participate in Congress deliberations at Allahabad in 1888. *INC* 1888, p. 95.

[44]*Akhbar-ul-Momnin* (Lucknow), 21 May 1890, UPNNR 1890.

[45]Abdul Majid and Abdul Rauf were the two prominent Muslim Congressmen. The latter addressed several public meetings with Kunzru who was their senior colleague in the Allahabad Bar. *Tribune*, 22 February 1888.

[46]*Ibid.*, 26 May 1888.

to prohibit the *tazia* processions altogether.[47] The Shias of
Lucknow, who were already disturbed by rumours of a government take-over of the Husainabad *Imam Barah* Trust,[48] elected
their representatives to the Congress sessions in 1890 and 1891
to protest against the government's intention and the 'high-
handedness' of the Sunnis.[49] Likewise, the Shias of Daryabad were
well represented at the Congress sessions in 1886 and in 1888. In
November 1888, they invited Mohammad Ali Bhimji, a Shia
from Bombay and a close associate of Badruddin Tyabji, to
address a Congress meeting. The Sunnis reacted by holding a
separate meeting. Maulana Mohammad Husain, the moving
spirit behind the anti-Congress campaign in Allahabad, declared
in his presidential address that anyone who pretended to be a
Congress delegate from Daryabad was not their representative.[50]
Thus existing sectarian jealousies explain why some Muslims
joined the Congress in Lucknow and Allahabad, while others
remained opposed to it.

The only two Muslims who attended the Congress in 1885
were Abdullah Mehrali and R.M. Sayani from Bombay.[51] Sayani,
who became president of the Congress in 1896, belonged to a
rich Khoja family of Kutch. He studied at Elphinstone College,
Bombay, and in 1886 passed his M.A. examination becoming
the first Muslim in the presidency to do so. Four years later,
he completed his law degree and joined the British firms of
Heath and Heath and Messrs Crawford and Company as a
solicitor. This brought him into contact with Europeans and
educated Hindus and Parsis. His subsequent participation in
municipal affairs, where he worked in close cooperation with
members of other communities, must have contributed to his
cosmopolitan outlook in public life. In 1888, Sayani's candidature as sheriff of Bombay was supported by both Hindus

---

[47]*Akhbar-ul-Momnin*, 12 January 1891, UPNNR 1891.

[48]*Oudh Punch* (Lucknow), 27 November 1891, *Ibid*. An *Imam
Barah* is a building in which the Muharram is celebrated, and service
held in commemoration of the deaths of Ali and his sons, Hasan and
Husain. At other times, the *tazias* are preserved in it.

[49]*Akhbar-ul-Momnin*, 21 May 1890, UPNNR 1890.

[50]See Bayly, *The Local Roots*, p. 130.

[51]At the second Congress there were two and at the third there were
seven Muslim delegates from Bombay.

and Parsis. In the same year, he was appointed member of the Bombay Council. In 1893 he presided over the Provincial Conference at Ahmedabad.[52]

The most influential supporter of Congress in Bombay was Badruddin Tyabji, a leading lawyer and an important public figure. His most difficult task after joining the Congress in 1887 was to persuade his co-religionists about the importance of the organisation and to allay their fears with regard to its objectives. Hume, one of the founding members of the Congress, impressed on him the need to counter the activities of Syed Ahmad Khan and his colleagues in order to 'neutralise their virulence and limit the evil consequences of their inherent and natural poisonous nature.'[53] Tyabji responded by writing to leading Muslims and explaining to them the requirements of the country.[54] 'I have always been of the opinion that in regard to political questions at large the Mussalmans should make a common cause with their fellow countrymen of all creeds and persuasions', he wrote to Ameer Ali.[55] If, however, the Congress followed policies prejudicial to Muslim interests, he suggested opposition 'from within [rather] than from without'.[56] 'We should thus', he wrote to Syed Ahmad Khan, 'advance the general progress of India, and at the same time safeguard our own interests'.[57] But Syed Ahmad paid no heed to his suggestions.[58] In fact, even among the Muslims of Bombay, there was considerable opposition to Tyabji's sympathy for the Congress. In August 1888, many Muslims of Bombay and Akola publicly declared themselves against the Congress.[59] The *Anjuman-i-Wahab*, an organisation devoted to religious and educational purposes, criticised Tyabji's sympathies for a 'Hindu

[52]Biographical information based on R.M. Sayani: *A Sketch of his life and career* (Madras, 1912), IOL Tracts: 1061.

[53]Hume to Tyabji, 22 January 1888, Tyabji Papers.

[54]Tyabji to Mahdi Ali, 14 January 1888, *Ibid.*

[55]Tyabji to Ameer Ali, 13 December 1888, *Ibid.*

[56]Tyabji to Mahdi Ali, 14 January 1888, *Ibid.*

[57]Tyabji to Syed Ahmad Khan, 18 February 1888, *Ibid.*

[58]See, for example, his blunt reply in Syed Ahmad Khan to Tyabji, 24 January 1888, *Ibid.*

[59]*Rast Goftar*, 12 August 1888; *Kaside Mumbai*, 12 August 1888, BNNR 1888.

organisation'.[60] Tyabji soon became despondent and frustrated at this attitude of his co-religionists. So in October 1888, he naively suggested to Hume that the Congress should be prorogued for five years because of the 'distinctly hostile attitude of the Mohammedans'.[61] This suggestion was an admission of Tyabji's failure to influence his community in Bombay and elsewhere.

In Bengal and the Punjab, only a few Muslims representing the intelligentsia supported the Congress. They were drawn mainly from important educational and administrative centres, where they shared with the Hindus a common educational background and often worked with them in newspaper offices, law courts, and local bodies. Some of the notable Muslim Congressmen in the Punjab, where the Congress gained few adherents even amongst Hindus,[62] were Muharram Ali Chishti, editor of the *Rafiq-i-Hind*, Syed Nadir Ali Shah, editor of the *Rehbar-i-Hind*,

[60]*Parsi Punch*, 19 August 1888, BNNR 1888.

[61]Tyabji to Hume, 27 October 1888, Tyabji Papers.

[62]Recent works on the Punjab have explained why there was little enthusiasm for the Congress in the province. Dr Jones has shown that the Arya Samajists, who commanded considerable influence, feared that the British might bring sanctions against them if they involved themselves in agitation and 'disloyal' activities. For the more militant Aryas, the Congress appeared pro-Muslim in its search for a transcendent nationalism. The years 1898 to 1900, however, marked the first upsurge of their interest in the Congress. This was the result of the controversy over the Punjab Land Alienation Act. Eager to use the Congress as a vehicle for voicing their opposition to the restrictions on land transfers, many Punjabi Hindus flocked to the 1899 Congress session and influenced the assembled delegates to carry a resolution condemning the proposed Land Alienation Act. But their enthusiasm was shortlived. In 1900, when the Congress Subjects Committee decided to drop the alienation discussion from the agenda as a concession to the feelings of Punjabi Muslims, almost all sections of the Hindu community were angered and disillusioned. Their hopes were shattered and they began to feel that a purely Hindu body was indispensable for safeguarding their political and economic interests. To the Punjabi Hindus, as Dr Jones has shown, the provincial world appeared far more real and relevant than the wider sphere of the Congress and national issues. Instead of national politics, factional struggles and communal competition commanded their attention. K.W. Jones, *Arya Dharm: Hindu Consciousness in 19th-Century Punjab* (University of California Press, 1976), pp. 241-50, 254-55; Also, see Barrier, 'The Arya Samaj and Congress Politics in the Punjab, 1894-1908', *JAS*, Vol. XXVI, May 1967.

Hakim Ahmad Ali and Munshi Nabi Baksh of the *Takmilul Hikmat* and the *Koh-i-Noor*, respectively. Amongst the well known lawyers active in the Congress were Shaikh Umar Baksh, president of the Hoshiarpur District Congress Committee, Shaikh Nabi Baksh, a municipal commissioner and president of the Gurdaspur Congress Committee, and Khan Mohammad Khan of Ludhiana.[63]

Similarly, the most prominent Muslim Congressmen in Bengal were professional men. Notable amongst them was Abdul Rasul, son of a rich zamindar of Guniank in Tipperah district. He went to St. John's College, Oxford, and was called to the Bar from the Middle Temple. On his return to India, Rasul enrolled himself as a barrister of the Calcutta High Court, where he came into contact with leading lawyers like W.C. Bonnerjee and Lal Mohan Ghose, who were active Congressmen. Among other leading Muslim Congressmen were Abdul Kaseem of Burdwan, who was elected a member of the Congress Constitution Committee in 1904, and Abdul Halim Ghuznavi, a petty zamindar of Tangail and Calcutta lawyer. Many of them played an important role during the Swadeshi movement in Bengal.[64]

One of the obvious conclusions that emerges from our analysis is that Muslims were sharply divided in their response to Congress for a variety of reasons, and that their reaction varied from province to province, and from city to city. In Bengal and the Punjab, for example, a numerically small group of professional men supported Congress, but the conservative landed interests consistently stood against it. Similarly, in the Bombay Presidency the Bohra and Khoja communities were plagued by faction and dissension in their attitude towards Congress. At the local level, the reaction of Shias and Sunnis in Lucknow and Allahabad illustrated how sectional rivalries often influenced political affiliations. These few instances seem to indicate that by the end of the nineteenth century, an all-India Muslim political consciousness had yet to emerge. Regional and local interests kept Muslims apart on the all-India

[63]*Tribune*, 14 October 1893, 25 November 1893, 13 December 1893.

[64]See S. Sarkar, *The Swadeshi Movement in Bengal, 1903-1908* (Delhi, 1973), pp. 426-35; Narain, *Press and Politics in India*, pp. 61-2.

level as well as in the provinces and localities. This affected
their reaction to Congress demands, as indeed to British
policies, which rested mainly on 'local, special and temporary
causes'.

As a political body, the Congress was viewed in different
ways by various Muslim groups. While the Muslim orthodoxy
in general regarded it as a Hindu body whose aim was to
drive out Islam from India,[65] men like Tyabji, Sayani and
Rasul saw Congress as a safe custodian of national interests.
According to them, it was a national organisation which
ventilated the grievances of all categories of Indians and had
'no concern whatever with the religion or the religious exercise
of any of its members'. Tyabji developed this argument in his
presidential address at the Madras Congress and in letters
written early in 1888 to Ameer Ali, Syed Ahmad Khan, and
the *Pioneer* of Allahabad.

To many aggrieved groups, such as the *wasiqadars* of Daryabad, the early Congress provided the only all-India forum
for voicing their particular grievances. But this was not so in
the case of many others who viewed Congress demands as a
potential threat to their material interests. Muslims in UP, for
instance, feared that the introduction of representative institutions, based on numerical representation, would leave them at
the mercy of the Hindu majority. Similarly, the Bengali and
Punjabi Muslims opposed the Congress demand for competitive
examinations; they favoured recruitment to the Civil Service
by a system of nomination because it served their interests
better.

III

GOVERNMENT ALIENATES THE MUSLIMS, 1900-1915

From 1900 onwards, the government introduced a series of
administrative and bureaucratic reforms in order to pacify the
Hindu revivalists in the UP and the anti-partition agitators in

---

[65] The emergence of Hindu revivalist movements with their militant
posture and their links with Congress gave credence to this belief in
many regions and at different social and economic levels.

Bengal. In doing so, it engendered widespread disaffection amongst dominant Muslim groups, threatened the Anglo-Muslim alliance in Indian politics, and provided a powerful stimulus for the growth of political radicalism. This, in turn, paved the way for the emergence of a pro-Congress group amongst Muslims, particularly in Bengal and UP, where government policies disturbed the *status quo* most. It stood for agitational politics as opposed to the politics of subservience advocated by Syed Ahmad Khan and other Aligarh Muslim leaders. It had no faith in the beneficence of British rule and emphasised the importance of claiming concessions through agitation and vigorous protest. The policies of Anthony MacDonnell in the UP, the reunification of Bengal, the rejection of the Aligarh Muslim University scheme, and the Kanpur mosque incident seemed to demonstrate the validity of the view that radical self-help was a better solution than mendicancy.

The drift into radicalism

In the UP, the policies of Anthony MacDonnell, who became Lieutenant-Governor in 1894, put a severe strain on Muslim loyalty to the government.[66] Unlike his predecessors, who made every effort to win over Muslims, MacDonnell adopted a prejudiced and unsympathetic attitude towards them. He regarded Muslims, quite wrongly, as a hostile and politically dangerous community, and, therefore, considered it important to reduce their strong position in government service. To achieve this end he fixed a communal quota for Muslims in public service (they were to be appointed in the ratio of three to five Hindus)—a measure which temporarily reduced the proportion of civil service posts occupied by Muslims.

Furthermore, in April 1900 the Devanagri script was placed

---

[66]*The Al-Bashir*, a pro-government paper from Etawah, was critical of MacDonnell's hostility to Urdu and the *Nadwat al-ulama* which was considered by the Lt-Governor as 'an association of narrow-minded, bigoted and conservative Mussalmans'. 'Taking his administration in general', the *Al-Bashir* observed, 'Sir Anthony MacDonnell has sowed the seed of discord between the Hindus and Muslims, disturbed the equanimity of the *zamindars*, and caused general unrest and distrust in the province'. *Al-Bashir*, 28 November 1901, UPNNR 1901.

on an equal footing with Urdu by providing for its optional use in court documents, and only those acquainted with both forms of writing were entitled to ministerial appointments.[67] This decision threatened Muslims more than any other vested interest in government service because, unlike the Hindus, they did not learn the Devanagri script in their normal course of education.[68] Muslims feared that the Hindus would not only gain ascendancy in government service, but would also displace them in course of time. Similarly, it would make life difficult for Muslim lawyers whose briefs would necessarily be reduced.[69] These fears were voiced at public meetings held in many cities of UP where Muslims expressed their resentment against the April resolution in unequivocal terms.[70] Realising the depth of the community's feelings, Mohsinul Mulk, secretary of Aligarh College, reorganised the Urdu Defence Association.[71] Leading barristers and pleaders of Allahabad established a similar association with the object of preserving the use of Urdu character and language.[72] In Lucknow, many eminent Muslims, led by Hamid Ali Khan, formed a committee for the same purpose. In August 1900, they organised a conference which was attended by an impressive array of journalists,

---

[67]'No person shall be appointed', stated the *Government Gazette* in its educational rules, 'except in a purely English office to any ministerial appointment henceforth unless he can read and write both the Nagri and the Persian character'.

[68]*Liberal* (Azamgarh), 16 April 1900, UPNNR 1900.

[69]*Report of the Indian Education Commission*, p. 123.

[70]Meetings were held in Mathura, Agra, Fatehgarh, Fatehpur, Amroha, Moradabad, Rampur, Allahabad, Lucknow, Aligarh and several other cities. Syed Raza Ali, who was much involved in the agitation against the Nagri resolution and toured many parts of the country to mobilise support, provides an interesting account of some of these meetings in his autobiography. S.R. Ali, *A'amaal Nama* (Delhi, 1943), pp. 88-91. Also, see *Rohilkhand Gazette* (Bareilly), 1 May 1900; *Azad*, 8 May 1900; *Mufid-i-Am* (Agra), 20 May 1900; *Riazul Akhbar*, 20 May 1900; *Oudh Akhbar*, 23 May 1900; *Jam-i-Jamshed* (Moradabad), 27 May 1900, UPNNR 1900.

[71]A meeting of Muslim barristers and some *ulama* held in Gorakhpur expressed its concurrence with the aims and objects of the Association. *Riazul Akhbar*, 16 August 1900, *Ibid.*

[72]*Aina* (Lucknow), 12 May 1898, *Ibid.*, 1898.

lawyers, *ulama*, and *taluqdars*.[73] This marked the beginning of an agitation which spread through most of the district towns of the UP. Over the years, the defence of Urdu became the cornerstone of Muslim separatist politics and its cause was espoused from several public platforms, including the All-India Muslim League.

Though the agitation in UP started off with great vigour, it collapsed within a year. Mohsinul Mulk, the mastermind behind the protest movement, succumbed to MacDonnell's pressure and reluctantly severed his connections with the Urdu agitation.[74] Lutf Ali Khan, president of the Urdu Defence Association, along with seven other *rais* from Aligarh, followed suit.[75] By 1901, MacDonnell had cut off all the tall poppies and only a small group of radical Muslims kept the agitation alive. This group, largely composed of young lawyers, journalists, and politically independent-minded Aligarh students, expressed its disillusionment with the politically conservative Muslim leadership and openly demanded militant action in defence of their interests. It also pressed for the establishment of a Muslim political association by demonstrating the inadequacy of mendicant tactics.[76] 'Owing to the want of such an association', wrote the *Asr-i-Jadid*, 'the interests of the Muslim community have already suffered in a variety of ways and are still being trampled under foot . . . .'[77] The paper also suggested greater

[73]On that occasion, Mohsinul Mulk referred to the genocide of Urdu in the following verse :

چل ساتھ کہ حسرت دلِ محروم سے نکلے
عاشق کا جنازہ ہے بڑی دھوم سے نکلے

[74]'By his abrupt secession from the Urdu Defence Association, he (Mohsinul Mulk) has shown himself to be a great coward and utterly unfit to be a leader. It was sheer cunningness, hypocrisy and deceitfulness on his part to decoy a people into a trap, and then quickly withdraw from it', wrote the *Azad*, 22 October 1901, UPNNR 1901.

[75]*Riazul Akhbar*, 24 September 1900; *Oudh Akhbar*, 17 September 1900, *Ibid.*, 1900.

[76]On this point, see a summary of Raza Ali's article published in the *Pioneer* of 24 November 1901 in S.R. Ali, *A'amaal Nama*, pp. 112-13.

[77]*Asr-i-Jadid* (Meerut), May 1903, UPNNR 1903.

cooperation with Congress on issues of common interest:
the reduction of salt duty, the raising of the minimum limit
of taxable income and greater employment of educated
Indians in the commissioned ranks of the army.[78] This view
received support from important journalists, such as Maulvi
Aqlab Mohani, Fazlul Husain, Maulvi Abdul Kazim and
Maulana Shaukat, editor of *Shahna-i-Hind*.[79]

Mohsinul Mulk and other Aligarh Muslim leaders, on the
other hand, were anxious to counter the moves towards joining
Congress. With this aim in mind, Musa Khan, a *rais* of
Datauli in Aligarh district, made attempts to found a regional
organisation.[80] Mohsinul Mulk suggested the revival of the
M.A.O. College Defence Association,[81] but the idea did not
strike a favourable chord after the disastrous failure of the
Urdu Defence Association.[82] He then approached Archbold,
Principal, M.A.O. College, Aligarh, and suggested the idea of
presenting a memorial to the Viceroy.[83] Two weeks later,
Mohsinul Mulk warned that 'if we remain silent . . . people
will leave us to go their own way . . .'[84] What he meant was
that the 'young educated Mohammedans' would join the

[78] *Asr-i-Jadid*, March 1903, UPNNR 1903.

[79] *Tribune*, 14 November 1906.

[80] *Jami-ul-Ulum*, 14 August 1900, UPNNR 1900.

[81] *Aligarh Institute Gazette*, 17 October 1903.

[82] See, for example, the reaction expressed in the Urdu newspapers in
Uruj (Bijnor), 14 July 1903; *Riazul Akhbar*, 1 February 1905; *Oudh
Akhbar*, 10 December 1903, UPNNR 1903.

[83] In his letter, Mohsinul Mulk wrote: 'You are aware that the
Mohammedans already feel a little disappointed, and young educated
Mohammedans seem to have a sympathy for the "Congress". . .Although
there is little reason to believe that any Mohammedans, except the
young educated ones, will join that body, there is still a general com-
plaint on their part that we (Aligarh people) take no part in politics,
and do not safeguard the political rights of Mohammedans. . . .' Mohsinul
Mulk to Archbold, 4 August 1906, quoted in R. Wasti, *Lord Minto and
the Indian Nationalist Movement, 1905-1910* (Oxford, 1964), p. 63.

[84] A fortnight later, Mohsinul Mulk referred to the letters received
from all over India telling him that 'Mohammedan feeling is very much
changed. . . , and saying that the Hindus have succeeded owing to
their agitation, and the Mohammedans have suffered for their silence.
The Mohammedans have generally begun to think of organising a
political association and forming themselves into political agitators.'
Mohsinul Mulk to Archbold, 18 August 1906, *Ibid.*, p. 231.

Congress. This was a prospect which neither the Viceroy nor his officials could possibly welcome. Consequently, the Viceroy agreed to receive a deputation of 'leading Mohammedans'. On 1 October 1906, a memorial was presented to Minto, the Viceroy, by thirty-five Muslims led by the Aga Khan, the head of the Ismaili sect. It formed the basis on which the All-India Muslim League came into existence on 30 December 1906. Forty years later, the same League led the movement for a separate homeland for the Muslims culminating in the tragic partition of the country.

Although Mohsinul Mulk and his pro-government supporters wrested the initiative from the 'young gentlemen' in forming a political organisation, they failed to discourage or prevent the growing demand for rapprochement with the Congress.[85] In fact, the demand gained impetus in the years following the establishment of the All-India Muslim League. This was partly because some Congressmen assiduously cultivated influential Muslim leaders and secured their support by identifying themselves with the Aligarh Muslim University project and the pan-Islamic movement. But more significantly the events in Turkey, the Kanpur mosque incident, the reunification of Bengal, and the rejection of the Muslim University scheme acted as a further irritant in the relations between the government and the Muslims and drove some of them into the Congress camp. Their aim was to forge a united front against the Raj.

Bengal and the Annulment of Partition

Bengal was partitioned in October 1905. The new province of East Bengal had a population of thirty-one million of which eighteen million were Muslims. It offered the Muslims new opportunities in education, government service, and the profes-

[85]Some of the important newspapers which advocated cooperation with Congress were: *Urdu-i-Moala* (Aligarh), December 1907; *Azad*, 10 December 1906. For pro-Congress feelings in the M.A.O. College, Aligarh, see *Tribune*, 9 May 1906; *Indian People*, 24 May 1906. For the Aligarh students' support for the Swadeshi movement in Bengal, see *Indian People*, 10 December 1905, UPNNR 1905.

sions. In a united Bengal, even though Muslims were numerically superior, they were handicapped because of their educational and economic backwardness which prevented them from securing adequate representation either on the Council or the local self-governing bodies. Nor did they fare well in the public services. In the Executive Service as well as the Judicial Service of the government of Bengal, Muslims in 1887 held only 9.6 per cent of the posts.

The partition of Bengal, however, proved to be a great boon to many Muslims in East Bengal. This is illustrated by some of the Muslim gains from 1906 to 1911. The number of literates in the province increased from 12,455 (14.53 per cent) in 1905 to 35,688 (21.43 per cent) in 1910-11. There was a corresponding increase in the number of Muslim educational officers and teachers.[86] There were similar gains in public appointments. In 1901, Muslims held one-eighth of the 1,235 gazetted appointments; in 1911, they occupied one-fifth of the 2,305 such posts. Muslims were also winning seats on the municipalities. In Commila division, they secured eight of the twelve seats, and in Sylhet six of the ten vacancies in 1906-7.[87] In the triennial election of Dacca Municipality, eight out of the fourteen candidates elected, were Muslims.[88]

Many Hindus, on the other hand, opposed the partition on the ground that it was an attack upon the 'growing solidarity' of Bengali nationalism.[89] But in actual fact their main grievance was that the new province threatened their dominance in the public services and professions. The Hindu-dominated Calcutta Bar feared that the creation of a separate High Court at Dacca would diminish its importance. Consequently, all the 'wealth and weight of the great horde of Calcutta lawyers and their

[86]See S. Ahmad, *Muslim Community in Bengal, 1884-1912* (Dacca, 1974), pp. 288-95.

[87]*Resolution Reviewing the Reports of the Working of the Municipalities in Eastern Bengal and Assam, 1906-7* (Shillong, 1908), p. 1.

[88]*Tribune*, 24 March 1909; For the overall improvement in Muslim representation on District Board, Local Boards and Union Committees in Burdwan, Dacca, Chittagong and Rajshahi divisions, see Rizvi, 'Muslim Politics and Government Policy', Table 46, p. 175.

[89]C.N. Basu, *The Partition Agitation Explained* (Calcutta, 1906); Basu, *The Partition Riddle* (Calcutta, 1906), IOL Tracts: 1048.

underlings was thrown into the fight against the scheme'.[90] The Maharaja Manindra Chunder Nundi lamented that in East Bengal 'the Muslim population will preponderate... [and] the Bengali Hindu will be in a minority. We shall be strangers in our own land'.[91] In other words, the hue and cry against the partition was raised mainly because Hindu professional groups wanted to perpetuate their dominance in a province where they were in a distinct minority.

The Viceroy, Hardinge, initially resisted suggestions for the modification of the partition. In January 1911, he opposed the idea of reverting to the *status quo ante Curzonem*, because he felt that such a move would be interpreted as 'a concession to noisy clamour', and would alienate the Muslims.[92] But by June 1911, Hardinge was converted to the proposal of revoking the partition. He endorsed the scheme outlined by J.L. Jenkins, the Chief Justice of the Calcutta High Court, for the revision of partition, and hoped that it would remove what the Bengali Hindus regarded as a 'flagrant injustice' to them.[93]

The government's decision, however, stunned many Bengali Muslims who had come to regard the partition as a settled fact. At widely attended public meetings, speaker after speaker forcefully protested against the government's 'utter disregard of Muslim feelings',[94] and explained how they felt betrayed and abandoned. 'Agitate and you will get what you want; remain calm and you will have your heads chopped. This is the moral we are given', observed Abu Saleh in the columns of the

[90]K.B. Krishna, *The Problem of Minorities* (London, 1939), p. 148. According to the Viceroy, the anti-partition agitation was due to the 'loss of certain amount of business, especially legal business, which now migrates from Calcutta to the large cities of Eastern Bengal, and that this feeling had been fanned into blaze by wirepullers at Calcutta under the influence of other wire-pullers at home connected with the National Congress.' Minto to Morley, 13 December 1905, quoted in Wasti, *Lord Minto and the Indian Nationalist Movement*, p. 27.

[91]Proceedings of the Town Hall Protest Meeting, 7 August 1905. *All About Partition*, IOL Tracts: 1037.

[92]Hardinge to Crewe, 25 January 1911, Hardinge to Crewe, 22 February 1911, Hardinge Papers (113), CUL.

[93]Hardinge to Jenkins, 11 June 1911, Hardinge to Crewe, 6 July 1911, *Ibid.*

[94]*Mussalman*, 12 June 1912.

Mussalman.[95] The message was loud and clear. The Bengali Muslims could no longer rely on government for concessions, and their young leaders demanded militant action in defence of their interests. Young lawyers and journalists like Fazlul Haq, Abdullah Suhrawardy and Mujibur Rahman saw possibilities of cooperation with the Congress, because its leaders, according to the *Mussalman*, 'were beginning to understand our problems and are willing to consider our special demands'.[96] They also felt that the political aims of the Congress and the Muslim League were the same and therefore there was scope for joint action on questions that affected the general political interests of the country.[97]

The Pan-Islamic Movement

Among Sunni Muslims, who formed an overwhelming majority of the Muslim population, the Sultan of Turkey was the *Amir al-Mu'minin* (Commander of the Faithful) and the protector of the Holy Places. The Khilafat, which in 1517 was transferred to Salim I of the House of Ottoman, was the viceroyalty of the Prophet of Islam, ordained by Divine Law for the perpetuation of Islam and the continued observance of its *Sharia* (Islamic law). The Khalifa, derived from the word '*khalafa*' (to leave behind), was both the religious head of the Sunnis as well as the ruler of an independent kingdom. Allegiance to him was obligatory, and that is why the Sultans of Delhi inscribed the names of the Khalifa on their coins and often received investitures as a legal sanction for their rule. The name of the Abbasid Khalifa, Al-Mustasim, continued on the coins for about forty years after the sack of Baghdad at the hands of the Mongols. It was

[95]*Mussalman*, 12 January 1912.

[96]Home Poll. A, March 1915, 45-55, NAI; Carmichael to Hardinge, 1 June 1913, Hardinge Papers (85). A correspondent suggested that Muslims should consider abandoning separate electorates in order to promote rapprochement with Hindus'. *Mussalman*, 19 January 1912.

[97]Notice, for example, Mujibur Rahman's comment that 'there is no room for the old time honoured arguments against the Congress, as there is no difference between the aims and objects of the Congress and those of the Muslim League'. *Ibid.*, 4 January 1915; FR (Bengal), 16 January 1915, Home Poll. March 1915, 53, NAI.

probably an expression of the sentiment: 'The Khalifa is dead, long live the Khalifa'.[98] Even as late as the eighteenth century many independent Muslim rulers turned towards the Khalifa as a source of legitimacy. Tipu Sultan, for example, sent an embassy to the Ottoman Khalifa in 1785. His emissaries secured for him letters of investiture allowing him to assume the title of an independent ruler.[99]

Throughout the nineteenth and twentieth centuries, Indian Muslims continued to show a solicitous interest in the welfare of Turkey.[100] During the Balkan wars, they were particularly disappointed with Britain's role. As the War progressed, it became evident that European politics had considerably changed since Britain fought side by side with Turkey against Russia half a century ago. The view gained credence, not unjustifiably, that Britain acquiesced in the Italian attack on Tripoli and concluded treaties with Russia and France under which the partition of the Ottoman Empire was decided. This aroused considerable anti-government feelings in India. 'There is a great agitation', reported the Viceroy, 'in Muslim circles over the war in the Balkans, and a general feeling that the Christians are combining to thrust the Muslims out of Europe'.[101] From Bengal it was reported that many Muslims were 'seriously anxious' about the future of Turkey,[102] and in the Punjab they closely followed 'every move in the game in the Balkans and every reference to the subject by British statesmen'.[103]

The Turko-Italian war proved to be decisive in bringing together the various sections of the Muslim community. In Bombay Presidency, conservative Muslims like Fazulbhoy Currimbhoy and Maulvi Rafiuddin lent their support to the

[98]R.P. Tripathi, *Some Aspects of Muslim Administration in India* (Allahabad, 1936), p. 37.

[99]Mohibbul Hasan (ed.), *Waqai-i-Manazil-i Rum*: *diary of a journey to Constantinople* (Delhi, 1968).

[100]For the historical antecedents of the Khilafat movement in India, see M.N. Qureshi, 'Pan Islamism and Nationalism: Muslim Politics in British India 1918-24' (Unpublished Ph.D. thesis, London, 1973), pp. 1-10, 15-18.

[101]Hardinge to V. Chirol, 22 October 1912, Hardinge Papers (84).

[102]Carmichael to Hardinge, 6 September 1914, *Ibid* (88).

[103]O'Dwyer to Hardinge, 11 August 1913, *Ibid* (84).

agitation against the 'unjust war'.[104] In UP, the agitation was kept alive by Zafar Ali Khan, the volatile editor of *Zamindar*, by Mohamed Ali who had recently launched himself in the world of journalism, by M.A. Ansari, the organiser of the Medical Mission to Constantinople, and by M.H. Kidwai, a lawyer from the Barabanki district.[105] These men joined the *ulama* in founding the *Anjuman-i-Khuddam-i-Kaaba* (The Society of the Servants of the Kaaba) in May 1913. The Society had its headquarters first in Delhi and later in Firangi Mahal, Lucknow, and its chief organisers were Maulana Abdul Bari, Kidwai, and Shaukat Ali.[106] Its main aim was to maintain the honour and safety of the Kaaba and to defend the Holy Places from non-Muslim encroachments.[107] Soon the *anjuman* established a wide network of branches in London, Constantinople, Cairo and Singapore, and its emissaries actively encouraged disaffection against non-Muslim powers.[108]

In its historical sequence, the *Anjuman-i-Khuddam-i-Kaaba* represented the first combined effort of the Muslim professional classes and the *ulama*. The alliance between the two was of great significance, because it illustrated that, on purely religious issues, the *alim* and the modernised Muslim could strive together for common ends.

The Aligarh Muslim University Movement

Founded in 1877, the M.A.O. College at Aligarh developed into an important centre for modern secular education. Its students, as Table 2.2 sets out, came from all parts of the country. This fact was continually stressed to raise funds for the College

---

[104]*Mahratta*, 20 October, 17 November 1912.

[105]In the UP, the reaction of the masses was reportedly 'sharp and bitter' towards the government. Home Poll. A, March 1913, 45, NAI; At Aligarh College, the students first mooted the idea of boycotting Italian goods. *Tribune*, 10 November 1911.

[106]For list of the founding members, see Abdul Bari Papers (1/42), Firangi Mahal, Lucknow.

[107]For the exchange of correspondence between Abdul Bari and the Viceroy on the aims and objects of the *Anjuman*, see Home Poll. Deposit, July 1914, 7, NAI; Home Poll. Deposit, April 1915, 19, NAI.

[108]Abdul Bari, *Khutba-i-Sadarat* (Erode, 1921), p. 10.

from different regions.[109] 'Aligarh', wrote Mohammed Ali, 'is not, has not been, and was never intended to be a provincial institution. It has striven, through good fortune and evil, for the strengthening of the communal bond that holds seventy million together as no provincial bond has hitherto done.'[110] During 1903 and 1911, the College had on its rolls 3,320 students.[111] In 1910, out of a total of 789 students, 366 (46 per cent) were from the U.P.; 130 (16 per cent) from the Punjab; 92 (11 per cent) from Bengal and Bihar; 33 from East Bengal and Assam, and 58 from Hyderabad.[112] In 1911 the College had an annual income of Rs 208,000—an increase of 165 per cent since 1897.[113]

The growing popularity of the College as well as its contribution to the educational development of the Muslims,[114] encouraged many Muslim educationists and politicians to argue the case for a University.[115] Aligarh was not only the ideological symbol of the educational, cultural, and political aspirations

[109]The contributions to the College fund came from all parts of the country as well as from different groups among Muslims. The common assumption that contributors were only from the landed aristocracy is untenable in the light of the available evidence. The list of contributors at the Aligarh Archives indicates that the College movement evoked great response among petty landowners, traders, shopkeepers, professional men and government servants. See, for example, S. Rashiduddin to Syed Ahmad, 25 December 1892; Abdur Rahman Khan to Syed Ahmad, 14 March 1894; Fazl Haq to Syed Ahmad, 9 March 1894; Nazir Ahmad to Syed Ahmad, 2 December 1875; Mohamed Hasan to Syed Ahmad, 1 June 1874, M.A.O. College Collection Fund Files, Syed Ahmad Papers, AMUA.

[110]*Aligarh Institute Gazette*, 20 November 1888; *Comrade*, 28 January 1911.

[111]*Statement Showing the Number of Students in the M.A.O. College, 1904-18*, Syed Ahmad Papers.

[112]*Comrade*, 4 March 1911.

[113]*Ibid.*, 14 January 1911.

[114]The percentage of Muslim undergraduates in the College (excluding those in Native States) affiliated to the Universities of Madras, Bombay, Calcutta and the Punjab was 1.7, 3.9, 6.6 and 21.8, respectively. The Aligarh College was responsible for the excellent figures of Allahabad University, where the percentage of Muslim undergraduates was 23.9. *Ibid.*, 14 January 1911.

[115]The idea of developing the College into a University was mooted time and again from several platforms. For details, see Rahman, *Consultation to Confrontation*, pp. 175-6.

of Muslims but was regarded as the future centre of a Muslim renaissance.[116] Optimists hoped that 'all roads will lead one day to Aligarh as all roads led in the best days of Islam to Cordova and Baghdad'.[117] The College would then be the 'Islamic Oxford' of India.[118] The pan-Islamists saw in the institution a glittering vision of a common centre, where Muslims from all over the world would congregate and promote a common 'Islamic consciousness', and revive the 'true spirit of Islam'.[119]

TABLE 2.2

PROVINCIAL DISTRIBUTION OF STUDENTS AT THE
M.A.O. COLLEGE, ALIGARH, 1893-1903

Year	Agra	Oudh	Punjab	Bengal & Bihar	Madras	Bombay	Central Provinces	Other States
1893	218	—	87	8	—	2	5	23
1903	220	81	86	44	15	12	14	59

Source : *Note on the Progress of the M.A.O. College*, 1893-1903 (Aligarh, n.d.), Syed Ahmad Papers, AMUA.

The government of India was favourably inclined to accept the proposals put forward by the Muslim University Foundation Committee. Harcourt Butler, in particular, believed that it would be politically expedient for the government to lead the educational movement and to encourage denominational universities, which would provide religious instruction and inevitably tend to keep 'alive the Hindu-Muslim feelings'.[120] But the Secretary of State and some members of his Council objected to the term 'Muslim' in the nomenclature of the University and

[116]C. Khaliquzzaman, *Pathway to Pakistan* (Lahore, 1961), p. 14.
[117]*Comrade*, 28 January 1911
[118]*Ibid.*, 14 January 1911.
[119]S.A. Qadir, 'The Proposed Mohamedan University', *Muslim Review* (Allahabad), October 1910, p. 288.
[120]Butler to the Aga Khan, 3 August 1911, Butler Papers, MSS. EUR. F. 116 (71), and Butler to Hardinge, 25 September 1911, Hardinge Papers (82).

the scheme to affiliate colleges outside the province. Montagu opposed the foundation of a denominational university maintaining that, by embarking on the enterprise of a new Muslim university, those who accused the government of a policy of 'divide and rule' would have a strong case.[121] Theodore Morrison, a former Principal of the M.A.O. College, Aligarh, and a member of the India Council at this time, opposed granting Aligarh the power of affiliation, because it was inconsistent with the idea of a teaching and residential university.[122]

By refusing the power of affiliation, the government 'pulled the main object underlying the University movement from under its feet.'[123] The promoters of the College such as Mohamed Ali, the Raja of Mahmudabad, Mazharul Haque, and Abul Kalam Azad were bitterly disappointed.[124] In July 1913, the Foundation Committee rejected the government's terms for the University.[125] The government's rebuff spurred them to agitate.[126] In the period after 1913, the campaigners for the Muslim University, with few exceptions, remained the most bitter critics of the Raj. Various attempts to assuage their feelings met with little success.

The Kanpur Mosque Incident

In August 1913, a serious riot occurred in Kanpur following rumours in the city that a portion of the Machhli Bazaar mosque was being demolished by the municipality.[127] The scene of disturbance was visited by several Muslim politicians, including Mohamed Ali, who allegedly used the incident to foment agitation against the government.[128] The *ulama* also joined in.

[121]A. Basu, *The Growth of Education and Political Development in India, 1898-1920* (Delhi, 1974), p. 164.

[122]*Ibid.*, pp. 165-7.

[123]*Comrade*, 20 July 1912.

[124]Montagu, *Indian Diary*, Vol. 1, p. 161, Montagu Papers, MSS. EUR. D. 523 (38), IOL.

[125]*Comrade*, 28 July 1913.

[126]Hardinge to George Ross-Keppel, 12 August 1912; Hardinge Papers (84); *Comrade*, 31 August 1912.

[127]For an account of the riots and the events leading to it, see Note by Meston, 31 August 1921, Home Poll. A, October 1913, 100-18, NAI.

[128]P.C. Bamford, *Histories of the Khilafat and Non-Cooperation Movements*. Reprint. (Delhi, 1975), p. 114.

Shibli Numani, formerly assistant professor of Arabic at the
M.A.O. College, Aligarh, and a leading spirit behind the foundation of the *Nadwat al-ulama* attended protest meetings
against the provincial government.[129] Among the 'leaders of
the localities', the Raja of Mahmudabad played a key role during the controversy. Then there was Nawab Ali Chaudhuri,
'a large landlord, much respected in his own district',[130] who
presided over a meeting of ten thousand Muslims held in
Calcutta. He declared at the meeting that he was not one of
those who would rush into the arena of political agitation for
the sake of notoriety, or who would consent to criticise the
action of the authorities unless he was sincerely and deeply
convinced, that it would be a mistake to suppose that an agitation of such a magnitude and importance was at all a local
affair or merely got up for the occasion.[131]

The agitation over the Kanpur mosque affair spread to
educational institutions too. At the Aligarh College, the poems
of Shibli,[132] Khwaja Hasan Nizami[133] and Hashim Faridi
on the evils inflicted upon Islam were recited in the Students'
Union and at the *mushairas* (poetry recitation sessions).[134]
Similarly, in *Nadwa* the students went on strike in March 1914,
ostensibly in connection with the expulsion of a student, but really, as would appear from the reasons given to the board of enquiry,

[129]Note by P. Biggane, 30 October 1914, GAD, 1908, 79, UPSA;
'History Sheet of Shibli Numani Shams-ul-Ulama', GAD, 1914, 55,
UPSA.

[130]Carmichael to Hardinge, 7 November 1913, Hardinge Papers (86).

[131]*Mahratta*, 10 August 1913.

[132]In 1913, Shibli wrote a moving poem on the Kanpur mosque
incident. It read as:

اگر چہ آنکھ میں نم بھی نہیں ہے اب باقی   اگر چہ صدمہ بلقان سے جگر شتی ہے
پکا رکھے ہیں مگر میں نے چند قطرہ خون   کہ کان پور کے بھی زمینوں کا کچھ حق ہے

See, Shibli to Azad, 20 August 1913, *Makatib-i-Shibli*, Vol. 1, p. 218.

[133]For a collection of poems on the incident, see K.H. Nizami,
Kanpur Ki Khuni Kahani (Meerut, 1913).

[134]K.M. Ashraf, 'Aligarh ki Siyasi Zindagi'. *Aligarh Magazine*,
1953-55.

the because the General Secretary of the institution prevented
students from taking part in a meeting in the Kanpur mosque
affair. The strike was eventually called off following the inter-
vention of Aftab Ahmad Khan, Nawab Ishaq Khan, and Hakim
Ajmal Khan.[135]

Muslim reaction to the Kanpur mosque incident needs to
be interpreted in terms of the sanctity attached to a *masjid*
(place of prostration). A *masjid* is the 'House of Allah' where
the faithful perform the public prayer. It is the local focus of
Muslim devotion and in some sense 'an epitome of Muslim life
and the Muslim story'. It is, therefore, not surprising that many
Muslims reacted violently to the news of the demolition of even
a portion of the Kanpur mosque. Admittedly, the incident
generated much tension because of events in the Balkans
and the rejection of the University scheme. But to argue that
the Kanpur affair would 'never have become an issue but for the
journalistic Mohamed Ali's search for agitational issue',[136] is
an assumption which has no basis whatsoever. Mohamed Ali
was neither the first nor the last man to recognise the sanctity
of mosques in India or in other Muslim countries.

III

Events between 1911 and 1914 led to important changes in
Muslim leadership and in its attitude towards the government and towards the Congress. The old school of aristo-
cratic Muslim politicians stood discredited because their policy
of collaboration had proved a failure. Ishaq Khan, Honorary
Secretary of Aligarh College, complained of being subjected to
various 'indignities' by the Ali Brothers.[137] What he probably meant was that the Ali Brothers were trying to get
rid of the pro-government lobby which dominated the
College administration, the Board of Trustees and the
Old Boys' Association. He also admitted in August 1913
that 'the moderate men amongst us have lost ground

---

[135]Note by P. Biggane, 30 October 1914, GAD 1914, 79, UPSA.
[136]Robinson, *Separatism*, p. 214.
[137]I. Khan to Meston, 20 November 1913, Meston Papers, MSS.
EUR. F. 136 (6), IOL.

with the public and are afraid of being ridiculed'.[138] Similarly, the Aga Khan, whose support for the reunification of Bengal made him a target for attack, found his position untenable and resigned from the presidency of the Muslim League.[139] The Nawab of Rampur, too, resigned from the visitorship of the Aligarh College which was increasingly coming under the influence of Mohamed Ali and Zafar Ali Khan.[140]

As the old leadership began to recede into the background, a new group of professional men and the *ulama* emerged which stood for cooperation with Congress and far less reliance on the government. Amongst the *ulama*, Azad and Shibli were forceful advocates of rapprochement with Congress. Azad was highly critical of Western imperialism which he considered both aggressive and anti-Islamic.[141] He urged Muslims not to be apprehensive of the Hindus, but to jointly strive for self-government.[142] The inspiration for these views was most probably provided by Shibli who was well known for his scholarly writings on Islamic history, literature, and religion. The only clue to his political views is provided by his articles published in the *Muslim Gazette*, edited by Maulvi Wahiduddin Salih of Lucknow. In these articles, Shibli argued the case for cooperation with Congress and criticised the League for pursuing sectional and communal policies. He suggested that the League should be freed from the domination of the titled gentry and the *jee-huzoors* so that it could identify itself with the political and economic interests of the country. Shibli observed that in pursuing a comprehensive and constructive economic pro-

[138]I. Khan to Meston, 21 August 1913, Meston Papers (6).

[139]'The time has come', wrote the Aga Khan, 'when the community must wake up and reorganise the League on a popular basis or it will degenerate into a self-appointed society of leaders without a following. If I continue any longer in the chair of President, I shall not be doing my duty. . .'. The Aga Khan to Wazir Hasan, 3 November 1913, Crewe Papers, I/14 (2), CUL; The Aga Khan to Butler, 3 March 1913, Butler Papers (71).

[140]Hamid Ali Khan to Ishaq Khan, 15 November 1913, Meston Papers (4).

[141]*Al-Hilal*, 9 October 1914; *Khutbat-i-Abul Kalam Azad* (Lahore, n.d.), pp. 18-19.

[142]*Ibid.*, 1 September, 18 December 1912.

gramme, the Congress, in fact was representing and promoting the best interests of the country.[143]

Similar views were expressed by a group of Western-educated Muslims. Mazharul Haque, who was probably the most respected leader of this group, urged Muslims to join the Congress and referred to 'a great powerful party of liberal Muslims. . .whose aims and ideals are the aims and ideals of the Congress'.[144] Also, the influential newspaper, *Comrade*, noted the importance of the Congress which embodied the 'genuine and vigorous aspirations which move educated India for a well organised and common national life'.[145] M.H. Kidwai, already famous for his role in founding the *Anjuman-i-Khuddam-i-Kaaba*, denounced the conservative Muslims for their 'sycophancy' and their adherence to 'archaic and obsolete' political notions. He suggested that Muslims should join Congress which 'has raised the political prestige of India in the eyes of the civilized world'.[146] An intelligence officer thus summed up the pro-Congress stance of Muslims in north India :

> A reliable correspondent who is clearly in touch with several classes of well-to-do Muslims in the north of India, has informed me that he has not met a single educated Muslim who is not in favour of combination between Muslim politicians in India and the Hindu Congress party.'[147]

In conclusion, then, the period from 1900 to 1915 witnessed notable changes in the relationship between various Muslim groups and the government. This was evident in the radical strain which marked the political activities of some Western-educated Muslims and their allies among the *ulama*. The shift

[143]See *Maqalat-i-Shibli* (Azamgarh, 1938), Vol. 8, pp. 148-84.
[144]*Tribune*, 21 January 1911; *Bengalee*, 27 December 1912,
[145]*Comrade*, 30 December 1911.
[146]*Mahratta*, 4 February 1912.
[147]WRDCI, 4 July 1912, Home Poll. B, August 1912, NAI; R.H. Craddock, Home Member, Minute 15 December 1912, Home Poll. A, March 1913, 45-55, NAI. Hardinge conceded in August 1913 that his government could not count on the loyalty of Muslims who were prepared to join 'any other faction in opposition to the Raj'. Hardinge to Crewe, 14 August 1913, Hardinge Papers (86).

from collaboration with the British government to cooperation with the Congress was the culmination of a process started soon after Syed Ahmad's death in 1898. It was partly because events from 1900 to 1915 proved the bankruptcy of the policy of reliance on the British, and partly because the Congress no longer aroused the kind of fears it did in its nascent stage. On the contrary, the Congress was regarded by some Muslims as a national body, representing a wide range of economic and political interests of the country. It was also seen as a powerful means of advancing and defending their material and religious interests and as a useful medium of articulating their immediate grievances. For this reason, the group associated with the leadership of Mohamed Ali, was referred to by the government as the 'extreme faction of the Muslim community', the 'Advanced Party', and the 'hot-headed Nationalist Party'. Their nationalist aim, even if impelled by religious motives and prompted by long-term material considerations, provided the *raison d'etre* for cooperation with Congress. Not surprisingly, they were able to play a major role in the politics of the subcontinent over the next decade.

CHAPTER THREE

THE LUCKNOW PACT

The year 1916 was marked by the culmination of the Congress-League negotiations and the formulation of a joint scheme of reforms, popularly known as the Lucknow Pact. This chapter will delineate the issues involved in the negotiations, identify those factors which paved the way for an agreement, examine Muslim reactions to the Lucknow Pact as they developed in Bengal, Punjab, and the UP, and finally, assess their impact on the national movement as well as on communal relations.

The negotiations which led to the Lucknow Pact must be set against the background of the Morley-Minto Reforms, the World War, and the reshuffling of political alignments in readiness for a further dose of reforms. Indian politicians, at first, generally welcomed the Act of 1909 as a major constitutional advance.[1] But within months of its operation, their imperfections and shortcomings became obvious. The expansion of Indian representation to the legislative councils was not followed by any measure of Indian control of public affairs. The non-official majorities in the enlarged councils were rendered illusory and ineffective by the system of nomination. In the Punjab, where the elective principle was introduced, the proportion of elected members was lower than any of the main provinces:

[1]According to Surendranath Banerjea, the Reforms were 'an honest effort to introduce the beginnings of parliamentary procedure in matters of local administration'. *Bengalee*, 19 December 1909.

it was 20 per cent as compared to 39.58 per cent in Madras, 40.81 per cent in UP, 43.90 per cent in Bihar and Orissa, 41.86 per cent in East Bengal and Assam, 43.75 per cent in Bombay and 51 per cent in Bengal.[2] Many Punjabi Hindus were also disappointed with the composition of the council which comprised, excluding the Lieutenant-Governor and two occasional 'experts' – ten officials (all Europeans), and 14 non-officials—two of them again Europeans, two Sikhs (both nominated), and three Hindus (one elected and two nominated). Thus in a province where Hindus formed 'the bulk of the educated, enlightened and public spirited community', they received only three seats in a council of twenty-four.[3] Consequently, the *Tribune* of Lahore which represented the interests of Hindu professional and commercial classes, decried the Reforms as a 'complete failure' and as 'totally insufficient'.[3]

Many Hindus decried the Reforms for another reason. This was related to the introduction of separate electorates as well as to what was later to be known as 'weightage', i.e., more seats than the Muslims were entitled to by numbers only. Muslims were allowed to vote in 'general' constituencies side by side with Hindus as well as in the separate and wholly Muslim constituencies. The Hindus feared that separate electorates would introduce 'an invidious distinction and an undesirable precedent whose perpetuation will only accentuate bitterness and irritation'.[4] Their main grievance, however, was that in the Punjab and eastern Bengal where Muslims were in a majority, the minorities would gain a bare electoral representation in proportion to their numbers and not to their importance. The Muslims, on the other hand, would receive a larger share simply because they were numerous, not because they were educated or wealthy. Surendranath Banerjea moved a resolution, which the Congress carried unanimously, objecting in no uncertain terms to

the excessive and unfairly preponderant share of representation given to the followers of one particular religion; the

[2]*Tribune*, 20 October 1910, 2 November 1910.
[3]*Ibid.*, 4 January 1910.
[3]*Ibid.*, 1 & 12 January 1910.
[4]*Ibid.*, 4 March 1910.

unjust, individious, and humiliating distinctions made between Muslims and non-Muslim subjects of His Majesty in
the matter of the electorate, the franchise, and the qualifications of candidates; the wide, arbitrary and unreasonable
disqualifications and restrictions for candidates seeking elections to the Councils; the general distrust of the educated
classes that runs through the whole course of the regulations; and the unsatisfactory composition of non-official
majorities in Provincial Councils, rendering them ineffective
and unreal for all practical purposes.[5]

The Muslim gains from the Reforms of 1909 were considerable. In six out of the seven councils, they secured representation in excess to their proportion of the population. But although the two main demands set out in the Simla Deputation
were conceded in the Act of 1909, the Muslim professional men
failed to receive adequate representation both in the Imperial
Legislative Council and the provincial councils.[6] Most of the
electoral qualifications favoured the rich, the title-holders, and
pensioned government servants. As a result, by 1914, professional men filled no more than two of the eight seats held by
Muslims in the UP Legislative Council.[7] In the local bodies too
their position was weak, and, after the municipal elections of
1910, separate electo rates were demanded in local government
on the grounds that Muslims were unlikely to be returned from
the mixed electorates.[8]
The Punjab Muslims had their own grievance against the
Morley-Minto Reforms. Separate electorates, which were the
main feature of the Reforms generally, were not made part of
the electoral system of the Punjab. As a result, when the elections were held in December 1912, Muslim candidates, particularly the professional men, fared badly. It was, therefore, not
surprising that after the elections they clamoured for communal
electorates. In December 1912, the Executive Committee of the

---

[5]*INC* 1909, p. 47.
[6]*Comrade*, 25 January 1914; *Paisa Akhbar*, 2 May 1916, PUNNR
1916.
[7]See Robinson, *Separatism*, pp. 222-23.
[8]For example, Ibni Ahmad to Mohamed Ali, 10 June 1911, Hasan
Ali Khan to Mohamed Ali, 14 May 1912, Mohamed Ali Papers.

Punjab Provincial League urged the provincial government to establish separate electorates.[9] Fazl-i-Husain, who was defeated twice from the Punjab University seat, sharply criticised the Reforms. 'That the Morley-Minto Reforms were grudgingly given', he observed, 'their working left in the hands of the bureaucracy, that in practice these reforms have proved to be quite illusory are facts by now admitted on all hands'.[10]

Thus, many Hindu and Muslim politicians had come to regard the Reforms as hopelessly inadequate. The outbreak of the First World War, however, opened up new possibilities of a further grant of political power. The British Government which was constantly emphasising that the Allies were fighting for the cause of freedom and liberty, could not ignore the persistent demand for a greater advance in self-government. Moreover, the government and a few British sympathisers of the Congress[11] were impressed by India's substantial contribution to the war effort and favoured some form of colonial self-government. 'The old regime *must* be changed', declared the Viceroy in July 1915, 'and the people must have more to say in their administration'.[12] Reginald Craddock, the Home Member, submitted a note to the Viceroy on possible measures to be adopted after the War in recognition of the support given by India to the war effort. 'The demand for political concession', he observed, 'is sure to be vigorously pressed when the War is over: it will be made by the active political sections of the educated classes, and is likely to receive considerable support in England.'[13]

Craddock was right in his judgement. Expectations of reforms raised new hopes amongst the politicians who set out to

---

[9] *Tribune*, 19 December 1912.

[10] Azim Husain, *Fazl-i-Husain: A Political Biography* (Bombay, 1946), p. 78.

[11] "It was but yesterday that our vision of India', wrote Henry Cotton, 'was a picture of danger, gloom and suspicion. Today the war curtain rises on a scene of enthusiasm and confidence. All is loyalty and devotion'. In February, he pleaded for the grant of provincial autonomy to India and its gradual admission into the Federation of the Empire. Henry Cotton, 'India : Now and After', *Contemporary Review*, February 1915, pp. 195, 200.

[12] Hardinge to Walter Lawrence, 29 July 1915, Hardinge Papers (94).

[13] Craddock to Hardinge, 25 March 1915, *Ibid* (89).

prepare a schedule of political demands.[14] In February 1915, two days before his death, Gokhale submitted his 'Political Testament' to the Governor of Bombay. In the same month, Wazir Hasan announced that the Muslim League was preparing a list of political demands to be made after the War. He emphasised the need for unity because of the 'shifting horizon and broadening political outlook about Indian affairs'.[15] In April, Annie Besant and, in July, Surendranath Banerjea, put forward their schemes. By mid-1915, Indian politicians had formulated their ideas on reforms. Over the next few months their efforts were directed towards achieving unanimity on the fundamental questions which had created a cleavage between the so-called 'Moderates' and the 'Extremists' in Congress. The search for unity also led to a process of rapprochement between the Congress and the Muslim League.

THE MAKING OF THE LUCKNOW PACT

Discussions between the Congress and the League representatives began in early October 1915. Reporting on their progress, Chintamani, editor of the Allahabad daily, *Leader*, informed Mohamed Ali that

> we are making satisfactory progress . . . and it is my earnest prayer that nothing may happen to bring back the old days of strife. Even on the question of representation we are most anxious to arrive at an understanding and I am hopeful that we shall succeed.[16]

In December 1915, the Muslim League session was held in Bombay at the same time and in the same place as that of the Congress. The idea, as Jinnah explained, was to provide both the organisations with an opportunity to confer together on the

[14]'During the war we Indians were looking forward to a great advance in self-government at its end . . . .Nationalism received a needed lift from talk of what was to come', Nirad C. Chaudhuri, *The Autobiography of an Unknown Indian* (London, 1951), p. 399.

[15]FR (UP), Home Poll. D, March 1915, 56, NAI.

[16]Chintamani to Mohamed Ali, 27 October 1915, Mohamed Ali Papers.

future of India.[17] The League appointed a committee of seven to prepare a reform scheme in consultation with Congress. During 1916, a number of joint meetings between the representatives of the All-India Congress Committee and the League were held.[18] The principal issues of discussion were separate electorates and the percentage of Muslim representation on the legislative councils. The Hindus had all along condemned separate electorates, but on this issue the Muslim leaders were unmoved. In July, Wazir Hasan had circulated a draft scheme which incorporated the principle of separate representation,[19] while Jinnah in his speeches regarded it as an indispensable safeguard.[20] In November, many Congress leaders gave in to the Muslim demands. For the first time, they accepted the principle of separate representation, which provided a basis for an agreement on the proportion of weightage for Muslims in the legislatures.[21]

Having accepted the principle of separate electorates, the main question left to be settled was the percentage of Muslim representation in the councils. The point in the case of Bengal was that, of the 12? members in the council, how many should be Hindus and how many Muslims? The Bengali Muslims argued that, as they were numerically stronger in the province, they should get half or at least 45 per cent. The Hindus, on the other hand, maintained that as the number of

[17] *Leader*, 13 June 1915.

[18] The Muslim League Reform Committee comprised Maulvi Abdul Majid, Syed Ali Nabi, Syed Raza Ali and A.A. Khan from the UP; Nawab Ali Chaudhuri, Mujibur Rahman, Abdul Rasul and Fazlul Haq from Bengal; Zulfiqar Ali Khan, Mohammad Shafi, Malik Barkat Ali and Syed Mohsin Shah from the Punjab; Ibrahim Rahimtullah; the Aga Khan, Jinnah, Bhugri, Faiz Tyabji and Abdul Husain Adamjee Peerbhoy from Bombay and Sind; Ali Imam, Mazharul Haque, Wasi Ahmad and Maulvi Fakhruddin from Bihar. Besides, there were three representatives from Madras; one from the Central Provinces and two from Burma. Home Poll. Deposit, January 1916, 36, NAI.

[19] S.S. Pirzada (ed.), *Foundations of Pakistan: All India Muslim League Documents: 1906-1947* (Karachi, 1969), Vol. I, p. 378.

[20] Presidential Address at the Bombay Provincial Conference, 1916, quoted in M.H. Saiyad, *Mohammad Ali Jinnah: A Political Study* (Lahore, 1953) p. 67.

[21] *Amrita Bazar Patrika*, 27 November 1916.

educated men in their community was larger, the Muslims were not entitled to more than 33 per cent. In the case of Bihar, Bombay, Madras and the Central Provinces, however, an agreement was reached without much haggling.[22] Significantly enough, Muslims in these provinces secured representation over and above what they were entitled to on the basis of population. In Bihar, for instance, where Muslims formed 13 per cent of the population, they were to have 25 per cent of the seats; in Bombay they formed 20 per cent of the population, but their percentage of seats was $33\frac{1}{3}$. In return for these concessions, the League representatives agreed to reduce Muslim representation in the Punjab from 55 per cent, to which they were entitled by their population, to 50 per cent.[23]

When the joint conference met again in the last week of December, it had to resolve the much disputed and controversial question of the proportion of Muslim representation in Bengal and the UP. After a somewhat acrimonious discussion, which lasted several days, the Bengali Hindus agreed to concede 40 per cent representation to the Muslims.[24] But the deadlock over UP remained. Chintamani and Malaviya were willing to concede only 25 per cent; Muslim delegates insisted on having 35 per cent. At that stage, Bhupendranath Basu, who played a vital role in breaking the deadlock over Bengal, suggested a compromise and proposed 30 per cent. This was carried without much opposition.[25] As an additional assurance to the UP Muslims, the All-India Congress Committee agreed to the proposal that if in any province two-thirds of a community was

[22]Fazlul Haq to Mohamed Ali, 23 November, 1916, Mohamed Ali Papers.

[23]*Amrita Bazar Patrika*, 27 November 1916.

[24]WRDCI, 25 November 1916, Home Poll. B, November 1916, 452, NAI.

[25]On 25 December 1916, the League Reform Committee demanded representation on a 40 per cent basis for Bengal and $33\frac{1}{3}$ for the UP Muslims. At the Joint Committee of the League and the Congress which met the same evening, Basu proposed a 40 per cent basis for Muslims of Bengal which was accepted. Malaviya proposed a 25 per cent basis for the UP Muslims, and he and Chintamani opposed Raza Ali's demand for $33\frac{1}{3}$ basis. UP Government, General Department, 1917, 140, UPSA; FR (UP), 6 January 1917, Home Poll. January 1917, 5, NAI.

against any measure or bill it should be dropped by both the communities.[26]

To sum up, the Congress-League scheme postulated representative government and Dominion Status for India. Among its provisions were: (a) that India should be raised from the status of a dependency to that of an equal partner in the Empire as a self-governing dominion, and (b) that the provincial legislative councils should consist of four-fifths elected and one fifth nominated members. The members of the council, according to the scheme, should be elected directly by the people on as broad a franchise as possible.

The scheme further recognised separate electorates for Muslims with a weightage of seats in excess of their proportion of the population in areas where they were in a minority. It laid down the proportion of Muslim seats in all provincial councils, except Assam, but including the Punjab and the Central Provinces where separate electorates had not previously existed. The following are the proportions of Muslim representation that were agreed to:

Province	Muslims in Population %	Number of Muslim Legislative Seats %
Bengal	52.6	40.0
Bihar and Orissa	10.5	25.0
Bombay	20.4	33.3
Central Provinces	4.3	15.0
Madras	6.5	15.0
Punjab	54.8	50.0
United Provinces	14.0	30.0

With regard to the Imperial Legislative Council, the Lucknow Pact provided that one-third of the Indian elected members should be Muslims, elected by separate electorates in the provinces, in the same proportion in which they were represented on the provincial legislative councils.[27]

[26]*Leader*, 28, 29 December 1916.
[27]For the text of the Reform Scheme, C.H. Philips (ed.), *The Evolution of India and Pakistan*, pp. 171-73.

The events between October 1915 and December 1916 and the principal issues of controversy involved in the negotiations raise several fundamental questions. Why did the Congress accept separate electorates after having consistently opposed the principle since 1885? Who were the promoters of the Lucknow Pact, and what was the motive behind their activities?

In 1909 and 1910, Congress had criticised the Morley-Minto Reforms for introducing separate electorates. The usual arguments against them dwelt on the identity of Hindu and Muslim interests, the danger of Muslim over-representation and the grave risks involved in emphasising racial differences.[28] But the climax to the opposition came in June 1911 when Richard Burn, the Secretary of the United Provinces, addressed a letter to divisional commissioners, asking for their opinion on four questions:

1. Separate electorates for Muslims on local boards
2. Proportion of seats which should be allotted to Muslims by separate electorates
3. Special qualification of Muslim voters and candidates
4. Participation of Muslims in general electorates.[29]

The Hindu-interest groups, hard hit already by the Legislative Council Regulations, viewed the Burn circular with 'feelings of dismay and despair'.[30] They feared that if his suggestions were accepted, then even in towns or districts where Muslims were in a minority, they would be in a majority on the local bodies. 'The logical consequence of this will be', observed the *Advocate*, 'that it will be impossible for the Hindus to secure entrance into the Councils. It was

[28]*INC* 1910, p. 84.
[29]The consensus among Hindus was that though apparently the Burn circular intended to invite opinions, in fact it was a definite statement of a policy suggesting the nature of the opinion that should be given. The *Leader*, for example, suspected that the government had made up its mind to concede separate electorates and excessive representation to Muslims as well as to allow them to take part in the general election. *Leader*, 7 June 1911.
[30]*Ibid.*, 22 June, 13 July 1911.

only by a majority of one vote that the Municipalities and the District Boards in the Bareilly Division could send a Hindu to the Council, under the present constitution. If the proposed changes come into effect, the Bareilly Division will have the privilege of being represented by Muslims both from separate and joint electorates. Such also might be the fate of six out of the eight large cities in the United Provinces. The Hindu middle class representation, meagre as it is in the Council, will thus be reduced to nullity.[31]

The opposition to the Burn circular was followed by yet another agitation in 1916 when the government pushed the United Provinces Municipalities Bill through the legislative council. The bill, which acknowledged the principle of separate representation, was based on a compromise between Motilal Nehru, Tej Bahadur Sapru, Jagat Narain Mulla, and the Muslim members of the legislative council.[32] Under its provisions, Muslims secured a disproportionately large representation both in parts where they preponderated in population as well as in parts where they were in a minority.[33] This was decidedly a strong grievance of the Hindus in cities—where they actually outnumbered Muslims—to be thus placed in a minority on the municipal boards. Malaviya and Chintamani, who led the agitation against the Municipalities Bill, urged the Hindu members of municipal boards to resign as a symbolic gesture of protest. Malaviya summed up his criticism of the Act in the following words:

[31]*Advocate*, 18 June 1911; 'If Mohamedans have more than proportional representation, Hindus will *ipso facto* have less than their proportional representation . . . . If, in addition, Mohamedans are empowered to get into local bodies through the general electorate, will not the less than proportional representation allowed to Hindus become less? Hindus very naturally and very properly resent this differential treatment which operates entirely to their detriment, and it is against this that their agitation will be principally directed.' *Leader*, 29 June 1911.

[32]For details, see Robinson, 'Municipal Government and Muslim Separatism', *MAS*, pp. 428-35.

[33]Under sections 11 and 12 of the Act, it was provided that when Muslims form less than 25 per cent of the municipal population, they receive 30 per cent of the seats; when forming 25 per cent to 38 per cent of the population they receive 38 per cent of the seats; above 38 per cent, according to numerical strength.

Though the Hindus were convinced that separate communal
representation on municipal boards was fraught with evil,
they were willing to consent that Muslims should have
separate representation. But they could not agree that they
should have an excessive representation too. If there were
70 per cent of Hindus in a town and 30 per cent of
Muslims it was utterly unfair that Muslims should have
nearly the same representation as Hindus, and yet that was
what the Act will bring about. The 30 per cent of Muslims
of Allahabad would be entitled to appoint eight out of
twenty-one elected representatives on the municipal boards,
while the 70 per cent of Hindus would have only ten such
representatives.[34]

The outcry against the Bill threatened the harmonious
progress of Congress-League negotiations. Motilal Nehru
and Sapru were quick to realise the danger, and consequently
supported the Jahangirabad Amendment of March 1916 in the
legislative council. Their principal interest in doing so was to
preserve the growing Congress-League alliance which almost
reached a breaking point early in 1916. Both Sapru and
Motilal were ardent champions of Hindu-Muslim unity and
were devoted to the cause of promoting a better understanding
between the communities. Sapru, who condemned separate
electorates in 1909,[35] came round to the view that if Muslims
were insistent on separate representation, there was no use
trying to have a united representation. 'In order to make it
possible for the Muslim community to cooperate with us . . .',
he declared in the legislative council, 'and in order to remove at
least one of the several causes of friction, I should not grudge
separate representation to the Muslim community.'[36] For
Sapru a satisfactory readjustment of inter-communal relations
was a pre-condition to India's political evolution.

Outside the UP, many Congress leaders recognised the
expediency of accepting separate electorates. Gokhale, for

[34]*Amrita Bazar Patrika*, 21 July 1916.
[35]See *Tribune*, 3 June 1909.
[36]*Proceedings of the UP Legislative Council*, 1916 (Allahabad, 1917),
p. 218.

example, explained in 1909 that, under the circumstances prevailing in India, separate electorates would minimise communal friction and ensure the representation of the minorities.[37] R.N. Mudholkar, President of the Congress in 1912, also recognised the expediency of conceding separate electorates to the Muslims.[38] During the negotiations at Lucknow in December 1916, Tilak, who was released from Mandalay jail on 17 May 1914, played a key role in resolving certain points of dispute. One of his biographers claims that on the question of separate electorates and Muslim representation, Tilak prevailed upon the intransigent Malaviya to reach an understanding rather than wreck the Congress-League scheme on the question of details.[39] Tilak echoed the sentiments of many Congress leaders which was succinctly expressed by the *Amrita Bazar Patrika*: 'The question of representation must on no account stand in the way of presenting a joint scheme of reforms to the government on behalf of the two great communities of India.'[40] The priorities of many Congress leaders were explicitly set out in this observation.

In its historical sequence, Congress recognition of the

[37] *Tribune*, 16 July 1909.

[38] *INC* 1912, p. 19.

[39] D.V. Tahmankar, *Lokmanya Tilak: Father of Indian Unrest and Maker of Modern India* (London, 1956), p. 244. 'There is a feeling among the Hindus', Tilak said at the theosophical convention held in Lucknow on 30 December 1916, 'that too much has been given to the Muslims. As a Hindu I have no objection to making this concession . . . . We cannot rise from our intolerable position without the aid of the Muslims. So in order to gain the desired end there is no objection to giving a percentage, a greater percentage, to the Muslims.' Quoted in D. Keer *Lokmanya Tilak: Father of Our Freedom Struggle* (Bombay, 1959), p. 365.

[40] *Amrita Bazar Patrika*, 27 November 1916. The *Hindoo Patriot* of Calcutta consistently maintained that separate electorates would help to minimise communal tension and secure the fair representation of the minorities. 'Concord cannot be established', the paper wrote on 11 March 1916, 'by mere platonic aspirations unaccompanied by mutual concessions'. During the agitation against the UP Municipalities Bill, the paper criticised the attitude of Hindu politicians. 'What a queer light is thrown open', it wrote, 'upon the so-called rapprochement between Hindus and Muslims by this exhibition of hostility to a compromise, which no one indeed claims to be an ideal or perfect one, but which is abundantly justified by the inexorable necessities of the case.' *Hindoo Patriot*, 20 May 1916.

principle of separate electorates in 1916 was an important step towards sweeping the way clear for rapprochement with the leading Muslim politicians. It was part of a continuous endeavour to gain their confidence and to secure their support in presenting a united front for demanding constitutional reforms from the government. Secondly, the Congress leaders were impressed by the transformation of the Muslim League, its adoption of the ideal of self-government, the success of Jinnah and other Muslims in holding the League session concurrently with that of the Congress in December 1915, and the easing of Hindu-Muslim tension.[41] These factors could not be ignored by Hindu Congressmen. Their opposition to the Muslim demands would have jeopardised the prospects of rapprochement, and would have given impetus to the anti-Congress movement among Muslims.

Thus the detractors of communal representation had, by 1916, come to believe in separate electorates, or at least in the expediency of accepting them. The Muslim politicians were pleased with the substantial concessions they received. What had been secured for them from the government in 1906, over the heads of the Hindus, had now, at least in principle, been conceded by the Congress, too. The Muslims regarded separate and adequate representation as the *sine qua non* for a popular franchise; the government had already accepted the condition, and now the Congress had given its blessing to it.

MUSLIMS COME TO TERMS WITH THE CONGRESS

The role of those Muslims who directed the Congress-League rapprochement from 1913 onwards is studied in this section. The government lumped them together as a group of 'ignorant and self-seeking men' whose motives were 'love of notoriety and the lust of gain'.[42] The key figures in the 'gang' were Mohamed Ali, Azad, Wazir Hasan and the Raja of Mahmudabad. Mohamed Ali was regarded as a 'mischievous agitator' and a 'dangerous element' in north Indian politics.[43] Wazir Hasan

---

[41]*Leader*, 4 January 1913.

[42]Sydenham to Hardinge, 18 March 1913, Hardinge Papers (86).

[43]FR (Delhi), 16 August 1914, Home Poll. A, September 1914, 1-3, NAI.

was declared a 'born intriguer and a mischievous fellow',[44] and the Raja of Mahmudabad was considered 'vain and unbalanced'.[45] They were dismissed as leaders of 'no importance' because their aim was only to "secure money and publicity'[46] Such uncharitable and jaundiced views betrayed the government's lack of understanding of the role and influence of a new generation of leaders like Azad, Mohamed Ali and Wazir Hasan. They also took no account of the intensity of anti-British feelings engendered by the revocation of the partition of Bengal and the Kanpur mosque incident, which unleashed a new flood of energy and organisational innovation. Leaders like Mohamed Ali and Azad neither felt the constraining hand of the moderates in the Muslim League nor were they committed to constitutional politics. Belief in, and commitment to, a religious ideal provided the driving force for their activities. Their aim was not to secure money and publicity for themselves but to bolster (what they considered to be) the political and religious interests of their co-religionists. They felt a pressing need to reorganise the Muslim League which would speak for, and defend, their community's interests, and to forge an alliance with Congress in order to combine against the government.

But not all the Muslim League leaders shared the political radicalism of Mohamed Ali and his followers.[47] This inevitably led to an intense personal and ideological conflict between those who saw their interests inextricably linked with the Raj, and those who represented a radical strain in Muslim League politics. In the UP, the conflict involved the landlords and government servants and a new group of Muslims who saw themselves as the 'younger men'—the men of *Nai Raushni* (New

[44]...Wazir Hasan is a born intriguer and a mischievous fellow. He is a Shia and plays on Mahmudabad's weakness and at present has great influence with him'. Butler to Allan, 6 April 1913, Butler Papers (71).

[45]Meston to Chelmsford, 20 August 1917, Meston to Lovett, 10 December 1916, Meston Papers (1).

[46]Viceroy to Secretary of State, 12 September 1913, Crewe Papers (I-14).

[47]See, for example, Butler's assessment of Muslim leadership, Butler to Hardinge, 30 April 1913, Hardinge Papers (85).

Light),[48] and the representatives of 'new ideals' and 'new forces'.[49] To the men of *Nai Raushni*, the 'old race of patriots' had the 'insolence of office' and the 'narrowness of outlook that comes over a mind esteemed as "practical" '. They saw themselves as champions of 'democracy against oligarchy, of freedom against convention, of idealism against opportunism, of faith against cynicism and compromise'. The ultimate result of their crusade, prophesied the *New Era*, would be the disappearance of the 'old order' into the 'museum of dead things called History'.[50]

In the Punjab, the provincial branch of the Muslim League was divided into two factions, one led by Mohammad Shafi, and the other by Fazl-i-Husain. Shafi was well known in the province because of his association with educational organisations like the *Anjuman-i-Islamia* and the *Anjuman-i-Himayat-i-Islam*. He was elected secretary of the Punjab Muslim League in 1907 and was nominated to the provincial legislative council in 1909. While the Morley-Minto Reforms were being formulated, Shafi emerged as one of the most important spokesmen of the claims of Punjab Muslims and the landed classes. In his correspondence with Dunlop Smith, he strongly argued in favour of separate electorates for Muslims and their 'real and adequate representation' on the expanded councils. He wrote:

Now, the Mohammedans of India form the most important minority in this country. By reason of their past history, the services they have rendered to the Empire in and out of British India and the fact that they are not a community confined to the four corners of Hindustan, their political importance far exceeds their numerical strength. Moreover, they constitute a distinct community having, in part, interests of their own which, while in line with those of their rulers, are separate from and often antagonistic to those of the majority.[51]

---

[48]Mohamed Ali, *My Life: A Fragment*, p. 39.

[49]Mazharul Haque, quoted in *Bombay Chronicle*, 27 January 1916.

[50]*New Era*, 14 April 1917.

[51]Shafi to Dunlop Smith, 18 June 1909, Dunlop Smith Papers, MSS. EUR. F. 166 (13), IOL.

Furthermore, Shafi justified his claims on the grounds that Muslims constituted 'a stable element in the political atmosphere of this country—an element on the solidarity and steadfastness of which, at all times, the British Government may safely and fully rely'. As a follower of what he called the 'Anglo-Mohammedan school of politics', Shafi regarded his community's interests to be identical with those of the government and refused to 'take part in anything calculated, in the slightest degree, to injure British interests and to weaken the stability and permanence of the British rule in India'. In his opinion, the political demands of the Hindu Congressmen threatened the stability of British rule and the cause of good government. And in order to counter the threat, he favoured the retention of the official majority in the provincial councils and the representation of the Muslims as well as the landed classes in 'sufficient numbers'.[52] Shafi was clearly the champion of conservative opinion in India, whose political survival depended on the government. He served the government till his death in 1932, and was steadfastly loyal to the Raj.[53]

Shafi's rival in the Punjab was Fazl-i-Husain, who had been a Congress supporter since 1905. Their first confrontation was in the *Anjuman-i-Himayat-i-Islam* in 1910, and it was due to the efforts of Nawab Fateh Ali Qizilbash, a landowner with large estates in Lahore and the Oudh district of Bahraich, that their differences were resolved.[54] A few years later, they were involved in a struggle for the capture of the Punjab Muslim League. Fazl-i-Husain was backed by a group of professional men led by Zafar Ali Khan, editor of the influential daily, *Zamindar*, and Malik Barkat Ali, editor of the Lahore *Observer*. He was also supported by the 'Lucknow members of the League' who were displeased with Shafi's

---

[52]Shafi to Dunlop Smith, 13 January 1909 & 13 April 1909, Dunlop Smith Papers (13).

[53]'I am sincerely convinced that the interests of the Muslim community in India are absolutely identical with those of the British Government, and the Anglo-Indian community and, in consequence, whenever any important change is proposed in the machinery of Government . . . ., the first question I ask myself is: How will it affect British Rule in India'. Shafi to Dunlop Smith, 8 June 1909, *Ibid.*

[54]*Tribune*, 27 April 1910.

opposition to the holding of the Muslim League session at Bombay in 1915. Wazir Hasan and the Raja of Mahmudabad opposed Shafi's election to the presidentship of the All-India Muslim Educational Conference,[55] a prestigious organisation founded by Syed Ahmad Khan in 1886. In December 1916, the Punjab Muslim League, of which Shafi was the secretary, was disaffiliated by the All-India Muslim League Council and the faction of Fazl-i-Husain was recognised as the 'Punjab Provincial Muslim League'.[56] This virtually sealed the fate of Shafi's political ambitions and paved the way for the emergence of Fazl-i-Husain as an important public figure.

Muslim politics in Bengal was dominated by the Nawab of Dacca and his protégés until the annulment of partition in 1911 led to dramatic changes which swept aside the conservative leadership. A new group of professional Muslims emerged as potential leaders. The most prominent amongst them were Fazlul Haq, Abdullah Suhrawardy and Mujibur Rahman, who advocated Hindu-Muslim unity and directed the Congress-League rapprochement in Bengal. They were helped by the pan-Islamic press in the province, which carried on anti-government propaganda during and after the Balkan Wars and the Kanpur mosque incident. By 1916, Fazlul Haq and his followers had gained control of the Bengal Muslim League. The Nawab of Dacca, the premier Muslim zamindar of east Bengal and president of the All-India Muslim League in 1912, died in 1915, and Shamsul Huda, a member of the Viceroy's Executive Council, failed in his bid to seize control of the League. Referring to the declining influence of the old style of leadership, the *Mussalman* triumphantly wrote:

> In every age, in every clime, and in every country there are reactionaries. Whenever any progressive movement is set on foot, they stand in the way, but they have never been

[55]FR (UP), Home Poll. Deposit, January 1917, 42, NAI.

[56]In justification of their action, the Council argued that, as the term of office under the constitution was limited to three years, the fact that there had been no election of office-bearers for four years, automatically terminated the existence of Shafi's League. FR (Punjab), Home Poll Deposit, February 1917, 49, NAI.

able to block the way; they only place temporary difficulties in the path of progress. . . .'[57]

Out of the political turmoil which characterised Bengal politics since 1911, Fazlul Haq emerged as a potential leader of a new kind. Unlike the traditional communal leader, whose influence was locally based on landholding and who was usually a member of one of the great Muslim families, Haq had made his way by personal ability. His education and his experience in teaching, law, administration and political organisation set him apart from the old leadership.[58] He was born in 1873 in a distinguished family of Barisal lawyers. After having studied Law and Mathematics at the University of Calcutta, he joined the Calcutta High Court in 1900 where he became an articled clerk to Ashutosh Mookerjee. In 1906 he attended the Muslim Educational Conference at Dacca and was entrusted with the responsibility of drafting a constitution for the Muslim League. His political involvement with the League began from that date.[59]

Fazlul Haq's patron was the Nawab of Dacca who had at his disposal a number of government appointments in the new province of Eastern Bengal and Assam. It was with his help that by 1908 Haq had become Assistant Registrar of Rural Co-operative Societies. Again, it was the Nawab who ensured his unopposed return for the Dacca Muslim seat in the legislative council. In 1913, however, Haq broke with the Nawab, rejecting his patron's policy of collaboration with government and favouring, instead, an alliance with the Indian National Congress. Later in that year, he was elected secretary of the Bengal Presidency League, which finally gave him an independent power base.

It is clear from the above analysis that by 1916 men like Fazlul Haq, Mujibur Rahman, Fazl-i-Husain, Zafar Ali Khan, Mohamed Ali, Wazir Hasan, Jinnah, and Mazharul Haque had emerged as the most articulate and influential group

[57]*Mussalman,* 23 January 1917.
[58]J.H. Broomfield, 'Four Lives: History as Biography', *South Asia,* August 1971, p. 80.
[59]A.S.M. Abdur Rab, A.K. *Fazlul Haq: Life and Achievements* (Lahore, n.d.), pp. 5-7.

amongst Muslims. They can be described as 'pro-Congress Muslims', as opposed to the 'anti-Congress Muslims', because their activities, since 1913, had a pro-Congress bias and were directed towards promoting a better understanding between the Congress and the Muslim League. Such categories are, of course, arbitrary and are useful only for explanatory purposes.

The pro-Congress Muslims generally belonged to the professional groups and were, therefore, less dependent on government support than the landowners and government servants in the Muslim League. As successful lawyers and journalists, they participated in political activities without the risk of losing official patronage. Their involvement with Congress followed soon after 1911 when they realised that the government had ceased to be a safe custodian of their religious, economic, and educational interests. The annulment of Bengal's partition alienated many Muslims in the province; the rejection of the Aligarh Muslim University scheme dashed the hopes of the UP Muslims; the Kanpur mosque incident and the events in Turkey offended the religious susceptibilities of many Muslim groups. In the words of Mohamed Ali, 'the Mussalmans felt themselves to be betrayed both in India and abroad'.[60] Their leaders tried in vain to explain the 'genuineness' of their religious cause to the government. When Wazir Hasan and Mohamed Ali visited London in 1913 to convey their community's feelings over the future of Turkey, the Secretary of State refused to grant them an interview. They were told that a meeting with them would be misunderstood by 'those of your co-religionists with whom you are not in accord, who claim equally with you to represent the political attitude and temper of the Mussalman community'.[61] As a reaction to this unsympathetic and hostile attitude of the authorities, leaders like Mohamed Ali saw the sense in joining Congress and using its platform for articulating their grievances. In May 1914, Mazharul Haque declared that 'there were no political questions in which the interests of both communities were not equally involved, or with regard to which they differed. As far as he himself was concerned, he would much

---

[60]Mohamed Ali, *My Life: A Fragment*, p. 35.

[61]Holderness, Under-Secretary of State for India, to Mohamed Ali and Wazir Hasan, 11 November 1913, Crewe Papers. (I/14/2).

rather be represented on the Council by his friend Gokhale than by anyone else. Our interests are practically identical'.[62] Rarely before was such a view expressed by a Muslim. It clearly illustrates that, in addition to a strong commitment to a nationalist ideology, British policies contributed substantially towards the growth of a pro-Congress trend amongst certain sections of Muslims.

Another important factor was the common educational background of most pro-Congress Muslims.[63] Leaders like Mohamed Ali, Wazir Hasan, Jinnah, Mazharul Haque, Fazl-i-Husain, Fazlul Haq. and Ansari were educated in British or Indian Universities where they interacted with Hindu students, educationists, social reformers and publicists. Abdul Majid Khwaja, Tassaduq Ahmad Khan Sherwani, Saifuddin Kitchlew and Syed Mahmud were contemporaries of Jawaharlal Nehru at Cambridge. They attended meetings of the 'Indian Majlis' which were often addressed by Indian politicians.[64] Mukhtar Ahmad Ansari studied medicine in London where he first met the Nehrus and established a life-long friendship with the family. Jinnah was called to the Bar at Lincoln's Inn, London, where he participated in political discussions held at Dadabhai Naoroji's residence. Fazlul Haq studied Law and Mathematics at the University of Calcutta and joined the Calcutta High Court in 1900, where he worked with the great lawyer, Ashutosh Mookerjee.

Wazir Hasan, who attended Aligarh College and Muir Central College, Allahabad, observed that education on similar

[62]*Bombay Chronicle*, 20 June 1914.

[63]Karl Mannheim suggests that 'Participation in a common educational heritage progressively tends to suppress differences of birth, status, profession and wealth, and to unite the educated people on the basis of the education they have received'. K. Mannheim, *Ideology and Uptopia: An Introduction to the Sociology of Knowledge* (New York, 1953), p. 138.

[64]J. Nehru, *An Autobiography*, (London, 1936), p. 22; Jawaharlal reported his impressions of a speech delivered by B.C. Pal at the Indian 'Majlis'. 'I objected greatly to his not taking the Mohammadans into consideration. Once or twice he did refer to them but then he was not very complimentary. . . .The Mohammadans here were, naturally, not very pleased with him'. J. Nehru to Motilal Nehru, 3 December 1908, *Selected Works of Jawaharlal Nehru* (henceforth *SWJ*) (Delhi, 1972), Vol. I, p. 62.

lines had produced a common understanding between the Hindus and Muslims of each other's problems and a recognition of a common destiny above the 'existence of separate entities and the din of communal claims'. It was owing to education that Muslims 'had begun to form conceptions of a broader obligation and wider responsibilities to their country as a whole'.[65] Henry Cotton in 1914 explained that the growing Hindu-Muslim cooperation on political questions was the direct result of a common educational background. 'Unity of ideas', he wrote, 'is due to uniformity of training, and the ideal which was present in Sir Syed's mind when he founded Aligarh College—but then was incapable of realisation—is at last attained. Mutual trust, a desire for the achievement of common ends and objects, nationalism and self-government — these are the inspiration of the rising generation not less of Mohammedans than of Hindus'.[66]

A common Western educational background not only helped to promote a better understanding between Hindus and Muslims, it also served as a link between Muslim leaders, who came from various regions, represented diverse cultures and spoke different languages. The English language alone could bring a certain degree of cohesiveness to an otherwise culturally heterogeneous group. This explains why many Muslim leaders generally corresponded with each other in English. Even some of the important newspapers such as *Comrade*, *Indian Daily Telegraph*, *Mussalman*, and *New Era*, which claimed to espouse the 'popular causes' of the Muslim community, were published in English.

As opposed to the Muslim professional groups, the Muslim landowners stood against the Congress.[67] They are best described

---

[65] *India*, 17 October 1913.

[66] Henry Cotton, 'India: Old and New', *Asiatic Review*, July 1914.

[67] The Raja of Mahmudabad was an exception He was a close friend of some leading Congressmen who enjoyed his hospitality at Mahmudabad House in Kaiser Bagh, Lucknow. He also supported the activities of Mohamed Ali and his friends, whom Meston described as the Raja's 'vile entourage'. But, except during 1915-16, when Meston became hostile and threatened to remove the Raja's *sanad*, the government took little notice of his activities. This was perhaps due to Harcourt Butler's friendship with the Raja. The pleasure-loving Lieutenant-Governor was

as 'conservative Muslims', a label which helps to represent their stance in politics. One of the important factors which determined their attitude towards Congress, as indeed towards agitational politics in general, was their relationship with the government. The landowners owed their wealth and status to the government which brought them forward as the 'natural leaders' of their areas. The *taluqdars* of Oudh, for instance, were endowed with full proprietary rights, title, and possession of their estates (*taluqas*); their interests were further protected by the *taluqdari* succession law of 1869 and the Encumbered Estates Act of 1870.[68] 'We must preserve', emphasised Harcourt Butler, an ardent champion of the cause of landlords, 'and develop a landed aristocracy, and work through it if we wish to keep an absolute foot in India, and I do not see how we could carry on without it'.[69] In the post-1909 period, the landowners were useful and important allies for working the reforms. They were effectively used to counterpoise the professional groups represented in the councils. In 1917, the UP government encouraged the landlords to put forward their claims before Montagu and Chelmsford.[70] This move was calculated to stifle the Congress-League scheme of reforms and to prevent professional men from gaining 'undue' representation in the councils.[71] And when the Reform proposals were published in 1918, the Viceroy suggested that the landlord

a frequent visitor to the palace in Mahmudabad where he wined and dined at the Raja's expense, listened to Urdu *ghazals* and was regaled by Indian dancing and music.

[68]T.R. Metcalf, 'Social Effects of British Land Policy' in R.E. Frynkenberg (ed.), *Land Control and Social Structure in Indian History* (Wisconsin, 1969), p. 148.

[69]Butler to H.E. Richards, 16 September 1906, Butler Papers (65).

[70]Meston to Tasadduk Rasul, 22 August 1917, Meston Papers (17). Over the next few months, Meston was in regular correspondence with the leading landowners and urged them to formulate their demands.

[71]Meston to Edward Gait, 8 September 1917, *Ibid.* One of the objections raised against the Montagu-Chelmsford Reform proposals was that it was 'designed to hand over the Legislative Councils bodily to the educated classes who have agitated against our Government, and to place the Executive Government under the control of the Legislative Council, with the results that the chief elements of British rule must inevitably be weakened'. Note on Indian Constitutional Reforms by John Hewitt 30 July 1918. *Ibid* (22).

organisations should be induced to throw their weight on the side of the proposals.[72]

The landlords, then, were the bulwark of the Raj. They could participate in agitational politics only at the risk of losing their position and power. The Chhataris and the Chaudhuris were brought up in the traditions of sturdy loyalty to the Raj whose 'salt they had eaten'; so they shunned Congress politics altogether.

REACTIONS TO THE LUCKNOW PACT

The Congress-League scheme evoked varied responses. Many politicians welcomed the political accord because it strengthened and enhanced the value of their constitutional and administrative demands which were to be put forward in the name of united India. 'There must be satisfaction all over the country', wrote the *Tribune*, 'that the question [of Muslim representation in Councils] has set at rest any further discussion in haggling which was already assuming an unseemly form, and that the scheme of post-War reforms prepared by the joint conference can now go to government, after the Congress and League sessions have approved it, with the seal of acceptance by the whole community.'[73] To others who had a vision of a united India free from communal animosities, the Lucknow Pact was a hopeful augury for the future. It ushered in a period of Hindu-Muslim fraternisation.[74]

There was mutual appreciation of the efforts of the promoters of the Pact. The Hindus eulogised leaders like Wazir Hasan, Jinnah, Mazharul Haque, and the Raja of Mahmudabad who were its principal architects. Jinnah, in particular, was hailed as the ambassador of Hindu-Muslim unity and acknowledged as the spokesman of the vast majority of educated Muslims. 'Young India', wrote a correspondent, 'ought to be proud of the fact that in the Hon'ble Mr. Jinnah it has found

[72]Chelmsford to Butler, 18 August 1918, Butler Papers (48).

[74]*Tribune*, 29 December 1916.

[74]See M.R. Jayakar, *The Story of My Life* (Bombay, 1958), Vol. I, p. 156, *Bombay Samachar*, 9 January 1917, *Gujarati*, 3 January 1917, BNNR 1917.

a leader who labours under no illusions as to what United India ought to have.'[75]

However, the Congress-League scheme did not go down well with some Hindus, especially in the UP and the Punjab. Their main grudge was that the scheme introduced a 'vicious principle', namely communal representation, intensified by election through separate electorates. Also, that the Muslims secured representation over and above what they were entitled to, and a veto over legislation to which they were entitled neither by their numbers, wealth, or influence nor by the constitution of the council. For instance, in the UP, they constituted 14 per cent of the population but were allowed 30 per cent of the seats in the provincial legislative council. On the other hand, Hindus and Sikhs of the Punjab were allowed only a small amount of weightage.

The All-India Hindu Mahasabha led the crusade against the Lucknow Pact. At its conference held in Lucknow, V.P. Madhav Rao, in his presidential address, attacked the principle of separate electorates and said that the object of the Hindu Mahasabha would be to 'educate the public mind on the evils likely to follow from a recognition of this principle and giving effect to it in the coming reforms'.[76] The local Hindu Sabhas in Allahabad, Benaras and Kanpur also denounced excessive representation given to the Muslim minorities in UP, Bombay, Bihar and Madras and the poor treatment of the Hindu minority in the Punjab.[77] But their opposition was ineffective, because some of their leaders like Sapru, Motilal Nehru, Jagat Narain Mulla, Malaviya, and Chintamani had taken a prominent part in the Congress-League negotiations as members of the All-India Congress Committee, and had endorsed the main provisions of the pact. After December 1916, these leaders urged, and in some cases successfully persuaded, their followers to take the pact in a generous spirit, and to subordinate communal interests to larger and more permanent national ends.

[75] *Amrita Bazar Patrika*, 6 December 1916; *Bengalee*, 4 January 1917; *Young India*, 3 January 1917.
[76] FR (UP), 1 January 1917, Home Poll. Deposit, February 1917, 26, NAI.
[77] *Leader*, 30 December 1916.

Compared to the Hindus, Muslim reactions to the negotiation of the Pact and its terms were far more varied. In the first place, many conservative Muslims vigorously opposed cooperation with the Congress, which they identified as a 'Hindu' body. The Secretary of State for India was told by one *alim* in Madras that there was no sanction in the Quran for an alliance with non-Muslims.[78] Secondly, they were also critical of the attempt to bring the Muslim League in line with the Congress ideals and policies. 'The stereotyped Congress slogans', observed Syed Husain Bilgrami, a former member of the Imperial Legislative Council, 'are a threat to our very existence'.[79] In 1913, Fateh Ali Khan Qizilbash condemned the ideal of self-government, adopted by the Muslim League and attempted to mobilise his forces against the radical group in that body.[80] In March 1914 he conceived the scheme of a Shia College. The aim was to counter the Aligarh Muslim University movement, and 'to produce an educated class with which will be associated every kind of healthy progress and which will produce members who will readily constitute a pious community of loyal subjects'. But the Raja of Mahmudabad, though a staunch Shia and a patron of education in the province, opposed the scheme. He suspected that the scheme was officially backed in order to weaken the Muslim University movement, and feared that a Shia College would aggravate Shia-Sunni tension in the UP.[81]

In May 1915, the Muslim opponents of Congress-League rapprochement joined hands in an abortive attempt to prevent the Muslim League session from being held concurrently with the Congress session at Bombay in 1915. Suleman Cassim Mitha, Fazulbhoy Currimbhoy, and Maulvi Rafiuddin launched a personal attack against Jinnah and Wazir Hasan and opposed their plan of holding the League session in Bombay.[82] Eventually, the Governor of Bombay, Willingdon, composed

[78]Montagu, *An Indian Diary*, p. 118, quoted in Hugh F. Owen, 'Negotiating the Pact', *JAS*, Vol. XXXI, No. 3, May 1972, p. 581.

[79]Bilgrami to Mohamed Ali, 12 June 1915, Mohamed Ali Papers.

[80]Fateh Ali Khan to Meston, 21 August 1913, Meston Papers (6).

[81]Interviews with the Maharajkumar of Mahmudabad, 10 July 1975.

[82]For details, see Owen, 'Negotiating the Lucknow Pact', pp. 571-72; Robinson, *Separatism*, pp. 242-45.

the differences between the two factions and the League session was held as scheduled.[83] But the campaign against the pro-Congress Muslims did not cease. In the UP, newspapers like *Al-Bashir*, *Al-Mizan*, *Zul Qarnain*, *Mashriq* and the *Aligarh Institute Gazette* continued their tirade against them. According to *Al-Bashir*, the pro-Congress Muslims were isolated from their community and were unaware of its problem.[84] Wazir Hasan was, quite uncharitably, singled out as an 'opportunist'. His ambition, according to *Al-Mizan*, was to achieve prominence through his alliance with the non-Muslims.[85]

However, in the years 1915 and 1916, these voices of protest enjoyed limited support; they took little account of the changed realities of Indian politics. Muslims were coming increasingly to see Congress in a more favourable light. In 1915 the government reported from Bengal, 'the Muslims have paid more attention than formerly to the proceedings of the Indian National Congress. A number of leading Calcutta Muslims attended the Congress at Madras'.[86] Also, Hindu-Muslim relations were generally cordial everywhere. Unlike the previous years, the *Bakr Id* festival and Muharram passed off peacefully

[83]Meston did not, however, consider Willingdon's action prudent. 'Lord Willingdon', he wrote to the Viceroy, 'in his good nature has given our Lucknow gang a somewhat inflated sense of their own importance by his action in personally composing their differences with the Bombay moderates . . . . Had we been asked earlier, I should have told Lord Willingdon that our people (and, as far as I know, the Punjab people also) do not want the League to meet at Bombay just now and be snapped up by the Congress; that the small clique, which Wazir Hasan organises and Mahmudabad feeds, are in no sense representative of the Muslims of North India; and that a triumph of this coterie will be taken as a triumph for Mohamed Ali and his followers.' Meston to Hardinge, 23 December 1915, Hardinge Papers (90).

[84]*Al-Bashir*, 8 June 1915, UPNNR 1915; Notice the reactions of *Medina*, 22 October 1916, and *Mashriq*, 19 December 1916, UPNNR 1916.

[85]*Al-Mizan*, 12 June 1915, UPNNR 1915. In a forceful criticism of the ideal of self-government adopted by the Muslim League, Syed Husain Bilgrami made it clear that he did not want to be 'ruled by men like Mr. Jinnah, Mr. Malaviya or even the Raja of Mahmudabad'. He described Jinnah as 'a man of very low birth'. Bilgrami to Meston, 14 November 1917, Meston Papers (4).

[86]FR (Bengal), Home Poll. Deposit, March 1915, 53, NAI.

in 1915 and 1916.[87] Furthermore, the group of 'conservative Muslims' was disorganised and lacked any widespread support. Many of their leaders like the Aga Khan were extremely unpopular because of their views on the Turko-Italian War and their role during the Aligarh University movement.[88] Meston summed up the strength of pro-Congress feelings amongst Muslims and the declining influence of 'conservative Muslims'. In a note submitted to the Viceroy, he observed:

In deciding either on the strategy of its *post bellum* policy or to handle the Home Rule agitation, the Government of India will no doubt have regard to the strength of the Nationalist feeling in India at the present moment. It is unquestionably greater than it has ever been in our time. The Christmas meetings at Lucknow caught up and consolidated popular sentiment as few political events have done. Extremists and Moderates have united after years of misunderstanding; and, greatest marvel of all, the Mahomedans also had come into the fold. A few Moderates may grumble here and there; and a few conservative Mahomedans may urge that the League does not represent their community. But they *do* nothing. They are voiceless in public; they do not hold meetings; they have completely lost command of the Press. For all practical purposes they have, for the time at least, disappeared as a separate party. The resultant union of all voices has filled educated India with a pride and a feeling of nationality which it is impossible to ignore.[89]

II

The terms of the Lucknow Pact provoked serious objections and opposition from the Bengali Muslims. They felt that their

[87]FR (Bengal), Home Poll. Deposit, December 1915, 25, NAI; FR (Madras), Home Poll. Deposit, December 1915, 26, NAI.

[88]According to Sydenham, Governor of Bombay, 'I imagine that the Aga Khan is dead as a leader, and from what he told me I think he realises that his power is gone. Anyhow he suddenly bolted, some weeks before he originally intended.' Sydenham to Hardinge, 18 March 1913, Hardinge Papers (85).

[89]Note for the Viceroy by Sir James Meston, 7 February 1917, Meston Papers (17).

interests were sacrificed to the claims of the minorities in Bombay, Madras, Bihar, and the UP for, although their population in the province was above 52 per cent, they were allotted only 40 per cent of the council seats. The Central National Mohammadan Association claimed a share for Muslims on the basis of their political importance and contribution to the Empire. Their claim in the matter of Muslim representation compared with the Congress-League scheme was as follows:

Province	Muslims in population (%)	Legislative seats allotted by Congress-League scheme (%)	Legislative seats demanded by the Association (%)
Bengal	52.6	40.0	52.0
Bihar & Orissa	10.5	25.0	25.0
Bombay	20.4	33.3	33.3
Madras	6.5	15.0	15.0
Punjab	54.8	50.0	55.0
United Provinces	14.0	30.0	35.0

In a memorial submitted to Montagu and Chelmsford in September 1918, the Association argued that as the trend of government's policy was towards granting autonomous administration to the various provinces and towards reduction of the British element in the personnel of the States, it was essential 'to have the rights of Muslims to share proportionately in such and future developments placed upon a firm and acknowledged basis, rather than leave the principle for settlement to a future time, and at the risk of bitter friction and fierce strife'. The spirit of the memorial was characterised by the concluding sentence of the Association's address: 'For England now to place the Indian Moslems, without proper, definite, and ample safeguards, under the heels of a hostile non-Moslem majority, would, your humble memorialists venture respectfully to submit, be a cruel act of breach of faith and violation of trust.'[90]

The Indian Moslem Association, formed in 1917 by Sirajul Islam and Nawab Ali Chaudhuri, rejected the Lucknow Pact

[90]Addresses Presented at Calcutta, Montagu Papers (34),

and demanded a more generous legislative representation for the Bengal Muslims. They proposed that the proportion of elected to nominated members be two to one, and that one half of the elected members should be Muslims. For the provincial executive councils, the association recommended six members in major provinces including three Indians of whom two should be Muslims, and four members in minor provinces, of whom two should be Indians with one Muslim.[91]

The increasing opposition to the Pact compelled the Bengal Presidency Muslim League — which negotiated with the Congress at Lucknow—to advocate certain modifications and to put forward additional proposals. In their memorial submitted to Montagu, Fazlul Haq and his supporters asked for 50 per cent of the council seats and 50 per cent representation in all branches of the public services.[92] They were in this way temporarily able to check the mounting criticism against them for selling out the Muslim community to the Hindus during the Congress-League negotiations.

Clearly, by December 1917, all the important Muslim organisations in Bengal were united in their opposition to the Lucknow Pact. 'The success of the scheme', wrote a Calcutta Urdu daily, the *Resalat*, 'will place the Muslims under the thumb of the Hindus. Muslim interests will not be safeguarded unless they get at least equal representation with the Hindus in the Councils. This is our and the Bengal Muslim League's opinion.'[93] The communal riots in Bihar in September 1917 intensified Muslim opposition to the Lucknow Pact. The *Resalat* warned the Muslims to 'learn a lesson from the universal ruin of their brethren in Bihar'.[94] This struck a sympathetic note in many provincial papers.[95] 'Those who apprehend that the Muslims will suffer political death if they do not unite with the Hindus are greatly mistaken', observed a correspondent. 'We have already stood alone 1,300 years. What is wanted is that we

---

[91]Addresses Presented at Calcutta, Montagu Papers (34).

[92]Addresses Presented at Calcutta, *Ibid.*

[93]*Resalat*, 2 December 1917, BENNR 1917.

[94]*Ibid.*, 7 December 1917, *Ibid.*

[95]For example, *Mohammadi*, 14 December 1917, *Ibid.*

should firmly abide by our religious laws and not become fainthearted'.[96]

In the Punjab, on the other hand, there was no serious opposition to the Lucknow Pact. The Muslim League, led by Fazl-i-Husain, Saifuddin Kitchlew and Syed Mohammad Umar endorsed the pact.[97] Similarly, contrary to the views of some historians, the Pact also enjoyed a fair degree of support in the UP.[98] This was because the UP Muslims secured more council seats than they were entitled to by their population in the province. The *Hamdam*, an Urdu weekly of Lucknow, welcomed the Pact because it secured the 'just rights' of the UP Muslims in the matter of representation.[99] Other leading Muslim newspapers, such as *Al-Bureed*, *Musafir*, *Rehbar*, *Nai Duniya* and *Malumat*, as well as many conservative Muslims like Shaikh Mohammad Abdullah of Aligarh, Hamidullah Khan of Allahabad, and Abdur Rahman Khan of Saharanpur also lent their support to the Lucknow Pact.[100] This was an ominous sign and the government moved in to counter the growing popularity of the Pact.

In the UP and Punjab, Muslim landlords and other

[96]*Resalat*, 17 April 1917, *Moslem Hitaishi*, 10 August 1917, BENNR 1917.

[97]*Tribune*, 17 January 1918; The only opposition came from Mohammad Shafi, who claimed representation for Muslims 'commensurate not only with their numerical strength but also with their political importance and the services they have rendered to the Empire'. He was backed by the pro-Government newspapers, such as the *Paisa Akhbar*, the *Kisan* and the *Urdu Bulletin*. Their criticism was that a Congress-League *entente* was prejudicial to Muslim interests, that the Lucknow Pact signified the merger of the League into the Congress, and therefore, the League had no right to represent the political interests of the Muslims. *Tribune*, 4 January 1918; *Paisa Akhbar*, 18 January, 13 February and 13 October 1917, PUNNR 1917.

[98]Dr Robinson and Dr Owen have argued that the Lucknow Pact received limited support in UP. The available evidence, on the other hand, proves beyond doubt that with the exception of men like Fateh Ali Khan and a few *ulama*, the UP Muslims received the Pact favourably. This was not at all surprising, for the proportion of representation negotiated for the UP Muslims was good value.

[99]*Hamdam*, 31 December 1916.

[100]Syed Raza Ali to *Pioneer*, 19 November 1917, quoted in *Leader*, 24 November 1917.

conservative Muslims were encouraged to put forward their
own scheme of reforms. In November 1917, Meston urged the
Nawab of Rampur, with whom he was very friendly, to consent
to be the patron of the UP Muslim Defence Association
organised by Nawab Fateh Ali Khan, Nawab Mohammad
Muzammilullah Khan, a prosperous landlord with large estates
in Aligarh and Etah districts, Syed Abdur Rauf, member of
the UP Legislative Council from 1913 to 1916, and Ibni
Ahmad, a landowner of Budaun and a practising lawyer at the
Allahabad High Court. 'It is assuredly time', he suggested,
'to stop a great deal of the nonsense that is preached by the
leaders. You will remember my parting prayer to you the other
day, and my earnest entreaty that you would come forward
and take your right position at the head of your community.
I never give advice which is likely to be embarrassing, and even
if I give it, I never resent its being rejected, but I do ask Your
Highness to think over this opportunity of taking a brilliant
and dominant part in organizing wise and moderate and
orthodox Moslem opinion in India.'[101] Meston also persuaded Nawab Abdul Samad Khan to join the Defence Association.
'Your adherence to the new association', he wrote 'would give
it strength'.[102]

Thanks to the government's encouragement, the Defence
Association presented an address to Montagu and Chelmsford
which declared 'that any large measure of self-government
which might curtail the moderating and adjusting influence of
the British Government would be nothing short of a cataclysm',
and claimed that, if devolution took place, Muslims should
have fifty per cent representation. This demand was unreal
because it failed to take into account the realities of political
life. British influence was gradually being curtailed in the
legislative bodies and there was no chance of the association's
demands being accepted.

An analysis of Muslim reaction to the Lucknow Pact
reveals clear ideological, strategic and factional divisions

[101]Meston to Hamid Ali Khan, 12 November 1917, Meston Papers (4).
[102]Meston to Samad Ali Khan, 12 November 1917; Also, see file
entitled 'Correspondence with Heads of Provinces and Others regarding
Constitutional Reforms', Ibid.

within the community. These divisions were more apparent at the end of 1917, when Montagu and Chelmsford received forty-four representations from Muslim bodies each claiming to speak for the community. A comparison of their demands makes it abundantly clear that the regional aspirations of the landed and the professional classes differed from province to province. The UP Muslims, who were in a minority in their province, were mainly interested in securing separate electorates and weightages so as to ensure their representation in self-governing bodies. The Bengali Muslims, on the other hand, though numerically superior, were backward as regards property, wealth, education, and employment in public service and the professions. So, they demanded not only separate electorates, but also representation on the basis of their population.

The religious groups, too, were sharply divided. The *Anjuman-i-Islam* of Bombay approved of the main provision of the Congress-League scheme, though the memorialists made larger claims for Muslims in the Bombay and the Imperial Legislative Councils. They demanded 36 per cent of the seats of which 28.8 per cent were to be elected by separate electorates and 7.2 per cent by joint electorates.[103] The *Anjuman-i-Islam* of Saharanpur, on the other hand, considered the scheme 'ruinous to the cause of Musalmans because of its hopelessly inadequate provisions for safeguarding Muslim interests'. 'Our instinct of self-preservation', stated the *Anjumans*' address presented to Montagu and Chelmsford, 'compels us to always keep at a safe distance from them [Hindus] in politics . . . . We are fully convinced that without *equal* strength, we are not for one minute safe with them in the political arena, because their interests happen to be so diametrically opposed to ours and their angle of vision so irreconciliably different'.[104] In the Punjab one group of the Ahmadiya community rejected the Congress-League scheme, but another group which called itself the *Ahmadiya Ishaat-i-Islam*, a 'body of about 50 persons

---

[103]Address of the *Anjuman-i-Islam*, Bombay, Montagu Papers (37).
[104]Memorial submitted by the *Anjuman-i-Islamia*, Saharanpur, Meston Papers (19).

established at Lahore', called for its immediate adoption by the government.[105] The *ulama* of Deoband wanted an *alim* to be appointed to each legislative council, the *wakfs* and the mosques to be placed under the charge of the *Sheikhul Islam*, and the disputes amongst Muslims to be settled in accordance with Muslim Personal Law.[106]

Such glaring divisions make it very clear that the political interests of Muslims were not alike; they varied from class to class and from region to region. The memoranda submitted to Montagu and Chelmsford indicate that, apart from the question of separate electorates, Muslims had no common political demands. This made nonsense of the communal categories created by the government. To treat Muslims as a distinct political interest was a conscious, but mistaken, policy pursued by the government. It superimposed artificial divisions in society. Moreover, in the years following the Non-cooperation movement, it also encouraged certain vested interests to assert their communal, as opposed to their class identity. This did not augur well for the future of the Indian national movement.

[105]Memorial submitted by the *Ahmadiya Ishaat-i-Islam*, Lahore, Montagu Papers (35).

[106]Maulvi Mohammad Ahmad to Sheweth, 30 October 1917, Meston Papers (19).

CHAPTER FOUR

REPRESSION, REFORMS AND HINDU-MUSLIM UNITY

The Lucknow Pact marked the beginning of Congress-League cooperation, which continued during the next few years. This is evident from Muslim interest in Congress affairs in several provinces. Sarfaraz Husain Khan, Mazharul Haque, and Hasan Imam were some of the leading members of the Bihar Congress. Many of the District Congress Committees in the Punjab had Muslim presidents and secretaries.[1] In the UP, many Western-educated leaders of the Muslim League, such as Ansari, Abdul Majid Khwaja, Wazir Hasan and Asaf Ali, played a prominent role in Congress activities.

Many leading Muslims also responded favourably to the Home Rule movement after Annie Besant's internment in June 1917. The Muslim League in Bengal, for example, allied itself with the provincial Home Rule League which was led by B. Chakravarti, I.B. Sen and H.N. Datta.[2] In Bombay, Jinnah and Omar Sobhani were the leading Home Rule Leaguers, and they campaigned actively to enlist the support of their co-religionists.[3] In the UP, too, there was considerable

[1]For example, Abdul Huq was president of the Ferozepur [DCC], Syed Ghulam Shah of the Gujrat [DCC] and Aziz Ahmad of the Rawalpindi [DCC] Shaikh Mohammad Ismail was secretary of the Hissar Congress Committee. *Tribune*, 23 & 25 October 1917.

[2]*Amrita Bazar Patrika*, 26 & 27 June 1917.

[3]For Jinnah's role in the movement, see J. Masselos, 'Some Aspects of Bombay City Politics in 1919' in Ravinder Kumar (ed.), *Essays on Gandhian Politics: The Rowlatt Satyagraha of 1919* (Oxford, 1971).

Home Rule activity.[4] Abdul Majid Khwaja established a branch of the Home Rule League in Aligarh.[5] Zahur Ahmad and Manzar Ali Sokhta were joint secretaries of the Allahabad Home Rule League, and Kamaluddin Jafri and Wahid Yar Khan were represented on the committee.[6] The Agra Home Rule League was led by Syed Ali Nabi, who had served as chairman of the Agra Municipal Board and was vice-president of the Agra District Congress Committee in 1916. In Lucknow, the Raja of Mahmudabad was the chief patron of the Home Rule League. According to Meston, the Raja supported the Home Rule movement with 'a clique of noisy and aggressive Muslims of the young party, who make the Raja's house their headquarters and live and agitate at his expense'.[7] This 'clique' included many young journalists, lawyers, and University students such as Raja Ghulam Husain, editor of *New Era*, Syed Abdul Jalib, editor of the Urdu daily, *Hamdam*, Shuaib Qureshi and Abdur Rahman Siddiqi. Reporting on the political events in his province, Meston wrote that the 'extremists' and the 'moderates' were united in the Home Rule agitation; and, the 'greatest marvel of all, the Muhammadans had also come into the fold'.[8]

Another notable feature of the period after the Lucknow Pact was the communal fraternisation in different parts of

---

[1]There were of course many Muslim landowners who arrayed themselves against the movement. The Nawab of Chhatari, for instance, presided over an anti-Home Rule League meeting. In September 1917, the landowners planned to form an anti-Home Rule League, but it failed to materialise. *Leader*, 20 September 1917; FR (UP), 18 October 1917, Home Poll. Deposit, November 1917, 29, NAI.

[5]A.M. Khwaja, *Home Rule se kiya matlab hai* (Aligarh, 1917). Other leading Home Rule Leaguers in Aligarh were Haji Mohammad Musa Khan, a *rais* of Datauli, and his son, Haroon Khan Sherwani, a well known historian of medieval India. In mid-July they issued a statement condemning the repressive policies of the government and urging Muslims to join the Home Rule Leagues. *Leader*, 15 July 1917.

[6]*Amrita Bazar Patrika*, 22 & 27 June 1917.

[7]Meston to Chelmsford, 20 August 1917, Meston Papers (1). The Raja doled out money to the Home Rule League and subsidised the *Observer* of Lahore to run it in the interest of the Home Rule agitation. Home Poll. Deposit, June 1917, 69, NAI; Home Poll. Deposit, September 1917, 6, NAI.

[8]Home Poll. Deposit, May 1917, 3, NAI.

the country. Hindus and Muslims of Allahabad embraced each other during the Dasehra and Muharram ceremonies and exchanged *pan* and cigarettes instead of fighting each other with *lathis*.[9] In Agra and Azamgarh, where communal tension was a common thing, no disturbances were reported.[10] At Peshawar, out of regard for Muslim feelings, the date of the Bharat Milap procession was shifted to avoid its observance on the tenth day of Muharram.[11] In Agra, the district Congress Committee and the Home Rule League took part in the Muharram procession and arranged six jars of *sharbat*, on which was written: 'Most revered Imam Husain, kindly have us granted Home Rule at an early date.'[12] According to the Nationalist Press, these were unmistakable indications of 'a growing consciousness of the fact that the national interests must be paramount, and the two communities must realize in an ever increasing degree the identity of their interests.'[13]

The period from January 1917 to April 1919 is important not only because it witnessed unprecedented scenes of Hindu-Muslim unity but also because it enables us to identify the issues and the circumstances in which the two communities cooperated with each other. This phase further reveals that an all-India political alliance helped to improve communal relations at the local level. In order to explain this connection, an attempt is made to discover the basis on which some of the leading Hindu and Muslim politicians forged an alliance at the all-India level, and the issues they raised for enlisting the support of their allies in the localities.

[9]*Leader*, 18 September 1917.

[10]J.C. Smith, the Collector and magistrate of Azamgarh, issued the following statement on 2 November: 'The district of Azamgarh is to be congratulated on the fact that the Dasehra and Muharram ceremonies passed off without disturbances of any kind. For more than three years past the government have been anxious regarding this matter and it is highly creditable to the people that at so critical a period there has been no sign of hostility between the different communities.' *Ibid.*, 15 November 1917.

[11]*Tribune*, 21 October 1917.

[12]*Leader*, 4 November 1917.

[13]*Tribune*, 30 October 1917.

GOVERNMENT RESORTS TO REPRESSION

Throughout the War years, the Home department was fed with exaggerated reports of a Turko-German conspiracy to incite the Indian Muslims against the British Government. In August 1915, Ubaidullah Sindhi, a converted Sikh who had studied at Deoband, worked with German and Turkish agents in Afghanistan to stir up tribesmen against the British on the north-west frontier. In March 1915, a 'Young Hindustan Association' was formed in Constantinople with the object of overthrowing the British Government in India.[14] But the Association evoked no response in India. Its organisers merely corresponded with Zafar Ali, Hasan Imam and Ajmal Khan and sent pan-Islamic literature to them which was circulated throughout India.[15]

Officials of the Raj were, however, alarmed by the spread of pan-Islamic propaganda, and so they interned many leading Muslims who were suspected of pan-Islamic connections.[16] This action was unnecessary because only a tiny section of the Muslim population at any time joined Sindhi or Mahmudul Hasan, or indeed preached in favour of militant action. In

[14]Maulana Abdul Hafiz and Maulana Maqbul Husain were among the members of the Association. They belonged to Kanpur and migrated to Constantinople after performing the hajj at Mecca and Medina. In Constantinople, they were employed by the 'Tashkilat-i-Makhsusa', a sub-section of the Turkish Ministry of War, which arranged and financed various anti-British missions. Home Poll. and Foreign Department B, August 1920, 441-449, NAI.

[15]Home Poll. Deposit, January 1916, 33, NAI. There is no evidence to suggest that any of these leaders ever replied to letters received from Turkey. They were probably aware of the watchful eyes of the Central Intelligence Department and were careful not to give it an excuse for curbing their political activities.

[16]Maulana Zafar Ali Khan, poet and journalist of Lahore, was one of the early victims of the government's repressive policy. On 12 January 1914, the Punjab Government forfeited the security of his paper Zamindar, and in December of that year, he was restricted to the area of his village near Sialkot. This was followed by the arrests of the Ali Brothers in May 1915, Abdul Kalam Azad and Hasrat Mohani. In December 1916, Maulana Mahmudul Hasan and his four companions of Deoband were arrested for taking part in the 'Silk Letter Conspiracy', a scheme devised by Ubaidullah Sindhi and his chief disciple, Mahmudul Hasan, to destroy British rule in India.

fact, the decision to arrest the pan-Islamic leaders turned them into martyrs in the eyes of the people and enabled their followers to use the issue of detenus as a lever to stir up an agitation against the government. In 1918, a Central Bureau was set up in Allahabad for this purpose.[17] In Bombay, various local *anjumans*, such as the *Anjuman-i-Aqaid* and the *Anjuman -i-Miamul Ghurba*, agitated for the release of Muslim detenus.[18] In the Punjab, the *Anjuman-i-Himayat-i-Islam,* Lahore, and the *Anjuman-i-Islamia* at Sialkot and Multan did likewise. In Bengal, too, the campaign continued with unabated zeal. Although the *Resalat* and the *Sedaqat* of Calcutta were opposed to the pro-Congress activities of the Ali Brothers, they nevertheless backed the efforts of the Bengal Presidency League to secure their release. This was because the Ali Brothers were popular and were admired for their vocal advocacy of Muslim religious interests.[19] The *Sedaqat* warned the government that if 'it laboured under the belief that it has succeeded in severing the bond of brotherhood between the Moslems and their detenus by interning them, then it has certainly shown a colossal ignorance regarding the religious beliefs of its Moslem subjects.'[20]

Clearly, Muslims in the early 1920s did not regard Mohamed Ali, Azad and Zafar Ali Khan as political agitators who whipped up popular discontent to achieve their personal ends. On the contrary, they were seen as selfless men who had the courage and determination to fight for the religious beliefs and practices of Muslims. An address presented to the Ali Brothers stated:

It would require a volume to enumerate in detail your services in regard to the M.A.O. College, the Muslim University, the galvanising of the Muslim community

[17]Home Poll. Deposit, January 1918, 59, NAI.
[18]*Ibid.* In Sind, G.M. Bhurgi elicited a clamorous endorsement of his condemnation of the treatment accorded to the Ali Brothers. Home Poll. Deposit, November 1917, 29, NAI.
[19]See, for example, *Resalat*, 27 October 1917, *Tirmizee*, 6 & 7 October 1917, *Naqqash*, 29 November & 4 December 1917, BENNR 1917.
[20]*Sedaqat*, 12 & 15 January 1920, *Ibid.*, 1920.

through your brilliant newspapers, the *Comrade* and the *Hamdard* . . . ., the raising of funds for Muslim victims in the Balkan War, the organising of a competent and well-equipped medical mission for the Turkish wounded. Your restoration to liberty is a mark of profound rejoicing to us. . . . Your presence in our midst will stimulate our community into the solidarity seriously imperilled during the last five years of agonizing ordeal.[21]

Government reports reveal the influence of Mohamed Ali, Zafar Ali, and Azad and the popularity of their newspapers. 'No paper has so much influence with the students as the *Comrade*, and no individual has the authority over them which is exercised by Muhammad Ali, reported the UP government.[22] Dr. Ziauddin, the officiating principal of Aligarh College, informed Reginald Craddock, Home Member of the Viceroy's Council, that he had great difficulty in keeping Aligarh in order because of Mohamed Ali's influence on the students.[23] Zafar Ali was equally popular in the Punjab. The *Zamindar*, published by him in Urdu, increased its circulation from 1,200 in 1910 to 15,000 in 1913. 'As soon as copies of this paper are brought into the bazaar, large crowds of people surround the news-shops and buy the copies',[24] a government report pointed out in testimony to the popularity of the paper in Lahore. *Al-Hilal* was an Urdu weekly published from Calcutta by Azad. It had a circulation of 11,000 within six months of its founding (i.e., by the end of 1912), and reached 25,000 during the War.[25]

What was the secret of Mohamed Ali, Azad, and Zafar Ali's success with the Muslims? A study of their role may provide an answer to the question, and also explain why many Congress leaders took up the cause of their release with great enthusiasm.

[21]*Leader*, 12 & 15 January 1920.

[22]FR (UP), Home Poll. D, December 1924, 31, NAI.

[23]Memorandum by R. Craddock, 15 October 1914, Home Poll. A, January 1915, 76-97, NAI.

[24]FR (Punjab), 28 January 1916, Home Poll. A, May 1916, 173, NAI.

[25]W.C. Smith, *Modern Islam in India* (Lahore, 1946), p. 226.

Zafar Ali was born in 1890. He graduated from Aligarh College before joining the Hyderabad Civil Service, where he rose to the position of Assistant Home Secretary.[26] A few years later, he returned to Lahore and acquired control of the *Zamindar*, a weekly newspaper published by his father Sirajuddin Ahmad. Within a few years, the paper increased its circulation in northern India by focussing on religious issues and giving extensive coverage to the Kanpur mosque incident, the Turko-Italian war and the Muslim University movement. Unlike *Paisa Akhbar* and *Vakil*, the *Zamindar* boldly criticised the British Government. The main thrust of the argument pursued in its columns was that, because the British were hostile to the Muslim kingdoms, it was the duty of Muslims to rise in their defence. The slogan of 'Islam in Danger' was raised to arouse the religious passions of the common people.

Like many of his contemporaries, Zafar Ali was a passionate pan-Islamist. This is reflected in his poetry and other writings.[27] According to him, the pan-Islamic concept was inherent in the Islamic idea of *Akhuwat* (brotherhood of Muslims), and its *raison d'etre* was to weld all Muslims, scattered over the world, into a compact whole, under the protecting aegis of the *Khalifa*.[28] He further maintained that the pan-Islamic movement was defensive in character, and its object was not 'to cherish projects of an aggressive nature against Christendom in spite of all that it has done to eliminate Islam, but to act purely on the defensive and to protect what little remains to the Muslims of their once splendid empire against further encroachments'.[29]

Zafar Ali's enthusiasm for promoting pan-Islamism was reflected in his activities. In 1912, he went to Constantinople to present to the Grand Vizier a part of the money raised by

[26]Shorish Kashmiri, 'Zafar Ali Khan', *Naqqush: Shakhsiat Number*, January 1955, p. 597,

[27]For the pan-Islamic content of his poetry, see Harun Rashid, *Urdu Adab Aur Islam* (Lahore, 1968), Vol. 1, pp. 313-30.

[28]Quoted in Celal Nuri, *Itehad-i-Islam* (Istambul, 1915), pp. 396-401.

[29]Z.A. Khan, 'Indian Muslims and Pan-Islamism', *Comrade*, 14 June 1913.

the sale of Turkish bonds.[30] He visited Turkey again in early 1913 with some members of the Indian Medical Mission and took an active part in furthering a Turkish proposal to provide a colony in Anatolia for Muslim refugees. On his return to India, he became involved in the Kanpur mosque affair and wrote articles condemning the British Government. 'A sacred portion of the Cawnpore Mosque', Zafar Ali announced, 'was demolished in the midst of guns and bayonets. In this way the funeral of that religious liberty, whose effigy has been shown as living and moaning for more than a century, was performed with full military honours'.[31] Towards the end of the year, the publication of an article entitled 'Come Over Macedonia and Help Us' prompted the Punjab government to forfeit the security of the *Zamindar* together with the Zamindar Printing Press.

Mohamed Ali was born into a family associated with the court of Rampur. He was educated at the M.A.O. College, Aligarh, and developed a life-long connection with the institution. In 1898, he won a government scholarship to Oxford, where he studied history. On his return to India, he took up employment first as the Chief Education Officer in his own state, Rampur, and later joined the Gaekwar of Baroda's service. But at Baroda he did not get on well with his colleagues and decided to leave. From 1907 to 1909 Mohamed Ali tried to find a job in government service, but was unsuccessful.[32] It was during this period that he first became involved in politics.

In February 1907, Mohamed Ali delivered two lectures at Allahabad—'The Present Situation' and the 'Muhammadan Programme'—in order to arouse interest in the Muslim League, founded in December 1906.[33] He was also involved in the 'great controversy which had gone on throughout the

[30]Michael O'Dwyer, *India As I Knew It, 1885-1925* (London, 1925), p. 172.

[31]*Zamindar*, 20 April 1913, quoted in Kumar (ed.), *Essays*, p. 271.

[32]See, for example, his correspondence with Harold Stuart, the Home Member, and George Clark, the Governor of Bombay. Mohamed Ali Papers.

[33]Home Poll. B, January 1913, 149, NAI.

Morley-Minto regime with regard to the claims of the Indian Mussalmans to be represented as a community in the Legislatures and the local bodies of the country'.[34] In his paper *Comrade*, launched on 11 January 1911, [he continued to defend the principle of separate electorates and its extension to local boards and the municipalities. 'Separate electorates have been found to be necessary at this stage', he observed, 'exactly because there exist at present distinct and well-defined Hindu and Muslim standpoints in regard to the common, immediate and every day affairs of Indian life.'[35]

However, Mohamed Ali's public career cannot be understood without reference to his religious beliefs, his concern for the Indian Muslims, and his romantic commitment to Islam. Like Zafar Ali and Azad, he too was a devout Muslim. As a schoolboy at Aligarh, Mohamed Ali attended Shibli's lectures on the Quran and made his first acquaintance with its meaning.[36] While at Oxford, he was attracted by Maulvi Nazir Ahmad's Urdu translation of the Quran, and, 'fired by my own religious zeal and financed by the affections of a generous brother, I had the Quran bound most sumptuously in calf by the book-binder of the Bodleian, and it looked superb on the otherwise meagerly furnished book-shelf in my college room.'[37] During the rest of his life, Mohamed Ali turned more and more to the Quran and found in it 'the consolation and contentment that was denied to us outside its pages'.[38] According to him, the Quran was a 'perennial of truth', and offered a 'complete scheme of life, a perfect code of conduct and a comprehensive social policy as wide as the human race and in fact

---

[34]Mohamed Ali, *My Life: A Fragment*, p. 33.

[35]*Comrade*, 11 January & 29 March 1913.

[36]Mohamed Ali, *My Life: A Fragment*, pp. 23-25.

[37]*Ibid.*, p. 29.

[38]Mohamed Ali, *My Life: A Fragment*, p. 45. During his internment in Chhindwara, Mohamed Ali spent most of his time reading the Quran and the works of Imam Ghazzali and Maulana Shibli Numani. It was probably during this period that he made a systematic study of Islam and steeped himself afresh in his Islamic heritage. A.M. Daryabadi, *Mohamed Ali: Za'ati Diary ke chund Auraq* (Hyderabad, 1943), p, 14; Mohamed Ali to Abdul Majid Daryabadi, 22 May 1916, 25 July 1916 (Urdu), A.M. Daryabadi Papers, JNML.

aswide asthe human creation'.[39] He revived Shibli's discourses
on the Quran at the Jamia Millia Islamia and made sure that
'our day began with a full hour devoted to the rapid exegesis of
the Quran'.[40] In May 1921, Mohamed Ali stated that he was
a 'Muslim first and everything else afterwards. As a Muslim,
I must be free and subject to no autocrat who would demand
from me obedience to his orders in defiance of those of God . . . .
Faith is my motive of conduct in every act . . . '.[41]

Mohamed Ali was deeply committed to the promotion of
pan-Islamism, which he regarded as the 'Supernatural Sangathan of Muslims in five Continents'.[42] At the M.A.O. College,
Aligarh, the writings of Shibli and T.W. Arnold on Islam and
its history made Mohamed Ali aware of the religious links
which bound Muslims throughout the world, and he saw himself
cast in the role of strengthening them. When he saw that the
Khilafat, which symbolised the temporal and spiritual glory
of Islam, was threatened by the Balkan Wars, he undertook
to save it. In September 1913, he went on a 'self-imposed
mission' to London to represent his community's views on
Khilafat, but received a cold reception from the Secretary of
State and his colleagues at the India Office.[43] But this did
not deter Mohamed Ali from his mission. By 1915, he was,
in the words of the Chief Commissioner of Delhi, 'the centre
and inspiration of the Pan-Islamic movement'.[44] Prejudiced
officials of the Raj referred to him as a 'notorious agitator' and
as dangerous element in North Indian politics,[45] though his

[39]Afzal Iqbal (ed.), Selected Writings and Speeches of Mohamed Ali,
p. 170.

[40]Mohamed Ali, My Life: A Fragment, p. 29.

[41]Mussalman, 13 May 1921.

[42]Mohamed Ali observed: 'Islam united Muslims by offering a set of
common ideals and offered the only rational basis for unity and cooperation among its followers. The sympathies of a Muslim are
co-extensive with his religion because they have been bred into him by
the inspiring spirit of his creed.' Comrade, 12 April 1913.

[43]See Holderness to Mohamed Ali and Wazir Hasan, 11 November
1913; Montagu to Mohamed Ali, 14 October 1913, Crewe Papers
(I/14:2).

[44]W.M. Hailey to H.H. Wheeler, 1 May 1915, Home Poll. D, May
1915, 36, NAI.

[45]FR (Delhi), 16 August 1914, Home Poll. A, September 1914, 1-3,
NAI.

co-religionists respected and admired his sincerity and devotion to the Khilafat cause.[46] This is why his was 'the only voice which was heard throughout India and by different Muslim groups'.[47] When, at the beginning of his internment, Mohamed Ali wanted to stop the *Hamdard*, Vilayat Ali urged him not to do so. 'I don't approve of your decision and I don't think many will . . . . You can't imagine what the loss of *Hamdard* will mean to us – the Mussalmans'.[48] Even during his internment, Mohamed Ali continued to inspire his colleagues in the Muslim League. In 1917 there was general agreement on his election as president of the League. 'It is imperative', Ansari proposed, 'to hold public meetings where popular voice should with all force and unanimity declare him to be the only person fit for the honour. . . . It would be disgraceful if someone else was allowed to supersede him.'[49] Similarly, a circular letter issued by Ansari and Mazharul Haque declared that Mohamed Ali's 'noble services rendered at the most psychological moment in the history of the community to which he belongs, mark him out as one of the most potent factors in the formation of the Indian nation'.[50] This illustrates the extent and range of support that Mohamed Ali enjoyed.

In some ways, Mohamed Ali was different from many of his contemporary politicians who sought political power in order to bolster their social status in society and to promote their class interests. In Mohamed Ali's case, on the other hand, politics was just a means to achieve certain higher social and

[46]Syed Abdul Has to Mohamed Ali, 19 July 1911, Mohamed Ali Papers. For the appreciation of Mohamed Ali's role by two of his contemporaries, Rashid Ahmad Siddiqi and Ijaz Askari, see *Aligarh Magazine*, 1960-61, pp. 100-10; *Aligarh Magazine*: Sir Syed Number, 1953-55.

[47]'Throughout the country, there was only one voice which was heard by the people of the north and the south, the east and the west, by the educated and the illiterate, the *ulama* and the ignorant. . . .' Abdul Majid Daryabadi, *Maqalat-i-Majid* (Bombay, n.d.), pp. 233-34.

[48]Vilayat Ali to Mohamed Ali, 20 August 1915, Mohamed Ali Papers.

[49]Ansari to A.M. Khwaja, 3 September 1917, Khwaja Papers, JNML.

[50]Circular Letter, 3 September 1917, *Ibjd*.

religious ideals.[51] These were, in his opinion, the protection of Islamic institutions in India and abroad, and the promotion of the concept of Muslim brotherhood—a concept which had a great emotional and religious appeal to Mohamed Ali as well as to his co-religionists. But neither of these ideals could be accomplished within the narrow framework of institutional politics. So, Mohamed Ali chose to stay out of legislatures and other self-governing bodies, and attempted to develop an independent base by reaching the man in the street, the *maulvi* in the mosque, the sufi in the *khanqah* and the zamindar in his *haveli*. In this way he bridged the wide gulf which separated the educated classes from other groups amongst Muslims, and succeeded in promoting the Khilafat movement, which embraced virtually all sections of the Muslim community. He used religious symbols, interspersed his speeches with extensive quotes from the Quran and the *Hadith*, and related the institution of Khilafat and pan-Islamic ideology to the religious beliefs and practices of the Muslims. This explains the secret of Mohamed Ali's success in agitational politics. His success should be measured in terms of his impact on political events and the extent to which he was able to mobilise popular support for the pan-Islamic ideology which he articulated with great force and fervour.

Anyone who passes from the pages of the *Comrade* to that of *Al-Hilal* becomes acutely aware of a sudden change in the intellectual climate. It is the change from emotional journalism to profound scholarship. Azad, the editor of *Al-Hilal*, was a prolific writer, a consummate stylist of Urdu prose and a persuasive speaker.[52] In his two weekly journals, *Al-Hilal* and

[51]Mohamed Ali was conscious of the fact that he was destined 'to make history' as is evident from his response to a suggestion to write a historical monograph. 'This is not the time for historical writing', he wrote, 'but to create history'. Mohamed Ali to A.M. Daryabadi, 1916, quoted in I. Askari, 'Mohamed Ali: Ek Sada-i-Shikast Saaz', *Aligarh Magazine*, 1960-61; Daryabadi, *Mohamed Ali: Za'ati Diary ke chund Auraq*, p. 14.

[52]Azad was associated with several journals and magazines. He wrote for the *Ahsan al-Akhbar*, a Calcutta journal, and started a literary journal, *Lisan al-Sidq*, in 1904. On Shibli's suggestion, he edited the *Al-Nadwa* and then joined the *Vakil* of Amritsar, an Urdu newspaper.

Al-Balagh, and his book *Masala-i-Khilafat-wa-Jazirat-ul-Arab*, Azad attempted to legitimise the institution of Khilafat on the ground that a 'political centre' (*siyasi markaz*) was necessary for the survival of a community and a nation. The Ottoman Empire provided such a centre.[53] It was the protector of the Religion of God (*din-i-ilahi*) and the symbol of the brotherhood of Muslims. To rise in defence (*difa*) of the Ottoman Khilafat was obligatory for the Muslims. 'So long as the whole world of Islam does not come together in an international and universal alliance', Azad declared, 'how can small tracts help the forty crores of Muslims.'[54]

In relation to India, Azad cited the instance of the Prophet Mohammad's covenant with some Jews in A.D. 622 as a historical precedent to justify Hindu-Muslim cooperation. He established, by citations from the Quran, *Hadith*, and the jurists' digests, that joining in common action with one category of non-Muslims, the Hindus, against another category of non-Muslims, the British, was an obligation upon every indi-

On 12 July 1912, Azad launched *Al-Hilal* under the patronage and financial support of Haji Nur Mohammad, son of a wealthy merchant who had brought Azad's father, Maulana Khairuddin Ahmad, to Calcutta. For the next four years, through *Al-Hilal* and *Al-Balagh*, Azad expressed his ideas on religious reforms, education and politics. In July 1914, he started a society known as the *Jamiat-i-Hizbullah*. Its object, according to *Al-Hilal* of 8 July 1914, was 'to send preachers to stay in cities, towns and villages where the religious condition of Muslims may be deplorable; where superstitions and intrigues are prevalent and where brotherhood and sympathy for the misfortunes of Islam and zeal for communal work are forgotten.' But the 'party of God' remained restricted in size and gained nothing like the publicity enjoyed by the *Anjuman-i-Khuddam-i-Kaaba*. In August 1915, Azad launched the *Dar-ul-Irshad* (College of Divinity) with practically the same objects as those of the *Jamiat-i-Hizbullah*. But this organisation also failed to secure any widespread support. By this time the career of *Al-Hilal* had ended (in November 1914), when its security deposit was forfeited by the Bengal government. In November 1915, Azad launched the *Al-Balagh*, but that too was closed in March 1926. Soon, afterwards he was interned in Ranchi in Bihar, where he remained until January 1920.

[53]A.K. Azad, *Masala-i-Khilafat-wa-Jazirat-ul-Arab* (Calcutta, 1920), pp. 26 & 119.

[54]Quoted in S.M. Ikram, *Modern Muslim India and the Birth of Pakistan* (Lahore, 1965), p. 146.

vidual Muslim.[55] Furthermore, Azad urged his co-religionists
to join the country's struggle for independence and tried to
allay fears of Hindu domination. Such fears, according to him,
were deliberately planted by the British government in order
to enlist Muslim support for consolidating its rule in India.[56]
The British were the enemies of Islam and the Maulana
condemned those who cooperated with the 'Satans of Europe
to weaken the influence of Islamic Khilafat and Pan-Islamism'.[57]
He cited the Quranic verse 'O believers, take not Jews and
Christians as friends' to provide a religious justification for
his hostility towards the British, and proclaimed that it was
God's wish that Muslims should stand up for the freedom of
India and it was His Pleasure (*marzi-i-khudawandi*) that they
should give new life to the forgotten duty of *jihad* (*farz-i-
jihad*).[58]

Religion was the fundamental cause which brought Mohamed
Ali, Azad, and Zafar Ali into the forefront of agitational
politics. They were devout Muslims with an abiding faith in
Islam which, in their opinion, embodied a complete set of rules
for human success and happiness.[59] Above all, they saw themselves as part of the larger Islamic community (*umma*) and
sought tenaciously to preserve and strengthen it against the
forces of nationalism and imperialism. In their attempt to achieve
this object, they developed a wide network of connections
ranging from educational institutions to political parties. They
had close links with the seminaries at Deoband, *Nadwa* and
Firangi Mahal which were the traditional centres of Islamic
education. No less important was their influence on the M.A.O.
College, Aligarh, where, despite the legacy of Sir Syed's opposition to pan-Islamism, they evoked a favourable response.

[55]Peter Hardy, *Partners in Freedom – and True Muslims: The Political
Thought of some Muslim scholars in British India 1912-47* (Scandinavian
Institute of Asian Studies, 1971), pp. 28-29.

[56]Badrul Hasan, (ed.), *Mazameen-i-Abul Kalam Azad* (Delhi, 1944),
Vol. 2, pp. 132-33.

[57]Quoted in A.H. Albiruni, *Makers of Pakistan and Modern Muslim
India* (Lahore, 1950), p. 136.

[58]Hardy, *Partners in Freedom*, p. 22.

[59]*Al-Hilal*, 23 October 1912: Mohamed Ali, *My Life: A Fragment*.
pp. 145-91.

Students flocked to the meetings addressed by Mohamed Ali and Zafar Ali and were swayed by the pan-Islamic ideology. Aligarh soon became one of the important centres of Khilafat activity.

Congress leaders attempted to forge an alliance with leaders like Mohamed Ali, Zafar Ali, and Azad. This was consistent with their strategy of first gaining the adherence of leaders who had a religious and emotional appeal, and then utilising their services to enlist the support of their followers. Having once realised that the Muslims were deeply troubled by internment of the Khilafat leaders, leading Congressmen made the issue of their release part of their campaign against the repressive policies of the government. This argument needs to be examined.

GANDHI CAMPAIGNS FOR THE RELEASE OF THE ALI BROTHERS

Tilak, Annie Besant and Gandhi were the leading Congressmen who supported the agitation for the release of the Khilafat leaders, particularly the Ali Brothers. They realised that, since the Ali Brothers enjoyed popular support amongst Muslims, by taking up their cause they would keep the Congress-League *entente* alive. Tilak, who had played a key role during the Congress-League negotiations in the winter of 1916, introduced a resolution at the Calcutta Congress demanding the release of the Ali Brothers.[60] In October 1917, Annie Besant went to Simla, after her conditional release from internment, with the intention of discussing the same question with the Viceroy.[61] Her main aim was to strengthen her alliance with the Muslims and to retain their support for the Home Rule League.[62]

[60]*Bombay Chronicle*, 31 December 1917.

[61]Willingdon, Governor of Bombay, interpreted Annie Besant's move as an attempt to secure the support of Muslims 'who hitherto have been indifferent or hostile to her pretensions'. Willingdon to Chelmsford, 28 October 1917, Willingdon Papers, MSS. EUR. F. 93 (1), IOL.

[62]It is noticeable that many of the Muslim Home Rulers joined the Home Rule Leagues after the internment of Annie Besant and occupied important positions in the organisation. In this respect, the names of Jinnah, Ansari, Asaf Ali, Syed Ali Nabi and Maulvi Abdul Ghaffor of Azamgarh need special mention.

It was Gandhi, however, who was the most active campaigner for the release of the Ali Brothers. He had worked with Muslims in South Africa and, after his return to India, he was keen to establish contacts with Muslim leaders.[63] He met the Ali Brothers in Aligarh and Delhi in 1915, and early in 1916. He attempted to see them in the Chhindwara prison, but was not permitted to do so by the government. 'The authorities have evidently failed', he wrote to Mohamed Ali, 'to appreciate my motive in wanting to see you. The only thing I as a passive resister can do in circumstances such as this is to bow to the decision of the Government of India.'[64] In December 1917, Gandhi assured the delegates at the Muslim League session that the Hindus were with them to a man in their just struggle for the Ali Brothers' release,[65] and in January 1918 he urged the Viceroy to release them.[66] But the Viceroy paid no heed to his requests. So, in July 1918, the Mahatma announced his decision to 'engage the Government in a duel' on the issue.[67] 'The fight for Mohamed Ali's release is a crushing burden', he wrote, 'though, I know it has but to be borne'.[68]

The question of the Ali Brothers, release brought Gandhi into contact with Abdul Bari, the founder of the *Madrasa-i-Nizamia* in Firangi Mahal, Lucknow, and one of the main organisers of the *Anjuman-i-Khuddam-i-Kaaba*. His first recorded meeting with Gandhi was in March 1918 in connection with

[63]In his autobiography, Gandhi noted: 'I was seeking the friendship of good Musalmans, and was eager to understand the Musalman mind through contact with their purest and most patriotic representatives.' M.K. Gandhi, *An Autobiography or the Story of My Experiments With Truth*, Reprint, (Ahmedabad, 1958), p. 325.

[64]Gandhi to Mohamed Ali, 14 April 1916, Mohamed Ali Papers.

[65]Speech at the All-India Muslim League Session, Calcutta, 31 December 1917, *The Collected Works of Mahatma Gandhi*, Vol. 14, p. 120 (*The Collected Works*, in process of publication in Delhi, are hereafter cited as *CWG*).

[66]'It is my firm opinion', Gandhi stated, 'that the continued internment of the two brothers and the refusal to discharge them is creating greater dissatisfaction and irritation from day to day. The Muhammadans, and also the Hindus for that matter, bitterly resent the internment'. Gandhi to J.L. Maffey, 1 January 1918, *CWG*, Vol. 14, pp. 141-42.

[67]Gandhi to Maffey, 12 July 1918, Chelmsford Papers (21).

[68]Mahadev Desai, *Day-To-Day With Gandhi* (Varanasi, 1968), Vol. 1, p. 93.

the release of the Ali Brothers.[69] A month later, the Maulana travelled to Bombay to meet Gandhi.[70] During the Khilafat movement, such meetings between the two became more frequent, and their extraordinary alliance was further strengthened.

Gandhi attached great significance to his relations with Abdul Bari, Ansari, and the Ali Brothers,[71] because he wanted to secure their cooperation to harmonise Hindu-Muslim relations in the interest of Swaraj. 'My interest in your release', the Mahatma wrote to Mohamed Ali, 'is quite selfish. We have a common goal and I want to utilise your services to the uttermost, in order to reach that goal. In the proper solution of the Mohammedan question lies the realisation of Swaraj.'[72] He was convinced that self-government could only be achieved if the Hindus and Muslims worked together; so he devoted his energies towards securing 'permanent unity' between them.[73] His inner voice told him that the two communities would unite as brothers one day because there was 'no other course open to them and they have but to be brothers'.[74]

What was Gandhi's impact on the Muslims during this period? Did he succeed in forging an alliance with them? Was he able to draw the Muslims into the countrywide Rowlatt Satyagraha which he launched in April 1919? Gandhi's efforts in connection with the release of the Ali Brothers earned him the popularity and adulation of many leading Muslims. He was extolled by Ansari as the 'intrepid leader of India, . . . who has...endeared himself as much to the Musalman as to the Hindu'.[75] His non-violent programme was endorsed by

[69]Robinson, *Separatism*, p, 298.

[70]Desai, *Day-To-Day*, Vol. 1, pp. 99-100.

[71]'After my arrival in India', Gandhi told a Khilafat meeting, 'I began to find out good Mohammedan leaders. My desire was satisfied when I reached Delhi, and found the Brothers Ali, whom I had the privilege of knowing before. It was a question of love at first sight between us. When I met Dr Ansari, the circle of Mohammedan friends widened and at last it even included Maulana Abdul Bari.' Speech on Khilafat, Bombay, 9 May 1919, *CWG*, Vol. 15, p. 295.

[72]Gandhi to Mohamed Ali, 18 November 1918, *Ibid.*, p. 64.

[73]*Ibid.*, p. 296.

[74]Desai, *Day-To-Day*, Vol. 1, p. 56.

[75]Speech delivered by Ansari at the Muslim League session in December 1918, Ansari Papers.

Mohamed Ali, who maintained that he had not found anyone
superior to Gandhi in any community.[76] To Mohamed Ali's
younger colleagues, Gandhi was 'a Tolstoy and Buddha
combined'.[77]

Gandhi's popularity amongst Muslims is also illustrated by
their response to the satyagraha launched against the Rowlatt
Bills.[78] Many followed the Mahatma's programme. Abdul Bari,
for example, supported the passive resistance movement against
the Rowlatt Bills. Satyagraha, he said, was quite in accord with
Islamic principles.[79] In Bihar, Hasan Imam and Mazharul
Haque were Gandhi's chief lieutenants. They helped to mobilise
'thousands' of Muslims to attend a public meeting held in
Patna in protest against the Rowlatt Act.[80] In Bengal, the
prominent feature of the *hartal* observed on 6 April was the
Hindu-Muslim fraternisation, of which the most striking
illustration was the attendance of Hindus at a meeting held in
the Nakhoda mosque.[81] 'Though the Rowlatt Act sits like a
dread nightmare on our breasts', the editor of *Amrita Bazar
Patrika* observed, 'it has united both Hindus and Mussalmans
in a way which has never been witnessed.'[82] In the Punjab,
Saifuddin Kitchlew, Pir Tajuddin, Mohsin Shah, Fazl-i-Husain

[76]Afzal Iqbal (ed.), *Select Speeches*, pp. 331-32; Mohamed Ali to
Shraddhanand, 26 March 1924, Mohamed Ali to Shaukat Ali, 15 May
1920, Mohamed Ali Papers.

[77]Abdur Rahman Siddiqi to Mohamed Ali, 24 March 1919, *Ibid.*
Maulana Ahsan Mirza, *Jazbat-i-Qaumi wa Mahatma Gandhi* (Lucknow,
1921). This is a collection of poems written between 1917 and 1918 in
praise of Gandhi.

[78]The Rowlatt Committee recommended that the government should
have powers to make arbitrary arrests and inflict summary punishments
for the suppression of revolutionary activities in certain parts of the
country. Accordingly, a Bill was introduced in the Imperial Legislative
Council in February 1919 and was passed in the teeth of opposition
from all the Indian members. On 24 February Gandhi informed the
Viceroy of his decision to launch satyagraha against the Rowlatt Act.
Two days later, he urged his countrymen to join the satyagraha. On 6
April, *hartal* was observed in different parts of the country.

[79]WRDCI, March 1919, Home Poll. B, April 1919, 148-52, NAI; also
see Daryabadi, *Mohamed Ali: Zaati Diary ke chund Auraq*, p. 20.

[80]*Searchlight*, 10 April 1919.

[81]Home Poll. B, May 1919, 514-15, NAI.

[82]M.L. Ghose to Mohamed Ali, 14 April 1919, Mohamed Ali Papers.

and Mohammad Iqbal threw their weight behind Gandhi in the satyagraha. The demonstration organised on the 9 April in Lahore included a substantial proportion of Muslims.[83] In Delhi, where Swami Shraddhanand was invited to address the Friday congregation at the Juma Masjid, Ansari, Arif Husain Haswi, editor of the *Congress* and the *Inqilab*, and Asaf Ali, a young barrister who had just returned to India after a successful academic career in London, were the leading Muslim satyagrahis. The most notable amongst them was Mukhtar Ahmad Ansari who belonged to a prominent family of Yusufpur in Ghazipur district. At the age of twenty he graduated from Madras University. A year later, he sailed for the United Kingdom and joined the University of Edinburgh as a medical student. He was the first Indian to be admitted as a Resident Medical Officer to Charing Cross Hospital, London, and as House Surgeon to Lock Hospital. On returning to India in 1910, he set up the medical practice in Delhi. Later, when the Balkan wars broke out, he led the successful Indian Medical Mission to Turkey.[84] 'His work in the Medical Mission', observed Meston, 'during the last Turkish war is a matter of pride to them [Muslims].'[85]

Ansari joined active politics soon after the arrest of the Ali Brothers with whom he first came into contact during the Turko-Italian war, and emerged as an important public figure only during the Home Rule movement.[86] In September 1917, he addressed a provincial Congress meeting at Lucknow and spoke on self-government and passive resistance and called for its immediate adoption.[87] This was the voice of a new generation of Western-educated Muslims, who were stirred by nationalist sentiments and were impressed by Gandhi's charismatic personality, his simplicity, and selflessness. Their participation in the Rowlatt Satyagraha was both the result of

[83]Kumar (ed.), *Essays*, pp. 281-82.

[84]In 1914, Ansari received an award from the Sultan of Turkey in recognition of the services rendered by the Medical Mission. Home Poll. B, July 1914, 17, NAI.

[85]Meston to Cleveland, 6 September 1916, Meston Papers (4).

[86]See, Donald W. Ferrel, 'The Rowlatt Satyagraha in Delhi' in Kumar (ed.), *Essays*, p. 196.

[87]Home Poll. Deposit, September 1917, 5, NAI.

their personal devotion to the Mahatma, and their conviction
that the Rowlatt Act was morally and politically reprehensible.

Gandhi's influence was not confined to the *ulama* or the
Western-educated Muslims, but extended to Muslim artisans,
merchants, millworkers and weavers, who participated in the
hartal organised on 6 April.[88] His success in securing their
adherence was due to two main reasons. First, Gandhi was able
to exploit the resentment nursed against the British government's policy towards the *Khalifa* of Turkey. Amidst rumours
that the Rowlatt Bills were 'intended to enable the Government
to coerce the Mohammedans and prevent them from giving
trouble so as to facilitate the dismemberment of Turkey',[89] the
Mahatma succeeded in arousing Muslim support for the
satyagraha. Secondly, the economic distress flowing from
the first World War also accounted for the favourable
response to Gandhi's call for satyagraha. During and after the
War there was a sharp increase in the prices of basic commodi-
ties such as rice, wheat, salt and cooking oil. In the UP,
because of lack of rain, foodgrain production fell sharply and
large areas of the province were hit by famine or scarcity. The
province, like other regions of India, was affected by the great
influenza which caused the death of at least five to six million
people. It was the great organisational leadership of Gandhi
which enabled him to canalise these local discontents into a
movement of protest against the government. The discontent
engendered by the Rowlatt Act acted as 'a touchstone for a
variety of grievances that would have otherwise remained
quiescent'.[90]

[88]For details, see Kumar (ed.), *Essays*; Judith M. Brown, *Gandhi's
Rise to Power: Indian Politics 1915-1922* (Cambridge, 1972), pp. 163,
173, 186.

[89]Govt. of Bombay, *Source Material*, Vol. 2, p. 739, quoted in James
Masselos, 'Some Aspects of Bombay Politics in 1919', in Kumar (ed.),
Essays, p. 176.

[90]Donald W. Ferrel, 'The Rowlatt Satyagraha in Delhi' in *Ibid.*,
p. 212; It has been suggested that 'in every place where *hartal* was well
observed and Gandhi's propaganda welcomed it seems that the tinder
of unrest had been drying for months and Gandhi's campaign was
merely the spark which started the conflagration'. Brown, *Gandhi*,
p. 185. This conclusion is supported by the graphic accounts of the course
of the satyagraha in the Central Provinces, and in the cities of
Ahmedabad, Bombay, Delhi and Lahore.

THE MONTAGU-CHELMSFORD REFORMS

Gandhi was also able to enlist the support of those Indian politicians who were disappointed with the Montagu-Chelmsford proposals, officially known as the *Report on Indian Constitutional Reforms*. I has been explained in chapter three that up to 1916, the political activities of Indian politicians— Hindus and Muslims alike—were largely determined by the prospect of reforms culminating in the Lucknow Pact. When the Secretary of State, Edwin Montagu, visited India in November 1917, the Congress and the Muslim League submitted a joint memorandum proposing reforms in the system of government. But many of their proposals were not accepted by Montagu and the Viceroy, Chelmsford. That is why from July 1918 onwards, when the joint *Report on Indian Constitutional Reforms* was presented to Parliament, the so-called 'extremists' in the Congress and Muslim League combined to attack the reforms. Significantly enough, it was this group of disgruntled Indian politicians which responded to Gandhi's call for satyagraha.

In order to understand the impact of the Montagu-Chelmsford constitution on Indian politics and particularly on the Congress-League concordat, we need to examine its recommendations.

By December 1916, the question of constitutional reforms was under discussion between the Government of India and the Secretary of State.[91] On 20 August 1917, Montagu, who succeeded Austen Chamberlain as Secretary of State for India in the preceding month, announced that his government had decided to take 'substantial steps' in the direction 'of the increasing association of Indians in every branch of the administration and the gradual development of self-governing institutions, with a view to the progressive realisation of responsible government in India as an integral part of the British Empire'. On 10 November 1917, Montagu reached India and, during his stay in the country, he received deputations, addresses,

---

[91]For a detailed account of the events leading up to the announcement of the Montagu-Chelmsford Reforms, see S.R. Mehrotra, 'The Politics Behind the Montagu Declaration of 1917', C.H. Philips (ed.), *Politics and Society in India* (London, 1963), pp. 89-92.

and memoranda from individuals as well as from various large
and small associations, including forty-four representations
from Muslim bodies.

By the end of 1918, a number of class, communal, and
religious demands were cascaded upon Montagu.[92] The
Secretary of State was personally opposed to the principle
of communal representation. He regarded their introduction in 1909 as a 'great mistake in the history of India and as
more harmful perhaps in its consequences than the permanent
settlement of Bengal, or the partition of that province'.[93] The
same thinking was reflected, at least on paper, in the *Report on
Indian Constitutional Reforms* in which communal representation was condemned on the grounds that it perpetuated class
distinctions, stereotyped existing relations, and constituted 'a
very serious hindrance to the development of the self-governing principle'.[94] Yet, the authors of the *Report*, like Morley
and Minto before them, felt constrained to accept communal
electorates. This was because Muslims regarded separate
representation and communal electorates as 'their only
adequate safeguards', and in 1909 they had obtained the
acquiescence of the government. In December 1916, the
Congress too accepted the principle as a basis of compromise.
So, the *Report* declared: 'Much as we regret the necessity, we
are convinced that so far as the Muhammadans at all events
are concerned the present system must be maintained until
conditions alter, even at the price of slower progress towards
the realisation of a common citizenship.'

At the same time, the authors of the reforms declared
themselves against any extension of the system, except in

[92]See Chapter three.

[93]E. Montagu, *An Indian Diary*, Vol. 2, p. 62, Montagu Papers (39).

[94]The *Report* observed that 'division by creeds and classes means
the creation of political camps organised against each other, and teaches
men to think as partisans and not as citizens; and it is difficult to see
how the change from this system to national representation is ever to
occur. The British Government is often accused of dividing men in
order to govern them. But if it unnecessarily divides them at the very
moment when it proposes to start them on the road to governing themselves, it will find it difficult to meet the charge of being hypocritical
or shortsighted'. *Report on Indian Constitutional Reforms* (London,
1918), Cd. 9109, p. 187.

the case of the Sikhs in the Punjab. As regards Muslims, they saw no reason to set up communal representation in any province where they formed a majority of the voters.[95] They also rejected the clause in the Congress-League scheme, according to which, 'no Bill, nor any clause thereof, nor a resolution introduced by a non-official affecting one or the other community (which question is to be determined by the members of that community in the Legislative Council concerned) shall be proceeded with, if three-fourths of the members of that community in the particular Council, Imperial or Provincial, oppose the Bill or any clause thereof or the resolution'. This clause, in the opinion of Montagu and Chelmsford, 'is so widely worded, and would in practice be so widely interpreted by those to whom its interpretation is specifically committed, that it would be unworkable. In a country like India it is impossible to say what proposals would not be capable of being represented as affecting communal interests'.[96]

The Montagu-Chelmsford Report's hostility to communal representation alarmed many Muslim politicians. A conference organised by Maulvi Abdul Jalil, secretary of the Darbhanga branch of the Central National Mohammedan Association, Shafa'at Husain, secretary of the Gaya District Muslim League, and Zamiruddin Ahmad, secretary of the Bihar and Orissa Provincial Hajj Committee, protested against the 'deprecatory language used in the *Report* with regard to separate Muhammadan representation and is alarmed to find that the scheme suggests a possible abolition of the same'.[97] In the Punjab, the reform proposals were denounced because they failed to provide 'substantial separate representation' to Muslims in the various constitutional and administrative bodies proposed to be set up under the scheme. The *Paisa Akhbar*, an organ of Muslim zamindars and government servants, warned the government against depriving Muslims of separate representation which would lead to their 'national extinction'.[98] In Bengal, the

[95]*Report on Indian Constitutional Reforms*, p. 135.
[96]*Ibid.*, p. 105.
[97]*Searchlight*, 5 September 1918.
[98]*Paisa Akhbar*, 17 July, 19 July & 22 December 1918, PUNNR 1918.

Central National Mohammedan Association feared that the recommendations of the report would lead to the 'political extinction' of their co-religionists.[99] Nawab Ali Chaudhuri, the president of the Association, criticised the report for having accepted the Congress-League compact as a guide in allocating the proportion of Muslim representation. He asserted that the Muslim population entitled them to at least 50 per cent of the Council seats.[100] W.H. Vincent, Member of the Governor General's Executive Council, went along with Chaudhuri's argument and proposed that Bengal Muslims should be represented in the Council in proportion to their population strength.[101] But the Southborough Committee (Franchise) was unimpressed. It recommended thirty-four seats, or 45 per cent of the territorial seats, to Muslims in the Bengal Legislative Council.[102] The question was referred back to the government of Bengal with a request that it prepare a scheme to increase Muslim representation, but it stood by its earlier recommendation that 45 per cent of the territorial seats was sufficient.[103]

In the UP, most Muslim politicians objected to the reform proposals because they excluded them from the general electorate without giving them the proportion which was secured to them by the Congress-League compromise.[104] They also resented the condemnation of communal representation. Voicing their protest over the issue, Harcourt Butler wrote:

[99]*Searchlight*, 1 September 1918.

[100]For an analysis of Chaudhuri's role, see J.H. Broomfield, *Elite Conflict in a Plural Society: Twentieth Century Bengal* (Berkeley and Los Angeles, 1968), pp. 126-29.

[101]Minute of dissent by W.H. Vincent, 23 April 1919, *Views of The Government Of India Upon The Report Of the Lord Southborough's Committee* (London, 1919), Cmd. 176, p. 18.

[102]*Report of the Franchise Committee* (Calcutta, 1919), pp. 9-10, 52.

[103]Broomfield, *Elite Conflict*, p. 127.

[104]The Raja of Mahmudabad observed that the reform proposals 'seize with avidity' the Muslim renunciation of participating in mixed electorates, 'but quietly gives the go-by to their instrument of requisition, viz., the explicitly fixed proportion which it conferred on them'. He appealed to the Secretary of State and the Viceroy to rectify this 'grave defect in their proposals'. *Tribune*, 10 August 1918; *Searchlight* 15 August 1918.

While your objections to the communal system . . . will
command universal assent, I have the gravest possible doubts
as to the suitability of justice, under present conditions, of
the application of the non-communal method to the people
of India even with the concession to Mohammedans which
you are prepared to recommend. It is admitted, as things
are, that it is not practicable to attempt the immediate
application of the non-communal method to the whole
population.[105]

The voices of protest raised by some Muslim politicians
were designed to assert what they perceived to be the 'distinct
Mussalman interests',[106] rather than to reject the Montagu-
Chelmsford scheme which was a definite improvement upon
the Lucknow Pact.[107] Separate communal electorates had been
preserved, and the Bengali Muslims had secured five seats more
than a rigid adherence to the Lucknow Pact would have given
them. In the rest of the provinces the division of seats between
the two major communities was based upon the Lucknow
Pact. In the Legislative Assembly, of the 105 elective
seats, 30 were reserved for Muslims, who also had the chance
of being returned from the eleven special constituencies. By the
end of 1918, the implication of these provisions became
apparent to some Muslim politicians on account of which, after
an initial period of diffidence, they began to rally round
the Montagu-Chelmsford Reforms. This was particularly
true of many politically conservative Muslims, who
recognised the crucial fact that the provinces were to
administer all those subjects which touched the daily
life of the common people. Among these were education,

[105]Butler to Montagu, 9 August 1918, Chelmsford Papers (4); Butler
to Chelmsford, 31 July 1918, Ibid (21).

[106]See, for example, the speech of Fazulbhoy Currimbhoy at the
Muslim League session in August 1918. Pirzada (ed.), Foundations of
Pakistan, p. 449.

[107]According to Nawab Ali Chaudhuri, 'the treatment accorded to
the Mussalmans by the British government has never been quite satisfactory in deed, but it has at any rate saved us from being swamped
by more powerful interests'. Quoted in Broomfield, Elite Conflict,
p. 128.

public health, sanitation and local self-government. These were not only to be provincially administered, but, by the arrangements known as dyarchy, were to be controlled by ministers chosen from among the elected members of the provincial legislative councils. This opened up the prospect for Indian politicians to enjoy a certain degree of power which they had never exercised before and to distribute patronage amongst their clients. 'From any improvement that we shall effect as the result of provincial autonomy', Fazulbhoy Currimbhoy declared optimistically, 'I expect we [Muslims] shall stand to gain more than the rest of the population —from better sanitation, from wider education and other larger opportunities for industrial growth'.[108]

Another reason which led the politically conservative Muslims to advocate acceptance of the reforms was due to their failure to undermine the Congress-League alliance and to wrest control of the Muslim League from the pro-Congress Muslims. Throughout the year 1917, they had been busy organising opposition against the Lucknow Pact, particularly in Bengal where Nawab Ali Chaudhuri resigned from the Bengal Presidency Muslim League and revived the moribund Central National Mohammedan Association.[109] The *Moslem Hitaishi*, owned by a wealthy merchant, Mulla Enamul Haq, announced that the Bengali Muslims had severed their connections with the League because of its failure to voice their 'rightful demands' for which it was created.[110] And in September 1917, when communal riots occurred in Bihar, the same paper attempted to arouse communal passions in order to discredit the Muslim negotiators of the Lucknow Pact.[111] 'The fanaticism . . . of the Hndus', the *Resalat* of Calcutta warned, 'will destroy all

[108]Pirzada (ed.), *Foundations of Pakistan.* Vol. I, p. 450.

[109]*Mahratta,* 13 & 20 May 1917. In the Punjab, Mohammad Shafi was the main anti-Lucknow Pact campaigner. He organised the All-India Conservative Association and presented an address on behalf of the Punjab Provincial Muslim League to Montagu and Chelmsford which claimed 50 per cent Muslim representation in the Executive Councils, and one-third in the Imperial Legislative Council. Montagu Papers (35).

[110]*Moslem Hitaishi,* 5 January 1917, BENNR 1917.

[111]Fazlul Haq was accused of sacrificing 'Muslim communal interests in order to win fame and position among the Hindus'. *Moslem Hitaishi,* 31 October 1919, *Ibid.,* 1919.

Muslim rites and customs. The Bihar riots have opened our eyes. We know what stuff the Hindus are made of. Such Muslims as still trust the Hindus are greatly mistaken'.[112]

In spite of all the hue and cry in the press, the Chaudhuris' and the Haqs' failed to capitalise on the riots to their advantage. This was mainly due to the efforts of many Congress and League leaders who prevented the Bihar riots from destroying the edifice of Hindu-Muslim *entente*. In an unprecedented gesture of goodwill, many Hindus of Calcutta, Basti, Gorakhpur, Benaras and Saharanpur raised funds in aid of the Muslim victims in the riots.[113] Similarly, although a Muslim meeting held in Rampur condemned the Bihar riots, it took care to add that its resolution 'has nothing to do with the Home Rule movement, nor does it mean hostility towards the Hindu population'.[114]

The September riots tarnished the image of many conservative Muslims, who were accused of inciting the 'lower classes' in the name of Islam.[115] This allegation did considerable damage to their prestige, particularly in Calcutta where the growth of communal tension in early 1918 was attributed to the activities of Nawab Ali Chaudhuri and his two supporters, Habib Shah and Fazlur Rahman, a Bihari Muslim whose chief influence was among the Urdu-speaking immigrant community of Calcutta: the Muslims traders, manufacturers, and lower-class factory labourers.[116] In addition to this, the government's recognition of the Congress-League compact as the 'most complete and most authoritative' settlement between the claims of the majority and the minority,[117] and as an 'accomplished fact and a landmark in Indian politics',[118]

[112]*Resalat*, 7 December 1917, BENNR 1917; *Medina*, 13 October 1917, UPNNR 1917.

[113]*Leader*, 12 & 21 November 1917; *Resalat*, 23 October 1917, *Oudh Akhbar*, 14 October 1917, *Ibid*.

[114]Home Police. A, December 1917 137--58, NAI.

[115]*Tirmizee* (Calcutta), 20 October 1917, BENNR 1917.

[116]*Nayak* (Calcutta), 19 October 1917, *Ibid*. For the role of Habib and Rahman in stirring communal trouble, see Broomfield, *Elite Conflict*, pp. 192-3.

[117]*Report on Indian Constitutional Reforms*, p. 77.

[118]Government of India to E. Montagu, 23 April 1919, *Views of the Government of India upon the Report of Lord Southborough's Committee*, p. 10.

took the sting out of the campaign against the pact and its negotiators. Nawab Ali Chaudhuri and his caucus were left with practically no issue by which they could whip up an agitation either against Congress or its Muslim supporters. Their loosely organised bodies fell into total disarray. They lost their credibility amongst Muslims and the influence to function as an effective group in the Muslim League. They were attacked in the press[119] and on public platforms.[120] They were dismayed by the pro-Congress and the anti-British tilt of the League, but could do nothing to influence its deliberations. That is why many of them sought refuge either in the councils or in the Nizam of Hyderabad's court. Nawab Ali Chaudhuri was elected to the Bengal Legislative Council, where he served as a minister from January 1921 until January 1924; Shafi was appointed to the Viceroy's Executive Council as the Member in charge of Education; Aftab Ahmad Khan was made a member of Secretary of State's Council;[121] the Rajas of Salempur, Jahangirabad and Pirpur and the Nawab of Chhatari were elected to the UP Legislative Council; Firoz Khan Noon, an Oxford graduate and a large landowner, was elected to the Punjab Legislative Council from Bhalwal tehsil of the Shahpur District; and the Tiwanas and the Daulatanas, who were active supporters of the Punjab Moslem Association, were returned to the Punjab Legislative Council.

Some of the pro-Congress Muslims, too, who had played

[119]For example, the *New Era* wrote a strongly-worded editorial against Shafi. 'He is trying', the paper wrote, 'to arrogate to himself the right to speak on behalf of the Mussalmans, and he intends in this garb to play the traitor and bring everlasting disgrace on his community. It is the duty of every true and honest citizen in this country to expose him and take the sting out of his action by demonstrating that he represents his own views and has absolutely no right to speak on behalf of this community or country. It appears to be the old game of the separatists by trying to set the Mussalmans against the Hindus and in the end ruin both.' *New Era*, 15 & 22 September 1917.

[120]Home Poll. Deposit, March 1920, 59, NAI.

[121]He was recommended by Meston as 'the soundest man we have. . . . He is an orthodox Muslim, clean-living and self-respecting; an enthusiast in education and a highly accomplished man himself. . . .On the whole he is friendly to the Government . . . ' . Meston to Chelmsford, 23 January 1917, Meston Papers (1).

an important role in negotiating the Lucknow Pact and in promoting the Home Rule agitation, landed up either in government service or in the Nizam's service. Leaders like Wazir Hasan and the Raja of Mahmudabad criticised certain aspects of the Montagu-Chelmsford Reforms, but did not reject them altogether. Like the so-called moderates in the Congress, they advocated a partial acceptance of the reform proposals. But the radical wing in the League paid no heed to their advice, and at the Delhi session of the League in December, Wazir Hasan and the Raja were bitterly condemned by Ansari, Ajmal Khan and the delegates from Bengal.[122] In the following months, they were subjected to more violent criticism and there were repeated demands for their resignation.[123] In March 1919, they resigned from the Muslim League.[124] The Raja of Mahmudabad was appointed Home Member in the UP government by Harcourt Butler, the newly arrived Lieutenant-Governor of the province, while Wazir Hasan became the first Indian member of the Oudh Bar to be appointed Second Judicial Commissioner. Khwaja Naziruddin Hasan, one of the founder members of the *Anjuman-i-Khuddam-i-Kaaba* and one of the twelve members appointed by the Muslim League Council to report on the Montagu-Chelmsford Reforms, entered the Hyderabad Service. Samiullah Beg, who was general secretary of the Congress Reception Committee in 1916 and a supporter of the Home Rule movement, gave up politics in 1918 and was appointed Chief Justice of the Hyderabad High Court.

However, most Muslim Congressmen found the Montagu-Chelmsford Reforms objectionable. 'To say that the report is highly disappointing and extremely unsatisfactory is to pass a very mild judgement on it', observed the *Mussalman* of Calcutta.[125] The government was warned that 'any attempt to reduce the proportions set forth in the Congress-League scheme or to do away with separate representation of the

[122]WRDCI, 9 November 1918, Home Poll. B, December 1918, 158-59, NAI; Home Poll. B, January 1919, 160-63, NAI.
[123]*New Era*, 15 February 1919.
[124]*Leader*, 6 March 1919.
[125]*Mussalman*, 19 July 1918; *Mohammadi*, 26 July 1918; *Jamhur*, 24 & 26 July 1918, BENNR 1918.

Muslims in the province in which they are in a minority will be resented . . . .'[126] Likewise, the *Jamhur* from Calcutta complained that, although the principle of separate electorates was accepted by Montagu and Chelmsford, 'the form in which this concession has been given to the Muslims is not at all satisfactory'.[127] The Bengal Presidency League declared the reform scheme 'disappointing and unsatisfactory in as much as the spirit in which they are conceived is decidedly unsympathetic and in some aspects hostile to Muslim interests'.[128] At the Punjab Provincial Conference held in Amritsar, Kitchlew and Barkat Ali spoke on similar lines.[129] At the Twelfth UP Provincial Political Conference, too, Muslim delegates joined other representatives in rejecting the reforms.[130]

These criticisms crystalised at the all-India level when a special session of the Muslim League was held in August 1918 in Bombay. The League, like the Congress, passed resolutions condemning the reforms. Both protested against the insinuation contained in the Montagu-Chelmsford proposals that the people of India were unfit for responsible government. Above all, both reaffirmed the principles contained in the resolutions relating to self-government (adopted at their annual sessions in Lucknow and Calcutta) and declared that 'the grant of self-government within the Empire is essential to strengthen the bond between England and India and also to satisfy the legitimate aspirations of the Indian people'.[131] The two resolutions adopted at the League and Congress sessions were practically identical. This identity, however, was no mere accident. It was the outcome of the joint deliberations of the Subjects Committee of the Congress and the Council of the Muslim League.

Why did the Muslim League reject the Montagu-Chelms-

[126]*Mussalman*, 26 July 1918.

[127]*Jamhur*, 10 July 1918, BENNR 1918.

[128]The resolution was introduced by Mujibur Rahman, seconded by Maulana Akram Khan and supported by Maulvi Nurul Huq Choudhry and Maulvi Habib Shah. *Searchlight*, 29 August 1918.

[129]*Tribune*, 30 July 1918.

[130]Haroon Khan Sherwani to Montagu, 12 July 1918, Judicial and Public (Reforms), 9-1, 1918, IOL.

[131]*Tribune*, 5 September 1918.

ford Reforms which had conceded most of its political
demands? Was it in the interest of keeping the *entente* with the
Congress alive? Or, was it due to the unfavourable conditions
which obtained at the time when the reform scheme was
published? When seen against the background of the economic
strains and stresses of the common people resulting from the
War, and the repressive policies of the government culminating
in the appointment of the Rowlatt Committee in December
1917 (which submitted its report at the end of July 1918), the
reluctance of most Muslim politicians to support the reforms
can be readily understood. The economic crisis engendered
disaffection amongst the peasants, traders, artisans and the
factory workers. This was reflected in the kisan movements in parts
of UP and Bihar, the millworkers strike in Ahmedabad and the
agitation against the Rowlatt Act in March-April, 1919. The
Sedition Committee's report, on the other hand, stirred nationalist sentiments and arrayed leading Indian politicians against
the government. Even the so-called moderates were outraged.
They pointed out reproachfully that nothing could be
better calculated to lend colour to the extremists assertion
that within the Jekyll of the reforms lurked the old Hyde
of repression.[132] They also failed to understand 'what
urgency was there to publish this outrageous Report almost
simultaneously with the Montagu-Chelmsford proposals, unless
it was to prejudice the legitimate demands of the people for a
real and substantial advance towards responsible government'.[133]

The Western-educated leaders of the Muslim League were
equally aghast at the implications of the government's repressive policies. They watched with suspicion the developments
that flowed from the reforms and were sceptical of the proclaimed 'good intentions' of the officials. They had
'experienced disappointment after disappointment' at the hands
of government,[134] while Congress leaders had consistently

[132]Broomfield, *Elite Conflict*, p. 141.
[133]*Amrita Bazar Patrika*, 22 July 1918.
[134]The Urdu newspapers explained this as the cause of Muslim
estrangement from government and their increasing participation in
Congress activities. See, for example, the observations of the *Al-Khalil*
as quoted in the *Paisa Akhbar*, 12 February 1919, PUNNR 1919.

supported their cause. Therefore, there was no reason for them to undermine their alliance with Congress by welcoming the reforms. Jinnah, Mazharul Haque, Hasan Imam, and Ansari were all-India politicians and their future in national politics depended on their success in maintaining the Congress-League *entente*.

Many Muslims League leaders had a further difficulty in accepting the reforms. They had so far campaigned relentlessly for the release of Muslim detenus and had, in the process, practically relegated all other issues to the background.[135] The acceptance of the reforms, therefore, implied not only an indirect endorsement of the government's repressive policies, but also an abandonment of the agitation in support of the detenus. Not surprisingly, most all-India Muslim politicians preferred to reject the reforms and earn the goodwill of their co-religionists. They were thus in the enviable position of enjoying both the confidence of the Congress and the support of their Muslim followers. This would perhaps explain why the Khilafat and Non-cooperation movements in the early 1920s were led by those Muslims who were not tempted by ¡the prospect of a seat in the council, but remained in the mainstream of agitational politics.

The period from January 1917 to April 1919 was in several respects one of the most important in the history of the Indian national movement. It was characterised by sharp conflicts and deep tensions between government and the radical wing of the Congress and the Muslim League. This was reflected in the controversy over the Montagu-Chelmsford Reforms and in the countrywide agitation against the Rowlatt Bills. In August 1918, the special Congress session held in Bombay pronounced the reforms 'disappointing and unsatisfactory'; this was followed by a similar pronouncement by the League. In April 1919,

---

[135]Notice, for instance, the reaction of the *Sedaqat* to the All-India Muslim Educational Conference held in November 1917. It observed that the Conference's cry 'for education seems to be a cry in the wilderness at a time when the attention of the Muslim community is fixed on the Muslim detenus'. *Sedaqat*, 18 November 1917, BENNR 1917.

Gandhi launched a satyagraha which, in spite of its limited success, paved the way for his emergence as a national leader. Moreover, his success in exploiting the local discontents quickened the process of mass politicisation which, in turn, gave a new dimension to the Indian national movement. In the years following the Rowlatt Satyagraha, the national movement was no longer confined to the English-educated elite; it involved a wide spectrum of Indian society, including those groups which had hitherto remained aloof and apathetic. The man who was responsible for drawing such groups was Gandhi. His techniques of mass mobilisation, which were essentially based on religious rituals, symbols, and popular indigenous traditions, go a long way in explaining his astonishing success in drawing individuals belonging to different castes, communities, and religions into the national movement.

Gandhi also succeeded in enlisting Muslim support for his political activities.[136] He was able to achieve this in part due to his remarkable organisational skill, and in part because he campaigned for the release of Ali Brothers and took an active interest in the Khilafat issue. Both questions greatly concerned Muslims and the intensity of their feelings was recognised by Gandhi. His early contacts with influential Muslims enabled him to understand the importance of religious institutions, rituals, and symbols in Indian Islam, and Gandhi never ignored them in his political calculations. In fact, he skilfully exploited them whenever the occasion demanded. No Hindu Congressman before Gandhi had made such an attempt—which may, perhaps, explain why no other Hindu before Gandhi commanded so much respect and influence amongst Muslims. Leaders like Aurobindo Ghose, Tilak and Bipin Chandra Pal introduced Hindu symbols and rituals which, instead of drawing Muslims into the revolutionary or Swadeshi movements, helped to drive a wedge between the Hindus and Muslims. Gandhi, on the

---

[136]See, for example, Chintamani's assessment of Mohamed Ali in 1924. He wrote to his Liberal Party colleague, Srinivasa Sastri: 'I had seen the latter [Mohamed Ali] more than a decade ago. How completely he has been transformed. Great I believe has been the Gandhian influence over him.' Chintamani to Sastri, 6 October 1924, T.N. Jagadisan (ed.), *Letters of V.S. Srinivasa Sastri*, 2nd edn. (Asia Publishing House, 1963), pp. 139-40.

other hand, played up the Khilafat issue; and by appealing to the religious sentiments of the Muslims he sought to win them over and enlist their support for his own political ends.

Another notable feature of the period covered in this chapter was the cross-communal alliance between different groups. The Congress and the Muslim League, which were the only two all-India organisations, were united in their opposition to the Montagu-Chelmsford Reforms and the Rowlatt Bills.[137] The few voices of dissent against the agitational politics of the two parties failed to have an impact in the midst of the popular upsurge which followed Annie Besant's internment. Attempts to foment communal tension in the districts were also thwarted by the Congress and League leaders. This is evident from the unique spectacle of friendly intercourse in different parts of the country. In an unprecedented gesture, Muslims invited Hindu leaders to address the Friday prayer congregations at the Juma Masjid in Delhi, the Sonepur mosque, Bombay, and the Nakhoda mosque in Calcutta.[138] Hindus and Muslims of Patnakhali in Bengal joined each others prayers in the local mosque and temple and resolved to work for the attainment of Home Rule.[139] These were impressive demonstrations of Hindu-Muslim unity. So long as the national movement rose above narrow sectarian and communal considerations it had the potentiality of embracing different sections of Indian society within its fold. In the post-1917 period, Indian politicians mobilised various groups on issues which were not the exclusive concern of any particular caste or community. That is why the response to their endeavours was not confined to any particular group; the Hindus and Muslims alike joined the protest movements against the Raj. By mid-April 1919, the scene was set for Hindu-Muslim cooperation in the Khilafat movement — a movement which marked the culmination of the anti-British tilt in Indian politics.

[137]'It is impossible to go through the proceedings of the session (Muslim League) without being struck by the fact that the national inspiration is as strong, as deep and as universal in the League as in the Congress and the country.' *Tribune*, January 1918.

[138]*Dainik Basumati*, 7 April 1919, *Nayak*, 14 April 1919, BENNR 1919.

[139]'Note on Patnakhali Satyagraha Movement' (Calcutta, n.d.), Jayakar Papers (436), NAI.

CHAPTER FIVE

SYMBOLIC UNITY AND KHILAFAT

No question agitated the Indian Muslims more during the early mid-twenties than the attempts of the Allies to dismember the Turkish Empire. Its future evoked sentiments of religious emotionalism among Muslims because the Sultan of Turkey was the *Amir al-Mu'minin* (Commander of the Faithful) and the custodian of the sacred places of Islam. To give expression to Muslim feelings, a Khilafat Committee was founded in March 1919 which aimed to secure not only a just and honourable peace for Turkey, but also the fulfilment of the pledges given by the British Prime Minister, Lloyd George.[1] The next important stage in the development of the Khilafat movement was the observance of 19 March as Khilafat Day; and on that day Gandhi, who had gone further than most Hindus in public life to work with Muslims, announced that he would launch a non-cooperation movement if the Turkish peace treaty did not satisfy the Indian Muslims. Accordingly, when the peace terms were announced in May 1920, the All-India Khilafat Committee adopted Gandhi's non-cooperation [programme. On 2 June, at Gandhi's suggestion, a conference of all parties was held at Allahabad which decided upon a policy of non-cooperation and appointed a committee to draw up a programme. On

[1]Lloyd George, in a speech in the House of Commons on 5 January 1918, declared that the British Government had no intention of depriving Turkey of the rich and predominantly Turkish lands of Asia Minor and Thrace.

1 August, the Khilafat Committee organised a *hartal* and entrusted Gandhi with the leadership of the Non-cooperation movement. Gandhi launched the movement by surrendering his titles and decorations to the government. 'Valuable as these honours have been to me', he wrote to the Viceroy, 'I cannot wear them with an easy conscience so long as my Mussalman countrymen have to labour under wrong done to their religious sentiments.'[2]

Various explanations of the Khilafat movement have been put forward by historians. According to some, it was engineered by a number of discontented groups in India. Their aim was to whip up an agitation against the government and to exploit the ideological issues in order to secure mass support. Such an interpretation is consistent with the recent trends in Indian historiography in which ideology is regarded as an inaccurate index of historical change, and great significance is attached to the competition between Indians 'for the loaves and fishes of political office and administrative place'. Within this framework the Khilafat agitation is treated as an artifact, a compound of material fears topped up by a dash of ideological whipped cream by the Ali Brothers in particular and the 'Young Party' Muslims, in general.

However, this interpretation ignores the importance of religious symbols in Indian Islam; underestimates the sense of religious unity amongst Muslims—a sentiment by no means all-pervasive but still extending beyond the narrow coterie of 'professional politicians'; and takes no account of the religious ties between the Indian Muslims and their co-religionists in other parts of the world which provided the driving force behind pan-Islamic ideology generally and the Khilafat movement in particular. This chapter focuses on these aspects with a view to explaining the nature and character of the Khilafat movement. It attempts to explain the reasons which underlay Muslim sympathy for Turkey and to identify the precise groups which were drawn into the movement. Furthermore, the aim is to examine the causes which led Gandhi to espouse the Khilafat

[2]Gandhi to Viceroy, 2 August 1920, Home Poll. Deposit Augnst 1920, 38, NAI.

cause, the significance of his involvement, and the Muslim
response to his initiatives.

II

The Indian Muslims share with their co-religionists elsewhere a set of common beliefs and practices. For this reason,
they have been conscious of their close religious links with
Muslim countries and often expressed their support and
solidarity with them through the pan-Islamic movement. The
educated Muslims, in particular, have also been keenly interested in the history, culture, and politics of medieval Arabia,
Moorish Spain, Turkey and Iran.[3] To the romantic historians
and poets such as Hali, Shibli, Ameer Ali, Khuda Baksh, and
Iqbal, the splendour of the Umayyad courts, the literary and
cultural accomplishments of the Abbasids, and the glories of
the Ottoman Empire formed the golden periods of Muslim
history.[4] In the nineteenth century, when the European powers

[3]The works of Shibli, Ameer Ali, Zakaullah and Khuda Baksh are
fairly well-known to scholars of modern Indian history. However, the
following publications, which form just a fraction of the writings on the
subject, are not so well known. They are listed here to give some idea
of the interest in Muslim countries. Maulvi Mohammad Inshaullah,
Sultanat-i-Usmania ki Maujuda Halat (Amritsar, 1897); Sirajuddin, *Hayat-
i-Salahuddin* (Amritsar, 1897); Mirza Hairat, *Khilafat-i-Usmani* (Delhi,
1901); Mohammad Farhatullah, *Tarikh-i-Ref* (Bijnor, n.d.), (this is a history
of Morocco); K. Mohammad Abdullah, *Damishq* (Amritsar, 1911); Abdul
Haleem Sharar, *Shaheed-i-Wa'afa* (Lahore, 1920), (this is a fascinating
play on the social and cultural life of the Muslims in Spain); N. Wajahat
Husain, *Anwar Pasha* (Lahore, 1921); Abdul Wahid Ibn Ali, *Khilafat-i-
Muwahhidin* (Madras, 1922), (this is a translation from the Arabic and
is a history of Spain and Morocco); A.R. Bulandshahri, *Sirat-i-Ghazi
Mustafa Kamal Pasha* (Bijnor, 1921); Asghar Ali Nizami, *Shan-i-Islam
aur Turki Talwar* (Lahore, 1923); Abdul Rab, *Sair-i-Undalus* (Allahabad,
1934), (a historical novel on the Muslims in Spain); Abdur Rahman
Shauq, *Hayat-i-Khalid bin Walid* (Lahore, 1936).

[4]One of the most eloquent instances of this nostalgia for the departed
glory of the Muslims is in Altaf Husain Halis' famous poem 'The Ebb
and Flow of Islam'. In many of Iqbal's poems, too, there is a constant
reference to the glorious traditions of the Muslim civilization. In his
poem *Bilad-i-Islamia*, he describes the grandeur of the great cities of the
Islamic world, such as Delhi, Baghdad, Medina, Damascus and
Constantinople.

threatened the heartland of Islam, the heritage of the past
stood forth as a symbol of community pride and distinction,
and Muslims began to find comfort in the civilized and once
powerful kingdoms of Moorish Spain, the Indian Mughals, and
the Abbasids of Baghdad. Iqbal was greatly moved by the sight
of Sicily, which was once held by the Arabs, and his poem
illustrates the extent to which some Muslims identified
themselves with the fortunes of Islam in other parts of the
world.[5]

Many Indian Muslims had a particularly strong regard for,
and a solicitous interest in, the welfare of Turkey which, as the
sole surviving independent Muslim kingdom, symbolised the
'temporal greatness of Islam's achievements' and whose Sultan
was the *Khalifa* of the Islamic world. That is why they viewed the
growing threat to the unity and integrity of the Turkish Empire
with concern.[6] In December 1918, Ansari warned his Muslim

---

[5]The poem read:

Once thou wast the cradle of the civilization of this race
The fire of whose glance was world captivating beauty
The nightingales of Shiraz wailed over Baghdad;
And Dagh wept tears of blood over Delhi.

To sing the dirge of ruin was to fall to my lot;
This torture—yea, self-torture was reserved for me.
Tell me of thy anguish; I am too full of pain;
I am the dust raised by that caravan which once broke its journey
here.

Paint me that picture of the old,
Rouse me by telling the tale of bygone days;
And I shall carry thy gift to India,
And make others weep as I weep now.

S.A. Latif, *The Influence of English Literature on Urdu Literature*
(London, 1924), pp. 111-13.

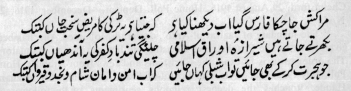

[6]Shibli to Editor, Aligarh Magazine, 17 November 1912, *Makatib-i-
Shibli*, Vol. I, pp. 342-43.

audience that Turkey, which had fought the battles of Islam for many centuries, was in imminent danger of being parcelled out into small states to the great detriment of the Muslim world. He went on to criticise not only the British government for its anti-Turkish policy, but also lashed out at the government of India for its alleged ill-treatment of the Indian Muslims, including the internment of their leaders, gagging of the press, and the slow pace of constitutional reforms.[7]

For most Muslims, however, no consideration outweighed their faith and religion. They were told in their local mosques or in the *madrasas* that, being the Prophet Mohammad's successor, the Sultan of Turkey was the *Amir al-Mu'minin*, and that obedience to him was obligatory. So they recognised him as their spiritual leader and offered prayers for his success and glory.[8] Moreover, the Sultan was also the defender of the Holy Places in the area known as Jazirat-ul-Arab which at one time extended—from Aden to the mountains of Syria—from Jeddah and the sea coast to the agricultural lowlands of Iraq.[9] The fear of this area passing into non-Muslim hands angered Muslims and drove them into the Khilafat agitation. Significantly enough, on this issue there was a high degree of unity which transcended

[7] Speech at the Muslim League Session, December 1918, Ansari Papers, JMIL.

[8] On 24 February 1904, the *Sadiq-ul-Akhbar* of Lahore wrote that the Indian Muslims 'look upon the Turkish sovereign . . . as their Caliph. Whenever they see that Government threatened with any danger, their hearts are filled with grief and they pray to God in mosques to avert the calamity, while their females offer similar prayers at home; fasts are also sometimes observed for the attainment of the end in view'. Quoted in I.A. Malik, *Punjab Muslim Press and the Muslim World, 1888-1911* (Lahore, 1974). Austen Chamberlain, Secretary of State for India, was surprised to learn that the Indian Muslims 'pray weekly for the Sultan, whilst they offer no prayers for their own sovereign'. Chamberlain to Chelmsford, 29 August 1916, Home Poll. Deposit, December 1916, 20, NAI.

[9] 'The mandate of Jazirat-ul-Arab', declared Mohamed Ali, 'has been given to us by the Prophet. No Christian or Jew can be the mandatory. The order to us is to expel the Christians and Jews from Arabia'. Home Poll. July 1925, 155, NAI. The Jazirat-ul-Arab, according to Mazharul Haque, 'touches the deepest religious sentiments of the followers of Islam. This country must remain under the suzerainty of the Muslim Khalifa'. *Motherland*, 19 January 1922, quoted in Q. Ahmad, J.S. Jha, *Mazharul Haque* (Delhi, 1976), p. 91.

regional or sectarian differences. In this respect, the attitude of the Shias was illuminating. They do not recognise the institution of Khilafat.[10] Yet, many of them decided to throw in their lot with the Khilafat agitation because of the impending danger to the sacred places of Islam.[11] Herein lies their significance; they provided a rallying point for virtually all sections of the Muslim community.

What was the significance of the Holy Places[12] to the religious life of the Muslims? The city of Mecca contains the *Baitullah* or the House of God, towards which the faithful turn their faces five times a day while offering *namaz*, and where thousands of them go every year to perform the pilgrimage at a given time in a given sequence of ceremonial actions.[13] Table 5.1 sets out the number of pilgrims who sailed from

[10]The Shias consider the first three Khalifas recognised by the Sunnis as 'usurpers' of the rights of Ali, since, according to them, the Prophet acting under divine guidance designated Ali and his descendants to a continuing authority.

[11]According to an intelligence report from Sind, the Shias there sympathised with the Angora Government 'in spite of their different religious standpoint as regards the Khilafat'. WR (Sind), 26 November 1921, 11 June 1921, J.C. Curry Papers, Centre of South Asian Studies, Cambridge. For further details on the involvement of the Shias in the Khilafat movement, see *Comrade*, 7 October 1911; *Paisa Akhbar*, 22 June 1920, PUNNR 1920; *Bombay Chronicle*, 7 May 1921.

[12]Constantinople was one of the holy cities, ranked next only to Mecca, Medina and Jerusalem. It was identified with the past glories of Islam, and regarded as a 'relic of a great national and religious value by the whole of the Muslim world'. Yaqub Hasan to Lloyd George, 1 July 1919, Foreign and Political Dept., External B, October 1920, 361-368, NAI; Home Poll. A, May 1919, 363-68, NAI.

[13]The following observation on the *Hajj* is useful: 'If the fatigues, privations, and difficulties of the pilgrimage to Mecca be considered, the distance of Hindustan must render the Hajj a formidable undertaking; yet, the piously disposed of both sexes yearn for the opportunity of fulfilling the injunction of the law-givers, and at the same time, gratifying their laudable feelings of sympathy and curiosity—their sympathy, as regards the religious veneration for the places and its purposes; their curiosity, to witness with their own eyes those places rendered sacred by the words of the Quran in one instance, and also for the deposits contained in the several tombs of prophets, whom they have been taught to revere and respect as the servants of God.' Meer Hassan Ali, *Observations on the Mussulmans of India*, Reprint of 1832 (edn. Oxford 1974), pp. 112-13.

Bombay and Karachi to the Hijaz. From 1919 to 1928, the average yearly number of pilgrims sailing from Indian ports was 19,464.[14] No discussion of numbers, however, would be complete without the observation that the rite of pilgrimage involves and affects more people than those who physically perform it. It is often a collective activity especially when the family, the village or the city quarter deputes a person to perform *Hajj* on their behalf and, in such cases, their participation is by proxy. On his return, the pilgrim is invited to especially arranged meetings, where his audience relives his tales and the experience he has had.[15] He is treated as a holy personage and is revered by all.

TABLE 5.1

NUMBER OF PILGRIMS WHO SAILED FROM BRITISH INDIA TO THE HIJAZ, 1907-1915

1907-8	1908-9	1909-10	1910-11	1911-12	1912-13	1913-14	1914-15
21,648	15,947	20,901	17,884	22,995	15,555	15,186	13,336

Source: *Statistical Abstract for British India*, 1916-17 (Calcutta, 1919), Vol. 4, p. 129.

To these Muslims, as indeed to the thousands of their co-religionists, the rumours regarding the desecration of the holy cities of Islam and the drinking of liquor in the sacred precincts came as a great shock.[16] The safety and sanctity of the Holy Places meant a great deal to their religious beliefs. This explains why they responded to the 'Islam in danger' cry with unprecedented enthusiasm. Money and ornaments poured into the Khilafat Fund, and thousands of Muslims from all walks

[14]See, J.A. Rahim, *Report of the Special Hajj Enquiry* in Home Public and Judicial Department, F. No. 8/758, IOL.

[15]See, for example, Mohammad Hamid Allah Khan, *Safarnamah-i-Medina-i-Munawarrah* (Lucknow, 1914); Ahmad Said Malihabadi, *Allah ke Ghar me* (Calcutta, 1972).

[16]Syed Ghafoor Shah, *Khun-i-Khirman* (Meerut, 1921); *Rasul Allah ke Roza-i-Mubarak pur Gola Bari aur Sada-i-Intiqam*, IOL Proscribed Publications (hereafter PP): 8; Munshi Wali Mohammad Wali, *Islam ki Faryad* (Delhi, 1921), PP: 142; Majid Ahmad, *Dard-i-Khilafat* (Aligarh, n.d.), PP: 44.

of life flocked to the Khilafat meetings. Their reasons for
doing so were entirely connected with their faith.[17]

III

The *ulama* were at the heart of Muslim concern over Turkey
and the Holy Places. From their *madrasas* and mosques they
suddenly emerged on the national scene to dominate the
course of the Khilafat agitation. Their presence on an all-India
platform was first noticed at the Muslim League meeting in
December 1918, where the prominent divines included Abdul
Bari, Azad Sobhani of Kanpur, Mohammad Ibrahim of Sialkot,
and Sanaullah of Amritsar. This was the first indication of their
determination to assume leadership of the Khilafat movement. 'In Islam', Maulvi Kifayatullah of Delhi declared, 'religion and politics are not two separate things. For a long time
they were together, but probably those who have received
modern education think that they are separate from one another.
This, however, is a wrong concept: they think that they should
monopolise politics and leave religion for the *ulama*'.[18]
Kifayatullah represented the voice of orthodoxy, which was confident and assertive. The *ulama* had come to the League
session to assert their views rather than to be led by the English-
educated Muslims. Politics to them had become all of a sudden
a necessary part of their religion,[19] and, during the next few
years, they appeared at almost all the Khilafat conferences and
influenced major policy decisions. They issued *fatawa* (religious
decrees) in order to enlist the support of their followers, and

[17]An intelligence report on the Khilafat movement in Sind admitted
that most Muslims in the area were impelled by religious motives, and
that only in the case of a few 'motives of personal vanity and the
necessity of making a living are the predominating influences'. WR
(Sind), 8 October 1921, Curry Papers.

[18]Quoted in Qazi Abdul Ghaffar, *Hayat-i-Ajmal* (Aligarh, 1950),
p. 185.

[19]'Until the *ulama*', observed Maulana Sajjad, 'take the reins of
politics in their own hands and cross their voices with those in autho-
rity, it will be difficult for them to establish their religious supremacy.
Moreover, the fulfilment of their higher aims [i.e., the protection of
Islam] will remain merely an empty dream.' A.M.M. Sajjad to Abdul
Bari, 4 December 1918, *Naqqush*, 1918, p. 91.

to demonstrate that they were united as a group on the Khilafat question. In March 1919, Abdul Bari issued a questionnaire which declared that, 'if there is any danger of infidels gaining possession of the Holy Places, all Muhammadans must fight. *Jihad* is as imperative as praying and washing'.[20] In the same month, the *maulvis* of Sukkur in Sind issued a *fatwa* declaring the Sultan of Turkey as the *Khalifa* of Muslims, and the Jazirat-ul-Arab as a sacred place 'wherein non-Muslim cannot rule or remain in possession'.[21] In Bengal, twenty-six *ulama* issued a *fatwa* forbidding Muslim participation in the Peace Celebrations, and Maulvi Najmuddin, who was one of the signatories, quoted the opinion of Abdul Bari that the violation of the *fatwa* would 'straightaway convert a Muslim into a *kafir*'.[22]

With these assumptions, it was inevitable for the *ulama* to employ a religious frame of reference. Everything was to be decided according to the *Sharia*; to join the Khilafat Committees was a religious duty; to wage *jihad* against the government was made obligatory by the *Sharia* and to boycott foreign goods as well as to migrate (*hijrat*) to the *dar al-Islam* was commanded by the *Sharia* and the Prophet Mohammad.[23] The *ulama* made it sound as if the religious texts had anticipated the dangers to the Khilafat and the holy cities of Islam, and had consequently laid down certain guidelines for the faithful to follow in the event of such dangers. They used the Quran and the *Hadith* as powerful weapons to gain the adherence of the masses who accepted them as infallible.

Who were the *ulama*? Where did they come from? What made them an important group in the Muslim community? It is

[20]WRDCI, 10 March 1919, Home Poll. B, April 1919, 148-52, NAI.

[21]*Tribune*, 21 March 1919.

[22]*Mohammadi*, 12 December 1919, BENNR 1919; The Governor of Bengal was informed that the *ulama* in the province travelled over eastern Bengal preaching *jihad* to the people and collecting considerable sums of money. Diary of Earl of Ronaldshay, 16 May 1919, Ronaldshay Papers, MSS. EUR. D. 609 (1), IOL.

[23]See, for example, A.M. Badauni, *Dars-i-Khilafat* (Meerut, 1919), p. 44; Shabbir Ahmad, *Tark-i-Mavalat* (Deoband, n.d.), PP: 53; A.K. Azad, *Boycott* (Meerut, 1921), PP: 106; Mahmudul Hasan, *Address Delivered at the Muslim National University, Aligarh, 29 October 1920*, PP: 54.

well known that Islam did not provide for a priesthood or a comparable religious institution. Gradually, however, a body of men developed with specialised religious functions—chiefly readers and reciters of the Quran, and also experts in recording the Traditions of the Prophet Mohammad. These men were the *ulama*—literally those who possess knowledge (*ilm*). They were not a separate class, but a body of people belonging to every social level. They formed an 'aggregate of academicians' who were supposed to have completed their education in a *madrasa* and studied a number of specialised subjects such as the Quranic exegesis (*tafsir*), the science of Prophetic tradition (*ilm-i-hadith*), jurisprudence (*fiqh*) and theology (*ilm-i-kalam*).[24] Indeed the hallmark of an *alim* was his learning in these subjects.

According to Fakhr-i-Mudabbir, a fourteenth century chronicler at the Delhi court, the *ulama* owed their special status to their knowledge. He observed:

All people know that after the apostles and prophets rank the truthful persons (*siddiqin*), martyrs (*shahidin*) and scholars (*aliman*). The scholars are included in the category of *siddiqis* and have preference over the martyrs. The Prophet has said: "The *ulama* are the heirs of the prophets." The world exists on account of the piety of the learned. The laws of *shariat* . . . are enforced by them . . . and things illegal and not sanctioned by the *sharia* are suppressed by them.[25]

---

[24]The following observation of Mohamed Ali is useful: 'Had I belonged to one of the families that specialise in religious learning, I would, no doubt, have spent half a lifetime in the study of the Quran and its *tafseer* or exegesis, or *Hadeeth* or the Traditions of the Prophet, or *Fiqh* or Muslim Jurisprudence, and *Aqaid* and *Kalam* or Dogmatics and Dialectics, which form the scholastic philosophy of the Musalmans regarding their creed . . . . As a necessary preliminary to these religious studies, I would have had to receive instruction for a number of years in Arabic grammar, and along with it in some secular Arabic literature. And after having finished . . . the entire syllabus of studies . . . , I would have set up as an *Alim* and teacher, giving instruction, in my turn, in the same, text-books to younger men similarly inclined or situated.' Mohamed Ali, *My Life: A Fragment*, pp. 2-3.

[25]Quoted in K.A. Nizami, *Some Aspects of Religion and Politics in India during the Thirteenth Century* (Bombay, 1961), p. 150.

Such a glorified image of the *ulama* was not entirely a product of Fakhr-i-Mudabbir's fantasy but was, indeed, grounded in Muslim ethics, and it helps to explain the special position the *ulama* occupied among Muslims. The *ulama* attained a position of moral and social superiority on the basis of their role as teachers, preachers, interpreters of the Islamic Law, and religious mentors. They were a powerful group in medieval India and dominated the upper echelons of religious hierarchy. They manned the judicial and ecclesiastical services, and wherever there was a mosque—and every Muslim locality had one — the *imam*, the *khatib*, the *muhtasib* and the *muftis* represented an interest which received state recognition. Some were actually an integral part of the state, and came to share in the control of the vast revenues of the land. They established matrimonial alliances with the ruling houses, purchased property and emulated the nobles (*amirs*) in lavish expenditure. Tradition classified them as *ulama-i-duniya* as opposed to the *ulama-i-akhrat*. The basis of this division was the difference in their attitude towards worldly affairs. The *ulama-i-akhrat* led an abstemious life of pious devotion to religious learning and eschewed entanglement in materialistic pursuits and political affairs. The *ulama-i-duniya*, on the other hand, were totally mundane in their outlook. They aspired for wealth and worldly prestige, and mixed freely with the ruling elite.[26]

In spite of the many religious grievances the *ulama* had against the anti-Islamic policies of the medieval Sultans, the relations between the two groups were generally marked by harmony, not hostility. Basically, ties of mutual self-interest bound them together. The *ulama* were an indispensable ally to the Sultans of Delhi, for they secured for them the one important element of authority which force alone could not command —legitimacy. The Sultans required a religious sanction for their monarchical and despotic rule and expected the *ulama* to give a favourable ruling in the light of the *Sharia*. Consequently, through bribes, flattery, and coercion, the Sultans turned the *ulama* into propagandists of their regime. The *ulama* never seriously protested against the misuse of their position and

[26]Nizami, *Religion and Politics*, . 152.

prestige among the Muslim masses.[27] On the contrary, many of them played to the tune of their masters no doubt because the entire religious structure was dependent upon their favours and support. They found excuses for praising and obeying the Sultans, knowing all the time that almost everything the Sultans did as persons and as rulers was repugnant to the *Sharia*. To protect their interests, the *ulama* delivered sermons in support of the Sultans and often acted as a channel of communication between the ruling elite and the Muslim masses. This is how they retained their social status.

The advent of British rule, however, brought a decline in the role of the *ulama* in Muslim society. The educational reforms, the reorganisation of the law courts, the growth of local governments and the spread of secular ideas weakened the power of the *ulama*. This was especially so in the cities, where these reforms had a direct impact. Yet, the *ulama* continued to make their presence felt among the Muslim masses through mosques and shrines, the *maktabs* and the *madrasas*. The Muslim community did not, and could not, have a church. But in spite of this, it was still possible for the *ulama* to mobilise opinion and to gather the community under its own banner.

The *ulama* were the guardians, transmitters, and the authorised interpreters of the Islamic Law, which comprehends Muslim beliefs, rituals, public and personal law. In other words, since almost every aspect of daily living was regulated by the *Sharia*, or required a ruling in the light of the *Sharia*, the services of the *ulama* became necessary in political, social, and economic affairs. They were called upon to play a variety of roles; and it is to them a Muslim turned, when in doubt, for the definition of controversial points of the doctrine. Their opinion was sought on a wide variety of subjects, ranging from the length of a *pyjama* while offering the *namaz* to the status of Muslims in a predominantly Hindu country. But the *ulama* were by no means united

[27]There were some notable exceptions. In the thirteenth century, for example, Nuruddin Mubarak Ghuznavi censured the Sultans of Delhi for pursuing anti-Islamic policies. The sufi saints, too, were the most vehement critics of the medieval state. This was particularly true of the sufis belonging to the Chishti order, who refused to be associated with the affairs of the state, in spite of pressures and inducements from the Sultans of Delhi.

ı n their views. A careful study of their *fatawa* reveals the deep ideological and doctrinal differences which divided them into several camps. Shah Abdul Aziz (1746-1824), for example, declared India to be a *dar al-harb* (abode of war) because 'in administration of justice, in matters of law and order, in the domain of trade, finance and collection of revenues everywhere the *kuffar* (infidels) are in power'.[28] Maulvi Karamatullah (1800-1873) of Jaunpur disagreed. According to him, India was a *dar al-Islam* because most of the injunctions of Islam in the sphere of marriage, divorce, and inheritance were in force under British rule, and Muslims enjoyed full religious liberty.[29] Such differences were not uncommon and they extended to various social and religious affairs as well.[30] With the establishment of the *Dar al-ulum* at Deoband and the *Nadwat al-ulama* in Lucknow, the doctrinal disputes were institutionalised. Each school developed its own group of followers, who vigorously challenged the validity of *fatawa* issued by the other side.[31]

[28]Quoted in Faruqi, *The Deoband School*, pp. 2-3.

[29]Hardy, *Muslims of British India*, pp. 110-11.

[30]For an insight into the nature of differences, see Robinson, *Separatism*, pp. 268-71. For personal rivalries amongst the *ulama* in Deoband, see Gail Minault, 'The Khilafat Movement: A Study of Indian Muslim Leadership 1919-24' (Unpublished Ph.D. thesis, University of Pennsylvania, 1972), pp. 66-70.

[31]For example, M. Manzar, R.A. Khan, *Deoband aur Bareilly ke ikhtilaf wa Naza par Faisla kun Munazara* (Sambhal, 1966). A number of leading *ulama* kept aloof from the Khilafat and Non-cooperation movements and criticised their fellow divines for associating with the Hindus. Maulana Ahmad Raza Khan of Bareilly was one of them. In 1921, he formed the *Jama'at-i-Ansar-ul-Islam* to counter pan-Islamism and convened a conference for that purpose. The first conference of the Jama'at was addressed by Maulana Mohammad Mian (1892-1956) of *Khanqah-i-Barkatia* in Marehra, a small town in Etah district of UP. The Maulana vigorously opposed the Khilafat agitation, advocated cooperation with the British and denounced the Khilafatists, including Abdul Bari, for associating with Gandhi and other Hindu Congressmen. See S. Jamaluddin, 'Religio-Political Ideas of a Twentieth Century Muslim Theologian—An Introduction', *Marxist Miscellany*, March 1977, pp. 13-18. In Sind, the *pirs* were equally divided. The *pir* of Kingri, for instance, not only opposed non-cooperation, but also advised his *murids* to remain loyal to the government. Pir Rashidullah, another influential Muslim divine, held aloof from the movement because it was 'initiated and controlled by Hindus'. WR (Sind), 9 April 1921, Curry Papers.

How did the *ulama* fit into the daily life of an individual? One can begin to answer this question by imagining what kind of contact an average Muslim had with an *alim*. As a young boy, he would attend a *maktab* or primary school where he would be taught to recite some portions of the Quran from memory, and also to read and write.[32] If he proved to be an apt pupil and was interested in pursuing the traditional Muslim education, he would go on for higher education at the *madrasa* which, like the *maktabs*, was staffed by the *ulama*. They were, thus, responsible for educating the Muslims, a role which not only provided them with a source of livelihood[33] but also enabled them to exercise a profound influence on Muslims in towns and the rural areas. They were the men of knowledge and their advice was sought on problems ranging from divorce and inheritance to disputes over property. In other words, they acted as counsellors to the people and their advice was rarely flouted—at least not openly.

The *ulama*, however, had the greatest influence in regulating religious life. On Friday, the average Muslim would attend the mosque service in his village or town and hear the weekly sermon given by the *khatib*, who was usually the prayer leader (*imam*). Here the *ulama* would come into contact with the rich and the poor; the Western-educated 'sahib' and the illiterate peasant; the town folks and the rural dwellers; and the young and the old. Similarly, when there was a death in the family the average Muslim would hire one of the professional Quranic readers or an *alim* to recite the Quran during the period of mourning. The *ulama* would also conduct the funeral service and the marriage (*nikah*) ceremony.

Thus the *ulama* were an important link between various Muslim groups; their educational and religious role enabled

[32]In 1916-17, the enrolment to the government-aided *maktabs* in the UP was 8,898. By 1926-27, the figure had risen to 43,973. This was a clear indication of the popularity of the *maktabs* amongst Muslims. *Report*, UP., 1921-28, Vol. 2, p. 140.

[33]The *ulama* were paid in various ways for their services. They were very often financially dependent on the government of the day or on other patrons. They were also remunerated either through financial endowments (*awqaf*) or donations. They supplemented their income by teaching in private houses, by copying books, by reciting the Quran, or by becoming a *khatib* or *Imam* of a mosque.

them to influence their co-religionists considerably. It is, therefore, not surprising that in small towns and villages, where the Muslim population was more susceptible to religious exhortation through local mosques and *madrasas*, the *ulama* led the Khilafat movement. From 1918 onwards, they appeared at all the Khilafat conferences, providing the inspiration behind a burst of Khilafat activity. They used the mosques, sufi shrines, and the religious seminaries and exploited all the available techniques of mass mobilisation to stir up religious passions in order to revive the pan-Islamic bogey. In Sind, for instance, the religious cry of 'Allah-ho-Akbar' was raised by the *ulama*. 'There is hardly any doubt', observed an intelligence officer, 'that the majority of the *Mullahs* in Sind have been won over by the agitators and are now beating the "drum ecclesiastic".'[34]

The *ulama* were able to secure the adherence of various Muslim groups laregly because they had an extensive network of social connections ranging from the Oudh *taluqdar* to the impoverished Muslim peasant in East Bengal. There is no doubt that they enjoyed a dominant religious hegemony which transcended class or caste divisions, and that they alone were able to enforce a uniformity in religious practices which, in its own right, was an amazing achievement. Successive Indian politicians realised their value, even if it was in the negative sense of preventing them from showing active opposition or from making adverse religious pronouncements.[35] The promoters of the Aligarh Muslim University, for instance, adopted a conciliatory attitude towards the Muslim divines in order to allay

[34]FR (Bombay), March 1920, Home Poll. Deposit, July 1920, 89, NAI.

[35]For example, there were vigorous attempts by the Congress leaders to enlist the support of the *ulama* during the civil disobedience movement in 1930-31. Note by D. Gladding, Officiating Deputy-Secretary to Government of India, 3 July 1931, Home Poll. A, August 1931, 189, NAI. The Government of India, on the other hand, was anxious to counter the efforts of the Congress leaders. The services of the Muslim landowners were utilised to keep the *ulama* 'straight'. In April 1930, the Nawab of Chhatari went on a mission to Deoband 'in order to use his own influence to keep them (*ulama*) from going astray.' This loyal servant of the Raj was obviously acting on the advice of his master. Hailey to Cunningham, 26 April 1930, Irwin Papers (24).

their fears about the future character of the University. Their support was necessary to convince the government that the University movement was backed by a wide spectrum of the Muslim community.

The Muslim professional men, who dominated the Muslim League after 1911, needed the *ulama* to rally public opinion around their brand of agitational politics,[36] and so they combined with them on all political and religious questions concerning the Muslim community.[37] The *ulama* were wooed and their fears about the irreligious character of the Muslim League removed. In December 1918, Ansari and Ajmal Khan went a step further in placating them. They tried to alter the aim of the Muslim League from protecting the political rights of Indian Muslims to protecting their religious interests as well both inside and outside India.[38] Clearly, some Muslim League leaders were willing to go a long way in their attempts to forge an alliance with the *ulama*, and through them carry on an intensive propaganda campaign.

The *ulama* responded favourably to these overtures mainly because they had no all-India organisation of their own and had

[36]In March 1915, Meston offered an interesting analysis of how the professional men and the *ulama* came to terms with each other. According to him, the 'young educated Muslim is restless and dissatisfied with everybody. His quest is for a cause, a call, something that he can be proud of, something which at small cost will retrieve his self-esteem and restore the glories of his race. This he finds in his religion. It gives him a link with great traditions. It may not be an ethical bond, but it is a militant bond; *in hoc signo vinces* . . . . At this point he comes in contact with the priest. Hence arises Pan-Islamism.' Meston to Hardinge, 25 March 1915, Hardinge Papers (89).

[37]The *Nai Roshni* of Allahabad, edited by Wahid Yar Khan, emphasised the importance of cooperating with the *ulama* in the struggle against the government's repressive policies. Similarly, the *Mohammadi* of Calcutta suggested that the task of rousing the Muslim masses to the impending danger to the Islamic world should be undertaken by the *ulama*. It observed: 'Let the *alim* betake themselves to work. Let the first steps in this great national work be begun in the mofussil, and let it be explained from each village mosque.' *Nai Roshni*, 23 December 1917, UPNNR 1917; *Mohammadi*, 23 April 1920, BENNR 1917; *Intikhab* (Gujranawala), 10 January 1920, PUNNR 1920.

[38]FR (Delhi), December 1918, Home Poll. D, January 1919, 42, NAI; WRDCI (Delhi), 18 January 1919, Home Poll. B, January 1919, 160-63, NAI.

little experience of techniques in mass mobilisation. Moreover, their bitter doctrinal disputes and mutual rivalries prevented them from uniting on any issue, a fact that had enabled the government to exploit their differences. By 1911, however, the *ulama* were rudely awakened by the growing threat to Islam—an awakening which coincided with, and was also to a large extent caused by, the political upheaval in Turkey. The first fruit of reaction was to come to terms with Muslim professional men and to utilise their political bodies and their experience in agitational politics to further the cause of pan-Islamism. The first significant move in this direction came from Firangi Mahal, Lucknow, where Abdul Bari helped to establish the *Anjuman-i-Khuddam-i-Kaaba* which, as a 'purely religious institution, selected for itself, from out of all religious duties, only one great duty, namely, service of the sacred places.'[39] For the first time the *Anjuman* was able to draw the *ulama* from different parts of the country as well as professional men representing a wide range of interests. Some of the leading *ulama* who joined the *Anjuman* were Shibli, Ubaidullah Sindhi, Abdul Majid Budauni, Shah Sulaiman of Phulwari Sharif, and Azad, while the formidable group of professional men comprised the Ali Brothers, Naziruddin Hasan, Ansari, and M.H. Kidwai.[40] Over the years these two groups worked in close cooperation in the Kanpur mosque incident, the Aligarh Muslim University movement, and the Khilafat agitation. Their religious fervour provided a strong base for an alliance, which created serious problems for the Raj.

By 1919, many professional men came to enjoy the trust and confidence of the leading *ulama* in north India where their activities were mainly concentrated. In March 1914, Mohamed Ali, Ajmal Khan and Ghulam-us-Saqlain, editor of *Asr-i-Jadid*, sat on the committee to enquire into the affairs of the *Nadwat-al-ulama*.[41] Mukhtar Ahmad Ansari was elected president of the *Anjuman-i-Islamia*, Ghazipur, a position which had always been occupied by the local *maulvis*.[42] In December 1918,

---

[39]Abdul Bari to J.H. DuBoulay, 17 March 1914, Home Poll. Deposit, July 1914, 7, NAI.

[40]Abdul Bari Papers, F.No. 1, FM.

[41]Note by Biggane, 30 October 1919, GAD 1914, 79, UPSA.

[42]*Leader*, 24 November 1917.

Ansari and Shuaib Qureshi, son-in-law of Mohamed Ali, were invited to address a meeting at Juma Masjid, Delhi, where they spoke in support of the Muslim League and proposed that Mohamed Ali and Maulana Mohammad Husain be represented at the Peace Conference.[43] In this way, leading professional men used the existing network of religious organisations and institutions to propagate pan-Islamism, and to bring themselves closer to the masses.

Since the *ulama* shared the pan-Islamic fervour of the professional men, they allowed them to use the religious organisations which, strictly speaking, came within their domain. But in return, the *ulama* expected them to orchestrate their specific religious demands set out in the memorandum submitted to Montagu and Chelmsford.[44] The future of their alliance depended on the extent to which the professional men were willing to support these demands.

THE DEVELOPMENT OF THE KHILAFAT MOVEMENT

If the participation of the *ulama* in the Khilafat movement was one significant development, the establishment of Khilafat committees from March onwards was another. For a community so unevenly distributed throughout the country, it was necessary to have both all-India and local organisations. That is why a Khilafat committee was formed in March 1919 at Bombay with Seth Mohammad Chotani, a prosperous government contractor and a timber merchant, as its president. A few months later, a committee was founded in Madras by Abdul Majid Sharar, editor of *Qaumi Report*. Likewise, Abdul Rahman Dinajpuri and Maulana Akram Khan launched a Khilafat committee in Calcutta. This inspired the local Khilafat leaders in Bengal to form affiliated branches in different parts of the province.[45]

[43]*Tribune*, 27 December 1918.
[44]A memorandum signed by 22 *ulama* from Deoband demanded that an *alim* should be appointed to each legislative council; *wakfs* and mosques should be placed under the charge of the *Sheikhul Islam*; and that *qazis* and *muftis* should settle disputes relating to the Muslim Personal Law. Maulvi Mohamed Ahmed to Sheweth, 30 October, Meston Papers (19).
[45]*Mahratta*, 7 November 1919.

Punjab, too, had its share of Khilafat committees which played a vital role in organising the boycott of the Peace Celebrations in November 1919. The intelligence reports especially referred to the activities of the Amritsar Khilafat Committee and described its president, Maulana Daud Ghuznavi, as the principal 'firebrand' in the region.[46] In the UP, there were Khilafat committees at Aligarh,[47] Jaunpur,[48] Lucknow, Bijnor,[49] and Allahabad. Their existence indicates that the Khilafat movement was not just confined to big cities but extended to towns as well. In fact, effective mobilisation of the faithful living in the villages was carried out from the towns, which formed the nucleus of all religious and educational activities. In each town the mosques attracted Muslims from neighbouring villages to the Friday prayers. Here they listened to the *khutba* which, during the Khilafat movement, was used to rouse religious passions. Moreover, the Khilafat leaders moved out from the towns into those areas which had hitherto remained untouched by any sort of political activity. In May 1919, the All-Presidency Conference of the *Majlis-i-Ulama* at Madras decided to tour the Presidency and stir up support for the *Khalifa*.[50] In early February 1920, Abdul Bari, Shaukat Ali, and G.M. Bhurgi, a Bohra Muslim from Bombay, addressed public meetings in Hyderabad (Sind) and Larkana. During the winter of 1921, Abdul Majid of Budaun who came into prominence during the Kanpur mosque agitation, and a group of

[46]FR (Punjab), 10 November 1919, Home Poll. Deposit, January 1920, 5, NAI.

[47]Hasrat Mohani was its president and Maulvi Anwarul Huda, a *vakil*, the secretary. The Khilafat Committee at Aligarh was particularly important because of the active involvement of the students at the University who displayed an unprecedented degree of enthusiasm in spreading pan-Islamic propaganda. Interviews with Mr. S.M. Tonki, a close associate of Abdur Rahman Bijnori and a non-cooperator, August 1973.

[48]The Jaunpur Khilafat Committee sponsored the publication of a collection of poems entitled 'Songs of the Nightingales' (*Bulbulan-i-Hurriyat ke Tarane*), PP: 47, IOL.

[49]See, for example, the collection of poems published by the Bijnor Khilafat Committee entitled *Gulshan-i-Khilafat*, PP: 152, IOL.

[50]K. Mcpherson, 'The Political Development of the Urdu and Tamil-speaking Muslims of the Madras Presidency 1901 to 1937' (Unpublished M.A. thesis, Western Australia, 1968), pp. 108-10.

Abdul Bari's disciples toured the villages of UP where they received an enthusiastic welcome.[51] On 14 January 1921, Maulvi Salamatullah, who was closely associated with Abdul Bari in all his religious and political activities, addressed a Kisan Sabha meeting at Malihabad where he declared that the grievances of the peasants would be redressed only after the dignity and prestige of the *Khalifa* was restored.[52] The Khilafat leaders exploited local discontent to stir up religious passions. For this end they used mosques, educational institutions, kisan sabhas, the Khilafat committees and the district Congress committees.

Another effective means for mass mobilisation was the press, particularly the vernacular newspapers, some of which appeared between 1918 and 1919. Prominent amongst them in the UP was the *Akhuwat*, founded by Abdul Bari and edited by Abdul Ghaffar, the biographer of Hakim Ajmal Khan and a journalist of repute.[53] In December 1918, Maulana Akram Khan established the Urdu-language, *Zamana*. At Allahabad, an English daily, *Muslim Herald*, made its appearance on 1 January 1919. In addition to this, in Bengal the pan-Islamic press included the *Mussalman*, founded in December 1906 with Abdul Kaseem as its nominal editor and Mujibur Rahman as the moving spirit, *Moslem Hitaishi*, *Hablul Matin*, *Jamhur*, *Naqqash* which was started early in 1918, *Mohammadi*, and *Sedaqat*. Delhi had two Khilafat papers, the *Qaum*, edited by Qazi Abbas Husaini, and *Inqilab*, edited by Arif Husain Hasvi, a close friend and associate of Mohamed Ali. In the Punjab, a daily journal by the name of *Waqt* appeared from Amritsar. It was the chief organ of the Punjab Khilafatists.

The increase in the number and circulation of these newspapers[54] meant that the politicians, the publicists and the *maulvis*

[51]*Bombay Chronicle*, 1 March 1921.

[52]The Government of the United Provinces, Police Dept., F.No. 51-N, 1921, UPSA.

[53]In December 1917, Qazi Abdul Ghaffar published the *Jamhur*, an Urdu daily, from Calcutta. But in October 1918 he was externed from the city and was forced to come to Delhi where he launched the *Sabah*, an Urdu daily.

[54]For the growth of Urdu newspapers and periodicals in UP, see F.C.R. Robinson, 'The Politics of U.P. Muslims 1906-1922' (Unpublished Ph.D. thesis, Cambridge, 1970), Table XXXV, p. 399.

could reach and influence a much wider audience than ever before. The existing religious networks, which gave a degree of cohesion to the Muslim community, were not themselves strong enough to maintain the momentum of an all-India movement. The newspapers performed this vital role. The extensive coverage of the events in Turkey, the machinations of European powers and the activities of Khilafat committees began to have a more direct impact on the Muslims. For the first time, they became aware of the relevance of the Khilafat in relation to their religious beliefs. The vernacular newspapers introduced the political and religious aspects of the Khilafat to every literate Muslim in the bazaars, mosques, and educational institutions, and served as a chief instrument of propagating pan-Islamic ideas.

The success of the Khilafat propaganda and the depth of its penetration among different groups of Muslims was well illustrated on 17 October 1919, when Muslims living in different parts of the country observed Khilafat Day.[55] In Madras city, shops of every description were closed.[56] In Bangalore, the district Muslim League acted on the instructions of the Bombay Khilafat Committee and organised a meeting attended by three to four thousand people.[57] In Mysore, Khilafat Day was observed by a branch of the Central National Mohammedan Association, which had earlier taken a lead in raising money for the Turkish Welfare Fund.[58]

In the North-West Frontier Province, Assam, the Central Provinces and the Punjab, however, there was little activity on

[55]The decision to observe Khilafat Day was taken at the All-India Muslim Conference on 21 September held in Lucknow. The Conference was attended by over 5,000 delegates, including a large number of *ulama*. *Tribune*, 27 September 1919.

[56]*Hindu*, 18 October 1919. Earlier Red Crescent societies were organised in Madras city and Ootacamund to collect funds to send medical aid to Turkey and meetings were held to pledge moral support for Turkey. In 1919, pan-Islamic sentiment in Madras Presidency received a boost when the All-India session of the *Nadwa* was held in Madras city. This was followed by the revival of the *Majlis-ul-ulama*, an association of Muslim divines, which remained in the forefront of Khilafat agitation. Mcpherson, 'The Political Development of the Urdu and Tamil-speaking Muslims of the Madras Presidency,' pp. 58, 91, 109.

[57]Brown, *Gandhi*, p. 199.

[58]Home Poll. Deposit, November 1919, 16, NAI.

Khilafat Day. The reason for this was mostly organisational. In the Punjab, the leading Khilafat leaders, including Zafar Ali and Saifuddin Kitchlew, were under internment. Consequently, the leadership fell into the hands of politically inexperienced men like Mahbub Alam, editor of *Paisa Akhbar*, and the poet Iqbal, who was the first secretary of the Punjab Provincial Khilafat Committee.[59] In the North-West Frontier Province, Assam, and the Central Provinces, on the other hand, there was no provincial Khilafat committee, and there existed no link between the Central Khilafat Committee and the provincial Khilafat leaders.

By contrast, in Bombay, Khilafat Day was observed more widely. Bombay city was a venue of several Khilafat meetings from March 1919 onwards. In late March an important meeting was addressed by Chotani and attracted over fifteen to twenty thousand Muslims. Gandhi, too, made a speech on that occasion. In mid-September he addressed another public meeting at which he assured his Muslim audience saying: 'You have the whole of India in your just struggle.'[60] Moreover, there was considerable political activity in Bombay during the Rowlatt Satyagraha which involved large numbers and a wide cross-section of the population. The effect of the agitation that had been carried on for several months, was that on Khilafat Day there was great excitement in the city. The streets in the city were deserted and shops in Crawford Market, Abdur Rahman Street, Chukla Pandvi, Mangaldas Cloth Market and Gokuldas Cloth Market remained closed. In the suburban areas, such as Bandra, Mahim and Matunga, Muslim butchers went on strike. In the afternoon, Muslims attended in great force the Friday *namaz* and offered prayers for the *Khalifa*.[61]

Bengal also had its share of Khilafat meetings. Here the pro-government and the pro-Congress Muslims set aside their political differences over the Montagu-Chelmsford Reforms and presented a joint front on the Khilafat issue. On 9 February 1919, Calcutta witnessed its first Khilafat meeting under Fazlul Haq, Abdul Kaseem, Akram Khan, Mujibur Rahman and

[59]*Leader*, 3 December 1919.
[60]Speech on Khilafat, 18 September 1919, *CWG*, Vol. 16, p. 151.
[61]*Bombay Chronicle*, 18 October 1919.

Maulvi Najmuddin. A few weeks later, a joint meeting of the Bengal Congress and the Muslim League held in Mymensingh declared its complete support to the Khilafat movement.[62] By September, the interest and anxiety regarding the fate of Turkey was at a high pitch in the province. It found expression on Khilafat Day. 'In all district and subdivisional towns', reported the *Amrita Bazar Patrika*, 'and in almost all important villages and hamlets of the Province, the Khilafat Day was observed in all solemnity and earnestness. The Hindus and Muslims vied with each other in showing their eagerness to keep the Turkish Empire intact.'[63]

In Bihar, Khilafat Day was organised by Safaraz Husain, a leading Congressmen, Maulvi Ghulam Ali and Syed Hasan Arzoo. Their great success lay in drawing the peasants and other rural folks to Khilafat meetings. A meeting held in Bahpura on Khilafat Day was attended by Muslim peasants from the neighbouring villages who joined in the prayers offered for the safety, dignity, and power of the Sultan of Turkey. In Gaya, shopkeepers, traders and legal practitioners suspended their business for the day. At Chapra, Bhagalpur, Monghyr, Darbhanga and Phulwari Sharif, Muslims assembled in mosques to pray for the divine protection of the *Khalifa*.[64]

In the UP, Khilafat Day was observed in most places as is evident from newspaper reports of public meetings, demonstrations, and prayers in mosques. At Allahabad, there was a public meeting which attracted over fifteen thousand people.[65] It was presided over by Maulana Wilayat Husain and was, significantly enough, attended by a large number of Shia *maulvis*. Similar meetings were held in Kanpur, Farrukhabad, Azamgarh, Benaras and Aligarh.[66]

The success of Khilafat Day in the UP was not surprising. The province had been the centre of every political agitation ever since the Turko-Italian war, and was the nucleus of all religious activities. It was also the homeland of the most vociferous pan-Islamists. At the first meeting of the Central Khila-

[62]Home Poll. Deposit, August 1919, 55, NAI.
[63]*Amrita Bazar Patrika*, 19 October 1919.
[64]*Searchlight*, 23 October 1919.
[65]*Leader*, 19 October 1919.
[66]*Ibid.*, 20 October 1919.

fat Committee, 50 out of the 107 delegates were from the UP.[67] The overwhelming majority of those who attended the All-India Muslim Conference on 21 September were UP Muslims.[68] In fact, they were chiefly responsible for rousing religious passions through the press and the platform, and providing direction to the Khilafat agitation in all its phases.

The observance of 17 October as Khilafat Day was significant in several respects. In the first place, it showed that the Khilafat movement enjoyed the support of many important groups among Muslims, and that its impact was felt in different regions. Secondly, it signified the beginning of a more militant approach on the part of some Khilafat leaders who were dissatisfied with the constitutional methods—submitting memoranda to the government of India and sending deputations to London. They were gradually becoming convinced that, inspite of petitions and prayers, the Turkish Empire would be 'ruthlessly dismembered in violation of all principles of equity, justice, freedom and self-determination and in direct conflict with all canons of political and international morality.'[69] The only way of saving the Khilafat, they felt, was to intensify the agitation with a view to keeping up pressure on the government. This would explain why the All-India Khilafat Conference, held in Delhi on 23/24 November, resolved to boycott the Peace Celebrations and British goods, and to withhold cooperation with the government if the Turkish question was not satisfactorily settled. The composition of the committee, appointed to work out the practical working of these resolutions, illustrates the dominance of what in official records were described as the group of 'extremists'.[70] The same men dominated the Muslim

[67]The number of delegates from each province were: UP 50, Bombay Presidency 20, Bihar and Orissa 10, Madras 6, Punjab 6, Delhi 5, Central Provinces 5. Home Poll. B, January 1920, NAI.

[68]*Tribune*, 27 September 1919.

[69]*Mussalman*, 27 February 1920.

[70]The boycott of British goods committee consisted of Zahur Ahmad, Hasrat Mohani, Zafarul Mulk Alvi, Akram Khan, Maulvi Muniruzzaman, Seth Abdullah Harmi, Haji Ahmed Khatri, Maulana Sanaullah, Agha Mohammad Safdar, Arif Husain Hasvi, Tajuddin and Maulvi Mohammad Sajjad. The Non-cooperation committee consisted of Abdul Bari, Abdul Majid, Sanaullah, Wilayat Husain, Ajmal Khan, Syed Husain, Raza Ali, Hasrat Mohani, Kamaluddin Jafri, Mumtaz

League session, which was notable for its 'display of virulent pan-Islamism', and where the 'anti-British spirit reigned supreme.'[71] According to an intelligence report, the 'loyalists were at a great disadvantage. They were abused very freely',[72] and criticised for their role in the Khilafat movement. This was an obvious reference to the attempt of the UP Muslims, led by Hasrat Mohani, Abdul Bari, and the Ali Brothers, to wrest control of the Central Khilafat Committee from the Bombay Muslims.[73] The main reason behind this was to make the Khilafat movement more anti-British and more agitational than it had been so far. To achieve this the 'moderates' had to give way to the 'extremists'.[74] The former believed in protesting through 'lawful' means, while the latter favoured militant action.[75] Their difference was expressed by Ibni Ahmad: 'No one can deny that every Muslim is concerned about the future of Turkey', he told Ansari in December 1919, 'we differ on one point, that is, how to convey our feelings to the authorities.'[76] The Raja of Mahmudabad made the same point

Husain, and Fazlul Haq and Seth Abdullah Harmi. *Leader*, 28 November 1919, *Amrita Bazar Patrika*, 26 November 1919.

[71]WRDCI, January 1920, Home Poll. Deposit, February 1920, 52, NAI.

[72]Report by Tasadduq Husain, Home Poll. Deposit, March 1920, 59, NAI.

[73]For details of the struggle between the UP Muslims and their brethren in Bombay, see Robinson, *Separatism*, pp. 300-1.

[74]The *Mohammadi* wrote the following on the resignation of Wazir Hasan and the Raja of Mahmudabad from the Muslim League: 'The *zamindars*, especially the taluqdars of Oudh, though independent in name, are really subservient to Government . . . . Hence it is not desirable for a *taluqdar* to act as the President of an extremist body like the League. But it is quite a different thing altogether with Wazir Hasan. He cannot be called fit to hold that responsible post (Secretary-ship) any longer as the Muslims have now reached a higher stage of advancement . . . ' *Mohammadi*, 14 March 1919, BENNR 1919.

[75]The difference between the 'moderates' and the 'extremists' were summed up by the *Moslem Hitaishi* of Calcutta. The paper observed: 'The moderates, if the Turkish peace terms go against Moslem opinion, will lawfully protest against them and continue doing so until redress is available. The extremists, on the other hand, will take immediate remedial measures.' *Moslem Hitaishi*, 23 April 1920, *Ibid.*, 1920.

[76]Ibni Ahmad to Ansari, 20 December 1919, Mohamed Ali Papers.

a few months later. He wrote to Shaukat Ali: 'It is [thus] clear that for the present division in the Muslim camp—a division which has, of course, nothing to do with the Khilafat question as such, in regard to which all are united, but was concerned with the question of strategy.'[77] Over the next few months, the 'moderates' and the 'extremists' maintained an uneasy alliance, though the latter remained the dominant group in deciding major policies.

The Khilafat Day was important for yet another reason. It brought Gandhi to the forefront of the Khilafat agitation, a position he continued to occupy until early 1922. We have earlier referred to his relationship with the *ulama* and several Muslim politicians, and his growing interest in the Khilafat issue, particularly after the collapse of the Rowlatt Satyagraha. In May 1919, he declared at Bombay that the Khilafat question was 'the greatest of all, greater even than that of the repeal of the Rowlatt Act, for it affects the religious susceptibilities of millions of Muslims.'[78] He urged Muslims to 'make a move at once in the desired direction', because 'time is running fast', and that soon 'it may be too late to do anything.'[79] He further appealed to Abdul Bari to organise the *ulama*, and warned him that 'the time for joint and firm action on our part is now. There will be disappointment and resentment after. But it will be to no purpose; everything is possible now, nothing *after* the publication of the terms.'[80]

Gandhi was obviously prodding the Khilafat leaders to intensify their agitation which, he hoped, would keep him in the forefront of national politics and enable him to regain the influence he had lost during the Rowlatt Satyagraha.[81] He was also determined to prove the efficacy of his technique of satyagraha over all other methods, a determination which propelled him to assume control of the Khilafat movement. Above all,

[77]*Tribune*, 21 March 1920.
[78]Speech on Khilafat, 9 May 1919, *CWG*, Vol. 15, p. 296.
[78]*Ibid.*, p. 297.
[80]Gandhi to Abdul Bari, 27 August 1919, *CWG*, Vol. 16, p. 70; Gandhi to Abdul Bari, n.d., quoted in Desai, *Day-To-Day*, Vol. 2, p. 35.
[81]For the declining influence of Gandhi after the suspension of civil disobedience, see Brown, *Gandhi*, pp. 182-87.

in taking up the Khilafat cause, Gandhi hoped to strengthen the bond of Hindu-Muslim unity, which he regarded as 'a thousand times more valuable than . . . our connection with the British.'[82] The theme of Hindu-Muslim unity was central in Gandhi's order of priorities and, after coming to India from South Africa, he wrote and spoke extensively on the subject, and cultivated influential Muslims in order to understand their fears and aspirations. Such initiatives were motivated by a genuine desire to make a contribution towards the solution of the communal problem. In helping Muslims in 'the hour of their peril', the Mahatma hoped to bring to an end communal animosities, secure Muslim friendship with the Hindus,[83] and gain their support for the national movement. 'If I kept aloof from the Khilafat question', he wrote in May 1920, 'I would consider myself as having lost all my worth. That work is my *dharma* par excellence. It is through the Khilafat that I am doing the triple duty of showing to the world what *ahimsa* really means, of uniting Hindus and Muslims, and of coming in contact with one and all . . . .'[84]

Gandhi's first opportunity to play an important role in the Khilafat movement arose at the All-India Muslim Conference on 21 September in Lucknow. He lent his support to the Khilafat Day resolution and appealed to his co-religionists to join the Muslims in fasting, prayer, and *hartal* and 'thus put a sacred seal on the Hindu-Mohammedan bond.'[85] Gandhi did so because he wanted to test the strength of Muslim feelings over the Khilafat, and the extent to which they were prepared for a confrontation with the government.[86] At the same

[82]Desai, *Day-To-Day*, Vol. 2, p. 237.

[83]*Young India*, 5 May 1920, *CWG*, Vol. 17, p. 391.

[84]Gandhi to Mangalbhai, 3 May 1920 in Desai, *Day-To-Day*, Vol. 2, pp. 154-44; On 7 September 1919, Gandhi wrote in the *Navjivan* that the Turkish question concerned the whole of India, because 'it is impossible that one of the four limbs of the nation be wounded and the rest of the nation remain unconcerned.' *CWG*, Vol. 16, p. 104.

[85]Letter to the Press, 10 October 1919, *Ibid.*, p. 227.

[86]This is clearly evident from Gandhi's speech on 18 September in which he stated that the shrewd and sagacious British rulers would take no time to assess 'whether we are serious or at play'. He, therefore, asked the Muslim audience to 'ask yourselves whether you are serious about this very serious matter . . . . Are you just? Are you sincere?

time, he wanted to assess the Hindu response to the Khilafat causewhich was important for the success of the Khilafat movemnet as well as for the future of Hindu-Muslim unity. 'You are my neighbours and my countrymen', he told a Muslim audience in Bombay, 'it is my duty to share your sorrows. I cannot talk about Hindu-Muslim unity and fail in giving effect to the idea when the test comes.'[87] This statement was a public announcement of his support to the Khilafat cause as well as an appeal to Hindus to follow his lead.

The impressive response to Khilafat Day provided Gandhi the much needed encouragement to speak and write on the Khilafat issue with greater confidence. At the same time, he realised that, in the prevalent political climate, many Hindu politicians were anxious to encourage pan-Islamic passions in the interest of mass agitational politics. This was evident from their participation in the public meetings held on Khilafat Day. In Allahabad, for example, Mohanlal Nehru and K.K. Malaviya appeared alongside the Khilafat is ts. In Delhi, Shraddhanand addressed a public meeting on Khilafat Day, while Lala Shanker Lal, managing director of the Delhi Swadeshi Stores, and honorary secretary of the Delhi Home Rule League, issued a message in its support.[88] In Madras, Rajagopalachari, G.S. Arundale, Ramaswamy Aiyer, G.A. Natesan and D.K. Telang joined the i m p r e s s i v e demonstration organised to condemn the proposed dismemberment of the Turkish Empire.[89] Their purpose was to cement an alliance with the Khilafat leaders and to enlist their support for various political objectives.

Encouraged by these developments, Gandhi began to take a more active interest in the Khilafat movement from October 1919 onwards. He attended the All-India Khilafat Conference in Delhi on 23/34 November and supported the resolutions to boycott the Peace Celebrations, to send a deputa-

---

The test is simple. A sincere and true man is ready to sacrifice himself for a cause. Are you ready to sacrifice yourself for a cause? Are you ready to sacrifice your ease, comfort, commerce and even your life?' *Young India*, 20 September 1919, *Ibid.*, p. 152.

[87]Speech on Khilafat, 9 May 1919, *CWG*, Vol. 15, p. 297.

[88]*Bombay Chronicle*, 19 October 1919; *New India*, 15 October 1919.

[89]*New India*, 17 October 1919.

tion to England, and to withhold cooperation from the government if the Khilafat question was not settled in accordance with the Muslim demands. However, Gandhi firmly opposed the resolution on the boycott of British goods, because it meant 'economic punishment' to the merchants and traders, which was against his principles as a satyagrahi.[90] He was also aware of the practical difficulties of organising a boycott and feared that it would provoke the opposition of Hindu and Muslim merchants.[91] These arguments prevailed. The only resolutions passed at the Khilafat Conference thanked Gandhi and other Hindus for their support and proposed a boycott of the Peace Celebrations. These resolutions are of particular interest as they mark the beginning of Gandhi's influence on the Khilafat leaders. The extent to which they had, by December 1919, come under his spell was apparent from the proceedings of the Muslim League in Amritsar. In deference to the wishes of Gandhi who held the cow sacred, the League resolved to prohibit the slaughter of cows on the occasion of *Bakr Id*. It also expressed gratitude to His Majesty the King for the spirit in which the Royal Proclamation had been issued.[92] In this resolution also the influence of the Mahatma is noticeable for he was at the same time carrying a similar motion through the Congress inspite of considerable opposition.[93]

January 1920 to 1 August, 1920

From January to March, the Khilafat protest reached a new level of intensity. This was largely due to the vigorous campaign of Azad, Zafar Ali Khan, and the Ali Brothers, all of whom were released from prison at the end of 1919. One of

[90]Speech at Khilafat Conference, 23 November 1919, *CWG*, Vol. 16, p. 307; On 24 November, while opposing Hasarat Mohani's resolution on boycott of foreign goods, Gandhi stated that 'there is a world of difference between withdrawal of cooperation and boycott. It is a man's privilege to withhold cooperation when he likes, but we must have regard for the opinion of the world before adopting any political step. What we intend to do cannot be effected through boycott'. *Ibid.*, p. 310.

[91]*Young India*, 14 January 1920, *Ibid.*, Vol. 16, p. 482.

[92]Pirzada (ed.), *Foundations of Pakistan*, Vol. I, p. 538.

[93]See Brown, *Gandhi*, p. 188.

their first acts on release was to muster greater support, particularly in Sind and the North-West Frontier Province which had, for the most part, remained aloof from all Khilafat activities. For this purpose, they organised tours, conferences, and public meetings. On 16 January, a group of students from Aligarh College was deputed to Peshawar and Kohat, where they addressed several meetings in mosques. At the end of their three-day mission, they raised Rs 23,000 for the Khilafat Fund.[94] In February, Abdul Bari, Shaukat Ali, Azad, and Bhurgi toured Hyderabad and Larkana in Sind and spoke at a Khilafat meeting, which was attended by fifteen thousand Muslims, including a large number of peasants.[95] This was followed by a tour of eastern Bengal. Several missions were also sent to different parts of Punjab and the UP.

In addition to such organised activity, the Khilafat leaders launched several newspapers, submitted numerous memoranda to the government, and organised conferences all over India. These activities were primarily designed to maintain the momentum of the agitation and to stir up the Muslims in those areas where there was comparatively less Khilafat activity. This was most certainly the aim of the conferences held in Hyderabad, Larkana, Nagpur, Burdwan, Mymensingh, Amritsar, and Multan. At all these places, the *ulama* were the most dominant group and also the most vehement advocates of non-cooperation.[96] On 4/5 January 1920, some *ulama* made fiery speeches in Hyderabad, and clamoured for a declaration of *jihad* against the enemies of Islam.[97] But perhaps the most important of these meetings was the Bengal Khilafat Conference held in Calcutta on 28 February. On that occasion, Abdul Bari, who until then had been noted for his policy of caution and moderation, delivered an extremely violent speech, which echoed the sentiments expressed a few weeks earlier at the Sind Khilafat Conference.[98]

[94]Proceedings of Aligarh Muslim University Students' Union, 9 December 1920, AMUA.

[95]*Amrita Bazar Patrika*, 18 February 1920.

[96]For example, the meeting at Amritsar on 12 March was attended by over ten thousand *ulama*. *Amrita Bazar Patrika*, 15 March 1920.

[97]Bamford, *Histories*, p. 147.

[98]For the text of the speech, see *Ibid.*, Appendix E.

In fact, he set the tone of the meeting which decided to boycott British goods, to withdraw cooperation from the government if the peace terms were unfavourable to Turkey, and to observe 19 March as Khilafat Day with a *hartal*.[99] Thus Gandhi's objections to the boycott of British goods were overruled because, by February 1920, it had become quite clear that Turkey would cease to exist as an independent state, that the Sultan of Turkey would be deprived of his territories in Europe and in Asia, and that the Holy Places of Islam would pass into non-Muslim hands.[100] 'The ship of the last independent state is about to sink in the sea of the terrible conspiracies of the alien in religion', warned the *Mohammadi*.[101] To prevent the sinking of the ship, the Khilafat leaders favoured the intensification of the agitation with a view to keeping up pressure on the government of India which, they hoped, would be able to exercise some influence on the Peace Conference. The resolutions passed at the Bengal Khilafat Conference can be interpreted in this light.

With a few exceptions, the decisions of the Bengal Conference went down well with the Khilafat leaders all over India. In early March, the United Provinces Ulama Association confirmed the Calcutta resolutions at the Conference held in Kanpur. During a meeting of the Subjects Committee of this conference, with Abdul Bari in the chair, the question of *jihad* was considered and it was resolved to send students to preach *jihad* in the mofussil.[102] On 10 March, the Aligarh Khilafat Committee expressed its readiness to enforce the boycott of British goods.[103] Two days later, the Punjab Khilafat Committee took the same decision. The notable feature of the meeting

[99] *Amrita Bazar Patrika*, 3 March 1920.

[100] This was particularly clear after the Khilafat Delegation to London found that it could make no headway with the British Government, and that public opinion in Britain was also arrayed against Turkey. (The delegation consisted of Mohamed Ali, Syed Husain, Syed Sulaiman Nadvi, and Abdul Kaseem.)

[101] *Mohammadi*, 16 January 1920. BENNR 1920.

[102] Bamford, *Histories*, p. 151.

[103] I owe this information to the late Syed Mohammad Tonki, who was an active campaigner during the Khilafat movement.

was the presence of ten thousand *ulama*.[104] Never before did
so many of them gather at one place, on one platform and for
a common cause. It was a striking demonstration of how
religion had roused the *ulama* from their slumber, and an
indication of their growing influence on the deliberations of
the Khilafat meetings.

In accordance with the resolution of the Bengal Khilafat
Conference on 28 February, a second Khilafat Day was observed on 19 March. Its effect was felt throughout the country.
In Madras city there was a fairly complete stoppage of business.[105] In Bombay Presidency, *hartal* was widely observed.
In Bombay city, there was a 'complete cessation' of business
which extended to the suburbs of Mahim, Dadar, and
Bandra.[106] In Poona, where the first Khilafat Day had
been ignored, shops remained closed from the early morning.[107]
In Sind, which had been the venue of several Khilafat meetings,
four honorary magistrates resigned in protest against the
anti-Islamic policies of the government.[108]

In Bengal the Khilafat Committee had been instrumental
in organising a systematic campaign since the meeting of the
Khilafat Conference on 28 February, and on the eve of the
hartal the province was full of leaflets, posters, and
circulars.[109] The effect of this was that Khilafat Day
was observed in most cities of Bengal. In Calcutta, shops
in the famous Hogg Market, which had remained open
even during the Swadeshi movement, looked 'airtight com-
partments, barred, padlocked and guarded.'[110] In Dacca,
Mymensingh, and Chittagong public meetings were held at
which resolutions passed by the Bengal Khilafat Conference
were unanimously adopted.

[104]This figure may well be an exaggerated one, but it is certainly
indicative of the impressive representation of the *ulama*. *Amrita Bazar
Patrika*, 15 March 1920.

[105]*Leader*, 21 March 1920.

[106]*Bombay Chronicle*, 20 March 1920.

[107]*Mahratta*, 21 March 1920.

[108]*Bombay Chronicle*, 20 March 1920.

[109]Report by an intelligence officer, 24 March 1920, Home Police.
513, UPSA.

[110]*Bombay Chronicle*, 21 March 1920, *Amrita Bazar Patrika*, 20 & 22
March 1920.

Hartal, fasting and prayer were some of the general features of Khilafat Day in the Punjab, while at most places public meetings were held and resolutions passed calling upon the British government to secure a settlement of the Turkish question in consonance with Muslim sentiments and ideals. Such meetings were reported from Amritsar, Lahore, Multan, Sialkot, and Peshawar.[111] In neighbouring Delhi, the notable feature of Khilafat Day was an impressive religious service at the Juma Masjid, and the suspension of all business. 'On the 19th', reported an intelligence officer, 'a very complete *hartal* was observed. Muslim League and other Muhammadan volunteers were posted in most of the bazaars and were insistent and almost aggressive in discouraging the collection of even the smallest crowd.'[112] In the UP, meetings were held in all the principal cities and prayers were offered for the *Khalifa*. In Allahabad a meeting was held in the *Idgah* which was attended, among a great many others, by Zahur Ahmad, Hyder Mehdi, Kamaluddin Jafri, Wilayat Husain, K.K. Malaviya, Jawaharlal Nehru, Purshotam Das Tandon.[113] Similar meetings were organised in Lucknow, Agra, Bahraich, Ballia, Hathras, Aligarh, Benaras, Fyzabad, and Firozabad;[114] and these provide some indication of how the Khilafat movement gradually spread from the big cities to the mofussil.

The publication of the Turkish peace terms on 14 May produced a blaze of resentment among every section of the Muslim community and gave a new dimension to the Khilafat agitation. Under the peace terms, Turkey was to be shorn of its Arab possessions—Syria, Palestine, Mesopotamia, and Hijaz, and other Turkish provinces in the Arab peninsula. The portion on the Asiatic and European shores of the Bosphorus was to be internationalised. The other half, extending from St. Stefano to Dalma Bagtche, was declared a port of international interest under a Commission 'on which Turkey was not even represented. In effect, the peace terms proposed to sever from Turkey provinces and districts predominantly inhabited by

[111]*Tribune*, 21 March 1920.
[112]Home Poll. Deposit, April 1920, 4, NAI.
[113]*Leader*, 21 March 1920.
[114]*Ibid.*

the Turks, and to impose suzerainty over the Turkish sovereign which, according to the Indian Muslims, would affect his status and prestige as the religious head of the community. Finally, the terms were designed to retain the protectorate of the sacred cities of Islam in non-Muslim hands.

Muslims regarded these terms as a blow to their religious feelings and sentiments. 'We Indian Moslems', declared the *Mohammadi*, 'vow in God's name never to accept these terms. Years will elapse and trials and ordeals in succession will confront us. But this resolve of ours will never change.'[115] *The Moslem Outlook* described the terms as 'a monument of hypocrisy and the blackest breach of faith', and added: 'Having won, through the sacrifices of their Moslem soldiers, their present position of dominance, the Allies, like the ungrateful monster of Shakespeare, Caliban, now turn round to the Mussalmans and say: "You have given us power and we know how to crush your most cherished religious sentiments".'[116] Even some of the Muslim landowners, who had generally kept aloof from the Khilafat movement, condemned the peace terms.[117]

Gandhi described the peace proposals as a 'staggering blow' to the Indian Muslims and declared non-cooperation as the 'only effective remedy . . . for healing the wounds inflicted on Mohammedan opinion.'[118] There was nothing new in this statement because, on 7 March 1920, Gandhi had already committed himself to non-cooperation as 'the only remedy left

[115]*Mohammadi*, 2 April 1920, BENNR 1920.

[116]*Moslem Outlook*, 20 May 1920. This weekly newspaper was published by the Islamic Information Bureau, London, which was run by Pickthal, Isphani and M.H. Kidwai.

[117]Nawab Ali Chaudhuri, for example, described them as 'outrageous' and 'unchivalrous', and lamented that 'the spoilation of the once glorious Ottoman Empire, the last resting place or repository of the remnant of all that was once acknowledged as Muslim power and civilization and the consequent destruction of the Khilafat which will inevitably lead in its train the downfall of Islam, so much disturbed the minds of the Indian Muslims that it threw in the background all other questions. The Muslims always accord the highest place to their religious sentiments which veritably form the apex of the pyramid of their lives'. Chaudhuri, *Views on Present Political Situation in India*, p. 1.

[118]Press Statement on Turkish Peace Terms, *CWG*, Vol. 17, pp. 426-27.

open to us'.[119] On 14 March, the Central Khilafat Committee endorsed non-cooperation. In early June, the Joint and Central Khilafat Conferences held in Allahabad reaffirmed the adoption of non-cooperation in four stages;[120] and appointed a committee with Gandhi as chairman, to give practical effect to that policy. The Conference further decided to extend the Khilafat volunteer organisation all over India in order to collect funds and prepare the masses for non-cooperation.[121] On 22 June, eighty-two Muslims submitted a memorial to the Viceroy, Reading, requesting him to impress upon the British government the vital necessity of revising the Turkish peace terms, and holding out the threat that, if their suggestions were not adopted, they would withdraw cooperation from the government with effect from 1 August 1920.[122] Gandhi sent a separate letter to the Viceroy, informing him that he was advising Muslims to adopt non-cooperation, because the peace terms violated ministerial pledges and disregarded Muslim sentiments. In justification of his decision, Gandhi wrote: 'I consider that as a staunch Hindu wishing to live on terms of the closest friendship with my Mussalman countrymen, I should be an unworthy son of India if I did not stand by them in their hour of trial.'[123]

By June 1920, Gandhi had gone a long way in his support of the Khilafat cause. From being a mere interested spectator in early 1919, he had assumed virtual dictatorship of the Khilafat campaign by the end of the year. How did Gandhi accomplish this? It was largely due to the skilful adjustment of his political strategy to the requirements of the situation and his rare ability to judge and understand the popular mood in the country. On 24 November 1919, for example, Gandhi opposed Hasrat Mohani's resolution on the boycott of British goods at the Khilafat Conference held in Delhi. But when the Bengal Khilafat Conference ignored his objections and declared in

[119]Letter to the Press, 7 March 1920, *CWG*, Vol. 17, p. 75.

[120]Gandhi's plan proposed several stages of non-cooperation. The first stage was the relinquishing of titles and honours, followed by the withdrawal of private servants and government employees (including the police and army), and the non-payment of taxes.

[121]Report from the Commissioner of Police, Bombay, Home Poll. B, 1920, 109, NAI.

[122]Home Poll. A, November 1920, 19-31, NAI.

[123]Gandhi to Viceroy, 22 June 1920, *CWG*, Vol. 17, p. 503.

favour of boycott on 28 February 1920, Gandhi, the astute
politician, decided not to press his objections. He realised that,
in view of the popular excitement which had been mounting
steadily since the observance of the first Khilafat Day on 17
October 1919, it was best to go along with the extremist Khilafat leaders, such as Hasrat Mohani, Abdul Bari, Azad Sobhani,
and the Ali Brothers, and retain their support. In fact, a
week after the Calcutta Khilafat Conference, Gandhi issued a
manifesto which was designed to achieve this objective.
Although he remained opposed to the boycott of British
goods,[124] Gandhi pressed the non-cooperation programme
more vigorously than he had ever done before. This was an
obvious attempt to keep up his alliance with the extremists
who, since the Muslim League session in December 1919, were
demanding action instead of words.

Gandhi had to encounter the further difficulty of persuading his own co-religionists to accept the non-cooperation programme. This was a hazardous job. Many Hindus were apprehensive that the Khilafat agitation would lead to violence—
a fea r which was strengthened by the fiery speeches
of some ulama and the Ali Brothers. 'The Khilafat movement',
wrote Srinivasa Sastri, 'would lead to disaster. I picture the
Mohammedans breaking out here and there in futile demonstrations'.[125] Furthermore, Gandhi's decision to launch
non-cooperation placed many Hindu politicians in a serious
predicament, for although they had paid lip-service to
the Khilafat rhetoric, they were totally unprepared for a
situation in which they would be asked to resign honours
and jobs. To them, non-cooperation was too heavy a price
to pay fo r the sake of Hindu-Muslim unity. 'If Gandhi's
motion of non-cooperation is adopted by Congress', the Nayak
observed, 'it will gradually become a part and parcel of the
Muslim League and the Khilafat Party. . . . The Congress will,
through Gandhi, pass into the hands of the Muslim League

---

[124]On 3 March, he said at the Khilafat meeting held in Bombay that
the Calcutta resolution on boycott 'does not command my sympathy
at all. We should keep away from the idea of boycott'. CWG, Vol. 17,
p. 68.

[125]To Sivaswami Aiyer, 13 April 1920, quoted in K. Dwarkadas,
India's Fight For Freedom (Bombay, 1966), p. 146.

and the Khilafat Muslims, and its predominant Hindu influence will be lost'.[126]

From May 1920, when Gandhi first explained his noncooperation programme to the All-India Congress Committee, till December 1920, there were serious differences and tensions between the champions of non-cooperation and their critics. The events of this period need to be examined, for they reveal Gandhi's impressive success in mobilising support for his programme, which eventually led to his complete domination of the Khilafat and Non-cooperation movements. But first let us understand why, in the first place, a section of Hindu politicians supported the Khilafat agitation at all.

Until June 1920, several Hindu politicians appeared alongside the Khilafat leaders at public meetings, demonstrations, and deputations. In Delhi, Swami Shraddhanand, Motilal Nehru, C.R. Das, B.S. Moonje, Kasturi Ranga Iyengar and Girdhari Lal were the vice-presidents of the Anti-Peace Celebration Publicity Board formed in November 1919.[127] In UP, especially in Allahabad, K.K. Malaviya, P.D. Tandon, Sundar Lal, Mohanlal Nehru, Motilal and his son, Jawaharlal, participated in Khilafat activities. In Bombay, Tilak and his lieutenants, Kelkar and Khaparde, assured Muslims of their support and, in March 1920, endorsed the decisions of the Bengal Khilafat Conference including the resolution on the boycott of British goods.[128] In Bengal, C.R. Das, who constantly stressed the unity of Hindus and Muslims, boycotted the Peace Celebrations.[129] Some Bengali newspapers, too, joined the campaign enthusiastically.[130]

These demonstrations of Hindu support were not at all surprising. The Hindu Congressmen were keen to maintain their alliance with Muslims, cemented at Lucknow in December 1916 and subsequently strengthened during the Home Rule movement and the Rowlatt Satyagraha. In parti-

[126]*Nayak*, 8 September 1920, BENNR 1920.

[127]*Amrita Bazar Patrika*, 1 December 1919.

[128]*Mahratta*, 14 March 1920; S.V. Bapat (ed.), *Reminiscences of Lokmanya Tilak* (Poona, n.d.), Vol. 3, p. 140.

[129]*Amrita Bazar Patrika*, 4 December 1919.

[130]For example, *Dainik Bharat Mitra*, 17 October 1919; *Viswamitra*, 17 October 1919, BENNR 1919.

cular, the radical wing in the Congress, which had rejected the Montagu-Chelmsford Reforms and was in the forefront of the anti-imperialist struggle, had nothing to lose by plunging into the Khilafat movement. On the contrary, it had the opportunity of securing new allies whose potential value, as the Rowlatt Satyagraha demonstrated, was considerable for promoting a mass movement.[131]

It was dangerous, however, to exploit religious sentiments for political purposes and to resuscitate the latent religious passions of the Muslims. This became evident by the end of 1919 when the radical extension of the Khilafat agitation, characterised by *hartals* and public demonstrations, gave rise to the fear of mob violence.[132] Likewise, the violent and fanatical outbursts of some Khilafat leaders caused grave concern to the Hindus, including Gandhi.[133] The *Tribune* warned the Khilafatists that they had 'everything to gain by confining their protests and their representation within strictly constitutional limits, and a very great deal to lose by deviating from their course.'[134] But Hasrat Mohani, M.H. Kidwai, and the *ulama* paid no heed to such warnings. They pressed their demands with or without the cooperation of Hindu politicians and, in early March 1920, it appeared that even Gandhi was unable to prevent them from taking decisions which were likely to alienate the Hindus.

[131]Lajpat Rai declared that the Khilafat issue provided a unique opportunity to the Congress 'to convince our Muslim brothers that we were and are sincere in our desire for Muslim friendship'. He added: 'The Hindu-Muslim unity betokens the dawn of a new day in the history of India and it will be extremely foolish and shortsighted to throw this chance which comes once perhaps in a century on the bidding of those who worship at the shrine of Dyerism.' P.D. Saggi (ed.), *Life and Work of Lal, Bal and Pal* (Delhi, 1962), p. 44.

[132]*Nayak*, 8 March 1920, BENNR 1920. The *New India* wrote the following on the eve of the first Khilafat Day: 'Madras does not want Hartal, it dare not have Hartals . . . , and Mahatma Gandhi's name must not be used to ask Madras to do that which it is unwise for it to do, and which might disturb rather than cement the good relations hitherto subsisting between the two communities.' *New India*, 15 October 1919.

[133]See, for example, Gandhi to Razima, 27 March 1920, *CWG*, Vol. 17, p. 293.

[134]*Tribune*, 23 March 1920.

By that stage many Hindu Congressmen realised that they had gone a little too far in their support of the Khilafat cause; but it was not too late to retrace their steps. They found the opportunity to voice their feelings at the Central Khilafat Committee meeting held in Allahabad on 1-3 June 1920. The meeting was attended by Motilal Nehru, Jawaharlal Nehru, Sapru, Annie Besant, Malaviya, Lajpat Rai, Satyamurti, B.C. Pal, H.N. Kunzru, Chintamani and Rajagopalachari, among others. C.R. Das, Tilak and his Maharashtrian followers were conspicuous by their absence. Gandhi explained the four stages of non-cooperation on the second day of the meeting, but Sapru, Besant, and Jamnadas Dwarkadas remained unconvinced. Malaviya, Lajpat Rai and Motilal were sceptical of the immediate adoption of non-cooperation. The only Hindu politicians who stood by Gandhi were Pal and Satyamurti, though a few months later even they changed their minds.[135]

Gandhi, however, brushed aside the opposition of his Congress colleagues and hastily appointed a sub-committee to give practical effect to non-cooperation. It is noteworthy that, besides Gandhi, there was not a single Hindu on the committee.[136] Even the resolution on non-cooperation adopted at the meeting was voted by Muslims.[137] That is why the Hindus who attended the conference did not find themselves committed to non-cooperation.[138] On 16 June, Motilal suggested to his son that it was time they selected for themselves constituencies for the UP Council to which elections were due later in the year.[139] By the end of July, there was a strong demand to postpone the carrying out of non-cooperation

---

[135]See Home Poll. B, 1920, 109, NAI.

[136]The sub-committee consisted of Gandhi, Azad, Mohamed Ali, Shaukat Ali, Hasrat Mohani, Saifuddin Kitchlew, and Haji Ahmad Siddiq Khatri.

[137]*Bombay Chronicle*, 7 June 1920.

[138]Jamnadas Dwarkadas, for example, strongly criticised Gandhi. 'I hope', he observed, 'I am not caricaturing Mr. Gandhi's programme, but it strikes me as an unnecessarily circuitous method of dislocating the functions of the State and paralysing Government, to the detriment of public safety and peace.' J. Dwarkadas, 'Non-Cooperation: A Cry for Halt', *Ibid*.

[139]Motilal to Jawaharlal, 16 June 1920, *A Bunch of Old Letters*, p. 17.

until the representative bodies in the country had announced
their views.[140]

This mood augured ill for the success of non-cooperation and posed a threat to Gandhi's alliance with
the Khilafatists. So he took the only possible course open
to him which was to formally launch the non-cooperation
movement a month before the Special Congress session was to
meet at Calcutta. This was an extraordinary step. It was
calculated to take the sting out of the campaign against non-
cooperation, and to give himself and his supporters enough
time to mobilise support before the Calcutta Congress where
he anticipated serious opposition.[141] Gandhi's decision was
also aimed at allaying the doubts of those Khilafat leaders who
felt uneasy over the Congress attitude towards non-cooperation.[142]

August to December 1920

By December 1920, Gandhi had outmanoeuvred his opponents
with the help of his allies in the provinces, and almost all the
leading politicians were marshalled on the side of non-cooperation. In September 1920, he presented his plan which
called for a surrender of titles and honorary offices;
refusal to attend levees and durbars; withdrawal from
council elections; withdrawal of children from government
schools and colleges; boycott of British courts by lawyers and
litigants; refusal to serve in Mesopotamia; and boycott of
foreign goods. After a prolonged debate this plan was

[140]*Bombay Chronicle*, 31 July 1920.

[141]Gandhi defended his decision of not consulting his colleagues in
Congress before launching the non-cooperation movement in the
following words: 'In my humble opinion it is no Congressman's duty to
consult the Congress before taking an action in a matter in which he
has no doubts . . .' *Young India*, 4 August 1920, *CWG*, Vol. 18, p. 112.

[142]The Muslim uneasiness followed from the Hindu-Muslim
Conference on 22 March 1920 held in Delhi and the Central Khilafat
Committee on 2 June, where Malaviya, Lajpat Rai and Sapru expressed
their opposition to non-cooperation. Prior to the CKC meeting, the
AICC meeting at Benaras had decided to defer their decision to adopt
non-cooperation to a special session of the Congress, which was to be
held in the middle of September.

approved by a vote of 148 to 133 in the Subjects Committee, and by 1,826 to 804 at the open session.[143] At the Nagpur Congress in December where there were attempts to rescind the policy of non-cooperation, Gandhi once more emerged victorious. His resolution was ratified with only two dissentient voices. This was undoubtedly a great personal triumph for the Mahatma and a vindication of his political methods and strategy. The Chief Commissioner of the Central Provinces reported:

> The outstanding feature of the Congress has been the personal domination of Gandhi over all political leaders and followers alike. He has carried through the policy that he had decided for this Congress without any material modification. . . . The moderates of Nagpur were not heard; the extremist opponents under Khaparde and Moonje were brushed aside; Pandit Madan Mohan Malaviya's efforts were negatory; Jinnah carried no influence; Lajpat Rai wobbled and then became silent.[144]

Historians have explained how Gandhi was able to muster support, and how he was able to count on the cooperation of certain aggrieved social and economic groups who displayed their resentment against government policies through non-cooperation.[145] They have also explained the reasons for the dramatic transformation of some veteran Congress leaders who went to Calcutta and Nagpur to offer stout resistance to non-cooperation, but came away as ardent champions of Gandhi's ideas. At the Calcutta Congress, Lajpat Rai, who had bitterly opposed non-cooperation at the All-India Congress Committee meeting in May, came under Gandhi's spell. Similarly, Motilal who was not convinced that non-cooperation was either necessary or practicable, executed a *volte face*.[146] At the Calcutta

[143]*Bombay Chronicle*, 11 September 1920.

[144]F. Sly to Chelmsford, 1 January 1921, Chelmsford Papers (26).

[145]For example, C.J. Baker, 'Non-Cooperation in South India', C.J. Baker and D.A. Washbrook, *South India: Political Institutions and Political Change, 1880-1940* (Macmillan, 1975), and Brown, *Gandhi*, Chapter 8.

[146]See his correspondence with Jawaharlal on 16 June and 5 July 1920, in *A Bunch of Old Letters*, pp. 17-18.

Congress, he was the front-rank Congress leader who supported Gandhi. Immediately after the Congress session he
resigned his membership of the UP Council and announced
that he would not seek election to the reformed legislature.
At Nagpur, C.R. Das made the dramatic announcement that
he would move the main resolution in support of non-cooperation. Das changed his attitude because the boycott of
the legislatures, to which he was chiefly opposed, was no
longer a live issue as the elections had already taken place.[147]

Gandhi's triumph at Calcutta and Nagpur was, however,
largely due to the overwhelming support of the Muslims
who, with few exceptions, had no reservations in accepting
the non-cooperation programme in its entirety.[148] In fact,
as soon as the Central Khilafat Committee adopted non-cooperation in early June, the Khilafat leaders undertook a
countrywide tour to enlist the support of their co-religionists. In the early months of 1921, the Ali Brothers, Abdul
Bari, M.A. Ansari, and Khaliquzzaman visited Madras to
stimulate support for non-cooperation. The presence of
Mohamed Ali at the Erode session of the *Majlis-ul-ulama* in
March 1921 gave a tremendous boost to the Khilafat movement, as did their presence in April, at various meetings in
Madras which attracted huge crowds of Hindus and Muslim.[149]
The *ulama* issued *fatawa* calling for *jihad* against the British and
migration (*Hijrat*) to the *dar al-Islam* (abode of peace) from
the *dar al-harb* (abode of war). Azad issued a *fatwa*[150] in which
he declared that 'from the point of the *Sharia*, the Muslims
of India have no choice but to migrate from India. All

---

[147]S.C. Bose, *The Indian Struggle 1920-42* (London, 1964), p. 44.

[148]It is noteworthy that the *Mussalman*, which represented a cross-
section of the *ulama* and the Western-educated elite, issued a stern
warning to the Muslim League and the Congress that 'no milk and water
non-cooperation will do. The policy of adopting non-cooperation by
being returned to the Legislative Councils and practising it within the
Councils must be abandoned. This is a sort of self-deception, and no
sincere patriot can be a party to such a policy'. *Mussalman*, 3
September 1920.

[149]For the activities of Mohamed Ali from 12 October 1920 to 27
October 1920, see Home Poll. 1922, 112, NAI, and *Hindu*, 4 April 1921.

[150]A.K. Azad, 'Hijrat Ka Fatwa', quoted in G.R. Mehr, *Tabarukat-
i-Azad* (Lahore, 1959), pp. 203-206.

Muslims who would like to fulfil Islamic obligations must quit India. The *Sharia* gives us no alternative course, except migration'. On 29 October, Maulana Mahmudul Hasan called for a total boycott of the educational institutions run by the government which, he said, was the 'greatest enemy of Islam and Moslems of India'.[151] In November, Abdul Bari collected five hundred signatures for a *fatwa* in favour of non-cooperation.[152] He had earlier declared his complete support to Gandhi and his non-cooperation programme. 'I have accepted his support in getting our aims fulfilled and for that purpose I think it is necessary to follow his advice . . . I know that the strength of Islam lies in association with him', he said.[153] In the Punjab, Pir Mohammad Husain, Sajjada Nashin of Almohar in Sialkot district, and the *Pir* of Sial Sharif in Hoshiarpur issued *fatawa* in favour of non-cooperation.[154]

In view of the activities which preceded the Calcutta and Nagpur Congress sessions, it was not surprising that Muslims attended the Congress in great strength. They had all along supported non-cooperation with the government in some form or the other, and they travelled to Calcutta and Nagpur to give their formal seal of approval. According to some estimates over two thousand Muslim delegates attended the Calcutta Congress[155] and their representation was so strong that they 'swamped the rest'.[156] Similarly, the Nagpur Congress was

[151]Address delivered at the Muslim National University, 29 October 1920; PP : 54, IOL; Maulvi Bashir Ahmad, *Tark-i-Mavalat* (Deoband, 1920), PP: 53, IOL.

[152]Some of the signatories were Azad, Kifayatullah, Azad Sobhani, Abdul Bari, Maulvi Sanaullah, and Mufti Azizur Rahman of Deoband. *Mutafiqa Fatwa-e-Ulama-i-Hind* (Bombay, 1920).

[153]Speech delivered on 15 October 1920 at the *Jamiat-ul-Ulama* meeting held in Lucknow, Abdul Bari Papers. Home Poll. Deposit, 1921, 4, NAI.

[154]Home Poll. 1922, 459, NAI.

[155]*Bombay Chronicle*, 10 September 1920, *Amrita Bazar Patrika*, 10 September 1920. Of the 217 Bombay delegates who voted for Gandhi's resolution on 9 September, 43 were Muslims. From Madras, of the 161 delegates who voted for non-cooperation, 125 were Muslims. *Bombay Chronicle*, 9 & 10 September 1920, *Hindu*, 16 September 1920.

[156]Willingdon to Montagu, 15 September 1920, Montagu Papers (20).

attended by a total of 4,582 delegates of whom 72 per cent were Muslims.[157]

The non-cooperation resolution had the overwhelming support of Muslims. Jinnah and Fazlul Haq created a mild stir when they expressed their disagreement, but their protests were a cry in the wilderness.[158]

IV

NON-COOPERATION IN PRACTICE

The impact of the Non-cooperation movement on Muslims can be tested by an analysis of its development from August 1920 until March 1922, when Gandhi called off civil disobedience after the outbreak of violence at Chauri Chaura in Gorakhpur district. During this period of intensive political activity, certain aspects of the non-cooperation programme had a fair measure of success in most areas—their impact was felt even amongst the masses which gives us some idea of the depth of the movement. In the North-West Frontier Province, the *ulama* established *Shariat* tribunals in a few places and a national school at Utmanzai.[159] In Sind, the *pirs* were in the forefront of the agitation. Here the support and sympathy for non-cooperation was not, as an intelligence officer noted, 'confined to those who joined the ranks of agitators but was growing in intensity among all classes of educated Muhammadans.'[160] In Bengal, popular feeling among Muslims was reported to be against the government, while the *ulama* 'who had formerly held aloof from politics have recently been drawn into the boycott movement'.[161] But perhaps the most striking response to non-

[157]G. Krishna, 'The Development of the Indian National Congress as a Mass Organisation', *JAS*, May 1966, Vol. 25, p. 418.

[158]Jinnah resigned from Congress in protest against the 'pseudo-religious approach to politics'. Fazlul Haq, on the other hand, came round to non-cooperation under pressure from Azad and Mohamed Ali. But it was not long before he defected and campaigned actively against non-cooperation.

[159]Bamford, *Histories*, p. 166.

[160]WR (Sind), 12 November, 26 November 1921, Curry Papers.

[161]FR (Bengal), November 1921, Home Poll. Deposit, December 1921, 18, NAI.

cooperation was in the form of *hijrat*, a movement stimulated by a *fatwa* issued by Azad in the middle of 1920.[162] The result was that thousands of Muslims, as many as twenty thousand in the month of August alone, migrated to Afghanistan.[163] Many of them sold their land and property to make the hazardous journey in the direction of the Khyber Pass.[164] But when the *muhajirins* reached Kabul, the Afghan authorities were alarmed by such an enormous influx and were compelled to turn them back. In consequence, the unfortunate emigrants returned to India penniless.[165]

Resignation from government service was another aspect of non-cooperation. By November 1921, the number of Muslim policemen who had resigned was thirty-one, forty and seventeen in the UP, Bengal and Bombay, respectively.[166] By mid-November 1920, out of the forty-six Indians who had given up their Honorary Magistracy, twenty-two were Muslims.[167] Several leading Muslims renounced their titles. These included Ajmal Khan who returned the Kaiser-i-Hind Medal of the First Class,[168] Maulana Badruddin of Phulwari, and Syed Ali Nabi who gave up his title of Khan Bahadur.[169]

The boycott of law courts was also carried out effectively.[170] Some of the leading Muslims who did so were

[162]For a detailed study of the *hijrat* movement, see Qureshi, '*Pan-Islamism and Nationalism*', Chapter 3.

[163]Chelmsford to Montagu, 11 August 1920, Chelmsford Papers (6); Chief Commissioner, NWFP, to Viceroy, 3 August 1920, *Ibid.*, (25).

[164]A lady correspondent reported her miseries caused by the departure of her husband, and sought financial assistance from Abdul Bari. Urdu Files, Abdul Bari Papers. Many years later, Husain Ahmad Madni compared the sufferings of the *muhajirs* with the hardships undergone by the Muslim refugees in 1947. To M. Siddique, n.d. in N. Islahi (ed.), *Maktubat-i-Shaikhul Hind* (Deoband, 1954), Vol. 2, pp. 262-63.

[165]For a vivid account of the hardships suffered by the *muhajirins*, see Mohammad Ghulam Husain, *Dastan-i-Hijrat* (Amritsar, 1921).

[166]Brown, *Gandhi*, p. 309.

[167]AICC Papers (5), 1920.

[168]Home Poll. Deposit, April 1921, 72, NAI.

[169]*Mussalman*, 6 August 1920.

[170]In Bengal, for example, the following Muslim lawyers suspended practice: Mohammad Yasin, Abdul Samad, Syed Abdul Majid, Syed Mohammad Mobin, Mohammad Shamsuddin, Chaudhuri Mohammad Isa and Maulvi Mohammad Husain. *Bombay Chronicle*, 14, 22 September 1920.

Mazharul Haque and Maulvi Mohammad Shafi from Bihar;[171]
Mohammad Husain, Mohammad Ismail Khan, Kamaluddin
Jafri, Moazzam Ali, Maulvi Zahuruddin, Khaliquzzaman,
T.A.K. Sherwani, A.M. Khwaja, Mohammad Azim and Raza
Mohammad from the UP;[172] Saifuddin Kitchlew and Barkat
Ali from the Punjab; and Asaf Ali from Delhi. In November
1920, twenty-two out of the forty-four lawyers who gave
up their legal practice were Muslims.[173]

The legislative council elections, which took place on
the eve of the Nagpur Congress, were also boycotted effectively
in the Muslim constituencies, particularly in the urban areas,
and more especially in the Punjab, UP, Bengal and Bombay.
In the UP, only 7 per cent votes were polled in the Muslim
urban constituencies as compared to 14 per cent in the non-
Muslim urban constituencies, and in many areas groups of
ulama and students prevented voters from going to the
polling booths. In the eastern and northern parts of Bengal,
there was a dearth of candidates and little polling was
reported from most areas. In Rajshahi and Dinajpur the
bulk of educated men, including pleaders, refrained from
voting. Almost all Muslims from Rangpur town abstained,
and so did large numbers of Muslims in Gaibandha subdivision of Rangpur district. In Bakarganj, very few
Muslims voted and in Mania district, not a single voter, Hindu
or Muslim, appeared.[174] Similarly, in Madras only six of the
provincial council seats were contested by Muslims, and only
a small number of enfranchised Muslims voted—6.6 per cent of
those eligible.[175]

Among those who resigned their seats from the legislative
councils or withdrew their candidature from various Muslim
constituencies were: Nur Mohammad, Kader Baksh, Kazi
Azimuddin, Sheriff Deoji Kanji, Mohammad Arif Mulla and

[171]Syed Mahmud, 'Looking Back' in *1921 Movement*: *Reminiscences*
(Delhi, 1971), pp. 143-43.
[172]AICC Papers (5), 1920.
[173]*Ibid.*
[174]R.K. Ray, 'Masses in Politics: The Non-Cooperation Movement
in Bengal, 1920-22', *IESHR*, December 1974, Vol. II, No. 4, p. 362.
[175]Mcpherson, 'The Political Development of the Urdu and
Tamil-speaking Muslims', p. 127.
[176]AICC Papers (5), 1920.

Salembhoy Karamji from Bombay; M.A. Masim, Maulvi
Wahid Husain, Mandud Rahman, Mazharul Haque, Mahbubul
Haque, Maulvi Nadir Ali, Mazharul Anwar, Hasan Suhra-
wardy, Abdul Karim, Fazlul Haq, Syed Sultan Ali, Azizul
Haque, Maulvi Shamsuddin, Maulvi Tamizuddin Ahmad,
Maulvi Mohammad Daud, Maulvi Saidullah, Maulvi Ikramul
Haque, Nuruddin Ahmad, Fazlur Rahman Adil, Abdur
Rashid Khan, Abdul Halim, Abdul Jabbar and Maulvi Abdul
Halim from Bihar and Bengal; and Kamaluddin Jafri, Sheikh
Zahur Ahmad, Hafiz Alam, Zahuruddin, Syed Zahur Ahmad,
Syed Hyder Mehdi and Aziz Ahmad Khan from the UP. These
names give a clue to the varied background of at least some
non-cooperators. They included rich merchants frcm Bombay,
petty landowners like Abdul Jabbar from Bengal and successful
lawyers like Kamaluddin Jafri and Syed Zahur Ahmad from
Allahabad. Most non-cooperators were Sunnis but there were
at least three well known Shias—Syed Sultan Ali, Kamaluddin
Jafri, and Syed Hyder Mehdi. They shared the view that non-
cooperation was the only way to prevent the Holy Places of
Islam from passing into non-Muslim hands.

Statistics for the boycott of schools and colleges by the
Muslims are not available in detail but reports from at least
three major educational centres in the UP indicate an impressive response to non-cooperation.[177] These were the *Nadwat-
al-ulama*, Lucknow; the *Dar al-Musanifin*, Azamgarh; and the
Muslim University, Aligarh.

The *Nadwa* had come under suspicion for its pan-Islamic
leanings during the Graeco-Turkish war, and after the outbreak of the Balkan wars there was a revival of pan-Islamic
activity in the institution.[178] This was intensified during the

[177]There were reports of strikes in the Calcutta Madrasa and
Government College, Lahore. At Amritsar, the *Anjuman-i-Islam* refused
the government grant for the maintenance of the institution. The
general situation in the educational centres was summarised by H. Sharp,
Secretary to the Government of India. On 19 February, he wrote:
'Within the last few weeks, strikes of students have occurred upon a
considerable scale in Bengal and it appears that in other provinces,
where the trouble seemed to have been scotched, it has now attained a
new lease of life.' Home Poll. B, 1921, 259, NAI.

[178]J.P. Hewitt to Dunlop Smith, 27 January 1908, and C.F. Della
Fosse to O'Donnell, 8 February 1914, GAD, 1908, 79, UPSA.

Khilafat and Non-cooperation movements. In November 1920, the students urged the trustees to refuse the government grant which was first sanctioned by J.P. Hewitt, Lieutenant-Governor of UP from 1907 to 1912.[179] From December 1920 to March 1921, they toured Bihar and the UP, where they raised money for the Khilafat Fund and formed Volunteer Corps in towns to intensify the non-cooperation campaign.

The *Dar al-Musanifin* was founded by Shibli in 1913 to promote the publication and translation of historical, religious, and scientific works. But like many other Muslim institutions, the *Dar al-Musanifin* was also used to foster pan-Islamism. This was mainly due to Syed Sulaiman Nadwi, one of Shibli's pupils at *Nadwa*. In April 1920 he spoke at Kanpur urging Muslims to give up their lives for the protection of the Holy Places. In 1920, he joined the Khilafat delegation to London, and from there he wrote to Abdul Bari that, if Muslims wanted to liberate Kaaba, they would have to liberate India first: 'The political emancipation of India', he wrote, 'was a religious duty.'[180]

Another leading non-cooperator at the *Dar al-Musanifin* was Masud Ali Nadwi, whose activities turned the institution into 'an extremist political institution', and a centre for the political activities of Azamgarh district.[181] His influence extended to many small towns in the region, such as Man, Sarai Mir, and Pharuja. Man was predominantly inhabited by Muslim *julahas* (weavers) who, under the leadership of Abdul Aziz, a barber, Maulvi Mohammad Sabir, the *imam* of the local mosque, Maulvi Abdullah, and Maulvi Zamir, worked zealously to make the non-cooperation movement successful. They pressed the honorary magistrates in the area to resign and compelled the local Islamia college to renounce its government aid. In Sarai Mir, on the other hand, all Khilafat activities were centred around the Arabic school, where the managers, the staff and the students worked enthusiastically in the

[179]*Hindu*, 4 November 1920.
[180]Gracey to Lambert, 8 January 1920, GAD, 1921, 1074, UPSA.
[181]*Ibid.*

neighbouring villages to explain the significance of the *fatawa* issued by Abdul Bari and Abul Kalam Azad.[182]

Among all the educational centres in the country, the non-cooperation movement evoked the most impressive response from the M.A.O. College, Aligarh, which later developed into the Aligarh Muslim University. Syed Ahmad Khan and his supporters wanted the College to be a vehicle for the diffusion of knowledge, while their British patrons were keen to implant 'in the minds of our students a conviction of the inestimable benefits India has derived from the British rule, and to foster in their hearts a sentiment of loyal devotion to the British Crown'.[183] This mission was carried out by Syed Ahmad's successors. However, during the first decade of the twentieth century the pro-government stance of the College came under severe attack from several quarters. This was in part due to the struggle for power between the Muslim trustees of the College and the European staff,[184] and in part because of the Hindi-Urdu controversy generated by MacDonnell's Nagri resolution of 18 April 1900. By 1907, Aligarh had become one of the most important nerve centres of agitational politics in the UP. This development was observed by William S. Marris, the district commissioner, who wrote in 1907:

How far the Aligarh movement has taken on a political colour is plain to any onlooker. The prominence of Aftab Ahmad Khan among the trustees, and of demagogues like Muhammad Ali and Shaukat Ali; the inception of the university movement as a counterblast to the Hindu University scheme; the enlisting of all national leaders like the Aga Khan; its association with the All-India Muslim League and All-India Muslim Educational Conference— these are all symptoms of one policy. Aligarh is destined

[182]Note by R.W. Bigg Wither, 7 December 1920, *Ibid.*
[183]Beck to Syed Ahmad Khan, 19 March 1896, Syed Ahmad Khan Papers, AMUA.
[184]For details, see Irene A. Gilbert, 'Autonomy and Consensus under the Raj: Presidency (Calcutta); Muir (Allahabad); M.A.O. (Aligarh)', S.H. Rudolph and L.I. Rudolph (eds.), *Education and Politics in India* (Delhi, 1972).

to be the focus of all Muhammadan intelligence and activity in India. Begun as a defensive move, it is already acquiring an offensive character . . . It has already lost its reliance on Englishmen and its trust in English methods and ideals. The danger I foresee is that if it is indulged and uncontrolled it will develop rapidly on decidedly anti-English lines.[185]

The prophecy of William Marris came true during the Turko-Italian war, the Muslim University movement, and the Kanpur mosque incident, when the College, under the leadership of some of its products like the Ali Brothers, Hasrat Mohani, Zafar Ali Khan and Raja Ghulam Husain, became the focus of agitational politics. Aligarh was gripped by pan-Islamic fervour.[186] On 11 January 1920, students raised Rs 6,000 for the Turkish Relief Fund, and many of them went out for propaganda purposes.[187] After the Calcutta Congress in September, Gandhi, the Ali Brothers, and Swami Satya Deva, a *kisan* leader, descended on the College campus to enlist support for non-cooperation.[188] But the real crisis came in September 1920 when the Ali Brothers pressed the trustees of the College to give up the government grant-in-aid and to reject the charter of the Muslim University.[189] This was the beginning of serious trouble. The College was closed, and the UP government proceeded to suppress the agitators.

The trustees met in mid-October to consider the Ali Brothers demand and decided, by an overwhelming majority, not to relinquish government grant or to refuse the Muslim

[185]Quoted in I.A. Gilbert, 'Autonomy and Cons nsus', pp. 198-99.

[186]See, for example, M. Ashraf, 'Aligarh Ki Siyasi Zindagi', *Aligarh Magazine*, 1953-55; Ziauddin to Honorary Secretary, M.A.O. College, 21 October 1919, Papers Relating to the Non-cooperation Movement (12), AMUA. The list of book issued from the College Library was indicative of the interest in Turkish affairs. The largest number of books issued between January 1919 to December 1920 related to Turkey. Mohammad Abdullah to Ziauddin, 29 January 1921, (SIX-14), *Ibid.*

[187]Mushtaq Husain to Principal, 17 January 1920 (62-B), *Ibid.*

[188]For speeches delivered by Satya Deva, see UP Government, Police. 1921, 104, UPSA.

[189]Ziauddin to Butler, 11 September 1920, UP Government, Education, 1921, 40, UPSA.

University Charter and also expressed their determination
'to run the institution on old established lines'.[190] Failing in
their first move, the Ali Brothers then tried to persuade
students to leave the College. Over seven hundred students
responded to their appeal.[191] These included Mohammad Ashraf,
a graduate student, who later became one of the leading
members of the Communist Party;[192] Abdul Hamid Khan,
son of a judge in Dera Ismail Khan;[193] Nurul Hasan of
Azamgarh who was 'so impressed by the speeches of Azad and
Azad Sobhani that I left College as a non-cooperator on the
27th October';[194] and Mohammad Abid Husain, an under-
graduate student who, on 24 October wrote to Ziauddin, the
principal of the College:

> Respectfully I beg to inform you that I have got my doubts
> removed within the last four or five days, and I am now a
> strong supporter of non-cooperation. . . . I can, and will
> read in your College only in case it is nationalised. Other-
> wise, I am ready to face the doom awaiting my non-
> cooperating brothers.[195]

The College authorities expelled the non-cooperators. But
when this failed to check the growing spirit of non-cooperation,
they decided to close down the College.[196] The UP government
went a step further to stem the tide of non-cooperation; it
suspended the scholarships of the non-cooperating students, and

[190]Those who voted in favour of rejecting the government grant
numbered eleven and consisted of Mohamed Ali, Ajmal Khan, A.M.
Khwaja, Ansari, Amir Mustafa Khan, Agha Safdar of Sialkot, Ismail
Khan, Syed Nasir Husain, T.A.K. Sherwani, Syed Mohammad Khan and
Kasim Husain of the Hyderabad State Service. Their opponents, on the
other hand, numbered forty-eight. Foreign and Political Dept., March
1921, 18-27, IOL.

[191]S.M. Abdullah, *Mushahidat wa Ta'asurat* (Aligarh, 1969), p. 295.

[192]For his activities, see UP Government, Police. 1920, 57, UPSA.

[193]A.H. Khan to Ziauddin, n.d., AMUA. This file is entitled 'Non-
Cooperation Acknowledgement Letters, 1920-21'.

[194]Nurul Hasan to Ziauddin, n.d., *Ibid.*

[195]M. Abid Husain to Ziauddin, 24 October 1920, *Ibid.*

[196]Proceedings of the Syndicate Meeting, 10 October 1920 (I-1), *Ibid.*
For a detailed account of the Non-cooperation movement at Aligarh,
see M.A. Zuberi, *Zia-i-Hayat* (Karachi, n.d.), pp. 68-76.

dismissed many teachers in the neighbouring areas who were allegedly responsible for stirring trouble on the campus.[197] Munshi Aziz Ahmad Zuberi, assistant master in the Government High School, Etah, was dismissed.[198] Similarly, Bhu Deo Sharma, a teacher in the Anglo-Vernacular High School, Anupshahar, was considered as 'an undesirable person for employment in recognised schools'.[199] The government also sought the help of several Muslim landowners and the ruling chiefs to combat non-cooperation at Aligarh.[200]

By the end of 1920, the College authorities in cooperation with the UP government had cut off all the tall poppies at Aligarh, and the non-cooperation movement lost its vigour after the College was closed. 'The repressive measure of the government', lamented a student, 'has struck terror into our hearts. If only God had given us enough strength to fight against this satanic government and its stooges in the University.'[201]

After the closure of the College on 26 October 1920, many students sought admission elsewhere, while others dissociated themselves from the agitation under parental pressures, as the following letter indicates:

My father has forced me to join your College once again, and I have reluctantly bowed to the parental authority. It is a mighty fall indeed. The whole enthusiasm ends in thin air. But you cannot realise under what great mental torture I am labouring today.[202]

The most determined, however, seceded from Aligarh and founded the Jamia Millia with the backing of Gandhi,[203] and

[197]Tafsir Ahmad to Ziauddin, 11 November 1920 (XX-37-d), AMUA.
[198]E.H. Richardson to the Inspector of Schools, 9 October 1920, Ibid.
[199]18 November 1920, Ibid.
[200]H. Sharp to Butler, 25 October 1920, Foreign and Political Department, March 1921, 18-27, IOL.
[201]Nuruddin to Naim Hasan, 3 February 1921 (XXX-38-E), AMUA.
[202]M. Ibrahim Khan to Mirza (a friend), 15 November 1920 (XX-37-b), Ibid.
[203]Gandhi campaigned actively for the Jamia Millia. On 24 October 1920, he urged the trustees of the Aligarh College to decline any further grant from the government, which was followed by an appeal to the parents to withdraw their sons from the College. On 11 October, he

with Mohamed Ali as its first Vice-Chancellor (*Sheikhul Jamia*).[204] Over the years, the Jamia Millia developed into a famous college and smybolised the best traditions of Indian nationalism. The Aligarh College, on the other hand, which witnessed considerable nationalist activity from 1916 to 1922, became one of the centres of the Muslim separatist movement.

visited Aligarh and spoke to the students on non-cooperation. In November, he returned to the city to participate in the committee for framing a constitution for the National Muslim University. The meeting was held on 22 November. For the role of Gandhi, see *CWG*, Vol. 18, pp, 221-22, 368-70; Home Poll. A, December 1920, 210-16, NAI.

[204] Abdullah Ghazi, 'Aligarh ki Tehrik aur Jamia Millia Islamia', *Aligarh Magazine*, 1953-55, pp. 271-72.

CHAPTER SIX

THE GROWTH OF COMMUNAL ANTAGONISM

Between 1916 and 1920, the Hindu-Muslim *entente* was one of the notable features of Indian politics. By the end of 1922, this was no longer true. The alliance between the Khilafatists 'and the 'Hindu politicians crumbled, and there was another spate of communal violence, originating either from disputes over the slaughter of cows, or over the playing of music before mosques. These developments proved that the assumptions on which Gandhi sought to unite Hindus and Muslims during the Khilafat movement were untenable. A number of groups with divergent and often conflicting aims were held together not because they had a common cause to unite for, but because it suited their various interests for the time being. Every further step in the progress of the non-cooperation movement tended to split them up into separate factions. Many leading Hindus were alarmed by the reckless enthusiasm of their Muslim allies, and their interest in the Khilafat cause was dampened by the Moplah riots in Malabar. Moreover, a group amongst them was eager to work the Montagu-Chelmsford Reforms, and consequently found that it was no longer expedient to support the Khilafat movement with its anti-British overtones. As a result, the 'Hindu Party' in the Khilafat campaign disintegrated. Some strayed into the new councils;[1]

---

[1] In 1922, Montagu, the Secretary of State, triumphantly observed: 'We have seen Bengal, which used to be one of the danger spots in India, become a Presidency, still exposed it is true to difficulties and

others drifted into the muddle of communal politics. This was
equally true of some of the Muslim politicians. The champions of
communal harmony and the architects of the Congress-League
alliance were cast in different roles after 1922. Many of the
non-cooperators deserted their more persistent colleagues and
adorned the government benches in the councils. This was a
cause of bitter controversy within the ranks of the Khilafat
leadership, which was eventually divided into two rival
camps.

The controversy over the question of Council entry was,
however, preceded by the collapse of the alliance between the
Hindu Congressmen and the Khilafat leaders. Since 1919 their
entente had been the most distinctive feature of Indian politics, because it had not only contributed to the spread of the
Khilafat movement but had also promoted the cause of communal amity. Its break up in 1922 sharpened communal
antipathies and encouraged the revival of various sectarian
organisations.

The first potential threat to the Hindu-Muslim alliance surfaced early in 1921, when serious differences cropped up over
the future course of the non-cooperation movement. Was it
to be conducted on the familiar lines of non-violence as
advocated by Gandhi? Or, was the use of force a viable method
for exerting pressure on the Raj? These questions had been
discussed and debated before and the general consensus was in
favour of following Gandhi's ideal of satyagraha. But the extremist wing of the Khilafat leadership, led by Hasrat Mohani,
Shaukat Ali, Zafar Ali and Azad Sobhani doubted the efficacy
of the Gandhian methods.[2] They did, however, pay lip-service

dangers which no human skill could have eradicated, but a Presidency
in which there is perhaps as little fundamental cause for concern as any
part of British India . . . . The greatest thing is to have got the co-operation of the people without whose co-operation Government would after
all be bound sooner or later to break down; the advanced thinkers, the
suspects of 1910 are the co-operators of today; some of them active and
strenuous participators in the work of the Government.'

Montagu to Ronaldshay, 23 February 1922, Ronaldshay Papers
(5-A).

[2]Gandhi himself admitted that not all Muslims accepted the principle
of non-violent non-cooperation. But he maintained that 'there has been
a distinct understanding with them that violence would never be allowed

to the principle of non-violence because they realised that any hope of gaining Hindu support lay only with Gandhi. In October 1920, Abdul Bari echoed their feelings when he declared that Gandhi's leadership was acceptable to Muslims because 'the strength of Islam lies in association with him'.[3] In February 1921, Mohamed Ali said publicly that he, Shaukat Ali, and Gandhi stood on the same non-violent platform, 'he [Gandhi] for reasons of principle and we for those of policy'.[4] So far all was well. Gandhi controlled the Khilafat movement and the Muslims followed his lead; all the major policy decisions were taken by him while the details were worked out by the Central Khilafat Committee and its provincial branches. But all this was to change over the next few months and the threat to Gandhi's leadership loomed large in the summer of 1921.

The first indication of the dramatic change in Muslim attitudes towards the Mahatma appeared at the Meerut All-India Khilafat Conference during 7-10 April 1921, when some *ulama* objected to the Hindu involvement in the Khilafat movement and demanded that its scope be defined according to the *Sharia*.[5] This was followed by a serious warning given by Abdul Bari that Muslims were ready to desert Gandhi and adopt violent methods for the redressal of their grievances.[6] The *ulama* demonstrated their impatience with the Mahatma's policy of caution and moderation and expressed dissatisfaction with the limited vigour with which he prosecuted the Khilafat agitation. These words were soon translated into deeds. In May 1921, some *ulama* set up *Darul Qaza* courts (House of Justice) in parts of Bihar and the North-West Frontier Province and

to go on side-by-side with non-violence'. He further added that even if Muslims accepted non-violence in a 'spirit of hatred', it was still possible 'to bring good out of even such non-cooperation, since it will save the country from bloodshed'. Gandhi to J. Mehta, 19 May 1920, Desai, *Day-To-Day*, Vol. 2, p. 161.

[3]Statement of Abdul Bari, n.d., Abdul Bari Papers· (From internal evidence it must refer to the *Jamiat-ul-ulama* session in October 1920.)

[4]Bamford, *Histories*, p, 166.

[5]WRDCI, 11 April 1921, Home Poll. D, June 1921, 54, NAI.

[6]Abdul Bari said in June 1921 that his community held that non-violent non-cooperation 'is a useful weapon to get our grievances redressed, but we never committed ourselves to always adhere to this principle'. Home Poll. 1921, 45, NAI.

preached *jihad* against the British in the countryside.[7] In March, the *Jamiat ul ulama* took a momentous decision which was of great importance for the Khilafat movement, though it received little public notice. It declared that it was *haram* (sinful) for a Muslim soldier to serve in the army.[8] The Karachi Khilafat Conference, 8-10 July, simply endorsed this resolution, which was introduced by Maulana Hasan Ahmad Madni, and supported by the Ali Brothers, Pir Ghulam Mujaddid, a Sindhi follower of Abdul Bari, and Maulana Nisar Ahmad of Deoband.[9]

Gandhi, although he supported the Karachi resolution and did not publicly express his disagreement with the *ulama*, did not sympathise with this radical strain in Khilafat politics. He feared that the militant posture adopted by some *ulama* would lead to the outbreak of violence and consequently destroy the credibility of his technique of non-violent non-cooperation. He was also aware of the signs of discontent amongst Hindu Congressmen following the Moplah riots in August 1921, and was anxious that the Khilafat leaders should not alienate them. But men like Abdul Majid Badauni, Ghafoor Ahmad and Nisar Ahmad were not convinced. On 21-22 December, they and their followers flocked to the Central Khilafat Committee and *Jamiat-ul-ulama* meetings in large numbers and demanded the immediate adoption of civil disobedience. Considerable friction occurred before Ansari, Azad, and Ajmal Khan could persuade the *ulama* to accept that Gandhi, 'the recognised leader of all Indians considered that the time was not yet ripe for civil disobedience'.[10]

The showdown came in December 1921. The Khilafat Conference, the Muslim League, and the Congress met simultaneously at Ahmedabad. Hasrat Mohani, representing the views of the more militant *ulama*, proposed that the Congress

---

[7] Bamford, *Histories*, pp. 168-69.

[8] The Conference was held in Bareilly from 24 to 26 March with Abul Kalam Azad as president. He announced that the *Jamiat-ul-ulama* had issued a *fatwa* to the effect that enlistment in the army was illegal according to the *Sharia*, and that those who disregarded this would be punished through the *Darul Qaza* courts. *Ibid.*, p. 165.

[9] See WR (Sind), 8 October 1921, Curry Papers. In September, the government arrested, prosecuted, and goaled all those who had a hand in introducing the resolution.

[10] Bamford, *Histories*, p. 177.

and Muslim League should strive to attain 'complete independence'. Without complete independence the Khilafat question
could not be settled, he said. Hasrat also declared that if
martial law was imposed Muslims would either have to abandon
non-cooperation or face the bullets and bayonets. In the latter
event, violence was the natural course to adopt in self-defence.[11]
At the Subjects Committee of the Muslim League, Azad
Sobhani, supported by Maulvis Fazlul Rahman, Abdul Majid
and Daud Ghuznavi, introduced a resolution for a change in
the Muslim League constitution in favour of securing complete
independence.[12]

Gandhi threw his weight against the resolution. He argued
that complete independence could not be incorporated in the
Congress creed unless and until Hindu-Muslim unity was completely accomplished.[13] This was another way of saying that
the idea of complete independence was premature, and that it
was unlikely to find favour with a section of Congress, especially the 'moderates'. Congress finally backed Gandhi rather
than Hasrat Mohani, as did the Subjects Committee of the
Muslim League on 30 December. Hasrat's resolution was
vehemently opposed by Ajmal Khan, Ansari, and Syed Raza
Ali and eventually rejected by thirty-six votes to twenty-three.

The *ulama* were enraged. In March 1921, the *Jamiat-ul-*
ulama had first mooted the idea of complete independence,
and its rejection by Congress and the League was infuriating.
'If Gandhi does not favour complete independence', stated
Maulana Abdul Majid, 'we would advise him to join the
illustrious group of *jee-huzoors* who would welcome him with
open arms'.[14] These were harsh words and they reflected the
growing rift between Gandhi and the Muslim priests. With the
Mahatma's influential allies like the Ali Brothers still in prison,

[11]*INC* 1921, pp. 55-6.

[12]For the text of the resolution and the Presidential Address of
Hasrat Mohani at the Muslim League session, see Pirzada (ed.),
Foundations of Pakistan, Vol. 1, pp. 557-58, 565.

[13]Gandhi said: 'Let us understand our limitation. Let Hindus and
Muslims have absolute, indissoluble unity. Who is here who can say
with confidence: Yes, Hindu-Muslim unity has become an indissoluble
factor of Indian Nationalism?'. *Young India*, 19 January 19 22, *CWG*, Vol.
22, p. 108; *INC* 1921, pp. 57-8.

[14]*Zul Qarnain*, 20 January 1922, UPNNR 1922.

there seemed little hope of a reconciliation.[15] His other supporters like Ansari, Ajmal Khan, and Syed Raza Ali did not
command as much influence amongst the *ulama* as the Ali
Brothers did. By the end of 1921, therefore, the Khilafat
movement was slipping out of Gandhi's control and his alliance with some of its influential leaders was under severe strain.

There was growing tension between some Khilafat leaders
and a group of Hindu politicians as well. It originated from
Mohamed Ali's statement in April 1921 that if the Afghans
invaded India the Indian Muslims would help them against the
British.[16] This speech created considerable apprehension among
Hindus,[17] especially among those who were already alarmed by
the growing militancy of the *ulama* and the Ali Brothers. In an
'Open Letter to the Maulana Sahebs', Jethmal Parasaram, editor
of *Bharatwasi*, announced his decision to oppose the Khilafatists
because of their violent outbursts and because they designated
themselves as 'Khadim-i-Kaaba' (Servants of Kaaba), and not
as 'Khadim-i-Hind' (Servants of India).[18] Brij Narain 'Chakbast'

[15]The Viceroy, Reading, assessed in July 1921 that Mohamed Ali
was 'a real factor in the situation', and that he was the 'link between
Mahommedan and Hindu'. He further added that if trouble arose between
Gandhi and Mohamed Ali, it would mean 'the collapse of the bridge
over the gulf between Hindus and Mahommedan'. The Marquess of
Reading, Rufus Isaacs, *First Marquess of Reading, by his son, 1914-1935*
(London, 1945), p. 199.

[16]Mohamed Ali's view was endorsed by Azad who stated that
'whatever Mohamed Ali said was quite compatible with the teachings of
Islam'. Home Poll. 1921, 45, NAI. Later, of course, Mohamed Ali
offered a clarification to remove the misunderstanding in the minds of
the Hindus. See his Presidential Address at the Allahabad District
Conference in May 1921, Home Poll. 1921, 10, NAI.

[17]'Surely it will be a very serious thing for the Hindus if, with the
declaration of *jihad*, Muslims go over to the side of the Amir of
Afghanistan', warned the Bengali language, *Bangali*. 12 May 1921,
BENNR 1921.

[18]'I ask you, gentlemen, whether in the circumstances it is possible
for you to join hands with the Swarajists of India. I am from among
those Indians who consider the attainment of Swarajya as their only
Dharma, but for you the Swarajya for India is not the first duty. You
build the whole edifice on religion, while we build the entire edifice on
patriotic considerations of Swarajya. Do you think it is possible, in the
circumstances, for both the parties to join hands?'. P. Parasaram to the
Ali Brothers, 8 July 1921, Mohamed Ali Papers, and see the comments of

a famous Urdu poet from Lucknow and a man with close connections with Malaviya, also reacted sharply to Mohamed Ali's
speech. He feared that the volatile Maulana and his followers wanted to establish the hegemony of Islam in India with the
help of Gandhi. 'I am convinced', Brij Narain stated, 'that at
this stage the Hindus must raise their heads and thwart all such
attempts. But our problem is that neither the students nor the
rural folks are willing to listen to us because of the magical
influence of Gandhi. Nevertheless, we must do something in
this situation.'[19] The message was clear. The Hindus had gone
too far in their support of the Khilafat movement and the time
had come to wriggle out of it. The Moplah riots along the
Malabar coast of South India were the last straw and deci-
sively weakened what little enthusiasm the Hindus had left for
the Khilafat cause.

In August 1921, the Moplahs in Malabar rose in rebellion
against their Hindu landlords, desecrated temples, and forcibly
converted some Hindus.[20] The reports of the events in this
remote corner of India caused serious tension between the
Hindu and Muslim politicians. The former asserted that hatred
of Hindus was at the bottom of the riots; that their temples
were marked out for destruction in order to overthrow Hinduism in Malabar, and that fanaticism was an instrument used by
the pan-Islamists to incite Muslims against the Hindus.[21]
Muslims, on the other hand, argued that the oppression and
exactions of the Hindu landlords were at the root of the trouble, and they denied that fanaticism entered into the picture at
all. In the meeting of the Congress Subjects Committee, Hasrat
Mohani said that the Moplahs suspected Hindus of collusion
with the government and were, therefore, justified in 'presenting the Quran to the Hindus. And if the Hindus became Mussal-

Lajpat Rai on the pan-Islamic trends amongst Muslims in Joshi (ed.),
Lajpat Rai: Writings and Speeches, p. 203.
[19]Brij Narain to Tej Bahadur Sapru, 28 April 1921, Sapru Papers
(Urdu), NLC. In early June, Brij Narain wrote an article in which he
examined the differences in the mental make up of Gandhi and
Mohamed Ali and observed that the unity between the two was
a 'political miracle' (*siyasi karishma*). *Aligarh Gazette*, 3 June 1921.
[20]For the causes of the Moplah riots, see Chapter seven.
[21]Moonje's Report to Shankaracharya of Puri on Malabar Riots,
Moonje Papers (35), NLC.

mans to save themselves from death, it was a voluntary change of faith and not forcible conversion'.[22] Syed Mahmud reporred to Gandhi that there were no forced conversions, while Abdul Bari accused the government of circulating false rumours in order to drive a wedge between Hindus and Muslims.[23] But Malaviya, Lajpat Rai, Moonje, and Shraddhanand were not satisfied with these explanations. They condemned the atrocities perpetrated on their co-religionists and demanded that the Hindus should be united, integrated and consolidated in defence against any such future occurrence. Moonje, the aggressively anti-Muslim leader from Nagpur, mooted the idea of settling 'our warlike races, such as the Marathas, Rajputs, Sikhs etc., in Malabar which alone, I think, can solve the problem of Moplah terrorism over the meek and helpless Hindus'.[24] This was in preparation for launching the *sangathan* movement which, as we shall see, greatly embittered Hindu-Muslim relations throughout the country.

In the midst of the heated controversy generated by the Moplah riots, Gandhi dropped a bombshell by suspending civil disobedience on 5 February 1922. This followed soon after the outbreak of violence in Chauri Chaura, near Gorakhpur. 'The whole conception of civil disobedience', Gandhi informed the Congress Working Committee, 'is based upon the assumption that it works in and through its non-violent character. . . . I personally can never be a party to a movement half violent and half non-violent.'[25] There seem to be two other reasons which might have influenced Gandhi to call off civil disobedience; firstly, the patchy success of the movement,[26] and, secondly, the growing strains in his alliance with the Khilafatists, and his inability to control their activities. The resolutions passed at the Karachi Khilafat Conference in July 1921 must have confirmed Gandhi's fears of a possible outbreak of

[22]Quoted in Gopal, *Indian Muslims*, p. 157.

[23]'Draft Statement on Malabar', Abdul Bari Papers.

[24]Moonje Papers (13).

[25]Gandhi to the Members of the Congress Working Committee, 8 February 1922, *CWG*, Vol. 22, pp. 350-51.

[26]See Brown, *Gandhi*, Chapter 9.

violence.[27] He was also aware of the effects of the Moplah riots on Hindus, and although he tried to soothe their feelings it was of no avail. Hindus were becoming increasingly apathetic to the Khilafat cause and were anxious to extricate themselves from the travail of non-cooperation. It would have been a blunder on Gandhi's part to disregard this fact in formulating his future political plans. The old postures seemed irrelevant, and the suspension of civil disobedience suddenly became a political necessity.

For Muslims, however, the future of Khilafat and the safety of the Holy Places was still an issue of 'life and death'. But Gandhi's decision to suspend civil disobedience took the sting out of their agitation. They were disappointed and angry, and at the meetings of the *Jamiat-ul-ulama* and the Central Khilafat Committee in March 1922, Gandhi was condemned for his decision. Hasrat Mohani rejected the Bardoli programme on the ground that, if religion enjoined violence, a policy of non-violence could not be adopted,[28] and at the *Jamiat-ul-ulama* Conference held in Ajmer, Abdul Bari attacked the Mahatma and the Bardoli resolutions adopted by the Congress Working Committee.[29] Such attacks continued even after Gandhi's arrest on 10 March 1922.[30] The Muslims were left to stew in their own juice. They felt betrayed and abandoned. When Gandhi returned from prison in February 1924, his interest—whatever little was left—in the Khilafat movement had evaporated. When asked to nominate a Hindu to join a Khilafat deputation to Angora, the Mahatma declined on the grounds that it would be 'out of place' for any Hindu to do so.[31] How ironical that less than five years earlier he

[27]It is noteworthy that this was one of the very few Khilafat conferences that Gandhi did not attend. He probably refrained from attending it because he was not in sympathy with the course that events would take.

[28]Home Poll. February 1922, 18, NAI.

[29]According to an intelligence report, Abdul Bari's speech was 'wild, impolitic and full of destructive programme'. Home Poll. 1922, 501, NAI.

[30]See, for example, the pamphlet written by Maulvi Abdul Hakim of Lahore in August 1922. It is entitled' *Mr Gandhi Mussalmanon ke hurgiz khair khwah naheen hain*'. IOL. Urdu. D652.

[31]Desai, *Day-To-Day*, Vol. 4, p. 22.

had urged his co-religionists to support the 'just cause of the Muslims', and said that 'for the Hindus not to support them [Muslims] to the utmost would be a cowardly breach of brotherhood.'[32]

The Khilafat movement was the first all-India agitation in which a wide spectrum of the Hindu and Muslim communities combined on an unprecedented scale. This combination, however, was just a passing phase in twentieth century Indian history. When Gandhi and his Congress followers suspended civil disobedience, almost immediately signs of Hindu-Muslim friction appeared. From February 1922 to December 1928, the contagion of communalism rapidly enveloped the country. The Khilafat movement appeared to some people to be a precursor of the 'worst form of a denationalising and even dehumanising movement of communalism, pure and simple',[33] and Gandhi was held responsible for breeding a spirit of intolerance, introducing religion into politics, and weakening respect for law and order.[34] M.R. Jayakar, member of the Bombay Legislative Council, observed at the height of Hindu-Muslim tension in 1925:

> To speak quite frankly to you, I regard it [Hindu-Muslim conflict] as the necessary reaction to Gandhi's policy during the last four years, which aimed at a most artificial and unreal unity between Hindus and Muslims, awakening sentiments and impulses in the latter community which, like the Frankenstein, it is now very difficult to allay. It makes me very sad to think that so great a patriot should have on this issue bungled so easily.[35]

DISINTEGRATION OF THE KHILAFAT PARTY

After the suspension of civil disobedience, there was yet another surprise in store for the Muslims. On 21 November 1922, the

[32]*CWG*, Vol. 17, p. 350.

[33]*Mahratta*, 4 July 1927, 26 June 1927; *Leader*, 2 January 1927.

[34]'One of the greatest disservices rendered by Gandhi is the sad undermining of the respect for authority which has been the consequence of his movement'. Shiva Rao to Lytton, 11 August 1924, Lytton Papers, MSS. EUR. F. 160 (22), IOL.

[35]Jayakar to Lajpat Rai, 8 September 1925, Jakakar Papers (405).

Turkish National Assembly at Ankara decided to separate the Khilafat from the Sultanate. And since the maintenance of the temporal power of the *Khalifa* was one of the main objects of the Khilafat movement, this action by a purely Muslim body completely took the wind out of its sails.[36] In March 1924, the final blow was struck by Mustafa Kamal Pasha who abolished the Khilafat and expelled the *Khalifa* from Turkish territory. Indian Muslims were stunned by this 'gross breach of religious injunctions'.[37] Their dream world crashed around them and they could do nothing except to raise loud voices of protest. The Turkish authorities simply ignored them. Mohamed Ali sought to keep the Khilafat agitation going in order to exert pressure on the Turks, but his colleagues saw no sense in fighting for a lost cause.[38] The institution of Khilafat was dead, never to be revived again. The Khilafat agitation in India lost its *raison d'etre* but its Committees survived for the next few months.

One of the immediate consequences of the abolition of Khilafat was the disruption of the Khilafat Party. From 1918 to 1922, religious zeal cemented an alliance between various Muslim groups, which were united perhaps for the first time in their history. But the collapse of the Khilafat agitation destroyed the edifice of Muslim unity and brought to the surface all the latent dissensions amongst them. In this section, we shall refer to some of these divisions and examine the role of the Khilafat leaders, particularly in relation to the Congress. What sort of careers did they choose for themselves? Did all the Khilafat leaders remain in the mainstream of national politics? What was their relationship with Congress? What was their role in Muslim League politics, and in the *tabligh* and *tanzim* movements? Answers to these questions

[36]For Muslim reaction to this decision, see Home Poll. 1923, 60, NAI.

[37]See, for example, the reaction of M.A. Ansari in Halide Edib, *Conflict of East and West in Turkey* (Delhi, 1935); Khaliquzzaman, *Pathway to Pakistan*, p. 74.

[38]Referring to Mohamed Ali's refusal to wind up the Khilafat Committees, Khaliquzzaman recorded: 'He was not a man to accept facts as facts. He was a born revolutionary aiming to destroy all that did not conform to his ideals, even though, he might not be able to reconstruct what he had destroyed.' *Ibid.*, p. 69.

might also help us to understand their reaction and response to an absolutely different political climate created by the operation of the Reforms Act of 1919 and by the revival of communal animosities.

One of the important groups which disappeared temporarily from the national scene was that of the *ulama*. The setback to the Khilafat cause had shattered all their plans and brought to an end their influence in all-India politics. Their period of glory—when they appeared at all-India conferences and influenced political decisions—was over. Their opposition to Council entry in pursuance of non-cooperation outside the legislature was disregarded, and they were told by Motilal Nehru not to dabble in politics.[39] Abdul Bari, the chief architect of the alliance between the *ulama* and the Congress, became increasingly despondent and isolated, and in August 1923, he complained that 'those who pretended to be our friends at one time and made a catspaw of the *ulama* now seem anxious to get rid of them.'[40] Abdul Bari was right. The *ulama* had been brought into prominence during the Khilafat movement because of their influence in the countryside, where the peasants, artisans, and weavers were greatly susceptible to their religious exhortations through the local mosques. But in 1923, when the issues confronting Indian politicians were political, the services of the *ulama* were no longer required. They were bluntly told to go back to the *madrasas* and *maktabs*.[41]

Early in 1924, Abdul Bari severed his connections with Congress and advised his disciples to avoid politics.[42] He did

[39]For controversy between the *ulama* and the professional men on the question of either joining the pro-Council entry group or pursuing non-cooperation outside the legislatures, see Robinson, *Separatism*, pp. 335-37.

[40]Statement to the Press by Abdul Bari, 20 August 1923, Abdul Bari Papers.

[41]Abdul Bari complained that he had heard this from several 'Western-educated sahibs, who have no respect for the guardians of Islam in India'. Abdul Bari to Mohamed Ali, 7 September 1923, in Urdu, Mohamed Ali Papers.

[42]In October 1923, Abdul Bari advised Hafizur Rahman 'Mujibi' (b. 1898), a non-cooperator from Farrukhabad, to abandon politics altogether because he thought that it was unreasonable to expect a fair deal from the Hindus. Interviews with Mr Rahman at Farrukhabad in December 1973.

so in protest against the role of some Hindu Congressmen in fomenting communal strife. He accused Malaviya and Lajpat Raj of provoking riots[43] and regretted that Gandhi not only associated with them but also justified their conduct and was susceptible to their influence.[44] Abdul Bari's statement to the press in August 1923 revealed the rift in Hindu-Muslim relations along with the growing strains in the alliance between the *ulama* and the Congress. He stated:

> I should like to call attention to the Muslims in general and the *ulama* in particular to the critical situation which has risen in India. The position of the Muslims has been rendered very awkward. Those who pretended to be our friends at one time and made a catspaw of the *ulama* now seem anxious to get rid of them. An invidious method has been adopted to aim a blow at their religion which is the only source of their pride and strength. I have nothing to say against the party which exploited the Muslims for their own purpose, for I knew what they wanted.[45]

After the setback to the Khilafat movement, brought about partly by the Treaty of Lausanne and partly by the deposition of the *Khalifa*, a group of professional men broke away from the Khilafat Committees realising the futility of continuing their agitation. Instead, they began to organise themselves into separate groups for different political, educational, and sectarian purposes. By December 1923, Ansari and Mohamed Ali gave up their opposition to Council entry and fell in line with Ajmal Khan, A.M. Khwaja, T.A.K. Sherwani and Khaliquzzaman. Sherwani and Khaliquzzaman served as secretaries of the Swaraj Party since its inception in January 1923, and Rafi Ahmad Kidwai, a comparatively new figure in UP politics, was elected convenor of the committee to revise the constitution of

---

[43]Abdul Bari to Mohamed Ali, 11 September 1923, Mohamed Ali Papers.

[44]Abdul Bari, *An Open Letter from Abdul Bari to the Mussalmans* (Lucknow, 1923), IOL. D. Urdu: 1911, and 'Fitna-i-Irtidad aur Mussalmanon ka farz', Abdul Bari Papers.

[45]Statement to the Press by Abdul Bari, 20 August 1923. *Ibid.*

the Swaraj Sabha in the UP.[46] M.H. Kidwai, one of the leading non-cooperators, also joined the Swaraj bandwagon and aspired to become president of the Legislative Assembly.[47] In Bengal, C.R. Das enlisted the support of many leading Khilafatists for the Swaraj Party, including Maulana Akram Khan, Mujibur Rahman, Wahid Husain, who represented the Urdu-speaking Muslims of Calcutta, and Maulvi Abdul Karim, an ex-government servant and former member of the Council of State. In the province at large his alliance with Muslims was a success. In the provincial elections of November 1923, the Swaraj Party captured an overall majority of seats including half the Muslim seats. Muslim support for the party was strongest in the eastern division of Chittagong and the northern division of Rajshahi, the storm centres of the Khilafat movement in Bengal.[48] In the Punjab, Muslims were split up into different parties but the dominant group rallied behind Fazl-i-Husain's 'Rural Party', which was strengthened by an alliance with the rural Hindus, mainly Jats, of the southern districts of Ambala division.

Another branch of the old Khilafat leadership, including Hasrat Mohani, Saifuddin Kitchlew, Shafi Daudi, and the Ali Brothers became more closely involved in communal politics. Their attempts to continue the Khilafat Committees had failed, and suddenly they found themselves isolated from the mainstream of politics. As time passed, they became increasingly estranged from the Congress as well. This was mainly because of what they considered to be the 'subservience' of Congress to the Hindu Sabha. Like Abdul Bari, Mohamed Ali complained that Gandhi was too much under the influence of Malaviya and Lajpat Rai, and that he was reluctant to take up

[46]Proceedings of the UP Swaraj Sabha, Allahabad, 1 February 1925, AICC Papers (76).

[47]Kidwai to Motilal, 1 May 1925, *Ibid* (71). But Motilal Nehru refused to consider his candidature because he feared that it would lead to the introduction of the 'Hindu-Muslim question into the Party—a question from which it has so far been absolutely free', Motilal to Kidwai, 2 May 1925, *Ibid.*

[48]R.A. Gordon, 'Aspects in the history of the Indian National Congress, with special reference to the Swarajya Party, 1919-1927' (Unpublished D. Phil. thesis, 1970, Oxford), p. 149.

the cause of Hindu-Muslim unity.[49] This was one of the causes
of his estrangement with Gandhi[50] and the Congress. Until his
death in 1931, Mohamed Ali remained a controversial figure,
but he could never regain the influence that he once had in
Indian politics. Instead, his communalism and his inconsistency
in politics became a source of embarrassment to his friends and
associates.[51] He appeared sometimes as a bigoted sectarian
leader and sometimes as a large-minded nationalist. A contemporary newspaper described him as 'a nationalist in the winter
season and a communalist in summer.'[52]

The Khilafat movement, however, furnished the Congress
with future stalwarts. Men like Ansari, Ajmal Khan, Azad,
A.M. Khwaja, T.A.K. Sherwani, Asaf Ali, and Syed
Mahmud were identified as 'Nationalist Muslims' as opposed
to the anti-Congress group led by the Ali Brothers. In the
aftermath of the civil disobedience movement, they were not
overwhelmed by the communal tide. They neither participated
in sectarian movements, such as *tabligh* and *tanzim*, nor were
they involved in the bitter communal controversies which
divided Indian politicians. The Nationalist Muslims were
genuinely committed to the ideals of Indian nationalism. They
adhered to the principles of secularism, and were proud of the
composite Indian culture which they saw as the logical consequence of a long process of intergration and assimilation
between different ethnic and religious groups. Above all, they
were unflinching supporters of the Congress. They identified
that body with Gandhi, Motilal, Sarojini Naidu, and Jawaharlal,
and considered them to be above narrow caste and communal
considerations. Loyalty to these leaders[53] and, more signifi-

[49]*Hamdard*, 3 May 1923.

[50]For details, see Mohibbul Hasan, 'Mahatma Gandhi and the
Indian Muslims', in S.C. Biswas (ed.), *Gandhi Theory and Practice: Social
Impact and Contemporary Relevance* (Simla, 1969), pp. 138-39.

[58]Maulana Arif Hasvi, who was joint editor of Mohamed Ali's newspaper, *Hamdard*, resigned in protest against Mohamed Ali's communal
posture in public life. *Forward*, 14 May 1926.

[52]*Ibid.*, 27 December 1927.

[53]In 1930, Ansari strongly disagreed with Gandhi's decision to launch
civil disobedience, but he said or did nothing against the Congress
policy and programme 'because of my loyalty and my deep attachment
to the Congress and to those who have got its reins in their hands.'
Ansari to Brelvi, 2 April 1930, Brelvi Papers (A-3), JNML.

cantly, to the Congress organisation was one of the most
distinctive features of their political creed. Even when they
disagreed with Congress policies and programmes, they did not
switch their loyalties. 'We must not leave the Congress', Ansari
pleaded with Sherwani at the height of his differences with
Gandhi, 'nor must we do anything to weaken the Congress . . .
To leave the Congress would be to commit political suicide, to
oppose the Congress would be a crime.'[54]

Mukhtar Ahmad Ansari was the leader of the Nationalist
Muslims.[55] He severed his connections with the Khilafat
organisation in July 1925,[56] and set out to reorganise the
Delhi Congress Committee, of which he was the president.[57]
His most important activities, however, were directed towards
the creation of a body which would act as an intermediary
between the Congress and the Muslims. With this aim in
mind, Ansari formed the All-India Muslim Nationalist Party,
which held its first meeting in July 1929.[58] The main organisers
of the party were A.M. Khwaja who, under pressure
from his creditors, had resumed his legal practice;[59]

[54]Ansari to T.A.K. Sherwani, 6 January 1930, Ansari Papers.

[55]When Ansari died in 1936, Sapru described him as 'a very true, a
very selfless, and a very earnest nationalist'. This view was shared by
leaders of all shades of opinion in India. Sapru to Asaf Ali, 12 May 1936,
Sapru Papers.

[56]In his letter of resignation, Ansari stated: 'On my return from
England in June, I found that communal passions had run amuck and
threatened to utterly destroy all that was noble and fine in this fortu-
nate Motherland of ours. I, therefore, felt impelled to do all that lay in
me to fight the demon of communalism. As an Indian owing allegiance
first to the Motherland, I feel I must sever my connections with all
communal sectional organisations.' Ansari to Secretary, Khilafat
Committee, 16 July 1925, Ansari Papers.

[57]Other office-bearers were Shuaib Qureshi, Asaf Ali, Abdul Aziz
Ansari and Qazi Najmuddin.

[58]The party had a two-fold objective. First, 'to organise the Muslims
for the purpose of enabling them to effectively discharge their duty to
the Motherland', and secondly, to 'create such relations between majority
and minority communities as would lead the former to consider the
rights of minorities in a spirit of broad-minded patriotism and the latter
in that of true nationalism'. Circular Letter, 17 July 1929, Ansari
Papers.

[59]Khwaja sought Gandhi's permission to resume his practice because
he had run into a debt of Rs 6,000. Gandhi reluctantly agreed 'to one of

Khaliquzzaman and Sherwani, secretaries of the Swaraj Party from 1923 to 1926; Syed Mahmud, a barrister from Bihar with close connections with Jawaharlal Nehru; Asaf Ali, the general secretary of the Delhi Congress Committee; Khan Abdul Ghaffar Khan, a Congressman from the North-West Frontier Province; Rafi Ahmad Kidwai, and Syed Abdullah Brelvi, assistant editor of the *Bombay Chronicle*.

But the going was tough for the Nationalist Muslims. The Ali Brothers condemned them for their association with Congress and for 'betraying' the Khilafat movement. 'In your blind adherence to Motilal Nehru and other Hindus', Shaukat Ali wrote to Ansari, 'you betrayed Muslims and your friends and co-workers.'[60] The Hindu Mahasabha leaders also suspected their intentions. Moonje saw the formation of the Nationalist Muslim Party as an attempt 'to enter the Muslims in the Congress in large numbers so that they may . . . exercise pressure from inside the Congress',[61] and particularly feared Ansari, Azad and Jinnah.[62] The Nationalist Muslims thus found themselves between the devil and the deep sea.

The fears expressed by Moonje and shared by many other Hindus were, however, unfounded. The Nationalist Muslim Party did not command any considerable support. It was composed of a small number of Muslim professional men—lawyers, doctors, and journalists—who did not operate in politics from an independent base. Its members depended on the support of leading Hindu Congressmen who encouraged them to counter the activities of the anti-Congress Muslims and patronised them in order to give credence to their claims of representing all Indians. As a result, the Nationalist Muslims exercised hardly any influence and remained on the fringe of national politics.

The Nationalist Muslims suffered from yet another drawback. Somehow their image became so firmly linked with that of the Hindus that they could hardly command any effective following from their own community. This was particularly true

the noblest of men doing the thing from which my whole soul recoils with horror'. Gandhi to Khwaja, 12 January 1926, Khwaja Papers.

[60]Shaukat Ali to Ansari, 19 May 1929, Ansari Papers.

[61]Moonje Diaries, 22 August 1929, Moonje Papers.

[62]Moonje to Jayakar, 31 July 1929, Jayakar Papers (437).

in the mid-twenties when communal feeling was rampant and mutual distrust and suspicion were widespread. In the midst of all this, the efforts of the Nationalist Muslims to restore communal harmony through drawing-room meetings and mutual pacts and agreements failed. According to Khaliquzzaman, who himself signed the death warrant of the Nationalist Muslim Party in the early 1930s, the party failed to achieve its objectives because:

> By its very nature it could have no roots in Muslim society and it did not make much headway either. Under its name no doubt several conferences were held .... but it had no rules or regulations; no separate membership and no separate office. Being backed by the Hindu Sabha press it lived in the newspapers all right but beyond that it had no positive existence. My idea that it might serve to bring about some discipline in Nationalist Muslim ranks did not materialize because the remedy was not potent enough to eradicate the evil.[63]

Thus the disintegration of the Khilafat movement led to a number of divisions within the 'Khilafat Party'.[64] Some Khilafatists stayed in Congress and held positions of responsibility in that organisation; others felt more at home in communal politics in which they were joined by politicians like Jinnah who had kept away from the Khilafat movement. The old Muslim League was resuscitated early in 1925. In spite of its limited membership,[65] the organisation provided the main

---

[63]Khaliquzzaman, *Pathway to Pakistan*, p. 102.

[64]Khaliquzzaman recorded: 'The disruption of the Khilafat organisation was like a breach in the embankment of the flowing stream of Muslim mass emotion, which diverted it into several petty streams some leading to desert lands there to dry up, some flowing by zig-zag routes to meet the original bed in their hoadlong march and some otners rushing towards the mighty ocean to drown themselves. To try to find any consistency, sound reasoning or logical method in Muslim politics during that period would be utterly futile.' *Ibid.*, p. 74.

[65]During the Khilafat days, the Muslim League, according to Khaliquzzaman, lived 'on paper, holding its session wherever Khilafat Conferences were held'. In January 1923, its total membership was only 1,097 and the income from subscriptions and donations was

platform for the articulation of Muslim political demands such as communal representation in the legislative bodies, extension of separate electorates to local bodies, and reservation of seats in public services. Indeed, these were precisely the issues which led to the growth of communal competition, particularly between Hindu and Muslim elites. But the scene of the conflict had shifted from the centre to the provinces where the Montagu-Chelmsford Reforms were in operation. It is to this scene of conflict that we must turn in order to explain the process which led to the growth of communal antagonism.

COMMUNALISM IN THE PROVINCES, 1921-1926

The collapse of the Hindu-Muslim alliance at the national level coincided with an intense struggle for power, influence, and patronage in the provinces. The roots of this struggle can be traced to the Morley-Minto Reforms which, by creating communal electorates, exacerbated Hindu-Muslim divisions and fostered the spirit of political exclusivism. Their impact was particularly marked on Muslims who saw the advantage of pressing for special safeguards and concessions in accordance with 'the numerical strength, social status, local influence and social requirements' of their community. This led to an artificial crop of associations which purported to represent all Indian Muslims, but which represented the interests of Muslim landlords, professional men, and government servants only. Their aim was to secure for themselves a strong position in the new power structure revolving around legislative councils, and their plea for the protection of the community's interests was, in fact, a veiled plea for a share in political power and patronage. Officials of the Raj turned a blind eye to this fact and never questioned the representative character of the supposedly all-India organisations like the Central National Mohammedan Association and the All-India Moslem Association. On the contrary, they were propped up

Rs. 1,681. By the end of 1926, the League's membership increased to a mere 1,184 in spite of the vigorous efforts of Jinnah to revitalise the organisation. *Ibid.*, pp. 137-38, and *Annual Report of the All-India Muslim League, 1928* (Lucknow, 1928) M.C. Chagla Papers, JNML.

and used to counterbalance the growing trend of revolutionary nationalism.[66]

However, the Morley-Minto Reforms did not destroy supra-communal connections in the politics of landlords' and professional men. This was due in part to the political and religious upheaval in the country from 1911 to 1918 which strengthened inter-communal alliances and paved the way for Hindu-Muslim cooperation, and in part because the Reforms fell short of Indian nationalist demands. There was no substantial extension of the franchise, the legislative councils' field of action—both in administrative and legislative spheres—was still severely circumscribed, and the non-official majorities in the councils were more nominal than real.[67] In addition to these imperfections, the benefits of reforms accrued mainly to the landowners and not the professional men who were subjected to special disabilities.[68] The professional groups in Congress and the Muslim League shared a common grievance against the Act of 1909 and, in December 1916, they formulated their own plan of constitutional reforms.

The Montagu-Chelmsford Reforms, on the other hand, initiated several significant changes in the structure of politics. On the legislative side, they increased the number of voters,[69]

[66]See, for example, Meston's correspondence with Nawab Hamid Ali Khan and Nawab Samad Ali Khan. Meston Papers (4).

[67]Although there were non-official majorities in all the provinces, they were more nominal than real, since a sufficient number of non-officials were appointed by the Chief Executive in every province to give them, combined with the official members, a majority over the elected members. For example, in Bengal there was a clear elective majority, but the balance of power was held by two or three European elected members who generally voted with the government on all the important issues.

[68]See Chapter three.

[69]The number of electors to the pre-reform legislative council was only 2,774, of whom 2,306 were Muslims and landholders, who returned six members by direct election, and the remaining 468 were members of district and municipal boards who returned thirteen members. But according to the first electoral roll drawn up in 1920, the number of voters was 1,347,922. By 1923, when the second election took place, the disqualification of females had been removed and the number of voters increased to 1,509,127, of whom 49,067 were females. *Report on the Working of the System of Government: United Provinces of Agra and Oudh* (henceforth, *Report*, UP) (Allahabad, 1928), p. 175.

TABLE 6.1

COMPOSITION OF THE PROVINCIAL LEGISLATIVE COUNCILS ESTABLISHED UNDER THE MONTAGU-CHELMSFORD REFORMS

Provinces	Total (ex-officio, nominated and elected).	NOMINATED			Total (elected).	ELECTED													
		Total (nominated and ex-officio).	Officials (nominated and ex-officio).	Non-officials.		By special electorates				By communal electorates.							By general electorates.		
						Total	University.	Land holders.	Commerce and Industry including mining and planting.	Total.	Muslims Urban.	Muslims Rural.	Europeans.	Anglo-Indians.	Indian Christians.	Sikhs.	Total.	Non-Muslims Rural.	Non-Muslims Urban.
1. Madras . .	127	29	23	6	98	13	1	6	6	20	11	2	1	1	5	..	65	56	9
2. Bombay . .	111	25	20	5	86	11	1	3	7	29	22	5	2	.	..	..	46	35	11
3. Bengal . .	139	26	20	6	113	21	1	5	15	46	33	6	5	2	..	..	46	35	11
4. United Provinces	123	23	18	5	100	10	1	6	3	30	25	4	1	.	..	..	60	52	8
5. Punjab . .	93	22	16	6	71	7	1	4	2	44	27	5	.	.	..	12	20	13	7
6. Bihar and Orissa	103	27	20	7	76	9	1	5	3	19	15	3	1	.	..	..	48	42	6
7. Central Provinces	70	16	10	6	54	7	1	3	3	7	6	1	.	.	..	..	40	31	9
8. Assam . .	53	14	9	5	39	6	.	.	6	12	12	.	.	.	..	..	21	20	1

Source: *Statement Exhibiting the Moral and Material Progress and Condition of India* (London, 1921), Cmd. 202, p. 249.

and established enlarged central and provincial legislatures with a majority of elected and non-official members [See Table 6.1]. On the administrative side, the reforms divided the functions of government between 'reserved' and 'transferred' departments. The 'reserved' departments were administered by the Governor-in-Council, but the control of such important departments as Education, Agriculture and Local Self-Government in the 'transferred' departments was handed over to ministers responsible to the legislature. This was the principle of dyarchy.

In the local self-governing bodies, too, the electoral qualifications were reduced,[70] the official and nominated element was curtailed, and the principle of election was widely extended. In 1920-21, the total number of municipalities in Bengal was 116 and, except in 5, the elective system was in force in all.[71] The reforms initiated in the Punjab set in motion the process of freeing the municipal committees from official tutelage. By 1922-23, there were at least 75 per cent elected members who were directly returned from a much wider franchise.[72] In the UP, the District Boards Act of 1922, which was carried through the first reformed Council, completely reorganised the district boards. The official element disappeared, the right to vote was extended to many more people, and the number of elected members was increased.[73]

These changes gave the idea of self-government a semblance of reality. For the first time, a large mass of work relating to public health, sanitation, and education came under the effective control of Indians, who received many powers which they could exercise to favour their friends, relatives, and members of their religious community. In the local bodies also the value of a seat was greatly enhanced. The chairmen and members of the district, local, and union boards and municipalities became masters of almost all local services. They provided

[70]A private bill introduced in the UP Legislative Council which became law in 1922 reduced certain categories of municipal qualifications to the level of those required of electors to the legislative council. *Ibid.*, Vol. 2, p. 190.

[71]*Resolution Reviewing the Reports on the Working of Municipalities in Bengal* (henceforth, *Resolution*, Bengal) (Calcutta, 1922), p. 1.

[72]*Report on the Working of the Municipalities in the Punjab, 1922-23* (henceforth, *Punjab Municipalities*) (Lahore, 1923), p. 1.

[73]*Report*, UP, Vol. 2, p. 230.

employment to various coveted posts, exercised almost complete control over primary education, issued contracts for public works undertakings, granted permission to organise bazaars and *melas*, regulated the route of religious processions, and had the power to impose local taxes. As the scope and functions of local institutions were enlarged, there was a corresponding increase in their powers and spheres of influence.[74] It was natural in such a situation for influential groups in the districts to contend for a seat on the local bodies, and for their allies to take an active interest in who got elected. The election results in different parts of the country demonstrated a fair degree of interest in district contests.[75] In the 1925-26 elections in Bengal, 61.3 per cent of the electorate voted in Dacca, over 70 per cent in the seven wards of Rajshahi division and about 75 per cent in the four wards of Comilla division.[76]

What was the impact of the changes introduced by the Montagu-Chelmsford Reforms on communal relations? Recent studies have clearly demonstrated that the enlargement of legislative councils, the broadening of the franchise and the extension of the scope and activities of the local bodies contributed to the growth of communal awareness, sharpened existing cleavages, and encouraged communal alignments. These developments, which are clearly evident from 1921 to 1926, were the consequence of several factors. The first was, undoubtedly, the retention of communal electorates in the Montagu-Chelmsford Reforms and their gradual extension to local bodies. The implications of this measure were not realised during the

---

[74]This was, of course, also related to increases in the income and expenditure of local bodies. From 1918 to 1922, municipal income rose by 40 per cent in Bombay, and by lesser amounts in other provinces. The increase was a reflection of the post-war boom following the rise in property taxes and increases in octroi and other levies on trade. One of the areas which benefitted most from these increases was education. There was an impressive expansion of schools, and an increase in education expenditure from 12.48 lakhs in 1920 to 17.60 lakhs in 1922. Hugh Tinker, *The Foundations of Local Self-Government in India, Pakista and Burman* (London, 1968), pp. 121-24.

[75]For Bombay Municipal Elections, see Tinker, *Ibid.*, p. 132.
[76]*Bengal Municipalities*, 1925-26, Appendix B, pp. 73-6.

Khilafat and Non-cooperation movements when the anti-
government spirit reigned supreme, and the majority of
Congress and Muslim League leaders boycotted the 1920 provincial elections. By 1922, however, the non-cooperation
movement had spent its force and the breach between Indian
politicians began to widen. In the councils, communalism
raised its ugly head, and on questions such as the slaughter of
cows, the representation of Muslims on local bodies and in
public service, there was a marked tendency towards communal
groupings. Muslims were committed to communal representation and reservation of seats for their community; Hindus, on
the other hand, were against these demands, and were particularly opposed to separate electorates for Muslims. Many UP
Hindus resigned from or boycotted the municipal boards
against the Jahangirabad amendment of March 1916, and in
1922 many Punjabi Hindus did the same. In both cases, the
protest was against the concession of separate representation.
Similarly, when Surendranath Banerjea, the first minister for
Local Self-Government in Bengal, agreed to concede separate
electorates in the Calcutta Municipal Bill of 1923, a massive
agitation was launched against him by the Hindu commercial
and professional classes.[77] 'How can he face a non-Muslim
constituency with this fatal record of pro-Muslim activities?',
wrote the *Amrita Bazar Patrika*, one of the leading campaigners against Banerjea's election to the Bengal Council in 1923.[78]

Another important factor which deepened communal
rivalries was the devolution of power to Indian hands which,
as recent studies have shown, led to a struggle for power and
patronage.[79] This situation would not have arisen had the

[77]In November 1921, Banerjea introduced a Bill in the Council in
which he avoided separate electorates because he regarded them as a
hindrance to the 'upbuilding of a united Indian nationality'. But Muslims
protested loudly against the exclusion of separate electorates, and in
February 1923, Banerjea was forced to accept a compromise: Muslims
were to have separate electorates for the first nine years, after which
they would have only reserved seats in general electorates.

[78]*Amrita Bazar Patrika*, 1 December 1923.

[79]Page has argued that the main effect of the introduction of
Ministerial responsibility was to increase competition for power at the
provincial level. He has shown how after devolution had taken place,
the desire to obtain office or to prevent others from obtaining office

two major communities been evenly developed. But this was not the case. The result was that in certain provinces, such as Bengal, where Muslims were economically and politically weak, they were less well represented within the council and less capable, for that reason, of utilising the Reforms to their best advantage.[80] The Bengali Muslims naturally felt that they should have the full benefit of their majority position and, therefore, they clamoured for concessions and safeguards. Hindus, on the other hand, were willing to concede only a temporary reservation of seats to Muslims wherever they were in a minority provided they agreed to joint electorates.

The scene was thus set for a keen competition in the struggle for power. The working of the Punjab and Bengal Legislative Councils provides a clue to the nature of the struggle. We propose to concentrate on these provinces where power was distributed, at least in some measure, according to population.[81] The majority communities, therefore, found the means of asserting their position, while the minorities were obliged to defend themselves by an insistence on their claims of recognition on the basis of their contribution to the province's revenues, their high level of literacy, and their overall dominance in public service and the professions. The legislative councils soon became the arena of innumerable battles.

Why is the UP excluded from the present discussion? The answer to this question is at hand. In the UP, the landholders constituted the largest single group and they held their position not as leaders of any community, but as leaders of landed interests. Under the Reforms, twenty-five out of twenty-nine Muslim members were returned by rural electorates, and a majority of these were leading zamindars of their districts who combined with Hindu zamindars on questions concerning

became the mainspring of political activity, and politicians who had worked together for reforms became competitors in a struggle for power. This argument helps us to understand the nature of communal politics in the 1920s. See Page, 'Prelude to Partition', Chapter I.

[80]In Bengal, where Muslims constituted 54.6 per cent of the population in the electoral area in 1921, they were allowed 39 seats, while the Hindus, with only 45 per cent of the population, had 46 seats.

[81]For an elaboration of this argument, see Page, 'Prelude to Partition', p. 13.

their class interests.[82] In 1921, the Nawab of Chhatari organised the Zamindar Party. This represented the first attempt by the landlords to come to terms with the political changes made by the Montagu-Chelmsford Reforms,[83] and to maintain their rural dominance, which was threatened by peasant movements from 1920 to 1922.[84] 'Formerly it was the tenants who were in need of protection', observed Shaikh Habibullah of Barabanki, 'now it is the landlords who need the protection of government.'[85] This feeling of insecurity was closely linked with the passage of the Oudh Rent Act in 1921 and the District Boards Bill, introduced in the same year by Jagat Narain Mulla, the minister for Local Self-Government. Both pieces of legislation were stoutly resisted by the landlords, and it was only Harcourt Butler's immense influence with the *taluqdars* which ultimately secured their passage.[86] But these developments suddenly made the disorganised and divided landlords[87] aware of the threat to their influence, prestige, and power. 'The landless agitator is out for the destruction of the landholders', warned the Raja of Jahangirabad, and criticised the 'self-constituted champions of the oppressed' for inciting the peasantry against the landlords. He urged his audience at the UP Landholders Conference to form a 'representative body' and to play a greater part in 'moulding public opinion.'[88] Similarly, Raja Durga Narain

[82]For example, the resolution for increased representation of the zamindars of the Agra province in the Council was introduced by the Nawab of Chhatari and was supported by Thakur Jagannath Bakhsh Singh and D.R. Ranjit Singh. *Proceedings of the UP Legislative Council*, March 1923, Vol. XIV, pp. 160-69.

[83]P.D. Reeves, 'The Landlords' Response to Political Change in the United Provinces of Agra and Oudh, India, 1921-37' (Unpublished Ph.D. thesis, Australian National University, 1963), p. 106.

[84]See M.H. Siddiqi, 'The Peasant Movement in Pratapgarh', 1920, *IESHR*, Vol. 10, September 1972, pp. 305-326; W.F. Crawley, 'Kisan Sabhas and Agrarian Revolt in the UP 1920-21', *MAS*, Vol. 5, 1971, 95-109.

[85]Habibullah to Butler, 6 March 1921, Butler Papers (80).

[86]See, for example, Butler's correspondence in Bulter Papers (80).

[87]Meston, the Lieutenant-Governor of the UP before Butler, was particularly distressed by the disunity amongst the landlords. On the eve of Montagu's mission to India, he made strenuous efforts to organise them to 'stir them up to realize the magnitude of the occasion'. To Willingdon, 22 August 1917, Meston Papers (17).

[88]Speech on 14 July 1922, Butler Papers (80).

Singh of Tirwa (Farrukhabad district) proposed the setting up of a Landholders' Association to promote solidarity among landholders.[89] These initiatives signified the beginning of the emergence of a united landlords' party both within and outside the Council. In 1923, as many as fifty-eight of the seventy-seven rural seats in the UP Council were won by landholders. They emerged as the largest single group. Yet, they were far from organised and united on any issue. The Zamindar Party was just a collection of individuals who had little or no allegiance to their organisation except in name; their members were unwilling to subordinate their personal interests or beliefs to those of the party, and if the party stood in their way they were willing to wreck it to clear the path.[90] Clumsy, naive and self-seeking, the Zamindar Party remained fragmented and out of touch with the changing realities of Indian politics.

COMMUNALISM IN BENGAL

By the end of 1922, the Civil Disobedience Enquiry Committee appointed by the Congress found that the country was not ready for civil disobedience. But this failed to settle the controversy between those who favoured the continued boycott of the new councils and those who urged the reversal of Gandhi's ban against Council entry. At the Gaya Congress in December 1922, C.R. Das made a vigorous plea for Council entry. This was turned down by the 'No-Changers.' The dissidents then constituted themselves into the Congress-Khilafat-Swaraj Party with Das as leader, and Motilal Nehru, with three others, as secretaries. Throughout the summer of 1923, the Swarajists steadily gained ground. The tide finally turned in their favour in September 1923. The Congress approved the modification of the boycott in favour of Council entry, and made it possible for them to breach the 'citadel of bureaucracy' both from inside and outside the councils.[91] In the elections, the

[89]Speech on 14 July 1922, Butler Papers (80).

[90]Reeves, 'The Landlords' Response', p. 186. 'It is very distresssing to me', wrote Harcourt Butler, 'to feel that the landowners are so divided among themselves and allow personal feelings to come before personal interests.' Butler to the Nawab of Chhatari, 20 December 1923, Chhatari Papers, JNML.

[91]*Forward,* 17 October 1923.

Swarajists won a clear majority in the Central Provinces. In Bengal, where Das had privately concluded a pact with Muslims as an electioneering device,[92] they represented the strongest individual group. In the UP and Bombay, though the Swarajists were returned in considerable numbers, they did not have the majority of votes. In the Punjab, Madras, Bihar, and Orissa they were very weak.

In Bengal, the Swarajists numbered forty-seven. More than one-third of their party members in the Council were Muslims. This meant that without their aid Das and his followers could not achieve their objective of wrecking the machinery of the Council from within. In an attempt to ensure Muslim support, Das concluded a pact with Bengali Muslim politicians between September and early December 1923. Its main features were:

1) For the provincial council representation on a population basis with separate electorates for Muslims.
2) For the local bodies—district boards and municipalities —representation in the proportion of 60 to 40 in every district: 60 to the community which was in majority and 40 to the minority. The question whether there should be separate electorates or not was kept open.
3) For government appointments 55 per cent seats were fixed for Muslims and the remaining 45 per cent for other communities.
4) To ensure religious tolerance and communal harmony, music was to be prohibited before the mosques and Muslims were to enjoy the freedom to perform cow-killing for religious purposes (*korbani*).[93]

Through these extraordinarily generous concessions, Das gained considerable Muslim support at the ballot box and in the Council, where he succeeded in organising the Swaraj Party on supra-communal lines. The party had quite a few Muslim

---

[92]'It seems strange', observed the *Amrita Bazar Patrika*, 'that these gentlemen should meet in a secret enclave and enter into a contract with one another in matters affecting the rights and liberties of more than four million of the people.' *Amrita Bazar Patrika*, 23 December 1923.

[93]*Forward*, 18 December 1923.

members who, in cooperation with their Hindu colleagues, obstructed the work of the Bengal Legislative Council. In fact, it was on the motion of Maulvi Nurul Huq Choudhry that the demand for ministerial salaries was rejected on 24 March 1924. A supplementary demand for a salary grant was also defeated on 26 August. The ministers then resigned and Lytton, the Governor, assumed temporary charge of the transferred departments. On both occasions Muslim votes enabled Das to make dyarchy unworkable.

However, Das's alliance with Muslims rested on shaky foundations, because it was bought at a very high price — a price which the Hindus were not prepared to pay. The Bengal Pact, which provided the basis for an alliance with Muslims, had serious implications for the Hindus who had for so long surpassed Muslims in Western education and various resultant economic and political benefits. It threatened the domination enjoyed by the Hindu landed, commercial, and professional classes, who faced the cheerless prospect of losing their advantages to a relatively new class of Muslim professional men and up-country merchants.

The Bengal Pact raised Muslim seats in the legislative council from 40 per cent, as provided by the Lucknow Pact, to 55 per cent. In other words, the Hindus were to lose 15 per cent of the seats to Muslims. In the local bodies, the principle of representation threatened to upset the balance of power in favour of Muslims, particularly in districts where they formed a majority of the population. In Dacca, for example, they formed 60 per cent of the population, but held only 27.2 per cent of the seats on the district boards. Hindus, on the other hand, held 72 per cent of the seats in spite of being in a minority. Under the Bengal Pact, however, the principle of 60:40 representation (60 to the majority community and 40 to the minority) meant an increase in Muslim representation from 27.2 per cent to 60 per cent, and a fall in Hindu representation from 72 per cent to only 40 per cent. Table 6.2 sets out the representation of Hindus and Muslims on local and district boards along with their population percentages, and reveals the implications of the 60: 40 principle on the communal composition of the local bodies in Bengal. Clearly, the Bengal Pact gave Muslims the opportunity of winning control of local bodies and improving

TABLE 6.2

HINDU AND MUSLIM MEMBERSHIP OF LOCAL AND DISTRICT BOARDS IN ALL BENGAL DISTRICTS (EXCLUDING DARJEELING), 1923

Name of Districts	Population (%)		Percentage of representation on District Boards		Percentage of representation on Local Boards	
	Hindu	Muslim	Hindu	Muslim	Hindu	Muslim
Burdwan	78.0	18.5	88.1	11.11	79.5	19.05
Birbhum	68.1	25.1	81.3	18.7	75.0	25.0
Bankura	86.3	4.6	91.7	8.3	86.7	13.3
Midnapore	88.2	6.8	91.7	8.3	94.1	5.9
Hoogly	81.9	16.4	84.7	15.3	81.3	15.38
Howrah	79.3	20.3	94.4	5.5	87.5	12.5
24 Parganas	64.2	34.6	76.7	23.3	63.5	36.5
Nadia	39.1	60.2	80.0	20.0	71.3	28.7
Murshidabad	45.1	53.6	55.6	44.4	50.8	49.2
Jessore	38.1	61.8	83.4	16.6	66.7	33.3
Khulna	50.0	49.8	81.3	18.7	62.1	37.9
Dacca	34.2	55.4	72.8	27.2	70.2	29.8
Mymensingh	24.3	74.9	54.2	45.8	39.0	61.0
Faridpur	26.3	63.5	58.4	41.6	54.6	45.4
Bakargunj	28.8	70.6	50.0	50.0	43.6	56.4
Chittagong	22.6	72.8	50.0	50.0	43.3	56.4

Contd....

TABLE 6.2. CONTD. . . .

Tippera	25.8	74.1	46.7	53.3	34.0	65.6
Noakhali	22.4	76.6	29.2	70.8	31.2	68.8
Rajshahi	21.4	76.5	45.5	54.5	33.4	66.6
Dinajpur	44.1	49.1	66.7	33.3	60.0	40.0
Jalpaiguri	55.0	24.8	85.7	14.3	88.9	11.0
Rangpur	31.6	68.0	55.6	44.4	46.3	53.7
Bogra	16.6	82.5	50.0	50.0	40.7	59.3
Pabna	24.1	75.8	58 4	41.6	52.8	47.2
Malda	40.6	51.5	66.7	33.3	—	—
[Province]	43.7	53.6	67.0	33.0	60.8	29.2

Sources: *Census*, 1921, Bengal, Part II; *Resolution Reviewing the Reports on the Working of the District Boards in Bengal, 1923-24* (Calcutta, 1925).

their position in others. The Montagu-Chelmsford Reforms had started the process by which Muslims could wrest control of local patronage from the zamindars and their clients;[94] the Bengal Pact went a step further in the same direction.

Das maintained that the Bengal Pact did not concede to Muslims 'more than they were entitled to get in fairness and justice', but few Bengali Hindus concurred. They regarded the pact as a one-sided bargain[95] and launched a massive agitation against it. This was led by Surendranath Banerjea and his group who were smarting under the crushing defeats they had sustained at the polls and were eager to pick up any stick with which to beat the Swarajists. The cow-protection societies in Bengal also protested against the provision relating to cow-slaughter. Meeting after meeting was held in Calcutta with Banerjea, Pal, and the Maharaja of Darbhanga—a patron of Hindu revivalist movements—in the forefront.[96] In December 1923, the Congress at Coconada rejected the Bengal Pact under pressure from Malaviya and Lajpat Rai who deprecated the attempt to solve what they regarded as an all-India question on provincial lines.[97] Das was furious. The Congress decisio nspelt danger to his alliance with Muslims in Bengal. 'You may delete the Bengal National Pact from the resolution', he said at Coconada, 'but I assure you, you cannot delete Bengal from the Indian National Congress or from the history of India. Bengal demands the right of having her suggestions considered. . . . She is an integral part of the Indian National Congress'.[98] This was mere verbal jugglery to conciliate the Muslim Swarajists whose loyalty to the party was, after all, based on tenuous links.

Das warded off the attacks against him by prevailing upon the Bengal Provincial Conference to ratify the Pact in May 1924 and succeeded in retaining Muslim votes in the Council. However, soon after his death in June 1925, the

[94]J. Gallagher, 'Congress in decline: Bengal 1930 to 1939', *MAS*, July 1973, Vol. 7, pp. 600-1.
[95]*Amrita Bazar Patrika*, 17, 19, 22 December 1923.
[96]*Ibid.*, 25, 29 December 1923.
[97]*Ibid.*, 21, 22 December 1923.
[98]Quoted in L.A. Gordon, *Bengal: The Nationalist Movement 1876-1940* (Columbia University Press, 1974), p. 197.

Congress leadership in Bengal was divided over the Pact. J.M. Sen Gupta, still anxious to retain Muslim votes for the Swaraj Party at the November 1926 elections, was in favour of continuing the Pact. At the stormy meeting of the Bengal Provincial Congress Committee on 13 June 1926, he saved it for the moment. But this proved to be one of the factors which led to a split in the Swaraj Party. On 25 June 1926, the 'Big Five' in Bengal politics[99] issued a manifesto which, apart from accusing Sen Gupta of having destroyed the 'solidarity and the prestige of the Congress and the Swarajya Party in Bengal', suggested that the Bengal Pact should be thrown to the winds because it was never ratified either by the Indian National Congress or by the majority of Hindus.[100] By November, Sen Gupta also came round to the same view. In one of his election speeches, he complained that his support of the Bengal Pact was being exploited by his opponents to discredit him. 'The Pact is not a live issue. . . . It might be wrong; in fact it has not found favour with 88 per cent of the Hindus', he declared.[101]

The Swaraj Party repudiated the Bengal Pact under the exigency of elections. Its decision to do so was in deference to its Hindu supporters who had consistently opposed any concessions to Muslim pressures, especially over tenancy legislation, the opening of Islamia colleges and schools, and the appointment of Muslims in the Calcutta Corporation.[102] It did not need any great degree of perception to understand that if the Swarajists were to maintain their ascendancy in Bengal politics, they had to abandon their policy of pandering to the Muslims. Any further attempt to enforce the Bengal Pact in the spirit of Das was bound to drive the new mass Hindu electorate into communal organisations, the most important being the Hindu Sabha.[103]

[99]They were: Tulsi Charan Goswami, Sarat Chandra Bose, Nirmal Chandra Chunder, Bidhan Chandra Roy and Nalini Ranjan Sarkar.

[100]*Forward*, 25 June 1926.

[101]*Amrita Bazar Patrika*, 4 November 1926.

[102]See K. Mcpherson, *The Muslim Microcosm: Calcutta, 1918-1935* (Heidelberg, 1974), pp. 84-6.

[103]In June 1926, Madan Mohan Burman and Jatindra Mohan Das Gupta of the Bengal Hindu Sabha convened an all-Bengal Hindu Conference to safeguard the Hindu interests'. This was one of the

The strategy evolved by the Swaraj Party was based on short-term political calculations which took no account of its impact on future communal relations in Bengal. Das had demonstrated the significance of an inter-communal alliance and provided the basis on which it could be sustained. He was able to do so in spite of the government's attempt to wean away his Muslim supporters, and the hostility of his co-religionists. But Das's successors failed to recognise the importance of carrying Muslim support in a province where the community was numerically preponderant. They neither attempted to reconcile the rival claims of the two communities, nor did they evolve an alternative scheme acceptable to the dominant Hindu and Muslim groups. As a result, the Swaraj Party in Bengal threw away its chance of building up a joint Hindu-Muslim front. Moreover, its failure to keep the electoral promises encouraged Muslim communalists to stir up a campaign against it and also alienated many influential Muslims who had enthusiastically joined Das's faction in Bengal politics. Maulvis Abdur Rashid, Mujibur Rahman, Ashrafuddin, and Abdul Matin Chowdhry resigned from the Bengal Provincial Congress Committee in protest against the rejection of the Bengal Pact.[104] In the 1926 elections, of the thirty-nine Muslims elected, only one was a Swarajist. The other thirty-eight members pledged themselves to work dyarchy in the interest of their class or community. The *Moslem Chronicle* summed up the attitude of Muslim politicians towards the Swaraj Party in June 1926:

> We confess we were never enamoured by the artificial alliance which Das's instinct of self-preservation prompted him to conclude with the Muslim community. The Muslims as a community never cared for the Pact and always looked upon it as a ha'poworth of political cheese which could be thrown into the dust bin any moment they liked.... We know that the Hindu politicians were playing a foul game, and when the pact was put to test within a few months of its

several attempts to take advantage of the growing discontent with the Bengal Pact. *Forward*, 8 June 1926.
[104]*Mussalman*, 10 September 1926.

birth, the astuteness of Hindu politics was quite apparent.[105]

After the collapse of their alliance with the Swaraj Party, some Muslim politicians found a viable alternative in communal organisations such as the *Tanzeem-ul-Mussalman*, formed by the Calcutta merchants and artisans; the *Anjuman-i-Difah-i-Islam* (Society for the Defence of Islam), organised and encouraged by Abdullah Suhrawardy, Y.C. Ariff and Mujibur Rahman; and the Bengal Muslim Party, established by Husain Suhrawardy and his father-in-law, Abdur Rahim. Bengal provided an ideal setting for these organisations to flourish. Most Muslims in the province, especially in the eastern region, were tenants of Hindu landlords and victims of their exploitation. The exploitation was in the form of seizure of land for rent arrears, collection of *puja* subscriptions from Muslim peasants,[106] and the harassment of those who sacrificed cows on *Bakr Id*.[107] Some Muslim politicians exploited these issues of peasant discontent in their struggle with the Hindus for jobs and seats in the legislative council. The 422,000 enfranchised Muslim rural voters, who were susceptible to religious and communal exhortations because of their grievances against the Hindu zamindars and *mahajans*, became cannon-fodder in the political battle. Muslim politicians found an excellent target for attack in the dominant Hindu community to which belonged the landholders and their agents, the money-lenders, the lawyers, the tax collectors, and other government officials with whom every Bengali Muslim, rural and urban, was obliged to have dealings. To charge this group with tyranny and to call for united backing to break its power was a sure way to arouse popular enthusiasm.[108] The crucial factor which added weight to this appeal was the ability of Muslim

---

[105]*Moslem Chronicle*, 18 June 1926.

[106]This was reported from a village in Champaran district, Bihar. *Zamindar*, 17 September, PUNNR 1923.

[107]There were reports of such harassment from Chandurani pargana in Mymensingh district from the agents of Rani Dinamani Chaudhrani. *Moslem Hitaishi*, 1 February 1918, BENNR 1918. There were similar incidents reported in 1890, when several powerful Hindu zamindars in East Bengal prohibited cow-slaughter in their jurisdiction.

[108]Broomfield, *Elite Conflict*, p. 328.

politicians to establish close links with their co-religionists in both rural and urban areas. The symbols of Islam—mosques, shrines and religious festivals—cut across the dividing lines of caste and class and simplified the task of mass communication. Muslim politicians took full advantage of these religious symbols in their political battle and used them to fan the fires of communal unrest.

The emergence of Muslim communal politics was also facilitated by the recrudescence of communal riots in different parts of the province which, as we shall see, were sparked off by a wide variety of factors. Whatever their cause, riots generated a feeling of insecurity, undermined trust and confidence between the two communities, and damaged the syncre‧tist tendencies in the countryside. The politicians, Hindu and Muslim alike, exploited the fears and prejudices of their respective followers to warp political issues.[109] They gave a communal colour to personal differences and tacitly encouraged revivalist groups to spread the virus of communal hatred. The effect of this was seen in the increasing number of communal riots, the worst of which was in Calcutta in April 1926.[110] This tragedy cast its shadow over the far off nooks and corners of Bengal and was even felt outside the province. Unscrupulous politicians like Fazlul Haq and Abdur Rahim thought it fit not only to swim with the current of communalism but to revitalise it and all even to perpetuate it, if possible.

During the all too brief honeymoon of Hindu-Muslim relations, Fazlul Haq was the most prominent Bengali Muslim in the Congress camp. From 1915 to 1919 he was in the forefront of agitational politics. But this phase in Haq's career ended in 1920 when he rejected Gandhi's non-cooperation programme and left the Congress. 'You know very well', he wrote in response to an invitation to attend a Congress meeting, 'that between me on one side and those representing the present-day

---

[109]Notice, for example, that once communal relations began to deteriorate, the Bengal Khilafat Committee came into action. On 29 May 1926, it held an emergency meeting to enrol volunteers for the defence of mosques, *dargahs* and other sacred places of the Muslims. *Forward*, 14 May 1926.

[110]Report by J.E. Armstrong, Commissioner of Police, Lytton Papers, MSS. EUR. F. 160 (46), IOL.

politics of the Congress, there is a gulf of difference which no worldly diplomacy can possibly bridge over. Your ideals and mine are different. You have adopted an ideal in the Congress to which I cannot subscribe'.[111] Haq was certainly the most prominent defector from the Bengal Congress. He had a strong base of support amongst the Bengali Muslims as opposed to the Urdu-speaking minority which was under the influence of Azad. He also had close links with some Muslim zamindars, such as the family of the Nawab of Dacca, and with the Western-educated elite in Calcutta and Dacca, and worked with them during the various phases of his political career. This gave Haq the unique advantage of commanding the support of two important groups in Bengal which, needless to emphasise, were the only effective ones in Bengal politics. In losing Haq's support, the Congress lost in Bengal an important spokesman for its cause.

In 1924, Haq was appointed Minister along with Abdul Karim Ghuznavi, a large landholder of Mymensingh, and Surendranath Mallick who had served as the first Indian non-official chairman of the Calcutta Corporation. But this ministry was overthrown by the Swarajists within six months of its being in office. During this period of confrontation, Haq and Ghuznavi used every means to stay in office—they offered bribes to some councillors and inducements to others. On 9 July 1924, Haq informed the Governor that Allabux Sircar, MLC from Dacca, had accepted a bribe of Rs 3,000 and had, in return, agreed to abstain from voting in favour of the Swarajists.[112] He also suggested that Rai Bahadur Pyarelal Das should be invited to join the Ministry because he commanded the votes of Bhusan Roy and Allabux.[113] The trump card, however, was communal. Aided and abetted by the government, Haq and Ghuznavi raised the cry that the aim of the Hindus was to get rid of the Muslim ministry with the object of supplanting it by a Hindu one. They also encouraged Khan Bahadur Musharraf Husain of Jalpaiguri to demand that 80 per cent of government appointments be provided to Muslims. This

[111]Fazlul Haq to Sarat Chandra Bose, 22 February 1921, quoted in A. Rab, *A.K. Fazlul Haq*, p. 56.
[112]Haq to Lytton, 9 July 1924, Lytton Papers (18).
[113]Haq to Lytton, 4 August 1924, *Ibid.*

was done on the assumption that the Hindu Swarajists would refuse to concede such a demand and, consequently, the Muslims in their disappointment would withdraw from the Swaraj Party, jeopardising any effective Swarajist opposition to the Ministry.[114] But these Machiavellian methods failed to produce the desired results and, on 26 August, the Legislative Council rejected the demand for ministerial salaries for the second time. As a result, the ministers resigned and Lytton reluctantly suspended the constitution. Haq was bitter and complained that he had 'fallen a victim to the vilest conspiracy' hatched by the Hindus.[115] This accusation was false. The ministry was overthrown by the combined opposition of the Hindu and Muslim members of the Swaraj Party.

By the end of 1925, Haq had tarnished his image in Bengal politics. The Swaraj Party made great play of the fact that he had offered bribes to several councillors in order to buy their votes; it launched a campaign against him which, in Haq's own words, 'had the effect of weaning away the sympathy of some of my best friends and supporters'.[116] Even the government ignored his claims when a new ministry was formed in 1926. Haq was disappointed. 'I sacrificed a position of assured success at the Bar to take to politics [more with a view to serve my community than anything else], and politics has given me but a poor return', he wrote to Lytton.[117] However, Haq had been in politics far too long to stay away now. He was proud of his past political career and was determined to regain the position he once occupied in Bengal politics.[118] But he was faced with the serious difficulty of having limited options: his connections with the British did not help him to boost his career in the legislative council; nor could he play a leading part in the Bengal Congress which, after Das's sudden death,

---

[114]Speaking on Husain's resolution, Das said: 'I distinctly see what is behind this resolution. What is behind the resolution is the shadow of a shadowy Minister and radiance of a great personage. Was it your direction or was it some malacious chance which dragged the mover and his supporters into what may be called the official block of this House . . . ?' *Forward*, 14 March 1924.

[115]Haq to Lytton, 2 September 1924, Lytton Papers (18).

[116]Haq to Lytton, 11 March 1925, *Ibid.*

[117]Haq to Lytton, 25 November 1925, *Ibid.*

[118]Haq to Lytton, 24 November 1925, *Ibid.*

had passed into the hands of the 'Big Five'. There was, however, one viable alternative. This was to play the role of a communal leader and perform a *volte face* on all political and constitutional issues.[119] Haq's scheme, as is evident from his political activities after his resignation, was to build up a strong and unified Muslim party which, he hoped, would enable him to assume the leadership of his co-religionists and provide him with a strong base to negotiate with the Bengal Congress and the provincial government.

Haq launched himself in this new role on the eve of the provincial elections in November 1926. With the help of Husain Suhrawardy, former Deputy Mayor of the Calcutta Corporation; Mujibur Rahman, editor of *Mussalman*; Haji Abdur Rashid Khan, Calcutta Corporation's Deputy Executive Officer; and Maulana Akram Khan, lawyer and defector from the Non-cooperation movement, Haq founded the Bengal Council Party in order to contest the elections independently of the Congress on a purely communal basis.[120] 'We have', wrote the organ of the new party, 'after all realised that the Congress is a Hindu organisation and Muslims have no chance of holding its leading strings. They are welcome within the ranks of Congress as long as they prefer to remain as the henchmen of Hindu leaders and slaves to their cunningly planned intrigues to keep Muslims out of real power.'[121] This was the voice of a few disgruntled politicians who had failed to make much profit out of the Hindu-dominated legislative council and were now willing to fan communal passions in order to foster their own political interests. In the prevalent tense communal atmosphere, this was like playing with fire. But it was by no means plain sailing for Haq—he had a rival in Abdur Rahim who was a

[119]Haq had consistently criticised the government for withholding parliamentary government from India. But in 1924 he preformed a *volte face* before the Reforms Advisory Committee by insisting that representative institutions were unsuited to India. He said that the 'incessant communal strife and the wider cleavages between class and class, creed and creed, create a political atmosphere in which the growth of self-governing institutions becomes an impossibility'. *Views of Local Government on the Working of the Reforms, 1924* (London, 1925), Cmd. 2362, p. 151.

[120]*Moslem Chronicle*, 24 September 1926.

[121]*Ibid.*, 20 August 1926.

potential threat to his dream of assuming the leadership of Muslims. Over the next two years, the two men were involved in a keen struggle for leadership.

Sir Abdur Rahim, a zamindar of Midnapore and a former judge of the Madras High Court, was more overtly communal than Haq and far more determined to exploit communal slogans as and when the occasion arose. After the expiry of his term on the Executive Council in 1925, he plunged into the muddle of communal politics. His first act was to address the Muslim League session in December 1925 at Aligarh, where he delivered an anti-Hindu and anti-Congress speech.[122] During the next few months, Rahim endeavoured to secure the support of the Urdu-speaking Muslims in Bengal,[123] the *ulama*, and the professional classes. By mid-April 1926, he had mustered enough support to launch the Bengal Muslim Party. 'The experience of the last three years', stated the party's manifesto, 'has shown how time after time the Muslim members of the Council belonging to the Swaraj or Nationalist parties, which are organisations controlled by astute Hindu politicians who supply the brains and the funds of the parties, had to sacrifice, at their behest, the clear interests of the Muslim electorate and the Muslim community.'[124] The Bengal Muslim Party, on the other hand, promised to remove the 'considerable disabilities and difficulties' faced by the community. It proposed to achieve this by ensuring that Muslims gained 56 per cent representation in the Legislative Council, local bodies, public services, universities, and various other professions. In other words, everything was to be organised along communal lines and Muslims *per se* were to have power and influence in proportion to their population.

With this distinctly communal platform, Rahim entered the elections in November 1926. Everything was working in his favour. The Calcutta riots in April 1926 had left a legacy of

---

[122]For the text of his speech, see Pirzada (ed.), *Foundations of Pakistan*, Vol. 2.

[123]This is evident from the fact that he actively championed the cause of Urdu in many of his speeches. See, for example, his speech at the *Jamiat-ul-ulama* session in March 1926. *Amrita Bazar Patrika*, 14 March 1926.

[124]N.N. Mitra (ed.), *The Indian Quarterly Register*, January-June 1926 (Calcutta, n.d.), Vol. 1, p. 67.

bitterness which Rahim exploited to the full. He went to the electors with a simple religious appeal: 'Mussalman! who are you going to vote for? For the servants of Rahim (Worshippers of God) or for the slaves of Rama (Hindus)?'[125] Most Bengali Muslim voters fell in behind Rahim, and his party gained a majority of seats in the Legislative Council. Rahim's own popularity is illustrated by the fact that he won the North Calcutta seat by securing 641 of the 648 votes.

In January 1927, Rahim was invited to form a ministry, but he was unable to recommend any Hindu member who would be willing to work with him.[126] He sought to win over the sympathy of Muslims MLCs by representing the intransigence of Hindus as a gross insult to the Muslim community. He said:

> There can be no doubt that this [namely, the unwillingness of the Hindus to cooperate with him] is the result of a combination among B. Chakravarti and P.C. Mitter and some other Hindu gentlemen of their ways of thinking to prevent me from forming a ministry. For some time past politicians of this class have been carrying on a ceaseless campaign against me simply because I sought to unite the representative men of my community in order to protect and safeguard its just interests.[127]

But this argument fell on deaf ears. Suhrawardy and Ghuznavi, who were themselves jockeying for a position in the ministry, refused to cooperate with Rahim. As a result, the Governor approached Ghuznavi who managed to form a ministry by weaning away some of Rahim's supporters and by securing the support of dissident Hindu Swarajists led by Byomkesh Chakravarti. Rahim was left high and dry.

[125] Quoted in Broomfield, *Elite Conflict*, p. 280.
[126] In fact, the Hindu press described Rahim as the 'high priest of communalism' and campaigned actively for his removal from the ministry. The *Amrita Bazar Patrika* wrote: 'In view of Sir Abdur Rahim's selection as Minister Bengal plunged again into the vortex of communal strife to unite and overthrow the ministry.' *Amrita Bazar Patrika*, 23 January 1927.
[127] *Ibid*,, 27 January 1927.

COMMUNALISM IN PUNJAB

Communal politics in the mid-twenties was a feature of many provinces including the Punjab. There were the usual squabbles over the distribution of seats in the council and local bodies, and the proportion of representation in government service. These differences, as we have seen in the case of Bengal, were often reflected in the resurgence of communal and revivalist bodies which purported to defend the interests of their followers. There were, however, certain important differences in the problems of Bengal and the Punjab. In Bengal, the Muslim majority had to settle its political claims with a relatively advanced Hindu community. In the Punjab, on the other hand, the Sikhs further complicated the problem. They formed about 14 per cent of the population, but claimed a far higher proportion of seats—about 30 per cent—on the grounds that they were the former rulers of the province and formed a large proportion of the army.[128] In other words, the struggle for power in the Punjab involved not two but three parties. There was one other significant difference between the two provinces. The Muslims in Punjab were far more advanced and prosperous than their co-religionists in Bengal. This factor placed them in a comparatively better position in relation to the existing power structure.[129] Punjab possessed a well-entrenched Muslim aristocracy which was nursed over the years by the British government. To the west of Lahore, Muslims were the main landholding group. In districts opened up by irrigation projects, notably Gujranwala, Lyallpur, and Montgomery, they shared this dominance with the Sikhs, but further west, in the districts where Muslims formed more than 80 per cent of the population, their pre-eminence was unqualified.[130]

[128]R.M. Sahni, 'Communal Representation', *Tribune*, 19 September 1924.

[129]In the Punjab, while the Muslims were not employed in the higher echelons of government service in numbers proportionate to their share of the population, they were employed to a much greater extent than their literacy, as a community, would warrant. In the Police Department, for example, they held 25 per cent of the appointments. In the scale of Rs 200 to Rs 300, they held 50 per cent of the posts, while the Sikhs and Hindus jointly held just over 16 per cent. *PSC*, 1913, Appendix XV, Vol. 12, Cd. 7901, pp. 156-58.

[130]Page, 'Prelude to Partition', pp. 21-22.

The government had a pronounced bias towards the landed aristocracy because it was heavily dependent on them for the recruitment of soldiers for the army, and because they could be effectively used as a counterpoise to the national move‑ ment. In the distribution of rural and urban seats, therefore, the government showed a strong bias towards the rural areas. Consequently, the chief beneficiaries of the Montagu‑Chelms‑ ford Reforms were members of the Punjab Moslem Association and the Punjab Central Association, representing the Sikh and Jat interests. Some of the notable Muslims who dominated the Council were Umar Hayat Khan Tiwana, Firoz Khan Noon, who represented Shahpur West from 1920 to 1923 and Shahpur East during 1923-36, Sikandar Hayat Khan, who came from a zamindar family of Wah, Ahmad Yar Khan Daulatana, who had an estate of 45,000 acres in East Multan, and Captain Mumtaz Mohammad Khan Tiwana.

The first Punjab Council, constituted in 1921, was composed of (besides twenty-three nominated officials and non-officials) seventy-one elected members of whom thirty-five were Muslims, fifteen Sikhs and the rest Hindus. As in the UP, the organisa‑ tion of the parties in the Council was on non-communal lines. 'The formation of parties', declared Fazl-i-Husain, leader of the rural bloc, 'has taken the line of the "have gots", and "have nots", with the result that there is a party existing of most of the Muslims and some of the landholding Hindus and Sikhs, because these are the communities which have been more or less excluded by the "have gots" who had enjoyed the monopoly of the public services under the pre-reform administration.'[131] The landlords in the Rural Party belonged to all communities and worked in close cooperation on questions which affected the dominant rural, as opposed to the dominant urban, interests. An attempt by the commercial group to repeal the Land Alienation Act, for example, evoked a storm of indignant protests from both the Hindu and Muslim landlords. They interpreted this as a move to undermine their rural dominance.[132]

The architect of the Rural Party was Fazl-i-Husain. He

[131]Quoted in Husain, *Fazl-i-Husain*, p. 152.
[132]*Punjab Administration Report*, 1922-23 (Lahore, 1924), p. 17.

had defected from the Congress in April 1920 on the issue of non-cooperation. In November 1920, he was elected to the Punjab Council from one of the four landholder constituencies and was appointed Minister of Education. In 1923, he was re-elected by the same constituency and entered the Council as leader of the Punjab National Unionist Party. The party cut across communal distinctions and held out a programme which aimed at preserving and fostering the dominant rural interests.[133] Some of its programme was later embodied in the Money-Lenders Registration Bill, the Punjab Court Fees (Amendment) Bill, and the Punjab (Urban Property) Rent Regulation Bill.

The programme set out by the Unionist Party evoked widespread opposition from several quarters, particularly from the moneylenders, the prosperous merchants, the traders, and the professional classes. At the same time, the inter-communal character of the party was threatened because of the policies of Fazl-i-Husain. As Minister of Education, he took a keen interest in promoting the cause of education amongst Muslims. He gave generous grants to the existing Muslim schools[134] and colleges, and encouraged the establishment of

[133]Some of the aims and objects of the Unionist Party were: (1) to attain dominion status within the British Commonwealth of Nations by constitutional means at as early a date as possible; (2) to secure a fair distribution of the burden of provincial taxes between agricultural and other classes; (3) to check the exploitation of economically backward classes by economically dominant classes; and (4) to preserve intact the Punjab Alienation Act as a measure of protection to backward classes. Husain, *Fazi-i-Husain* pp. 154-55. For a useful analysis of the Unionist Party in its early years, see Ashiq Husain Butalvi, *Iqbal ke akhri do saal* (Karachi, 1961), pp. 163-93.

[134]By the close of the nineteenth century, Punjab had a large number of special Muslim schools which were mostly under private management. In places like Lahore, Multan and Sialkot there were local *anjumans* whose main function was to further the cause of education in the local community, and they maintained a college as well as a number of high, middle or primary schools. The *Anjuman-i-Himayat-i-Islam*, for example, was entirely supported by private subscriptions and donations, and it maintained a college, a high school and a primary school for boys and girls. Other similar institutions were the M.A.O. High School, Amritsar, and Mamuje High School, Rawalpindi.

new ones.[135] In November 1924, he sanctioned a grant for setting up three new intermediate colleges at Lyallpur, Gujrat, and Campbellpur for the benefit of the large Muslim population in western Punjab.[136] He also laid down that places at the Government College and the Medical College in Lahore should be distributed amongst Hindus, Muslims and Sikhs in the ratio of 40: 40: 20.

Fazl-i-Husain also made some significant changes in the working of the municipalities and local boards. He introduced communal electorates in eleven municipalities in addition to the thirty-eight already existing in January 1921, and adopted a new formula of representation according to which the elected seats were distributed among the communities in proportion to their population. This policy was obviously calculated to benefit the numerically preponderant Muslim community at the expense of the educationally and economically advanced Hindus. Between 1917 and 1920, the Punjab government had greatly increased the number of municipalities which possessed communal electorates and the percentage of Muslim seats rose from 40 to 44 per cent. As a result of Fazl-i-Husain's bill, however, Muslims improved their position still further.[137] The

[135]In justification of his policy of giving financial aid to Muslim schools and colleges, Fazl-i-Husain argued that there was an unequal distribution of grants to the government-aided institutions. He provided the following figures for 1921-22 to illustrate his point. These figures set out the amount of grants sanctioned (in Rupees) to the government-aided schools in five districts.

	Hindus	Muslims	Sikhs	Christians	Total
Ambala	55,245	15,800	8,698	20,887	100,430
Jullundur	52,396	13,741	30,943	27,287	123,367
Lahore	97,413	61,954	88,189	117,224	364,780
Rawalpindi	46,220	37,015	60,039	40,253	183,527
Multan	35,287	30,249	17,073	250	83,333
Total	286,561	158,929	204,942	205,901	856,333

Source: *Punjab Legislative Council Debates*, 5 March 1924, (Lahore, 1924), Vol. VI, No. 8, p. 315.

[136]*Ibid.*, 18 November 1924, Vol. VII, No. 7 p. 470.

[137]Muslims formed 53 per cent of the municipal population; from 1920 to 1923 the proportion of Muslims was increased from 44 per cent to 49 per cent. Tinker, *The Foundations of Local Self-Government*, p. 135.

same applied to the district boards of which Muslims controlled over 53 per cent in 1925 (See Table 6.3).

The Punjabi Hindu elite viewed Fazl-i-Husain's policies as
an assault on their social and economic position. 'Muhammadans under the leadership of Mian Fazl-i-Husain are out
to relegate Hindus to an insignificant position in the Punjab',
lamented Amar Nath Chopra, a High Court *vakil* in Lahore.[138]
When the Municipal Amendment Act was passed,
it aroused a storm of indignation among the Hindus.
Lala Duni Chand, member of the Legislative Assembly, and
Lala Ganga Ram, member of the Punjab Legislative Council,
persuaded Hindu voters and the candidates to withdraw from
the municipal elections (held on 17 December 1923) in protest
against the increased Muslim representation on the municipal
boards.[139] The Sikhs also joined in the boycott in order to press
their demand for separate representation instead of representation by election jointly with the Hindus.[140] In Lahore, Rawalpindi and Ferozepur, where Muslims gained control of the
municipalities, Hindu members resigned as a symbolic gesture
of protest.[141] But in places like Gojra, Hissar, and Rohtak,
where their dominance was maintained, they kept quiet.

The growing communal squabbles were also reflected in
the Legislative Council. Here the Hindu councillors set aside
their class and caste differences in a determined and organised
effort to oust Fazl-i-Husain. Their grievance against him was
that he had not only unfairly and unjustly distributed patronage to his community,[142] but had also extended the principle

---

[138]*Tribune*, 28 December 1923.

[139]The Ambala municipality contained an equal number of Hindu
and Muslim members, but in pursuance of Fazl-i-Husain's reforms, the
Muslim element increased from six to eight while Hindus remained at
six. *Punjab Legisaltive Council Debates*, 4-5 August 1924, Vol. VII, No. 1,
p. 89.

[140]For the arguments advanced by the Sikhs in support of their
demand, See *Punjab Legislative Council Debates*, 29 February 1924, Vol.
VI, No. 5, p. 205.

[141]FR (Punjab), 1 July 1923, Home Poll. 1923, 125, NAI.

[142]Lala Sevak Ram alleged that, since 1920, Hindu schools had not
received any grants-in-aid in Multan division. According to him, Fazl-
i-Husain 'gives grants-in-aid to the old Hindu schools and goes on
opening new Mussalman schools. Because there are innumerable Hindu

TABLE 6.3

COMMUNAL COMPOSITION OF THE PUNJAB DISTRICT BOARDS, 1925

Name of District Boards	Distribution of Population			Total Number of Members Elected or Nominated		
	Muslims	Sikhs	Hindus & Others	Muslims	Sikhs	Hindus
Hissar	18,571	42,956	487,620	11	—	27
Rohtak	91,854	432	604,291	5	—	34
Gurgaon	189,119	846	420,933	16	—	24
Karnal	235,618	12,280	580,828	11	3	26
Ambala	157,338	95,155	311,122	9	—	27
Kangra	38,197	1,830	722,600	1	—	37
Hoshiarpur	279,450	132,250	495,326	13	12	18
Jullundur	303,427	199,923	202,347	15	21	3
Ludhiana	147,336	230,777	111,519	10	24	1
Ferozepur	437,462	291,788	251,580	14	22	7
Lahore	227,198	90,684	88,599	20	17	4
Amritsar	343,073	262,067	144,887	12	22	2
Gurdaspur	385,661	133,892	269,259	15	15	12
Sialkot	580,532	74,939	282,352	20	12	5
Gujranwala	387,152	45,027	99,782	21	10	4
Sheikhpura	357,797	85,253	110,023	19	7	4
Jhelum	422,979	18,626	35,463	25	3	2

Contd.........

TABLE 6.3 Contd.........

Rawalpindi	214,070	10,819	11,254	24	4	2
Attock	436,418	14,631	15,840	32	2	2
Mianwali	288,451	2,242	33,281	25	—	5
Montgomery	497,945	93,297	91,827	17	5	6
Lyallpur	515,122	145,063	177,868	27	11	3
Jhang	475,388	9,376	85,795	24	1	5
Multan	671,307	16,342	105,432	29	3	4
Muzaffargarh	482,134	4,530	57,697	24	1	5
Dera Ghazi Khan	385,104	670	39,557	29	3	4
Shahpur	552,014	24,490	65,692	32	3	1
Gujrat	670,340	47,105	50,609	35	2	2

Source : *Punjab Legislative Council Debates*, 30 November 1925, Vol. VIII, No. 26, p. 1319.

of separate representation to public services, local bodies, and educational institutions. In March 1923, Raja Narendranath, a rich landowner and president of the Punjab Hindu Sabha, moved for a cut in Fazl-i-Husain's 'salary as a protest against his policies.[143] The motion received the support of all the elected Hindu and Sikh members, but it was defeated because of the solid opposition of the Muslims and the British officials. Following this event, Muslims in the Legislative Council supported Fazl-i-Husain *en bloc*, thus forcing party divisions to run along the lines of communal cleavage. Many Hindu councillors, on the other hand, remained hostile to Fazl-i-Husain. In the summer of 1925, when Fazl-i-Husain officiated as member of the Viceroy's Executive Council, the *Tribune* echoed the feelings of many Punjabi Hindus:

> The disappearance of Sir Fazl-i-Husain from the stage of Punjab politics, even though temporary, will undoubtedly make many people heave a sigh of relief . . . . The tide of communalism among the educated and politically minded Mussalmans of the Punjab, thanks largely to Sir Fazl-i-Husain's policy, has been so high during the last four years, that it is no easy thing for any individual or group . . . to go against the tide.[144]

Another issue which aroused communal passions in the Punjab Legislative Council centred around the Money-Lenders Registration Bill.[145] Introduced by Mir Maqbool Ahmad of

schools he can always show that he is giving grants to as many Hindu schools as to Muslim schools'. *Ibid.*, 14 March 1925, Vol. VIII, No. 11, p. 559.

[143]For the role of Narendranath, see B. Cleghon, 'Religion and Politics: The Leadership of the All-India Hindu Mahasabha in Punjab and Maharashtra, 1920-1930', in B.N. Pandey (ed.), *Leadership in South Asia* (Delhi, 1977), pp. 400-404, 411-12, 418-19.

[144]*Tribune*, 26 August 1925.

[145]Most moneylenders in the Punjab were Hindus and their debtors were either petty Muslim zamindars or poor peasants. In western Punjab, the money lenders belonged to the Agarwal, Khatri and Arora castes, and their borrowers were mainly Muslim peasants. In the western Dera Ismail Khan district, 86,000 acres (8 per cent) of the cultivable land was transferred during 1880-85 from the Muslim culti-

Amritsar, the Bill aimed at preventing the moneylenders from biting too deep into their debtors flesh. It laid down that all moneylenders should be registered and keep accounts—their failure to do so would absolve the debtors of all legal liability to pay the principal amount or the interest rates. But certain vested interests, led in the press by Gulshan Rai, the secretary of the Punjab Hindu Sabha, and in the Council by Raja Narendranath, howled down the Bill simply by labelling it a Muslim measure.[146] Pandit Nanak Chand, who represented the non-Muslim rural constituency of Hoshiarpur and had wide connections with the city bankers and traders, declared that the Bill was 'a Muhammadan measure because in the Quran people are asked not to lend money on interest because it is unlawful to do so.'[147] He was supported by Chaudhri Ram Singh of Kangra and other Hindu councillors.[148] The entire discussion in Council proceeded so strongly on communal lines as to cloud the real issues involved in the Bill. It was a clear illustration of how the communal bogey was raised by certain groups to protect and promote their vested interests.

The growing dissensions in the Punjab Legislative Council encouraged the growth of revivalist and communal movements, the most important of which was the Punjab Provincial Hindu Sabha. Formed in 1907, the Provincial Hindu Sabha held its first conference in Lahore in October 1909 under the presidentship of Protil Chandra Chatterjee, a retired judge of the Punjab High Court.[149] Its aim was to oppose the 'extravagant and unwarranted demands of Muslims regarding

vatois to the Hindu moneylenders. S.S. Thorburn and M.L. Darling had constantly drawn the government's attention to the growing indebtedness of the cultivating class and the transfer of landed property by mortgage and sale to the urban moneylenders. The Punjab Land Alienation Act of 1901 had disqualified the non-agricultural classes from owning land, but it did not go very far in relieving the peasants from the clutches of the moneylenders. The Punjab Money-Lenders Registration Bill was an important step in the right direction.

[146] *Tribune*, 25 October 1924.

[147] *Punjab Legislative Council Debates*, 18 November 1924, Vol. VII, No. 7, p. 514.

[148] *Ibid.*, p. 523.

[149] Indra Prakash, *Hindu Mahasabha: Its Contribution to India's Politics* (Delhi, 1966), p. 11.

representation in the reformed legislative councils', and to protest against the concessions received by Muslims under the Act of 1909.[150] By following an overtly and specifically Hindu politics, the Sabha was able to secure the support of Hindu traders, lawyers, merchants, and bankers who nursed a grievance against the Land Alienation Act and the Morley-Minto Reforms.[151] 'The Hindus have organised themselves', announced the *Indian Patriot*, 'into a separate body in the belief that by such separate organisation alone can they safeguard the interests of their community.'[152] The issues raised at the Sabha sessions provided topics for excited discussions as Hindus hoped for a better future—one in which they could maintain their status and prevent further governmental action against their interests.[153]

From 1916 to 1922, the Punjab Hindu Sabha lay low on account of the Congress-Muslim League rapprochement, the Home Rule movement, the Rowlatt Satyagraha and the Khilafat movement. But in the aftermath of the Non-cooperation movement, the All-India Hindu Sabha and its provincial branches launched themselves with renewed vigour. In the Punjab, the Sabha gained the adherence of a wide spectrum of the Hindu community because of the policies of Fazl-i-Husain, and claimed to speak for and defend the interests of Punjabi Hindus. Its revival, therefore, must be explained chiefly in terms of the political struggle which characterised Punjab politics since 1922.

The key figure in the revival of the Punjab Hindu Sabha was Lala Lajpat Rai, whose inclination, according to Jawaharlal Nehru, 'was somewhat to the right as well as towards a more communal orientation.'[154] The Lala was an all-India politician with a strong political base in Punjab, where he had strong links with the Arya Samaj, the cow-protection societies, and the

[150]*Tribune*, 6 April 1909, and 3 November 1909.

[151]For the composition of the Hindu Sabha in 1909, see *Ibid.*, 5 October 1909, 7 October 1909 and 16 November 1909.

[152]Quoted in *Ibid.*, 3 November 1909.

[153]*Panjabee*, 26 October, 1909, quoted in Jones, *Arya Dharm*, p. 291.

[154]Nehru, *An Autobiography*, p. 158.

Hindu Sabha.[155] According to him, the Arya Samaj taught the 'true and genuine Hinduism of the Vedas, it works in the interest of the Hindus, and it defends the Hindu community from the onslaught of alien religions'.[156] He also defended the *shuddhi*[157] and *sangathan*[158] movements. 'The principle of *shuddhi*', he wrote, 'has now been accepted by the Hindu Sabha, and I am free to confess that the idea at the back of this decision is partly political, partly communal, and partly humanitarian'.[159]

As a spokesman of Punjabi Hindus, Lajpat Rai campaigned actively against the principle of communal representation, and sought to unite 'Hindu opinion' against it. In 1924, he initiated a move to involve Hindu leaders of other provinces in an effort to 'arrange for a permanent machinery to clarify and crystallise Hindu public opinion on all political questions'.[160] Such a machinery already existed in the Hindu Mahasabha, but the Lala was anxious to revitalise it and turn it into an effective national body. In 1925, he appealed to various Hindu groups to set aside their differences and unite under the flag of the

[155]According to the *Tribune* of 7 December 1923: 'In the Punjab and at the present time the Congress and Lala Lajpat Rai are inseparable terms. His influence, authority and prestige are the influence and authority of the Congress itself.' Although this is an exaggerated assessment, it gives us some idea of Lajpat Rai's influence in the Punjab.

[156]Lajpat Rai, *A History of the Arya Samaj* (Bombay, 1967), p. 183.

[157]*Shuddhi* is a Sanskrit word which means purification. In religious terminology it was applied to (1) conversion to Hinduism of persons belonging to 'foreign religions'; (2) reconversion of those who adopted one of the 'foreign religions', and (3) reclamation, i.e., raising the status of the depressed classes. The *shuddhi* movement received direct inspiration from the Arya Samaj movement, launched by Dayanand Saraswati in 1875. The proselytising work of the Samaj was effected largely by a branch of the Arya Pratinidhi Sabha established in 1909. Later other organisations such as the Hindu Ashrams, the Hindu Sabhas, the Rajput Shuddhi Sabha and the All-India Khatri Sabha also joined in.

[158]The *sangathan* movement aimed at consolidating and uniting the Hindus. Moreover, it sought to efface the image of Hindu as a *dhoti*-wearing coward and to replace it with the image of a militant Hindu who would be willing to maintain his honour and that of his commnnity. G.R. Thursby, *Hindu-Muslim Relations in British India* (Leiden, 1975), p. 159.

[159]Lajpat Rai, 'Hindu Muslim Problem', *Tribune*, 13 December 1924.

[160]Lajpat Rai to Purshotamdas Thakurdas, 13 December 1924, Thakurdas Papers.

Hindu Mahasabha.[161] This appeal was consistent with the desire of many Hindu Mahasabhites, who wanted the organisation to be a 'Hindu Rashtra Sabha' which would shape the destiny of the 'Hindu Nation' in all its social, political, and cultural aspects.[162] In terms of ideology, therefore, there was little difference between Lajpat Rai, a leading Congressman, and many Hindu sectarian leaders.

The Punjab Hindu Sabha also served as a rallying point for a multitude of Hindu revivalist groups: the Shuddhi Sabha, the Arya Samaj and the orthodox Sanathan Dharma Sabhas. A prominent leader of the Shuddhi Sabha was Mahatma Munshi Ram, known as Swami Shraddhanand. He came under the influence of the Arya Samaj leader, Dayanand Saraswati, early in his life. In the 1890s, he was active in the Antaranga Sabha, a branch of the Shuddhi Sabha, and later he renounced his legal career to conduct a *Gurukul*, an educational institution, with the object of reviving ancient Indian philosophy, history, and literature.[163] But during the Rowlatt Satyagraha, Shraddhanand was stirred by the nationalist upsurge and took a leading part in organising a *hartal* at Delhi. He also joined the Khilafat movement, and was invited to speak from the Juma Masjid pulpit in 1919. In 1922, however, Shraddhanand severed his connections with the Congress in order to revive the Shuddhi Sabhas. Encouraged by Malaviya and Lajpat Rai, he concentrated his efforts on converting the Malkhana Rajputs settled in Multan and Agra.[164] This aroused the hostility of the UP

---

[161]*India Quarterly Register*, January-June 1925, Vol. 1, pp. 378-80. From April to December 1925, the Lala was busy enlisting support for the Hindu Sabhas and the *sangathan* movement. He presided over the Calcutta session of the All-India Hindu Mahasabha, visited Assam, Burma and Sind to organise *sangathan* and local Hindu Sabhas, and chaired a meeting of the Bombay Hindu Conference held in Bombay city.

[162]Prakash, *Hindu Mahasabha*, p. 8.

[163]See M.R. Jambunathan (ed.), *Swami Shraddhanand* (Bombay, 1961).

[164]The Malkhana Rajputs were converted under the Afghans, and settled as military colonies in the Jumna tract in the neighbourhood of Agra and Delhi. Their origin, however, is not clear. Malkhanas—a title and not a clan name—were probably Jadon Rajputs formerly, some were Jats and others were Agarwal *banias*. Many Malkhana Rajputs in the Mathura district were descendants of Tarkar Brahmans.

and Punjabi Muslims and Shraddhanand's career as an active politician and social reformer was cut short as he eventually fell at the hands of a Muslim fanatic.[165] This marked the beginning of a prolonged period of communal violence which took a heavy toll of human lives when Hindus and Muslims embarked on a mutual orgy of violence.

When C.R. Das, Motilal Nehru, Sarojini Naidu, Ajmal Khan and Azad visited Punjab in March 1923, they found the communal situation virtually hopeless. 'On our arrival here, we found that the relations between the Hindus and Muslims, both educated and uneducated, were so greatly strained that each community had practically arrayed itself in an armed camp against each other', ran their report.[166] In 1926, the communal situation in the Punjab remained unchanged.

---

[165]Although many Muslims condemned the murder of Shraddhanand, they did not consider it as a 'national tragedy'. Some Hindus, however, regarded the Swami as 'an apostle of unity'. A Shraddhanand Memorial Trust Fund was raised and till September 1927, Rs 118,678 were collected with Bombay contributing Rs 29,177, UP Rs. 14,613, Punjab 39,530, and Bengal and Assam 2,626. Jayakar Papers (436).

[166]'The conclusion to which we have arrived', continued the report, 'is that while it is true that almost the whole of Hindu and Muslim population of the Punjab is more or less affected, the reasons which apply to the so-called educated classes are entirely different from those which apply to the masses and we feel constrained to say that the latter have to no small extent been exploited by interested persons among the former for their own selfish purposes'. AICC Papers (3).

CHAPTER SEVEN

COMMUNAL RELATIONS IN THE LOCALITIES

One of the striking developments in the mid-1920s was the recrudescence of communal riots, involving loss of life and property. The record of such riots dates back to 1810, but in no period were they as widespread as in the 1920s. From 1922 to 1928, generally, Hindu-Muslim riots involved many more people, took a heavier toll of human lives and left a permanent legacy of hatred in the Indian subcontinent. From March to July 1923, there were communal outbreaks in Amritsar, Multan, Moradabad, Meerut, and Allahabad. In August and September there were further outbreaks at Amritsar, Panipat, Gonda, Jabalpur, Agra and Rae Bareilly. The most serious one during this period was a disturbance which occurred at Saharanpur in connection with the Muharram festival. In 1924, the frequency of riots increased in many parts of the country. From April to October, there were violent clashes in Hapur,[1] Delhi, Lahore, Lucknow, Moradabad, Bhagalpur, Nagpur, Shahjahanpur, and Allahabad. The most serious outbreak of all, which was followed by an exodus of the Hindu population, took place at Kohat in the North-West Frontier Province.[2] It was against this

[1] Report on Hapur riots by P.W. Marsh, District Magistrate, 16 April 1924, Home Poll. 1924, 249-I, NAI.

[2] Kohat was, next to Dera Ismail Khan, the most sparsely inhabited district of the North-West Frontier Province. It was the home of a Pathan tribe, the Khattaks, who constituted more that one-half of the total population. There was a small Hindu and Sikh population as well, which was mainly engaged in trade and petty business. The spark which

background that Gandhi declared, on 18 September 1924, that he would fast for three weeks; but even this did not stem the tide of communal violence. According to official statistics, there were eighty-eight communal riots from 1923 to 1927, in the course of which over four hundred were killed and five thousand injured.[3] From September 1927 to June 1928, there were nineteen riots which affected all the provinces except Madras.[4] This was a far cry from the communal fraternisation of the early 1920s. In January 1927, even an optimist like Gandhi told a meeting at Comilla in Bengal that the Hindu-Muslim problem had passed out of human hands into God's hand, and confessed at the end of the year that his methods were 'out of tune with the present temper of both the communities'.

What were the factors which caused communal riots? Were they simply a manifestation of local economic and social grievances which acquired a communal colour? Or, were they the result of the supposedly ancient, inherent, ineradicable religious antagonism between the two communities? If so, why were communal disturbances becoming more frequent in this period than in earlier times? And finally, where did they occur most, and why? These questions need to be examined in order to study the communal situation in the largely unexplored arena of the localities.

The immediate occasions, though not the deeper causes, which sparked off communal outbreaks were: music before mosques, cow-slaughter, and disputes connected with the obser-vance of religious festivals or ceremonies. Muslims maintained that the playing of music before mosques not only interrupted their prayers, but interfered with the canons of Islam. Hindus, on the other hand, argued that their religion and social customs

---

caused the explosion in August and September 1924 was a poem published by the Sanathan Dharam Sabha, which was considered by Muslims as an outrageous insult to Islam. For details, see Report on Kohat Riots by Charles A. Innes, Home Poll. 1925, 31-II, NAI.

[3]Quoted in W.R. Smith, *Nationalism and Reform in India* (London, 1938) p. 353; *Report*, U.P. p. 79.

[4]*Indian Statutory Commission*, Vol. I, p. 27.

required processions to pass through public streets with music.[5] They further maintained that a ban on music would threaten their civic right of leading processions along roads. Muslims contended that mosques were not so numerous as to make recognition of their demand a negation of any civic right of the Hindus.[6]

The government tried to settle the rival claims of the two communities by laying down certain general rules to regulate the processions. But these were changed from time to time partly because of the opposition of communal bodies, and partly because of the difficulties of enforcing them in those areas where the local leaders had worked out their own arrangements.[7] However, in March 1927 the government took the initiative in issuing two specific instructions to the district authorities which were to be enforced 'in the absence of any clear evidence as to the existing practice or any definite agreement between the two communities to which they conform'.[8] But by the time those instructions were enforced, the dispute over music before mosques had already taken a heavy toll of human lives. In the course of the Calcutta riots early in April 1926, which were caused by the playing of music by an Arya Samajist procession before a mosque, 44 people died and 584 were injured. Over 197 shops were looted and 151 cases of fire were reported.[9] These details were sufficient to shatter one's faith in Hindu-Muslim unity.

Another cause of quarrel between the two communities was the slaughter of kine, whether for food or religious sacrifice, by the Muslims. Islam enjoins the faithful to offer animal

[5]D.R. Sharma, General Secretary of the Delhi Hindu Sabha to Secretary, Government of India, Home Department, 20 July 1926, Home Poll. 1926, 179, NAI.

[6]*Moslem Chronicle*, 4 June 1926.

[7]Home Poll. 1926, 179, NAI.

[8]The orders were (1) that processions with music would not pass mosques, temples and churches during the hours of public worship; (2) in case of disputes whether a building came within the above categories, it would be referred to the district officer for decision. Home Poll. 1927, 166, NAI.

[9]For an account of the riots, see The Earl of Lytton, *Pundits and Elephants: Being the Experiences of Five Years as Governor of an Indian Province* (London, 1942), pp. 167-73.

sacrifices at the *Id al-Zuha* or as it is called in India, the *Bakr Id*. It also lays down that, while the minimum obligatory offering for a Muslim is a sheep or goat, the offering of a camel, cow, or buffalo is equivalent to seven sheep or goats, and thus by such a single offering seven persons can participate in the sacrifice. In India, horned cattle were numerous and cheap, and it was much less costly to use one of them for the sacrifice than to provide the equivalent number of sheep or goats.[10] For these reasons, it was the general practice of Muslims to sacrifice cows. In 1922, the *Anjuman-i-Zahirin-AlalHaq* of Jabalpur published a *fatwa* setting out these reasons in great detail. The *fatwa* was signed by several *ulama*, including Maulana Abdul Hadi Mohammad Zahid who was a close friend of Maulana Abdul Bari.[11] A pamphlet on similar lines was published and circulated by the *Anjuman-i-Islamia* of Panipat soon after a bloody riot in the city over the cow question.[12]

The Hindus, on the other hand, regarded cows as sacred and worshipped them in many parts of the country. The sanctity of cows was recognised even in the pre-British period, but the first recorded society for their protection was formed in 1882 by Dayanand Saraswati in Calcutta. By 1818, cow-protection societies were active in the Punjab and the UP. In June 1893, the riots in Ballia, Azamgarh, and Gorakhpur were attributed to the activities of these societies.[13] In the Punjab, the Arya Samajists campaigned for the protection of cows, a cause which was later taken up by the Hindu Sabha. In Bombay, Tilak made the cow symbol an integral part of the Shivaji festival which he had instituted and popularised. In the twentieth century, the same issue remained the spark which ignited the Hindu-Muslim cow-riots which were to occur with unfailing regularity year after year until the Partition in 1947.

The cow-protection movement had the support of many Hindu Congressmen, including Tilak, Lajpat Rai, Malaviya, Shraddhanand, Jayakar, and Moonje. The most prominent

---

[10]A. Raoof, *Submission About the Korbani Question* (Calcutta, 1911), IOL Tracts: 1084.

[11]See *Adalat Gaushala Parastan* (Jubbulpore, 1922).

[12]*Mussalmanan-i-Panipat ki Bipta aur Afsana* (Delhi, 1926).

[13]S. Krishnaswamy, '1893: A year of Unrest in India', *Quarterly Review of Historical Studies*, Vol. 6, 1966-7, p. 155.

among them, however, was Gandhi. He regarded the cow with the same veneration as he did his mother, and declared that 'protection of the cow is an outer form of Hinduism and I would not regard him a Hindu, who is not prepared to give his life to save a cow. Cow-protection is dearer to me than life itself'.[15] He hoped that by virtue of the Hindu support to the Khilafat cause, Muslims would reciprocate the favour by protecting the cow.[16]

Gandhi's hopes were realised during the Khilafat movement, when the Muslim League urged the Muslims to refrain from cow-slaughter. Abdul Bari informed the Mahatma that in appreciation of the Hindu support to the Khilafat cause, 'we ourselves have determined not to sacrifice cows in future'.[17] But the 'cow-caliphate formula' did not work long.[18] As soon as the non-cooperation movement petered out and the Hindu pressure for cow-protection increased, the Muslims began to asserted their right to perform cow-sacrifice. The *Jamiat-ul-ulama* gave its support to cow-slaughter.[19] Encouraged by the stand of the local *Jamiat-ul-ulama* leaders, the Muslims in Delhi insisted on using the Pahari Dhiraj route (in violation of a previous informal agreement) for taking sacrificial cows to the slaughter house.[20] Even Abdul Bari performed a *volte face* by declaring that if Muslims agreed to giving up cow-slaughter, they would then have to yield on the issue of music before mosques as well.[21] This was a signal to Muslims to practice cow-slaughter and to disregard all previous commitments. The results were unfortunate. The riots over cow-slaughter, which had considerably subsided from 1918 to 1922, became more frequent and widespread. It should be clear that the new round of conflict was precipitated by the breakdown of the alliance between the Muslim politicians and the *ulama*,

[15]Desai, *Day-To-Day*, Vol. 3, pp. 154-55.
[16]Speech at Calcutta, 26 January 1921, *CWG*, Vol. 19, p. 283.
[17]Abdul Bari to Gandhi, 1919, Abdul Bari Papers.
[18]See Anthony Parel, 'Symbolism in Gandhian Politics', *Canadian Journal of Political Science*, December 1969, pp. 523-24.
[19]*Akhbar-i-Am* (Lahore), 21 February 1923, PUNNR 1923.
[20]Abdur Rahman Siddiqi to Mohamed Ali, 1 July 1925, Mohamed Ali Papers, and *Comrade*, 17 July 1925.
[21]Circular Letter, n.d., in Urdu, Abdul Bari Papers.

on the one hand, and the Hindu Congressmen on the other. It was a symptom of a malaise which followed the suspension of civil disobedience.

There were, however, certain basic causes which led to communal riots in different parts of the country and in different periods of modern Indian history; often the sudden blaze was produced by some chance spark. In some cases, the cause was mainly economic. This was particularly true of Bengal where a large proportion of Muslim peasants were victims of the exploitation of zamindars and money-lenders who happened to be predominantly Hindu. (There were a number of cases in which they revolted against the land-lords' demands of enhanced rents, exactment of unauthorised cesses and the attempts to tamper with their rights of occupancy.) In Mymensingh district,[22] which was the scene of communal riots in 1907, the landlords forced their *raiyat* to pay illegal *abwab* amounting to 50 per cent over and above the lawful rent. There was also a system in force by which the rents of occu-pancy rights were enhanced by extra-juridical contract after seven, or sometimes every five, years. In addition, money-lenders not only realised compound interest at a rate which was often 50 and sometimes 100 per cent per annum, but also forced their clients to contribute illegal subscriptions over and above the already extortionate interest. One of the subscrip-tions was known as *Ishwar Britti* and was devoted to the up-keep of Hindu idols. Muslims resented paying this subs-cription. This is illustrated by the fact that both at Bakshiganj and Dewanganj the rioting in 1907 began by an attack upon the idol which had been erected with the hated *Ishwar Britti*. After demolishing the idol, the mob turned its attention to the shops of the moneylenders who had been most prominent in their oppression and in exacting illegal taxes.[23] Similarly, riots in Kishoreganj subdivision, Pabna, Madaripur and Barisal

---

[22]Mymensingh district was in the Dacca division and was the largest district in the Bengal Presidency in terms of area and population. In 1911, it had a population of 4,526,422. The Muslims formed nearly three-quarters of the total population. F.A. Sachse, *Bengal District Gazetteer: Mymensingh* (Calcutta, 1917).

[23]Report by R. Nathan, Home Poll. A, December 1907, 57-63, NAI.

were essentially peasant uprisings against landlords.[24] 'Discontent always prevails', observed a peasant leader, Muzaffar Rahman, 'amongst those who are exploited and the discontent finds vent in class struggles'.[25]

The riot of August 1921 in Malabar was another example of a peasant revolt against the landlords. Willingdon, Governor of Madras, tried to establish a connection between non-co-operation and the Moplah 'rebellion' and argued that 'the outbreak is entirely due to the persistent preaching, generally in the mosques of the wickedness of the British Government over the Turkish Peace Terms, of the danger to the Moplah's religious faith, and to the fact that Gandhi and Mohamed Ali were everywhere declaring that Swaraj was coming at once, and did this with complete impunity, which showed that the British Raj was dead or dying.'[26] The root cause of the trouble was, however, economic. The Moplahs, who consisted of the descendants of Arab traders and of converts to Islam from low Hindu castes, were mainly peasants who were ruthlessly exploited by Namboodri landlords and Nayar moneylenders. The British land settlement policies in Malabar gave the landlords an arbitrary power of eviction and rent-raising which severely affected the Moplahs. Reduced to insecure tenancy, vulnerable to rack-renting and eviction at the hands of Hindu landlords who were sustained by British Indian courts, the Moplahs reacted in a series of outbreaks. These have been described as 'social protests conducted as religious acts'.[27] Mac-Gregor, District Collector of Malabar in the 1880s, observed that the Moplah 'outrages' were agrarian, and that 'fanaticism is merely the instrument through which the terrorism of the landed classes is aimed at'.[28] The Logan Commission of 1881

[24]*Mussalman*, 2 August 1927. For a useful analysis of the Hindu-Muslim riots in the winter and early spring of 1906-07, see Sarkar, *Swadeshi Movement*, pp. 444-62.

[25]*Ganavani*, 28 April 1927, BENNR 1927.

[26]Willingdon to Reading, 13 September 1921, Reading Papers (23).

[27]Stephen Dale, 'Islam and Social Conflict: The Mappilas of Malabar 1498-1922' (Unpublished Ph.D. thesis, California, 1972), p. 109, quoted in Robert L. Hardgrave Jr., 'The Mapilla Rebellion, 1921: Peasant Revolt in Malabar', *MAS*, Vol. 2, February 1977, p. 61.

[28]E. Thurston, *Castes and Tribes of Southern India* (Madras, 1909), Vol. 4, p. 478.

reached a similar conclusion and recommended a series of changes in the land tenure of Malabar to mitigate the plight of the Moplahs.[29] But these were never enforced and Malabar continued to suffer under an oppressive system of land tenure and subinfeudation. As late as 1900, South Malabar—where the situation was most serious —earned the 'unenviable reputation of being the most rack-rented country on the face of this earth'.[30] The failure of the Madras government to implement the recommendations of various investigation commissions worsened the agrarian situation in Malabar and exacerbated discontent.

In August 1921, the Moplahs were up in arms for a fresh bout against all forms of authority—the Hindu landlords as well as the British Raj.[31] The trouble was caused by the arrest of some Khilafat leaders in Tirurangadi. This provoked the Moplahs in other areas to block the roads, cut telegraph lines, attack post offices, police stations, and railway stations. The Hindus, too, had to face the brunt of their attack because they assisted the local authorities in quelling the disturbances.[32] There were numerous instances of forcible conversions, desecration of temples, and killings. By November 1921, the troops were able to control the mob frenzy and restore order in the difficult and extensive tract of the Malabar country. But by that time, over three thousand Moplahs had died. Their uprising was, quite wrongly, given a communal colour and interpreted as a manifestation of Muslim hatred for the Hindus.

In addition to the economic factor, communal tension was also caused by Hindu and Muslim revivalist movements which sought to modify or transform the life of their followers in accordance with the basic tenets of Islam and Hinduism. The Muslim revivalists stressed the need for reforming Indian Islam

[29]See *Correspondence on Moplah Outrages for the years 1849-50* (Madras, 1863), p. 107.

[30]Quoted in Hardgrave, 'The Mapilla Rebellion', p. 65.

[31]For the events leading to the August uprising, see *Ibid.*, pp. 65-74.

[32]Telegraphic Information and Correspondence regarding the Moplah Rebellion, 24 August to 6 December (London, 1921), Cmd. 1552; C.G. Tottenham, 'The Mapilla Rebellion and Malabar Operation', Indian Police Collection, MSS. EUR. F. 161-4, IOL.

by purging it of various Hindu customs and practices and restoring the puritanical spirit of early Islam. This was the aim of the movements launched by Shah Abdul Aziz and Haji Shariat Allah, the founder of the Faraizi movement. In the second half of the nineteenth century, a number of theological seminaries sprang up in the UP and Punjab with revivalist overtones.[33] The most important of these were the *Nadwat al·uluma*, the *Dar al-ulum* at Deoband, the *Madras-a-i-Ilahiya* in Kanpur, the *Anjuman-i-Taleem*[34] the *Anjuman-i-Itehad-wa-Taraqqi* (Association for the promotion of unity and progress)[35], the *Anjuman-i-Islamia* founded at Lahore for the purpose of protecting Muslim religious endowments, and the *Anjuman-i-Himayat-i-Islam*.[36] The object of many of these organisations was to repel attacks of the Arya Samaj, to protect Islam from the Christian missionaries, and to preach Islam among non-Muslims.[37]

[33]The last quarter of the nineteenth century also witnessed many Muslim revivalist movements which aimed either to defend the faith or to revive the pristine purity of Islam. In the Punjab, Mirza Ghulam Ahmad (1883-1908) founded the Ahmadiyah movement to reform and revitalise the Islamic tradition and to counter the activities of the Christian missionaries. He was also involved in a bitter and acrimonious debate with some Arya Samaj leaders. See S. Lavan, *The Ahmadiyah Movement: A History and Perspective* (Delhi, 1975).

[34]It was founded by Mohammad Shafi and Nawab Fateh Ali Khan Qizilbash in 1910. *Tribune*, 6 May 1911.

[35]*Ibid.*, 30 April 1911.

[36]This was founded at Lahore in 1885. Its aim was to disseminate western learning along with religious education and to improve the 'social, moral and intellectual condition of the Muslims'. By 1905, the *Anjuman* had established a number of schools in different parts of the Punjab, including one in Lahore which had 1,582 students on the rolls. Its income also increased from Rs 758 in 1885 to Rs 1,10,546 in 1905. In 1910, a Provincial Muslim Educational Conference was organised under the auspices of the *Anjuman* and was attended by many leading Muslim politicians, including Fazl-i-Husain. *Ibid.*, 10 July 1906, 1 April 1910.

[37]The activities of some Arya Samaj leaders contributed greatly to the growth of communal tension in the Punjab. In the 1880s, Pandit Lekh Ram (1858-1897), a devoted follower of Dayanand Saraswati (1824-1883), used his paper, *Arya Gazette*, as a vehicle for venting his wrath against Islam, particularly the Ahmadiyahs. He was also the chief spokesman on the issues of cow-protection and the promotion of Hindi in government departments. See Lavan, *Ahmadiyah Movement*, pp. 76-82; Jones, *Arya Samaj*, pp. 149-51.

The Hindu revivalists, such as the Arya Samajists, looked back to the glories of Hindu civilization before the advent of Islam in India, and attempted to restore Hinduism to the purity of Vedic times by eradicating caste and idol worship.[37] They campaigned for the protection of the cow and initiated the *shuddhi* movement.[38] Har Dayal, an exiled revolutionary, declared in 1925, that the future of India rested on Hindu *sangathan*, Hindu Raj, and *shuddhi* of the Muslims and Christians. The Muslims and Christians were far removed from the confines of Hinduism because their religions were alien to India. 'Thus, just as one removes foreign matter from the eye', he observed, '*Shuddhi* must be made of these two religions.'[39] Har Dayal was merely setting out the objectives of the All-India Shuddhi Sabha which was established in 1909 by the Arya Samajists in the Punjab.

Hindu and Muslim revivalist movements, which initially emerged as a reaction against the activities of the Christian missionaries, had many features in common. Both were founded on the assumption that their religion comprehended a set of beliefs and values which were infallible, and both derived inspiration from the past, adopted a set of heroes, and popularised historical myths. Muslim revivalists dwelt on the five centuries of Muslim rule in India and maintained that 'the real history of India commences with the entry of Mussalmans'.[40] Their heroes were the great iconoclast, Mahmud of Ghazni, and Aurangzeb, the puritan Mughal ruler who reversed the policy of *Sulh-i-kul* (peace for all) initiated by Akbar. Many Hindus, on the other hand, turned to Asoka, Rana Pratap, and Shivaji for inspiration and regarded them as heroes. In Maharashtra, Tilak revived the memory of the Maratha ruler, Shivaji, as a means of stimulating resurgent Maratha nationalism, and since then he has been elevated,

[38]From mid-1884 onwards, the Samaj sponsored and gradually came to perform ceremonies of readmission. Although individual reconversions had little impact on the general standing of Hindus in relation to other communities, they possessed great symbolic value. They offered hope and signified a new world in which Hindus could fight to maintain themselves and their religion. Jones, *Arya Samaj*, p. 131.

[39]Quoted in Emily C. Brown, *Har Dayal* (Tueson, 1975), pp. 233-34.

[40]Ameer Ali, quoted in K.K. Aziz, *Ameer Ali: His Life and Work* (Lahore, 1968), p. 376.

without any justification, to the status of a national hero. So, while the Hindu and Muslim revivalists drew strength from certain historical figures, they idolised different people for different reasons. This is how revivalism also tinged the interpretation of Indian history[41] which reinforced existing ideological differences. To some Hindu revivalists, the medieval period in Indian history was characterised by destruction, murder, and proselytisation of the Hindu population, and they contrasted it with the assimilative capacity of the Hindus, their tolerance, and their rich cultural and religious heritage.[42] Many Muslim revivalists, on the other hand, glorified the achievements of the Turks, Afghans, and the Mughals and regarded the medieval period as the high point of civilization in India.

Revivalist movements had their principal centres in towns and in the cities, and it is no coincidence that communal riots occurred mostly in urban areas. The most serious riots in the UP took place at Agra, Shahjahanpur, and Saharanpur in 1923; at Allahabad and Lucknow in 1926; and at Bareilly, Kanpur and Dehra Dun in 1927. In Bengal, Calcutta had its largest share of riots also in the 1920s. In the Punjab, Multan, Lahore, and Amritsar figured as rioting centres. Western India had comparatively few riots although in the late 1920s its record was marred by as many as ten in Sholapur and the neighbouring areas.[43] In South India there is evidence of only three riots—in Malabar, Nellore, and Bangalore.

[41]See R. Thapar, H. Mukhia, B. Chandra, *Communalism and the Writing of Indian History* (Delhi, 1969).

[42]This view was encouraged by the writings of some British historians in the nineteenth and the first quarter of the twentieth centuries. Their aim was to emphasise that the British did more 'for the substantial benefit of the people' than the 'despotic', 'intolerant' and 'cruel' medieval Sultans. Henry Elliot, one of the leading British historians of the medieval period, referred to 'the few glimpses we have, even among this single volume, of Hindus slain for disputing with Muhammadans, of general prohibitions against processsions, worship and ablution, of other intolerant measures, of idols mutilated, of temples erazed, of forcible conversions and marriages...'. His purpose, as he confessed frankly, was to make 'our native subjects more sensible of the immense advantages' of British rule.

[43]Figures quoted in N.C. Kelkar's speech in December 1935, Jayakar pers (65).

It would thus seem that the riots were not only an urban phenomenon, but were generally confined to the UP, Punjab, and Bengal. The reason is that these provinces were the centres of revivalist movements. The Arya Samaj, the Shuddhi Sabhas and the cow-protection societies flourished there and were a constant source of irritation to communal relations. The Hindi-Urdu controversy was stirred in north India. The pan-Islamic movement had its origin in the same region before spreading to other parts of the country; and the citadel of Muslim orthodoxy lay in places like Deoband, Lucknow, Bareilly, and Aligarh—all in the UP.

Furthermore, towns were more exposed to the press, the publicists, and the politicians. The improved system of transport, the greater frequency of communication, and the interchange of news by post and telegraph increased the mobility of zealous religious revivalists and enabled them to reach audiences in different parts of the country. The press and better means of communication had another impact. A riot which occurred in any place, even the most remote, was speedily heard of all over India. But often exaggerated and even false reports of what happened were spread and, as most newspapers belonged to one or the other of the contending parties, the accounts published were unabashedly partisan. Every possible incident was given a communal twist and minor events were exaggerated until they appeared to be events of major importance.[44] The natural effect was that even in places where communal harmony prevailed controversies and conflicts arose and hostility was engendered. This rapid dissemination of news and the increasing use of the press by various revivalist organisations added a new dimension to communal disturbances.

Who were the organisers of revivalist movements in the 1920s? What did they strive to accomplish, and what was the extent of their influence? Among Muslims there is no evidence of any organised and effective revivalist activity after the

[44]For example, a trivial incident in Sasaram (Bihar) as a result of a drunken brawl between a Hindu and Muslim was seized upon to excite religious passions with the result that in the space of two or three days eighteen riots occurred in addition to minor affrays and assaults. *Report on the Administration of the Police in the Province of Bihar and Orissa*, 1926, p. 14.

Khilafat movement. In response to the *shuddhi* and *sangathan* movements, there were a few isolated efforts to establish *tabligh* (propagate) and *tanzim* (organise) societies. But these were merely in the form of local organisations to counter the activities of the Arya Samaj. The *Jamiat-ul-ulama* formed the *Tabligh-ul-Islam* (Society for the propagation of Islam) to combine the various schools of thought for joint action, but this effort proved unsuccessful. The Deobandis and the *Anjuman Raza-i-Mustafa* (Society to win the favour of Mohammad) of Bareilly refused to cooperate with the Qadianis in the organisation. Various other bodies arose with objectives similar to the *Tabligh-ul-Islam* under such names as *Anjuman-i-Tahaffuz-i-Islam, Anjuman Hifazat-i-Islam*, and *Anjuman-i-Hurriyat-i-Islam*, but they were all divided by doctrinal disputes and, consequently, secured no following.[45] In the Punjab, Kitchlew organised the *tanzim* movement which failed to survive after a brief spell of popularity. It gained no substantial support outside the Punjab because of the paucity of funds and the lack of organisation.[46]

Compared to the *tabligh* and *tanzim* societies, the *shuddhi* and the *sangathan* bodies were better organised and had the support of many influential groups among Hindus. The *shuddhi* sabhas, which were founded by Pandit Bhoj Dutt Sarma of Amritsar in 1907, were patronised by a number of socio-religious organisations in north India. Their initial success was due to the support of the Kshatriya Upkarini Mahasabha, the movement for inter-clan unity among the Rajputs, and to the association of Rampal Singh and Raja Durga Narayan Singh of Tirwa with their activities.[47] In 1907, the Rajputs in Agra division were associated with the *shuddhi* sabha and joined the Arya Samaj in an attempt to reconvert the Muslim Rajputs, particularly the Malkhanas.[48] In the wake of the Moplah riots in Malabar, the sabhas gained more

[45]'Communal Friction in the United Provinces, 1924', Home Poll. 1925, 140, NAI.

[46]For Bengal, see Mcpherson, *The Muslim Microcosm*, p. 89.

[47]R. Gordon, 'The Hindu Mahasabha and the Indian National Congress, 1915 to 1926', *MAS*, April 1975, Vol. 9, p. 172.

[48]Between 1907 and 1910 the society claimed to have converted 1,052 Muslim Rajputs. Lajpat Rai, *A History of the Arya Samaj*, p. 121.

recruits. Chief among them was Shraddhanand who was mainly responsible for reconverting many of the Malkhana Rajputs and for bringing in eighty-four 'non-Hindu villages' into the fold of Hinduism.[49] In August 1923, the *shuddhi* campaign was officially included in the All-India Hindu Mahasabha programme. This gave further strength to the movement. It could now count on the active support of leading all-India politicians, such as Malaviya, Lajpat Rai[50] and Moonje.

The object of the *sangathan* movement was to consolidate and unite Hindus into an organic nation. This was a new phenomenon, for the idea of unity could hardly appeal to the caste-ridden Hindu society.[51] But the extraordinary increase in communal violence provided a rationale of self-defence for the organisation. The organisers of the *sangathan* movement proceeded on the assumption that Hindus were by nature docile and submissive and, consequently, they were bullied by the 'aggressive' Muslims.[52] Their remedy was to organise Hindus on militant lines—to infuse in them a spirit of aggression, and to reverse the principle of non-violence advocated by Gandhi and some of his followers.[53] Moonje was the most vehement advocate of this view, and it was almost entirely due to him that the *sangathanists* gained a foothold in parts of northern and central India.

[49]*Forward*, 6 January 1927.

[50]For Lajpat Rai's views on *shuddhi*, see *Tribune*, 13 December 1924.

[51]Notice, for example, the response of Bhasker Rao Pandit, a Brahmin lawyer from Poona, to the idea of unity with the untouchables. He bluntly told Moonje that the Brahmins would not 'lower our civilization by trying to assimilate them into ourselves. We shall fight the Muslims and the untouchables combined and it does not matter if all Brahmins perish eventually in the attempt'. 8 August 1939, Moonje Diaries (2).

[52]Shraddhanand quoted in the *Amrita Bazar Patrika*, 17 August 1923.

[53]Moonje was of the view that Gandhi's philosophy of *Ahimsa* was 'highly suicidal' to Hindus. He noted: 'In one word I have been saying to Gandhi's followers that I consider my mission in life now to be to do everything possible so that the teachings of Love and Ahimsa. . . may not take root at least in Maharashtra . . . . Gandhi's philosophy will lead to destruction and extermination of the Hindus from the face of the world'. 13 July 1926, Moonje Diaries (1).

Moonje was a revivalist and a communalist in every sense. He believed that 'until the Hindu youth are again inspired with the same ambition of Hindu Raj in their land of Hindustan, the Hindus cannot put forth the best energy that they are capable of in the present struggle for Swaraj'.[54] The fight for Swaraj was not only against the British but also against the Muslims. 'It was merely a continuation of the struggle which was initiated by Prithviraj Chauhan when the Hindu Raj, culture, and religion was first assailed under the Muslim impact.'[55] Frequent were his lamentations over the disunity prevailing among his co-religionists; he sought to base Hindu solidarity on the Hindu hatred of Islam and its followers. In his view, Muslims were aggressive and intolerant,[56] and so he stressed the necessity of organising Hindus in 'self-defence'.[57] In his diary, Moonje proudly noted: 'I told (a group of Maharashtrians) that Maratha young men must always remember their national and historical peculiarity which consisted in fighting the Muslims with success.'[58] His aggressively anti-Muslim posture gave a new dimension to the *sangathan* movement. As time passed, the activities of the enthusiastic *sangathanists* were not merely confined to strengthening and consolidating Hindus, but extended to a well organised anti-Muslim propaganda. Such antagonism towards the Muslims, almost inevitably, had important political implications. They stimulated an increased awareness of the need to protect Muslim interest, strained the links which held together the supra-communal connections, and led to vicious communal rioting in many parts of the country. In Allahabad, the steady deterioration of communal relations was caused by the *shuddhi* and *sangathan* movements,

[54]3 May 1929, Moonje Diaries (1).

[55]*Ibid.*

[56]Moonje to Bapuji, n.d., Moonje Dossier (26).

[57]'I am glad to tell you that I have been able to organise the Hindus of Nagpur for self-defence. It was a sight for Gods to see when well-built Hindus. . .with lathis in their hands paraded the streets of Nagpur. . .Besides in two well organised street fights, the Hindus succeeded in repelling the attacks of the Muslims. . .I am sure you will be delighted to hear of the Hindu Sangathan of Nagpur which is purely of a defensive character'. Moonje to Sinha, 18 December 1923, *Ibid.*, (19).

[58]20 April 1926, Moonje Diaries (1).

which were patronised by the Hindu Sabha. 'This body', noted the Commissioner of Allahabad, 'with its doctrine of *sangathan* has aroused an aggressive spirit, which has spread to the small towns and villages'.[59] Similarly, vigorous anti-Muslim propaganda carried on by the *sangathanists* eventually led to communal riots in Ajmer in July 1925.[60]

The great strength and popularity of the *shuddhi* and *sangathan* campaigns was largely because of their close association with the All-India Hindu Mahasabha and its provincial branches.[61] The Mahasabha was founded in 1915 in order to safeguard the 'separate and distinct interests of the Hindu community'. It helped to draw the already existing provincial Hindu Sabhas together and provided a common platform to various religious and cultural movements in different parts of the country. Among its patrons were rich bankers, landowners, and professional men. The executive committee of the UP Hindu Sabha, for example, contained twelve lawyers, three zamindars who were also lawyers, and six commercial and landed magnates. They were all drawn from the large trading centres, such as Allahabad, Kanpur, Benaras, and Lucknow and were men of influence in their districts as well as in provincial politics.[62] In Bihar, the Hindu Sabha was founded by the Maharaja of Darbhanga in 1907 and popularised by two leading lawyers, Parmeshwar Lal and Sachidanand Sinha.[63] In

---

[59] Home Poll. 1924, 249, NAI.

[60] Home Poll. 1925, 368, NAI.

[61] The Provincial Hindu Sabhas were established in the Punjab in 1907, Bihar in 1907, UP 1914, Delhi 1918, Central Provinces 1923, Bombay and Maharashtra 1924, Berar and Bengal 1924, and in Sind in 1926. The All-India Hindu Mahasabha was formed in April 1915 with headquarters at Dehra Dun, the home of the first secretary, Deva Ratan Sarma.

[62] Some of the important members of the Executive Committee in 1915 were: Rampal Singh, *taluqdar* of Rae Bareilly, T.B. Sapru, Madan Mohan Malaviya, C.Y. Chintamani, Motilal Nehru and Hriday Nath Kunzru, lawyers from Allahabad, and Lala Bishambhar Nath and Ram Charan Das, bankers and zamindars from Kanpur and Allahabad, repectively. See R. Gordon, 'The Hindu Mahasabha and the Indian National Congress', pp. 152-53.

[63] J.S. Jha, 'An Unpublished Correspondence relating to the Bihar Hindu Sabha', *Journal of the Bihar Research Society*, January-December 1968, pp. 339-44.

the Punjab, the Sabha comprised a number of important groups, such as the Lahore bankers and traders, journalists like Gulshan Rai, landowners like Raja Narendranath, and all-India politicians like Lajpat Rai.

The Mahasabha came into prominence soon after the Lucknow Pact was concluded in December 1916. The concession of separate and increased representation to Muslims in the UP and Punjab provoked a spate of protest meetings. But this agitation ran out of steam. Anxious to remain in the mainstream of national politics, Hindu Mahasabha leaders like Malaviya and Lajpat Rai joined the Khilafat bandwagon. From 1921 onwards, however, the Mahasabha received a new lease of life because of the steady deterioration of communal relations. The first sign of its revival appeared in December 1922 at the Mahasabha session held in the Congress pandal at Gaya. The conference passed resolutions establishing a Hindu Relief Committee to render financial assistance to the victims of communal riots, the Hindu Raksha Mandal to organise local bodies to protect Hindu interests in communal riots, and an organising committee to establish Hindu Sabhas in all provinces.[64] This was followed by another conference in August 1923 when the Mahasabha officially included the *shuddhi* campaign in its programme. By taking this decision, the Mahasabha brought a more specifically religious emphasis to its platform. *Shuddhi* was to be conducted by the All-India Shuddhi Sabha of the Arya Samaj, and actively supported by the different strands in the Mahasabha.

The key figure in the revival of the Mahasabha and in pushing through the *shuddhi* resolution (at the conference in August 1923) was Madan Mohan Malaviya. His activities were of special interest because he had beenn an important figure in Congress politics since 1886 and had a profound influence on Hindu revivalism in the UP. Malaviya founded one of India's most well-known English dailies, the *Leader*, and also a Hindi newspaper, *Abhyudaya*. He conceived and carried out the

---

[64]Among the members of the various committees were Malaviya, Rampal Singh, Lala Ram Saran Das, Moonje, Jamnalal Bajaj, Lala Hansraj, N.C. Kelkar, Shraddhanand, G.S. Khaparde, C. Vijaya-raghavachariar, former president of the Congress, S. Satyamurthi, K. Natarajan, editor of *Indian Social Reformer*, and Pandit Neki Ram Sarma. See, Gordon, 'The Hindu Mahasabha', pp. 168-69.

project of a Hindu university at Benaras, propagated the cause of Hindi, and actively campaigned for the protection of the cow. Malaviya also had close connections with the Prayag Hindu Samaj, the Sanatan Dharm Mahasammelan and the UP Hindu Sabha which gave him a wide range of contacts among the professional men, commercial magnates, and the land-owners of North India. It was on the strength of their support that Malaviya was able to command considerable influence in local, provincial and all-India politics. There was no contem-porary politician in Allahabad who could match Malaviya's enthusiasm for the cause of Hindu religion and culture, his extraordinary missionary zeal, and his immense organising capacity. He was a Hindu first and foremost, and dedicated himself to the promotion of Hindu interests in the Hindi-speaking areas.

After the suspension of civil disobedience in March 1922, Malaviya revived his interest in the Hindu Sabha (which gave organisational form to the politics of Hindu communalism) and the Shuddhi Sabhas. In his presidential address at the Hindu Sabha session held at Gaya, Malaviya dwelt at length on the disintegration of the Hindu community, the need for a strong communal organisation, and the revival of the Hindu Mahasabha. In August 1923, he was mainly responsible for passing a resolution in favour of the *shuddhi* campaign and included it in the Mahasabha programme. Over the next few years, he addressed various local and regional conferences where he spoke in support of the Hindu Sabhas and the *shuddhi* and *sangathan* movements.[65] In December 1925, he urged his audience at Kanpur to establish local branches of the Hindu Sabhas and to maintain *akharas* in every village and thus bring about complete *sangathan*.[66] Following the decision of the Mahasabha in August 1925 to contest the provincial elections in November 1926, Malaviya used communal slogans against his arch Swarajist rivals, espe-cially Motilal Nehru,[67] and incited communal unrest, parti-

---

[65]For details, see S.L. Gupta, *Pandit Madan Mohan Malaviya: A Socio-Political Study* (Allahabad, 1978), pp. 293-96, 298-99.

[66]'Note on the Activities of Malaviya', Home Poll. 1926, 187, NAI.

[67]'Publicly I was denounced', complained Motilal Nehru, 'as an anti-Hindu and pro-Mohammedan but privately almost every individual

cularly in Allahabad where his activities led to a steady deterioration of Hindu-Muslim relation.[68] In this way, Malaviya kept alive the tradition of militant Hindu nationalism, which was taken up more effectively by the Rashtriya Swayamsevak Sangh (RSS) and the Jana Sangh after Independence.

The riots from 1922 to 1927 and the growth of communal antagonism, in general, set off an acrimonious debate on the question of responsibility. The favourite British theory was that the introduction of reforms precipitated the struggle for power between the two communities and that communal riots were a violent expression of that struggle.[69] The nationalist leaders, on the other hand, pointed out that the government deliberately tried to maintain the feud on the principle of *divide et impera*, and that its agents instigated communal riots. There is, however, no evidence to prove the government's complicity in riots.[70] On the contrary, it seemed anxious to prevent violence in the interest of maintaining law and order, and adopted a series of measures to cope with the problems arising out of disputes over cow-slaughter and music before

voter was told that I was a beef-eater in league with the Muslims to legalise cow-slaughter in public places at all times'. Motilal Nehru to Jawaharlal Nehru, 2 December 1926, *A Bunch of Old Letters*, pp. 51-52. A correspondent from Bijnor reported on 5 November 1926 that Malaviya and Bhai Parmanand were trying to 'create and fan the communal fire among the electorate'. AICC Papers (21/ Part 2), 1926.

[68]Home Poll. 1926, 26, NAI.

[69]The Governor of Bengal observed: 'This growing antipathy between the two great communities was one of the fruits of the Reforms ... When Indians became Ministers and not only controlled policy but had a monopoly of patronage, the influence of Government was apt to be exercised in favour of the community to which the Ministers belonged to the detriment of the other community.' Lytton, *Pundits and Elephants*, pp. 165-66. This was also the view of many British writers associated with the Government of India in different capacities. See, for example, J. Coatman, *India in 1926-27* (Calcutta, 1928), p. 19, and R. Coupland, *The Indian Problem, 1833-35* (Oxford, 1942), pp. 33-34.

[70]This is not to suggest that the district authorities were not guilty of negligence of duty and bad judgement. In the case of Kohat riots the Governor of Punjab admitted that the local authorities neglected the situation and delayed the use of troops at their disposal. Hailey to Vincent, 30 November 1924, Hailey Papers (6-B).

mosques.[71] In 1924, Reading, the Viceroy, suggested the formation of a Central Board in each province and district with a view to invoking the help of influential local leaders in the settlement of religious disputes.[72] His government also adopted stringent measures against those newspapers which incited communal tension by openly disseminating false or exaggerated reports of communal riots.[73] Reading's successor, Irwin, devoted his address at the Chelmsford Club in Simla on 17 July 1926 to the Hindu-Muslim tension, which he termed 'the dominant issue in Indian life today'. In his view, the remedy for the situation lay with the Hindu and Muslim leaders, and he urged them to take the first steps towards fostering 'a new atmosphere of trust'. To help create this 'new atmosphere of trust', Irwin convened a Unity Conference in September 1927, but the conference proved to be a dismal failure. This was because the Hindu delegates wanted to restrict the discussion at the Conference to religious and social issues, while the Muslims insisted on an agreement on political and economic issues which lay at the root of the communal problem.[74] Zafar Ali Khan refused to allow the 'nimble-witted' Hindus to outwit the 'slow-witted' Muslims by limiting the discussion to comparatively 'trivial matters' and shelving the 'real point', such as the extent of Muslim representation in the legislative bodies and in the services.[75]

On religious issues, the Government of India did not tamper with Queen Victoria's momentous proclamation of 1858 which was an emphatic commitment to religious neutrality. Its general policy was to let the district authorities decide methods of dealing with local issues of dispute. This was largely the result of the view that it would be dangerous to fetter the discretion of local officers and quite impracticable to prescribe general formulas which would most

[71]See, for example, the compromise reached over cow-slaughter at Ayodhya owing to the efforts of the Lieutenant-Governor, Meston. Home Poll. A, October 1915, 258-59, NAI.

[72]Home Poll. 1925, 140, NAI.

[73]Home Poll. 1926, 210, NAI.

[74]Amrita Bazar Patrika, 25 September 1927.

[75]Mussalman, 16 December 1927.

likely prove unsuited to varying situations.[76] Moreover, there was the further danger of offending the religious susceptibilities of one or the other community by laying down general rules for the playing of music or cow-slaughter. So, the government scrupulously avoided meddling in affairs which were likely to arouse the religious passions of either community. The traumatic experience of 1857 had not altogether been forgotten in the nineteen-twenties.

However, the government cannot be exonerated of the charge of fostering Muslim separatism and exploiting the existing differences.[77] Since the introduction of the Reforms Act in 1909, the government offered a number of political concessions to various Muslim groups as part of its strategy to seek allies in governing the country. When the Montagu-Chelmsford Reforms were launched the support of the Punjabi and Bengali Muslims became as important as that of the landowners in the UP. The effective representation of the Swarajists in the legislative councils and their determination to wreck the Reforms from within made it necessary for the Raj to depend on certain groups. The British wanted to work the constitution and they were willing to forge tactical alliances in order to thwart the attempts of their opponents. For example, the Bengal government's primary aim was to whittle down the Swarajists, and their best hope of doing so lay in encouraging communal divisions. The Swaraj Party had gained the adherence of some leading Muslim politicians, but they were, as events later proved, notoriously fickle in their attachments and could be easily detached from their Hindu colleagues in the party.

The government's first attempt to wean away Muslims from the Swaraj Party was made in March 1924 when

[76]Memorandum by H.W. Emerson, 13 April 1931, Home Poll. 1931, 10, NAI.

[77]A somewhat crude expression of this policy came from Birkenhead, the Secretary of State for India, in response to the Nationalists' demand for a further instalment of reforms. He wrote: 'I have placed my highest and most permanent hopes upon the eternity of the communal situation .... All the conferences in all the world cannot bridge over the unbridgeable, and between these two communities lies a chasm which cannot be crossed by the resources of modern political engineering.' Birkenhead to Reading, 5 March 1925, Reading Papers (9).

Musharruf Husain, MLC from Malda, introduced a motion calling for the implementation of the Das Pact, particularly the provision relating to Muslim representation in government service. But this attempt failed. Das moved for an adjournment of the discussion on the motion, which was carried through the Council. This did not, however, deter the government from exploiting communal slogans in order to secure tactical advantages over their Swarajist opponents. In March 1924, when the demand for ministerial salaries was rejected, the government made much of the fact that the two ministers—Fazlul Haq and Ghuznavi—were Muslims, and it retained them in office and encouraged them to make communal profit out of the issue.[78]

Similarly, the Punjab government depended on the support of those members in the Council who represented rural constituencies. It threw its weight behind Fazl-i-Husain, who not only led the 'Rural Party' but also controlled Muslim votes. Both these groups were patronised in order to contain the Swarajists and the powerful urban Hindus, who were mainly connected with the Hindu Sabha. Edward Maclagan, Governor of the Punjab, appointed Fazl-i-Husain and Lal Chand, a Jat agriculturist from Rohtak, as ministers in spite of the opposition of the non-agriculturists.[79] Malcolm Hailey, who succeeded Maclagan as Governor of the Punjab, continued the policies of his predecessor and appointed Chhotu Ram, the co-founder of the Unionist Party, as one of his ministers. This was in recognition of the strength of the Unionist Party in the Punjab Legislative Council.

Hailey was able to solve the ministerial crisis with ease.[80]

[78]Broomfield, *Elite Conflict*, pp. 252-56.

[79]According to the *Tribune*, 'the re-appointment of Fazl-i-Husain is bound to accentuate the existing tendency [of communalism], while the appointment of Chaudhri Lal Chand will materially aggravate the evil by introducing a further element of unhealthy division. To the Hindu-Muslim problem will now be added the rural-urban problem, and the Council which has during the last three years, been the battleground of Hindu-Muslim rivalries will now be also the battleground of rural-urban jealousies'. *Tribune*, 31 December 1923.

[80]The ministerial crisis was caused following the resignation of Lal Chand after a successful petition was filed against him by the non-agriculturist groups in the Punjab.

But over the next few years there was a significant change in his relationship with Muslims in the Unionist Party. He was apprehensive of their growing popularity and influence as reflected, for example, in the appointment of Abdul Qadir as president of the Legislative Council, and was anxious to contain them.[81] At the same time, Hailey wanted to avoid a confrontation with the powerful urban-based Hindus, and was keen to secure their support in order to maintain a balance between the different parties.[82] Consequently, he attempted to woo the non-agriculturist Hindus by extending patronage to them and by ignoring, at least temporarily, the claims of the Unionists and the Muslim members.[83] Fazl-i-Husain was made Revenue Member and was relegated to the reserved half of the government. He was no longer the popular leader of the Council. Manohar Lal, who had been Fazl-i-Husain's arch critic, was chosen as one of the ministers. Hailey explained his policy thus:

To have carried on with the old arrangement would have meant that the Hindu party as such was to be permanently excluded; it would have driven them back on opposition and ultimately to swaraj; and the condemnation of the

[81]Hailey was interested in the re-election of Casson as president of the Council, but Fazl-i-Husain favoured Sir Abdul Qadir. And as Fazl-i-Husain's supporters were in majority, Hailey was forced to yield to the wishes of his minister. For details, see Husain, *Fazl-i-Husain*, pp. 159-60.

[82]Hailey's policy in this respect and the measure of his success is evident from the following: 'In the political world the balance between Muhammadans on the one hand and Sıkhs and Hindus on the other created a position which, if on occasions led to communal troubles embarrassing the government, on the other hand placed Government in a strong situation as holding the balance between the parties. As a consequence, the politically-minded Hindus found themselves unable to maintain a consistent opposition to government and, at all events, during the last three years came definitely to the view that they would have to depend on Government if they were to maintain their position vis-a-vis the Muslims.' Hailey to Irwin, 16 October 1928, Hailey Papers (14-A).

[83]For example, Hailey vetoed the Registration of Money-Lenders Bill and obstructed the passage of the Land Revenue (Amendment) Bill, both of which were among the important items on the programme of the Unionist Party.

Hindus to the position of a minority which to all appearance would be permanently excluded from government would have made it difficult to hope for any improvement in the communal tension in the Province.[84]

Hailey's judgement was consistent with British policy in India. The imposition of British rule, as Seal has suggested, meant a 'shuffling of the elites in British India; its continuance meant that they had to be continually reshuffled. Collaborators came and went; new allies and new enemies envenomed the rivalries inside the country'.[85] In the first reformed council, the government was dependent on the support of the 'Muslim Party'; in the second it was not. This meant a reshuffling of allies. The old familiar figures disappeared giving way to new ones. In affecting this change, Hailey was confident that he had taken the 'right course, not only in regard to the interests of the Punjab, but in regard to Indian politics generally'; but he was less sure about the success of his policy in future.[86] His fears came true in the nineteen-thirties, when the political climate in India, as indeed in the Punjab, changed dramatically and the government was once again forced to rely on Muslim support in order to stem the growing tide of nationalist feelings. In return, the Muslims received concessions first in the Communal Award and later in the Act of 1935.

---

[84]Hailey to Alexander Muddiman, January 1927, Hailey Papers (10-A).

[85]Seal, The Emergence, p. 343.

[86]Hailey to A. Muddiman, January 1927, Hailey Papers (10-A)

CHAPTER EIGHT

'THE PARTING OF THE WAYS'

When one thinks of the numerous differences, political as
well as communal, that separate the various parties in the
country, one is almost overwhelmed with a feeling of despair. Dominion Status or independence, music before mosques, cow-slaughter, separation of Sind, joint electorates
or separate electorates, reforms for the Frontier Provinces,
representation of minorities in the legislature and services,
are all baffling problems, and have, each one of them,
proved a stumbling block in the way of the success of past
conferences.

This excerpt from the *Hindustan Times* of Delhi, 20 May 1928,
encapsulates the existing differences between the men connected
with the Congress and the Muslim League. We have discussed
the implications of the Montagu-Chelmsford Reforms and
their impact on communal relations. We have also examined
how the suspension of civil disobedience led to an unceremoni-
ous breakdown of inter-communal alliances and how even
those groups which had previously worked together in political agitations, such as the Rowlatt Satyagraha and the Khilafat
movement, disintegrated. Communal animosity became the
order of the day and Hindu-Muslim relations steadily deterio-
rated. This was an evil omen for the future of India's national
movement.

The issues which drove Indian politicians into communal
camps came to the fore again in 1928 when the All-Parties

Conference met to draw up a constitution for India. Its deliberations brought into sharp focus the fears and aspirations of several Hindu and Muslim groups about the future political structure of India. Were they to accept a unitary or a federal system of government? What would be the position of minorities in either system? Were they to receive special constitutional safeguards in the form of communal representation? If so, what would be the principle of distribution of seats in the legislative bodies? And finally, was the constitution to be framed on the lines of dominion status or complete independence? These questions were discussed and debated during the All-Parties Conferences from February to August 1928 and are of great value in understanding the widely different angles from which both Hindus and Muslims regarded their respective political interests.

The meetings of the All-Parties Conference led to the appointment of a committee which produced a report, popularly known as the Nehru Committee Report. As the report claimed to offer a solution to the communal tangle, it received considerable attention from the government and the Indian politicians. The report was important for another reason: it laid bare the assumptions on which some Indian politicians sought to resolve the communal crisis. This chapter seeks to understand those assumptions by analysing the report and its implications for various Muslim groups and their reactions to it.

BACKGROUND TO THE ALL-PARTIES CONFERENCE

From the early days of their entry into the legislative councils, the Swarajists pressed for the revision of the Montagu-Chelmsford Reforms. Motilal Nehru, leader of the Swaraj Party in the Legislative Assembly, called for the dismantling of the half-way house of dyarchy and for the setting up of full provincial autonomy. In September 1925, when the Report of the Muddiman Committee was considered by the Assembly,[1] he

---

[1]The Muddiman Committee was appointed in May 1924 'to enquire into the difficulties arising from or defects inherent in the working of the existing Act'. In September 1925, it produced a Majority and a Minority Report. The Majority Report, signed by Alexander Muddiman

moved an amendment to the government motion. He proposed fundamental changes in the constitutional machinery in order to make the Government of India fully responsible to the legislative bodies. His motion was adopted. The government recognised the 'ever increasing claims of Indian Nationalism', and the Secretary of State for India announced the appointment of a Statutory Commission in November 1925.[2] From April 1926 to November 1927, the Viceroy and the Secretary of State worked out the details regarding the form, the terms of reference, and the composition of the Commission. The results of these discussions were announced by the Conservative Prime Minister, Baldwin, on 8 November 1927: a Royal Commission was to be sent to India two years before the time laid down by the Act of 1919.[3]

As soon as it became clear that a commission was on its way to India, and that political reforms were imminent, Indian leaders began to formulate their political demands. There was the usual clamour for Hindu-Muslim unity and a series of paper pacts were concluded which were directed less to the reconciliation of rival policies than to the maintenance of an outward unity, or some working formula of compromise.[4] In

(Chairman), Mohammad Shafi, B.C. Mahtab of Burdwan, A.H. Froom and H. Moncrief Smith, found the necessary scope for improvement within the Act of 1919. But the signatories to the Minority Report—Jinnah, Sapru, P.S. Sivaswamy Aiyer and R.P. Paranjype—did not agree and rejected the existing Act outright.

[2]The Earl of Birkenhead, Frederich Edwin, *Earl of Birkenhead: The Last Phase* (London, 1935), Vol. 2, p. 245.

[3]The Act of 1919 provided for the appointment of a Statutory Commission after ten years in order to examine the working of the system of government, and to report as 'to whether and to what exent it was desirable to establish the principle of responsible government, or to extend, modify, or restrict the degree of responsible government existing therein'.

[4]For example, Abdul Qadir, President of the Muslim League session in 1926, declared: 'If between 1927 and 1929 we do not behave more reasonably than we have done during the past six years, the future appears to be very gloomy. If, however, we spend the next three years in doing constructive, instead of destructive work, in uniting the various communities in India instead of disuniting them . . . , we will stand a fair chance of getting substantial advance in our rights and privileges.' Pirzada (ed.), *Foundations of Pakistan*, Vol. 2. p. 82.

this situation, many of the old familiar figures emerged from political wilderness. Jinnah was one of them. He had played a crucial part in negotiating the Lucknow Pact and from 1924 onwards he was cast again in a similar role. His main aim was to bring the Congress and Muslim League leaders together and to evolve a common basis for an agreement between them. By playing the role of a mediator, Jinnah hoped to stay in the mainstream of national politics and to regain some of the influence he had lost during the Khilafat and Non-cooperation movements. That is why he was anxious to establish new connections with various groups and to renew his contacts with others.[5]

On 20 March 1927, Jinnah presided over a conference of Muslim politicians held in Delhi.[6] The conference agreed to forego separate electorates if their four demands (which were later endorsed by the All-India Muslim League, the All-India Khilafat Conference, and the *Jamiat-ul-ulama*) were endorsed in *toto*. The first of these demands was that Muslim representation in the Bengal and Punjab Legislative Councils would be in proportion to their population. The second was that Muslims would be allowed one-third of the seats in the central legislature. And the last two demands were that Sind be separated from Bombay Presidency and constituted as an independent province,[7] and reforms be introduced in the North-West Fron-

[5]See, for example, Jinnah to Mohamed Ali, 30 November 1927, Mohamed Ali Papers; Jinnah to P. Thakurdas, 22 May 1925, Thakurdas Papers (4/Part 4); Jinnah to Jayakar, 22 May 1925, in S. Pirzada (ed.), *Quaid-e-Azam Jinnah's Correspondence* (Karachi, 1966), p. 169.

[6]Among those who attended the conference were Mohamed Ali, Ansari, Mohammad Yaqub, Mohammad Ismail, Ali Nabi and the Raja of Mahmudabad from UP; Mohammad Shafi, Mohammad Nawaz Khan, Raja Ghazanfar Ali Khan, Mohammad Shah Nawaz, Abdul Qadir and Abdul Qayyum from the Punjab; C.H. Ariff, H.S. Suhrawardy, Abdul Matin Chowdhry, Maulvi Mohammad Shafi from Bengal and Bihar; Syed Ahmad Shah, the *Imam* of Juma Masjid, Delhi; and, Jinnah from Bombay. *Leader*, 23 March 1927.

[7]Sind formed the extreme north west portion of the western Presidency with an area of nearly 50,000 square miles and a population of just over three million in 1921. In 1843, it was annexed by the British and was made part of Bombay Presidency. Since then various proposals were formulated to either constitute Sind into a separate province or to incorporate it with the Punjab. The Hindus of Sind, who

tier Province.[8] Clearly, the strategy of Muslim politicians was
to press for further Muslim-majority provinces being carved
out of British India so as to form a northern bloc in which the
Hindus would be, as it were, hostages for the good behaviour
of their co-religionists in the centre and south.[9] The issues of
Sind and the North-West Frontier Province were used as pawns
in the chessboard of all-India communal politics, and they remained the corner-stone of Muslim politics until 1935 when Sind
was finally constituted into a separate province.

Anxious to maintain the facade of Hindu-Muslim unity, the
Congress Working Committee and the All-India Congress Committee accepted the Delhi Proposals in order to pave the way
for rapprochement with leading Muslim politicians. But this

formed just over 25 per cent of the population, were opposed to an
independent province on the grounds that Sind would not be able to
bear the cost of running its own administration. The Muslims, on the
other hand, hoped that if Sind was constituted into an independent
province, they would have a greater say in administration and would
enjoy a fair share in government service and the professions because of
their numerical strength. For details, see 'The True Facts Regarding the
Separation of Sind from the Bombay Presidency', Ronaldshay Papers
(609), and Deputation from the Sind Muhammadan Association in *Indian
Statutory Commission*, Vol. 6, Part I, p. 208.

[8]The North-West Frontier Province was carved out by Curzon in
1901. In 1921, the province had a population of 2,062,786, with Muslims
constituting 91 per cent of it. The Morley-Minto and the Montagu-
Chelmsford Reforms were not introduced in the province because of its
limited economic resources. But in 1922, the government appointed a
Committee which recommended the establishment of a legislative council.
The implementation of this recommendation was, however, postponed
by Denis Brays, chairman of the Committee and later Governor of the
NWF Province. This encouraged the Muslim League to take up the
issue of reforms in the province. In May 1924, the League passed a
resolution urging the government to introduce reforms in the NWF
Province. In February 1926, Syed Murtaza of Madras introduced a
resolution in the Legislative Assembly on similar lines. It was supported
by Jinnah and the Muslim members of the Independent party, and was
eventually passed with the help of the official majority.

[9]Mohamed Ali bluntly stated that the presence of the Hindus in the
Muslim-majority provinces would guarantee the safety of Muslims in the
Hindu-majority provinces, and that the establishment of Sind as an indepen
dent province was necessary for the so-called 'balance of power' between
Hindus and Muslims in British India. *Hamdard*, 4 April, 28 April 1927,
and Qamar Din to Motilal, 16 April 1928, in Urdu, AICC Papers (4).

was done at the risk of alienating many Hindus, who launched a massive agitation against the proposals.[10] Motilal Nehru and Srinivasa Iyengar, who persuaded the AICC to adopt the proposals, were attacked bitterly. The *Surya* wrote: 'The Congress has become a handmaid of Motilal Nehru and the sole function of the AICC is to register his decrees. It was, therefore, a foregone conclusion that his views in the matter of Muslim offer would prevail, and it is an open secret that he favours the Muslims.'[11] Congress was also condemned for accepting the Muslim demand for representation in the legislatures in proportion to their population,[12] and for recognising the principle of partition along the 'permanent lines of religious cleavages'.[13]

[10] The centre of this agitation was in Sind, where it was jointly organised by the Sind Provincial Hindu Sabha, the Sind Hindu Association and the Sind Zamindar Association. These bodies represented the interests of rich traders, landowners and professional men, who played an important role in the economic, political, and social life of Sind. Most traders in the region were Hindus. In government service, the Amils of the Lohana caste held the great majority of posts and they occupied in Sind a position analogous to that of the Kayasthas in UP or the Pandits in Kashmir. As a result of their strong economic position, the voting strength of the Hindus was greater than that of Muslims, and under the provincial franchise they formed a majority of the population. That is why, as Table 8.1 sets out, they dominated the municipalities in at least six districts in Sind. The continued amalgamation of Sind with Bombay Presidency ensured Hindu dominance in many spheres. But the creation of an independent province meant the setting up of a legislative council where power would be distributed, at least in some measure, to the Muslim majority. It further meant that Muslims would have greater opportunities to compete with Hindus in education, government service, and in the professions. And as this impending danger threatened Hindu domination in Sind, they vigorously opposed the separation of Sind. The All-India Hindu Mahasabha and its provincial branches also joined their co-religionists in Sind in order to gain a foothold in the region and to assert their right to be consulted on all political issues. For details, see *True Facts*, pp. 9-20; *Should Sind be joined with the Punjab* (Hyderabad, 1916), IOL: 1111; *Leader*, 25 March 1927, and Copy of the Hindu Mahasabha resolution, enclosed in Ijaz Husain to Mohamed Ali, 9 April 1927, Mohamed Ali Papers.

[11] *Surya*, 5 June 1927, BNNR 1927; Moonje to Jayakar, 10 June 1927, JayakarPapers (436).

[12] *Basumati*, 19 May 1927, *Hitavada*, 10 June 1927, BENNR 1927.

[13] *Servant of India*, 2 February 1928, BNNR 1928.

TABLE 8.1.

COMMUNAL COMPOSITION OF THE MUNICIPALITIES IN SIND, 1927

Name of the Municipality	Total population of Municipal Districts	Population		No. of Elected Members		No. of Nominated Members	
		Hindus	Muslims	Hindus	Muslims	Hindus	Muslims
	1	2	3	4	5	6	7
Karachi	238,516	109,746	112,623	54	44	6	5
Hyderabad	96,883	62,268	34,414	65	51	5	9
Sukkur	114,497	71,705	41,577	70	41	8	13
Larkana	37,657	20,013	17,449	42	38	6	7
Nawabshah	15,265	11,612	3,644	22	10	2	3
Thar Parkar	9,886	7,324	2,564	20	8	1	3
Upper Sind F District	10,583	5,244	5,268	10	10	1	2
Total	308,287	287,912	180,539	283	202	29	42

Source: *Bombay Legislative Council Debates*, 20 July 1927 (Bombay, 1927), pp. 276-7.

While the agitation against the Delhi Proposals was gaining momentum, the Secretary of State for India dropped a bombshell by announcing the appointment of an all-British Statutory Commission on 8 November 1927.[14] The exclusion of Indians from the Commission aroused much indignation and resentment among leading Indian politicians who, then, united in opposition to the Commission. When the Congress met in Madras at the end of the year, it voted to boycott the Commission, proclaimed independence as its goal, and resolved that a draft constitution should be placed before a Special Convention to be held in early spring. The All-India Khilafat Conference, the All-India Muslim League, and the *Jamiat-ul-ulama* also joined the Congress in boycotting the Commission.[15] The *Mussalman* summed up the decision of these organisations: 'No one—no self-respecting Indian—should come forward to give evidence before the Statutory Commission or to cooperate with it in any other way. The larger interests of the nation demand it; our sense of national self-respect urges it.'[16]

In the midst of this patriotic outburst, the agitation against the Delhi Proposals subsided. But the controversies remained unresolved; they surfaced again when the All-Parties Conference was convened on 18 February 1928.

[14]The Statutory Commission was composed of Sir John Simon (Chairman), Lord Burnham, Lord Strathcona & Mount Royal, Edward Cadogan, Vernon Hartshorn, Col. G.R. Lane Fox and Major C.R. Altee. According to Stanley Reed, editor of the English daily, *Statesman*, with the exception of Simon and Burnham, all the other members of the Commission were 'absolute mediocrities'. To Hailey, 8 June 1928, Hailey Papers (12-A).

[15]The British Government was counting on the support of landowners and Muslims, and the Secretary of State for India had taken special care to advise Simon, Chairman of the Statutory Commission, to advertise his interviews with the non-boycotting Muslims. But the government's expectations were only partially fulfilled in the Punjab where Shafi and Firoz Khan Noon committed the Muslim League in favour of the Statutory Commission. As a result, the All-India Muslim League Council, which was dominated by the boycotting Muslims, reversed its decision of holding the annual League session at Lahore and chose Calcutta as the venue. This move was bitterly opposed by Shafi and his followers, and in the end two separate sessions were held, one in Lahore and the other in Calcutta.

[16]*Mussalman*, 18 November 1927.

ALL-PARTIES CONFERENCE, FEBRUARY-JULY 1928

The first meeting of the Conference was attended by over a
hundred delegates including Malaviya, Motilal, Lajpat Rai,
Ansari, Mohamed Ali, Sapru, Hasrat Mohani, Moonje, Jinnah,
Shafi Daudi, Nawab Ismail Khan, Seth Hajı Abdullah Haroon
of Sind, H.N. Kunzru. Jairamdas Daulatram, and the Raja of
Mahmudabad.[17] Amongst them were representatives of the
Congress, the Liberal party, the Hindu Mahasabha, and the
Muslim League which had appointed a committee consisting
of the Raja of Mahmudabad, Jinnah, Hasrat Mohani, Abdullah Haroon and Ismail Khan to confer with other political
organisations on the basis of the Delhi Proposals.

The Conference faced serious difficulties over the question
of Sind. Jairamdas Daulatram, Moonje, and Lajpat made
spirited speeches against its separation and rejected the
Congress resolution relating to the creation of an independent Sind province.[18] They demanded that the issue of Sind
should be reviewed again but Jinnah, Hasrat Mohani, and
Mohamed Ali refused to agree. The Mahasabha delegates also
objected to reservation of seats for Muslim majorities in the
Punjab and Bengal. On this point they were supported by
the Sikh delegate, Sardar Mangal Singh, as well as Motilal,
and Jawaharlal Nehru, and other Hindu Congressmen.[19] This
volte face performed by Congress leaders did not go down well
with the Muslim delegates. They argued that having once accepted the Delhi Proposals Motilal and the others had no justification in changing their views. So, they decided to boycott

[17] *Leader*, 15 February 1928.

[18] A few days after the All-Parties Conference opened, Moonje,
Jayakar, and Kelkar issued a manifesto in which they condemned the
'attempts to constitute new provinces in India with the object of
creating a number of provinces in which a particular community is in a
majority. *Ibid.*, 13 February, 28 February 1928.

[19] Jawaharlal to Syed Mahmud, 30 June 1928, *SWJ*, Vol. 3, pp. 50-1.
It is interesting to note that Gandhi, who took no part in the All-Parties
Conference, was also opposed to separate electorates and to reservation
of seats. But he did not express his views publicly for fear of antagonising the Muslims. For the views of Gandhi on the future constitution of India, see Gandhi to Motilal, 3 March 1928, Motilal
Papers (G-I).

the All-Parties Conference.[20] The rejection of the Delhi Proposals by the Mahasabha in April 1928 was the last straw. Jawaharlal Nehru informed the Congress Working Committee that after the Mahasabha decision, 'no help can be expected under the circumstances from the representatives of the Mahasabha and probably of the Muslim League. In regard to one or two matters the attitude of the Sikh League is also uncompromising'. He further wrote : 'it is too much to be hoped that these conflicting viewpoints will be able to accommodate themselves and will agree to a common formula. We are therefore to prepare ourselves for this conflict and to decide on our course of action'.[21]

It was in these circumstances that the All-Parties Conference met in May 1928 at Bombay. But it again failed to resolve the disputes. The Conference appeared to be on the verge of disruption. It was, however, rescued by Annie Besant, Motilal, Sapru and a small group of Nationalist Muslims led by Ansari. By June, some kind of unanimity was reached. But, as Motilal informed Gandhi, it was 'neither complete nor of the genuine type but something we can stand for both in the All-Parties Conference and the country at large'.[22] A committee, consisting of Motilal, Sapru, Ali Imam, Shuaib Qureshi, Jayakar, M.S. Aney, G.R. Pradhan, Mangal Singh, and M.M. Joshi was formed to draw up a constitution for the country.[23]

The deliberations and decisions of the committee, popularly known as the Nehru Committee, were influenced by the views

[20] In response to Ansari's invitation to attend the next Conference at Bombay, Mohammad Yaqub referred to the Muslim League's decision not to participate in its deliberations unless the Delhi Proposals were accepted by all the political parties, including Congress and the Mahasabha. 'The strength of opposition on the part of these important organisations', he wrote, 'cannot be overlooked and it seems nearly impossible to obtain support of majority organisations to a reasonable plan providing safeguards for all interests.' *Hindustan Times*, 16 May 1928.

[21] Jawaharlal to Members of the Congress Working Committee, 3 May 1928, *SWJ*, Vol. 3, p. 38.

[22] Motilal to Gandhi, 11 June 1928, Motilal Papers (G-1).

[23] Of the ten members of the committee elected by the Conference, Jayakar expressed his inability to act on it. Joshi did not attend the meetings at all, and Ali Imam and Pradhan attended only a few meetings. Motitlal to Gandhi, 27 June 1928, Motilal Papers (G-1).

of Motilal and Sapru who, in all fairness, were the authors of the Nehru Report.[24] To arrive at a correct estimate of the report, it is therefore necessary to examine their views on the communal problem.

Motilal and Sapru had a great deal in common. Both were lawyers of great distinction in Allahabad. Both were Kashmiri Pandits and had grown up in an 'Indo-Persian cultural atmosphere' which was the legacy of the Mughal Court in north India. They had studied Urdu and Persian and could speak, read, and write both the languages with ease. 'In the days of my boyhood', recalled Motilal in 1924, 'my earliest impressions were received at the feet of the Muslim professors and teachers and the more than half a century that has since elapsed has not in the least blunted the effect which those first impressions produced upon my young mind.'[25] Sapru was also a scholar in Urdu and ardently championed its cause through articles and speeches. In a passionate appeal to his audience at Lucknow University, he said:

> Let not the language in which Atash, Nasikh, Insha, Wazir . . . wrote, or the language in which the genius of Ratan Nath (Dar), Sharar, Sajjad Husain and Jwala Prasad 'Barq' found its expression only a generation ago be despised; let it not perish or even languish because the message from the West is more pressing or profitable. Cultivate the language and develop it. . . .[26]

In public affairs, Motilal and Sapru evinced a breadth of vision and freedom from a communal and sectarian approach. They adhered to the secular traditions of the Indian national movement as opposed to the Hindu revivalist trends represented by leaders like Malaviya and Lajpat Rai. To Motilal religion

[24]The Viceroy aptly referred to the Nehru Report as the 'Nehru-Sapru Constitution'. Irwin to Birkenhead, 6 September 1928, Irwin Papers (152/4).

[25]*Legislative Assembly Debates*, February 1924 (Delhi 1924), Vol. 4, No. 14, p. 784.

[26]K.N. Raina, *Welding the Nation: Academic Addresses and Selected Writings* (Bombay, 1974), p. 13.

signified bigotry, intolerance, and narrow mindedness 'It puts artificial barriers', he declared at the Calcutta Congress in 1928, 'between man and man and prevents the development of healthy and cooperative national life. . . . Its association with politics has been to the good of neither. Religion has been degraded and politics has sunk into the mire. Complete divorce of one from the other is the only remedy.'[27] This was the thinking which had gone into the making of the Nehru Report.

The phenomenon of communalism was inconsistent with their secular strand in politics, and a threat to their vision of a united and secular India. Hence, Sapru and Motilal made several attempts to tackle the communal problem.[28] They believed in an equitable settlement of inter-communal claims, and stressed the importance of allaying the fears and satisfying the political aspirations of Muslims. This attitude was reflected during the debate on the UP Municipalities Bill in 1916 when they did not make the abandonment of separate electorates the pivot of a settlement with Muslims. Speaking in the UP Legislative Council, Motilal pronounced separate electorates as a pernicious principle in public life, but recognised that, 'we cannot by preaching these principles keep off the actual separate representation for Muslims for any length of time. It must come. It has come already in the elections to Councils and it must go on and filter down to . . . the lowest rungs of the ladder of public life.'[29] Sapru, also, recognised separate representation as a 'necessary evil' and argued that in order to enlist Muslim support for the national movement and to remove at least one of the several causes of friction, 'I should not grude separate representation to the Muslim community'.[30] These views were often misunderstood by some of their Hindu

---

[27]*Congress Presidential Addresses, 1911-1934*, New Series, p. 864.

[28]In July 1926, Motilal and Sapru took the lead in forming the 'Indian National Union' which aimed to create a 'national consciousness and a national atmosphere in which religious and communal conflicts will be relegated to a subordinate plane'. Other members of the organisation were the Raja of Mahmudabad, Srinivasa Sastri, Sarojini Naidu, Ajmal Khan, Azad, S. Iyengar, and Sen Gupta. *Indian Quartetly Register*, July-December 1926, Vol. 2, pp. 90-5.

[29]*Proceedings of the UP Legislative Council*, 1916, pp. 27-8.

[30]*Ibid.*, p. 218, and Sapru to E. Thompson, 22 August 1932, Sapru Papers.

colleagues who accused Sapru and Motilal of pro-Muslim proclivities. During the election campaign in 1926, Motilal's opponents declared that he was 'denationalized', and Sapru's colleagues in the Liberal Party criticised him for his pro-Muslim sympathies.[31] The attempts on the part of Motilal and Sapru to dispel such an impression were of no avail.[32] In fact, even today they are regarded by some Hindus, quite unjustifiably, as the earliest supporters of Muslim separatist claims.

THE RECOMMENDATIONS OF THE NEHRU REPORT

The Nehru Committee Report was published on 15 August 1928. It was an impressive document which covered a wide range of constitutional issues. An introductory chapter made out a case for full Dominion Status while three chapters dealt with the communal problem. The final recommendations, which bore the impress of a considerable amount of labour and thought, were given in Chapter seven. These include definite proposals relating to reservation of seats, the form of electorate, and the future status of Sind and the North-West Frontier Province. In addition to this, there was a Declaration of Rights which guaranteed religious liberty and cultural autonomy to each individual and group. It aimed at allaying Muslim fears of Hindu domination: 'We cannot have one community domineering over another', declared the report. It went on to add: 'We may not be able to prevent this entirely, but the object we should aim at is not to give domination to one over another but to prevent the harassment and exploitation of any individual and group by another.' The authors of the report assumed that if religious liberty was guaranteed and cultural autonomy provided for, the communal problem would be solved.[33]

The Nehru Report conceded some of the Muslim demands embodied in the Delhi Proposals. Motilal persuaded Aney and

---

[31]V.S. Srinivasan to D.V. Gundappa, 15 December 1930, Jagadisan (ed.), *Letters of V.S. Srinivasa Sastri*, p. 203.

[32]Sapru to Thompson, 29 December 1930, Sapru Papers.

[33]*All-Parties Conference 1928: Report of the Committee appointed by the Conference to determine the principles of the Constitution for India* (Allahabad, 1928), p. 29.

Mangal Singh, who represented the Hindu Mahasabha and the Sikh League respectively, to agree to the separation of Sind from Bombay and its elevation, in company with the North-West Frontier Province, to the status of full province.[34] The report, however, rejected the Muslim demand for reservation of seats in Bengal and the Punjab.[35] Its verdict was that reservation of seats for majorities was 'incompatible with real representative and responsible government'. Moreover, on the basis of statistics provided by Jawaharlal Nehru and Subhas Chandra Bose, the report concluded that the Bengali and Punjabi Muslims did not require any 'adventitious aid' to secure the full benefit of their natural majority. Their population was so distributed that in whatever way the electorates were formed, they were sure to capture a majority of seats in the legislative councils and the local bodies.[36] And finally, the argument that the Hindus who were a minority in population in the Punjab and Bengal but were a majority in voting registers ceased to have any validity under a system of adult franchise recommended by the Nehru Report.

In the Hindu-majority provinces, however, the authors of the Nehru Report were compelled by 'force of circumstances to introduce a temporary element of communalism' in the form of reservation of seats for Muslim minorities in proportion to their population both in the central and the provincial legislatures. This meant that the weightage fixed for Muslims under the Lucknow Pact and the Montagu-Chelmsford Reforms was done away with. Separate electorates were also abolished. According to the report, the principle of weightage had no place in joint or mixed electorates:

> It is of course not physically impossible to reserve a large proportion of seats for Muslim minorities than their popula-

[34]Motilal to Gandhi, 27 June 1928, Motilal Papers (G-1).

[35]At the All-Parties Conference, this was one of the controversial points. Shuaib Qureshi, who argued on the basis of the Delhi Proposals, maintained that the Muslim population in the Punjab and Bengal should be reflected in the legislatures. But the Hindu and Sikh delegates were unanimously opposed to this demand. See Motilal Nehru to the Members, All-Parties Conference Committee, 20 July 1928, Ansari Papers.

[36]*All-Parties Conference*, pp. 43-4.

tion would justify but, apart from the obvious injustice of
such a course not only to the majorities but to the minorities as well, it will in our opinion be harmful to the development of Muslims themselves on national lines. We have
allowed them their full share on the population basis by
reservation and anything over and above that share they
must win by their own effort. We do not propose to impose
any restrictions on their right to contest a large number of
seats than those reserved for them.[37]

And finally, there was the thorny question of Muslim
representation in the central legislature. Muslims claimed that
their population was one-third of the total and entitled
them to a similar proportion of seats in the central legislature.
Their population, however, was so unevenly distributed that
they could not be certain of securing one-third of the members
by election. They, therefore, demanded that one-third of the seats
be reserved for their community. This argument was pursued
by Shuaib Qureshi at the All-Parties Conference and unanimously adopted by the All-India Muslim League and its
provincial branches. But, with the exception of Sapru, no
member of the Nehru Committee accepted this demand. In
fact, it was maintained that Muslims formed less than one-fourth
of the total population of British India and were not entitled to
have reservation over and above that proportion in the central
legislature.[38]

In sum then, the Nehru Report recommended reservation of
seats for Muslims only in provinces where they were in a
minority. By a stroke of pen its authors abolished separate
electorates, discarded reservation of seats for Muslim majorities
in the Punjab and Bengal, and rejected the principle of
weightage for Muslim minorities. This was an extraordinary
decision in the light of the Lucknow Pact and the subsequent
Congress-League negotiations. In May 1927, Motilal Nehru
and Srinivasa Iyengar had taken the lead in persuading
Congress to accept the Delhi Proposals which contained the
provision for one-third representation in the central legislature

[37] *All-Parties Conference*, p. 52.
[38] *Ibid.*, p. 54.

as well as reservation of seats for the Muslim majorities in Bengal and the Punjab. So, why did Motilal and his Congress colleagues perform a *volte face*? Was it intended to undo the 'wrongs' done to Hindus in UP and the Punjab by the Lucknow Pact? Or, did Motilal and other Hindu Congressmen succumb to the Hindu Mahasabha pressures, as alleged by some Muslims? To answer these questions, we must examine the reactions of the leading Hindu politicians to the Nehru Report.

To many Hindus, the report was 'the most authoritative statement and exposition of national demands', and its recommendations relating to the communal problem were regarded as 'bold, outspoken and fearless'.[39] Its great merit was that, unlike the Lucknow Pact, it did not propose any abrupt changes in the relative position of the various communities in the legislatures. In the Hindu-majority provinces, there was relief at the abolition of separate electorates and weightages for Muslims.[40] The report was also welcomed by the Punjabi and Bengali Hindus who had consistently campaigned against the reservation of seats accorded to the Muslim majorities by the Lucknow Pact.[41] Thus Lala Lajpat Rai, who was one of the important leaders in the campaign,[42] urged his followers to

[39]*Hindustan Times*, 15, 17 August 1928, and *Amrita Bazar Patrika*, 17 August, 28 September 1928. According to the *Tribune*, 'never before has the communal problem been dealt with either a more singular freedom from communal bias or prepossession or in a spirit of greater comprehensiveness and statesmanship than in these pages'. *Tribune*, 16 August 1928.

[40]Jayakar welcomed the report because its recommendations were 'more beneficial to the Hindus than any scheme so far suggested on the Congress side'. Jayakar to Kelkar, 28 August 1928, Jayakar Papers (442).

[41]'Since the Muslim League Pact of 1916', observed Raja Narendranath, 'Punjab Hindus have had a grievance against the Congress and the advanced politicians. The Pact of 1916 for the first time allowed communal representation through separate electorates for Muslims in Councils even for Provinces in which they were in a majority.' Narendranath to Cunningham, 5 July 1927, Hailey Papers (11-A). For further details, see Proceedings of the All-Parties Conference held in Delhi on 23/24 January 1925, AICC Papers (G-72).

[42]In December 1924, Lajpat Rai declared that he considered the acceptance of the principle of communal representation in the Lucknow Pact as a 'great blunder'. 'It must be conceded', he wrote, 'that the Lucknow Pact was more or less a patch up affair between the Muslim

accept the Nehru Report.[43] So did leaders of the Arya Samaj Sabha like Narendranath and Gulshan Rai.[44]

While preparing the report, Motilal and his other colleagues could not have ignored the strength of Hindu opposition to the Lucknow Pact. They must have realised that an attempt to prepare an agreement on similar lines would alienate Hindus from the Congress and drive them into the Hindu Mahasabha camp. So, the only way of taking the steam out of the Hindu Sabha campaign and of gaining widespread Hindu support for the Nehru Report was to reject those terms of the Lucknow Pact which were unpopular amongst Hindus in Punjab and the UP.

As regards Muslims, Motilal assumed that the introduction of adult suffrage would satisfy them in Bengal and the Punjab, and the detailed statistics on their performance in the district board elections would allay their fears of Hindu domination. This assumption was not, as we shall see, without basis. Motilal's hopes that the Nehru Report would be welcomed by Muslims in the Punjab and Bengal came true. The UP Muslims, on the other hand, did not figure prominently in Motilal's calculations. He was confident of gaining the support of the Nationalist Muslims, but for the rest he showed no concern. He was convinced that if the Punjabi and Bengali Muslims were won over, Muslims elsewhere 'would be settled by throwing a few crumbs here and there'.[45] In this case, Motilal's expectations were not fulfilled. The men he expected would settle for a few crumbs eventually led a massive agitation against the Nehru Report and even succeeded in enticing away its Muslim supporters in other provinces. Over the years, they remained in the forefront of the Muslim separatist movement and were, indeed, the creators of Pakistan. The controversy

League and the Indian National Congress.' Lajpat Rai to Thakurdas, 13 December 1924, Thakurdas Papers (40/2).

[43]Extracts from the Presidential Address of Lajpat Rai delivered at the Provincial Hindu Conference held in Etawah on 27-28 October 1928', Shaukat Ali Papers, JMIL.

[44]*Some Reflections on Nehru Report Recommedations* (Lahore, n.d.), *Ibid.*

[45]Motilal to Annie Besant, 30 September 1928, *A Bunch of Old Letters*, p. 65.

over the Nehru Report started a debate which ended only in
1947. A study of the debate might help to highlight some of the
important elements of the Muslim separatist movement.

MUSLIM REACTIONS TO THE NEHRU REPORT

Muslim reactions to the Nehru Report varied from province to
province, and it is important to stress this point in order to
understand their distinct political interests. The conventional
argument that Muslim reaction was a 'swift, unmistakable and
unqualified rejection'[46] is untenable because it is based on the
assumption that Muslims had common political interests
throughout the country. We have earlier explained that this was
not true.[47] The so-called all-India Muslim political interests
differed from region to region and that is why the All-India
Muslim League could never evolve a set of demands acceptable
to all its members. In 1918, there was not one but several
organisations which submitted their reform proposals to
Montagu and Chelmsford. Each one of them purported to
represent all Muslims. But their claims were hollow. They
simply represented narrow group interests as opposed to the
supposedly all-India claims of the Muslim community.

The conventional argument about the Muslim rejection of
the Nehru Report is also based on the assumption that its
implications were the same for Muslims all over India, and
presupposes that the political and economic standing of Muslims
in relation to the Hindus was similar in each province. A careful
study of the Nehru Report, however, reveals that its recommendations affected Muslims of each province differently. That
is why they were so sharply divided into 'pro-Report' and
'anti-Report' camps. Both groups viewed the report from the
point of view of their communal interests, and these were by no
means the same. This argument needs to be closely examined.

Under the Acts of 1909 and 1919, Bengali Muslims were
placed in a disadvantageous position. There were but a few
Muslim landlords in the province, and, compared to the Hindus,
fewer Muslims in trade, public services, and the professions.

---

[46]K.K. Aziz, *Britain and Muslim India* (London, 1963), p. 92.
[47]See pp. 96-97,

As a result, they were in a minority in voting registers and in the provincial legislative council. The Bengali Muslims therefore insisted on separate electorates and reservation of seats so that their numerical strength in the province could be reflected in the council and the local bodies. According to the *Mussalman*, these two demands were the 'corner-stone' of Muslim politics and were needed 'exactly for the reason for which protective tariff is necessary for the infant or nascent industries of India'.[48]

The Nehru Report, however, explained that Bengali Muslims did not require any 'artificial protection' because their population was distributed in such a way that they were sure of securing effective representation in the council and the local bodies.[49] The results of the Bengal District Board elections (See Table 8.2) were produced to support this argument. Muslims did well in the elections even though the electorate for the District Boards was mixed and the electoral roll was based on a property or tax-paying franchise. They won all the twenty-two seats in Mymensingh district[50] and the twenty seats in Chittagong. In Jessore district, they won fifteen of the sixteen

---

[48]*Mussalman*, 30 July 1927, 27 December 1927.

[49]Muslims had a majority of 4 per cent over all the other communities put together. But they were not evenly distributed over the province. Hindus were largely concentrated in one part of Bengal—the Burdwan division and part of the Presidency division—with the result that the Muslim majority elsewhere was far more than 4 per cent. The authors of the Nehru Report argued that, like the Punjab, Bengal had definite zones of Hindu or Muslim population. Examining those zones roughly by divisions they found that three divisions (Chittagong, Dacca, and Rajshahi) were 'Overwhelmingly Muslim zones', one was an 'Overwhelmingly Hindu zone', and one was a 'moderately Hindu zone'. Now, the Muslim zone had 291 seats in it, the strong Hindu zone 80 seats, and the moderately Hindu zone 95 seats. The total number of seats if one member was to be elected from every 100,000 population came to 466. Thus, the Muslims would have a clear majority with 291 seats. They would also win seats in the Hindu zones. In other words, the distribution of Muslim population was such that they were bound to get more seats than their numbers warranted. 'They may suffer from economic causes or educational backwardness but the loss from this cannot outbalance the gains from solid majorities in the Muslim zone.' *All-Parties Conference*, Appendix B, pp. 148-49.

[50]S.C. Bose to Motilal, 12 July 1928, AICC Papers (2).

TABLE 8.2

STATEMENT ABOUT ELECTED MEMBERS OF THE DISTRICT BOARDS IN
BENGAL, 1927-8

Names of districts	Total no. of seats	No. of Hindu members	No. of Muslim members
1. 24 Parganas	20	16 (64.2)	4 (34.6)
2. Bogra	15	4 (16.6)	11 (82.5)
3. Bakargunj	20	5 (28.7)	15 (70.6)
4. Midnapore	22	1 (88.2)	1 (6.8)
5. Rajshahi	18	7 (21.3)	11 (76.6)
6. Rangpur	18	7 (31.5)	11 (68.1)
7. Khulna	16	11 (50.0)	5 (49.8)
8. Hooghly	20	17 (81.9)	3 (16.0)
9. Mymensingh	22	Nil (24.3)	22 (74.9)
10. Pabna	16	3 (24.1)	13 (75.8)
11. Noakhali	16	6 (22.3)	10 (77.6)
12. Jalpaiguri	16	14 (55.0)	2 (24.8)
13. Tippera	19	13 (25.8)	6 (74.1)
14. Nadia	20	15 (39.1)	5 (60.2)
15. Burdwan	16	14 (78.0)	2 (18.5)
16. Murshidabad	15	7 (45.1)	8 (53.6)
17. Faridpur	20	8 (36.3)	12 (63.5)
18. Malda	15	8 (40.6)	7 (51.6)
19. Howrah	12	10 (79.3)	2 (20.3)
20. Beerbhum	16	15 (68.1)	1 (25.1)
21. Bankura	10	9 (86.3)	1 (4.6)
22. Jessore	16	1 (38.2)	15 (61.7)
23. Dacca	22	16 (34.2)	6 (65.4)
24. Chittagong	20	Nil (22.6)	20 (72.8)
25. Dinajpur	18	4 (44.1)	14 (49.1)

N.B. The figures given in brackets are ratios to the total
population.

Source: *All-Parties Conference*, Appendix C, pp. 154-5.

seats. In districts where the two communities were in about
equal strength, Muslims often managed to win seats in excess
of their population. This was so in the case of Dinajpur.

Here Muslim formed 49 per cent of the population. Yet, they won fourteen seats as against four of the Hindus who were over 44 per cent of the population.[51] On the evidence of these results, the Nehru Report concluded that Muslim fears, based on the superior economic and educational standards of the Hindus, were largely imaginary. It added: 'We have seen that this superiority has not helped the Hindus of Bengal at the District Boards elections and we are sure that the result of council elections will be even more strikingly in favour of Muslims.'[52]

The Nehru Report made it clear that Muslims in East Bengal had nothing to fear from joint electorates;[53] in West Bengal, where they were generally in small minorities, Muslim candidates had a fair chance of winning some seats through an alliance with the Congress and various regional parties.[54] These arguments made sense and it was not long before the Bengali Muslims veered round to mixed electorates. Abdur Rahim, who had vehemently supported separate electorates at the Muslim League Session in December 1925, suddenly turned into an advocate of joint electorates. As president of the Bengal Muslims All-Parties Conference, he declared that it would be a 'political blunder' if Muslims were to reject the Nehru Report. He went on to assure his audience that the introduction of adult suffrage would ensure Muslim representation in the legislature either equal to, or in excess of, their population.[55] The Bengal Muslim League and the Provincial Khilafat Committee also fell in line with these arguments.[56] Both these organisations represented a cross-section of the Muslim leadership which included Abdur Rahim, H.S. Suhrawardy, Maulana Akram Khan, Mujibur

[51] *All-Parties Conference*, p. 47.

[52] *Ibid.*, p. 48.

[53] *Mussalman*, 16 August 1928.

[54] *Khadem*, 22 August 1928, *Mohammadi*, 23 August 1928, *Soltan*, 7 September 1928, BENNR 1928.

[55] Speech on 23 December 1928, *Indian Quarterly Register*, 1928, Vol. 2, p. 418. Abdur Rahim had earlier stated that 'if adult suffrage is established, there would be very little risk, if any at all, of communal majorities oppressing the minorities'. *Bombay Chronicle*, 21 August 1928.

[56] *Mussalman*, 2 October 1928.

Rahman, Chowdhry Ashrafuddin, and Abdul Karim. Their favourable response was, therefore, of considerable importance. Compared to the Lucknow Pact, the Nehru Report offered a better deal to Bengali Muslims and they were determined to campaign in its favour.

In the case of the Punjab, the Nehru Report identified three natural belts or areas: the predominantly Muslim area, the neutral area but with Muslim majority, and the Hindu-Sikh area. In the north and north-west of the province where Muslims were overwhelmingly strong, no other community could 'encroach on their reserve'.[57] In the south there was a small 'Hindu-Sikh zone' where the two communities were equally strong. This zone included the districts of Hissar, Rohtak, Gurgaon, Karnal, Ambala, Simla, Kangra, Hoshiarpur and Ludhiana. Between these two zones there was a third area where Muslims were predominant, such as Lahore and Gurdaspur districts, but they were not so many as in the north and north-west. The authors of the Nehru Report presumed that the Punjabi Muslims would capture 47.3 per cent of the legislative council seats from the 'overwhelmingly Muslim zone', while the Hindus and Sikhs would jointly capture nearly 30 per cent. The remaining 23 per cent of seats lay in either a predominantly Muslim area or in districts where Muslims were numerically strong. 'Allowing for every contingency', ran the report, 'we cannot conceive of Muslims not capturing enough seats in this area to give them a clear majority in the provincial legislature.'[58]

Many Punjabi Muslims were convinced by these arguments. Barkat Ali, the vice-president of the Punjab Muslim League, stated that after the introduction of adult franchise the question of reservation of seats for the majority communities would lose all practical significance.[59] Sardar Habibullah Khan,

---

[57]The districts included in the overwhelmingly Muslim zone were: Gujrat (86.2%), Shahpur (82.8%), Jhelum (99.7%), Rawalpindi (82.6%), Attock (90.9%), Mianwali (86.3%), Montgomery (71.8%), Lyallpur (60.8%), Jhang (83.3%), Multan (82.2%), Muzaffargarh (86.8%), Dera Ghazi Khan (88.3%), Sialkot (61.9%), Gujranwala (71.9%), Sheikhapura (63.3%). The figures given in brackets are ratios to the total population.

[58]All-Parties Conference, pp. 44-45.

[59]Tribune, 17 August 1928, and Bombay Chronicle, 11 September 1928.

deputy president of the Punjab Legislative Council, and Mohammad Alam, leader of the Nationalist Party in the Council, agreed that the Nehru Report recommendations were beneficial to Punjabi Muslims.[60] Even leading members of the Punjab Khilafat Committee like Kitchlew, Zafar Ali Khan,[61] and Abdul Qadir[62] rallied round the Nehru Report.

By September 1928, 'barring a few die-hards of the Shafi school the great bulk of the Mussalmans' had endorsed the Nehru Report.[63] Ansari, president of the Madras Congress held in December 1927, commended the efforts of the 'Punjabi Khilafatists' in enlisting support for the report. 'They have almost overwhelmed the forces of reaction', he triumphantly wrote to Motilal Nehru.[64] This raised great expectations amongst many Congress leaders who seemed optimistic of reaching a final agreement on the communal problem. Motilal, for instance, was confident that having secured the support of the Muslim-majority provinces the remaining provinces would be 'easily settled by throwing a few crumbs here and there'. He informed Gandhi that the UP Muslims were fighting 'for the supposed rights of the Muslim majorities in the Punjab and Bengal. The most effective answer to them would be that the Punjab and Bengal have accepted the Lucknow resolutions and do not need the other provinces to champion their cause'.[65] Neither this nor any other argument helped to convince the UP Muslims who spearheaded the crusade against the Nehru Report. Motilal had underestimated their potentiality to stir up trouble and to wreck any constitutional agreement which did not protect and foster their political interests.

[60]*Tribune*, 21 and 28 August 1928.

[61]He introduced a resolution in support of the Nehru Report at the Delhi Provincial Conference held in October 1928. *Indian Quarterly Register*, 1928, Vol. 2, p. 437.

[62]On 20 September, Abdul Qadir moved a resolution at the Punjab Provincial Conference congratulating Motilal Nehru and other members of the Committee on drafting the report. He also expressed his support for its recommendations. *Ibid.*, p. 436.

[63]Motilal to Annie Besant, 30 September 1928, *A Bunch of Old Letters*, p. 65.

[64]Ansari to Motilal, 19 September 1928, AICC Papers (105/ Supplementary Files).

[65]Motilal to Gandhi, 24 November 1928, Motilal Papers (139).

The UP Muslims objected to the Nehru Report for several reasons. In the first place, they criticised the ideal of Dominion Status postulated in the report. Leaders like Hasrat Mohani, Azad Sobhani, Shafi Daudi and the Ali Brothers stood for complete independence because they considered Dominion Status inconsistent with the independent spirit of Islam.[66] At the All-India Khilafat Conference held in Calcutta on 25 December, they rejected the Nehru Report and declared that complete independence, outside the British Empire, was the goal of Muslims.[67] During the course of this Conference, Mohamed Ali said that 'today Mahatma Gandhi and Sir Ali Imam would be sitting under our flag and over them would fly the flag of the Union Jack. The Nehru Report in its preamble has admitted the bondage of servitude'.[68]

A far more serious criticism levelled against the Nehru Report was that it discarded the idea of a federal system of government and recommended a unitary central government in which all residuary powers were vested. Muslim politicians demanded a decentralised federal government in which the residuary powers would be vested in the component provinces. This was the only means of ensuring that a Hindu-dominated central legislature would not legislate against 'Muslim interests'.[69] The Nehru Report not only rejected the principle of a federal government but also fixed Muslim representation in the central legislature at 25 per cent and not 33 per cent as claimed by the Muslim League and the All-India Muslim Conference held in March 1927. Muslims in the UP were outraged. 'You make compromises in your constitution every day with false doctrines, immoral conceptions and wrong ideas', Mohamed Ali said, 'but

---

[66]For views of Shaukat Ali, see *Hamdard*, 23 August 1928. Hasrat Mohani had declared in 1924 that Muslims would never accept Dominion Status because they would then have to live under the double dominion of Hindu majority and British suzerainty. 'For an honest compromise between the Hindus and the Muslims' he said, 'the elimination of the Britishers is essential . . . . The real Muslim feeling is for independance.' *Hindustan Times*, 14 November 1924.

[67]*Indian Quarterly Register*, July-December 1928, Vol. 2, p. 403-404.

[68]*Ibid.*, p. 402.

[69]*Ibid.*, p. 404, and *Haqiqat, Sada-i-Muslim*, and *Mansur*, see UPNNR 1928.

you make no compromise with our communalists—with separate electorates and reserve seats. Twenty-five per cent is our proportion of the population and yet you will not give us 33 per cent in the Assembly. You are a Jew, a *bania*.'[70]

Separate electorates and weightage were two other crucial issues which concerned the UP Muslims. Firstly, they pointed out that the system of joint electorates would enable Hindus to elect only those Muslims who were under their influence.[71] Secondly the experience of joint electorates in many places was unsatisfactory. Shafa'at Ahmad Khan, member of the UP Legislative Council, gave instances to show that because the number of non-Muslim voters in certain mixed constituencies was large, Muslim candidates failed to get elected.[72] The message drawn from those examples was loud and clear. Separate electorates, stated the memorandum submitted to the Statutory Commission, were vital 'to our political existence as our experience of those constituencies where the joint electorates obtain has convinced us that Muslims will disappear from all legislative bodies unless separate electorate is guaranteed to us'.[73]

As regards weightage in any future representative system, the UP Muslims justified their claim in terms of their past historical and political importance rather than in terms of their numbers.[74] Although the Lucknow Pact had recognised this claim, the Nehru Report rejected it. The UP Muslims were indignant.[75] Without weightage, Mohamed Ali said, Hindus

[70]Speech at the All-India Khilafat Conference, Calcutta, 25 December 1928. *Ibid.*, p. 403.

[71]*Hamdard*, 23 August 1928.

[72]See S.A. Khan, *What are the Rights of the Muslim Minority in India* (Allahabad, 1928), p. 89.

[73]'Memorandum Submitted by the Muslims of the United Provinces' *Indian Statutory Commission: Selections from Memoranda and Oral Evidence by Non-Officials,* Vol. 6, Part I, p. 338.

[74]*Representation of the Muslims of the UP to the Indian Statutory Commission* (Allahabad, 1928), p. 172.

[75]The *Mashriq* characterised the Nehru Report as sweet poison for the minorities and pointed out that there would be serious dangers to the Muslims if their representation was reduced from 30 per cent to only 15 per cent. The *Aligarh Mail* observed that the report was a 'nefarious attempt to cut the jugular vein of political Islam in India

would establish a 'legalised tyranny of numbers'.[76] Many UP
Muslims also feared that it would usher in a 'Brahmin or
Kayasth domination'.[77] This remark is significant because it
reveals the Muslim anxiety of a potential threat to their privi-
leged position in the UP. To what extent was this fear justified?
To answer this question, we must examine the position of the
UP Muslims in public services and the local self-governing
bodies.

In the public services, the UP Muslims generally held on to
their position because of the UP government's practice of
securing, either by definite rule or by convention, a proportion
of Muslims which in most cases was fixed at 30 per cent. In the
UP Civil (Executive) Service, for instance, one-third of the
vacancies filled by competitive examinations were reserved
for Muslims. Similarly, under the rules regulating
appointments to the UP Police Service, the Governor-in-
Council was empowered to announce, with a view to preventing the preponderance of any community in the service, the
number of vacancies which would be reserved for particular
communities. Although no definite proportion was laid down,
the government extended its patronage to Muslims who actually
preponderated in this service. In the Subordinate Revenue
Service, it was laid down that not less than two and not more
than four Muslims would be taken for every five Hindus, the
ratio being determined each year according to the comparative
merits of the candidates. In the Subordinate Educational Service, on the other hand, there was an established convention
that 30 per cent of the total number of appointments were
made from among the Muslims.[78] The results of this policy are
evident from Table 8.3 which sets out the proportion of Hindus
and Muslims appointed to some of the services.

and murder it in cold blood by doing away with all the safeguards which
Indian Muslims can claim in any system of government'. For further
reactions, see UPNNR for the week ending 8 and 15 September 1928.

[76]Quoted in R.A. Jafri (ed.), *Nigarishat-i-Mohamed Ali* (Hyderabad,
1944), Vol. 2, p. 23.

[77]Representation of the Muslims, p. 149; *Moslem Outlook*, 19 August
1928.

[78]Note by T. Sloan, 10 December 1928, *Indian Statutory Commission*,
Vol. 6, Part I, pp. 346-47.

TABLE 8.3

PROPORTION OF HINDUS AND MUSLIMS APPOINTED TO CERTAIN
SERVICES, 1918-1923

Name of Service	Hindus	Muslims
1. Listed Posts of Collectors	—	1
2. Deputy Collectors	75	55
3. Tahsildars	87	87
4. Naib-tahsildars	104	73
5. Inspectors of Police	25	32
6. Sub-Inspectors of Police	333	238
7. Registrars of Co-operatives	37	23

Source: *Proceedings of the UP Legislative Council*, February
and March 1923, Vols. 12 and 14, p. 30 and p. 420.

The available figures on Muslim representation in elected
self-governing bodies are also revealing. They show that in
1925-26, one-fourth of the 1,408 elected members of districts
boards were Muslims.[79] In March 1928, the UP government
revealed that 66 out of 240 members of Notified Area committees,[80] or 27.5 per cent, and 391 out of 935 members of
municipal boards, or 4.8 per cent, were Muslims.[81] In the legislative council, 30 per cent of the members were Muslims in
addition to the government-nominated members.

Now, the Nehru Report threatened the privileged position
of the UP Muslims in several ways. It recommended that in
addition to being given fourteen per cent of the elected seats by
a system of reservation Muslims would be free to contest other

[79] *Report*, UP., Vol. 2, p. 231.

[80] The Municipalities Act of 1900 for the first time recognised the
non-municipal urban areas as distinct units of local self-government.
They were designated 'notified areas' and their status was, with many
important reservations, modelled on that of the municipalities. The
question whether a town would be set up as a notified area was
decided on a combination of various factors—population, industrial
development, importance for commerce, or as junctions for railways or
roads. By 1928, the UP had 54 notified areas, and each notified area
committee consisted of four elected and one nominated members.
Ibid., p. 224.

[81] Brass, *Religion and Politics*, p. 172.

seats. Muslims stood to gain under this arrangement because
in several urban areas they were in a majority and in others they
formed a strong and influential minority.[82] The UP Muslims,
however, were not convinced. As a minority in every single
district, they feared that if elections were held on a district
basis they would have no chance of winning a 'fair proportion'
of representation from mixed electorates. Even if the electoral
unit was smaller than the district, they would still not improve
their representation. This was because even in those parts of
the UP where Muslims were most numerous, such as Budaun
and Moradabad districts, their proportion in the rural areas
was so low that they had few chances of gaining seats in a
system of straight voting by mixed electorates.[83] Inevitably,
Muslims in the UP saw the Nehru Report as a potential threat
to the benefits they had secured under the Montagu-Chelmsford
Reforms.

One of the important groups which had every reason to
condemn the Nehru Report was that of government servants
and Muslim landowners. As they had gained their position in
the legislative councils either through government nomination
or through separate electorates, their strategy was to work in
close cooperation with the government and to press for the
retention of separate electorates. In March 1927, when the
Muslim Conference agreed to forego separate electorates,
Muslim legislators of the UP, Madras, and Bihar Councils
rejected joint electorates as detrimental to the 'political advancement of the Muslim community'.[84] This was another way of
saying that in a system of joint electorates their chances of
being elected would be considerably reduced. There was yet

[82]Muslims were in a majority in fourteen municipalities. These
were Deoband, Kairana, Nagina, Najibabad, Bijnor, Chandpur,
Sahaswan, Tilbar, Saharanpur, Moradabad, Budaun, Sambhal, and
Amroha. The large towns in which they formed nearly 50 per cent of
the population were Meerut, Aligarh, Bareilly, and Lucknow. For
distribution of Muslim population by district, see Robinson, *Separatism*,
pp. 12-13.

[33]For details, see *Report*, UP., Vol. 3, pp. 6-7.

[34]They included Maulana Shafi Daudi, Sarfaraz Husain Khan and
Abdul Bari from Bihar, and Raja Syed Ahmad Al i Khan, Nawab
Jamshed Ali Khan and Shafa'at Ahmad. *Leader* 29 March, 30 March,
11 May 1927, and *Searchlight*, 3, 8 April 1927.

another danger. The introduction of adult suffrage meant the disappearance of reserved seats and the further enfranchisement of over fifteen million voters, mainly tenants, so that the landlords faced the prospect of being ousted from the general constituencies as well. Hailey informed John Simon, Chairman of the Statutory Commission, that

> Curiously enough, the Nehru Committee's Report is likely to work in our favour, for the landowners are not unnaturally perturbed at the prospect of adult suffrage and the abolition of the reserved seats which they now hold.[85]

In November 1928, some landowners and government servants submitted a memorandum to the Statutory Commission on behalf of the 'Muslims of the United Provinces'. They included Nawab Jamshed Ali Khan, president of the Muzaffarnagar Zamindar Association, Munshi Ihtisham Ali, president of the UP Muslim League and a petty landowner, and the Raja of Jahangirabad, an affluent landlord from Barabanki district. They were joined by Shafa'at Ahmad Khan and Sheikh Abdullah of Aligarh, who were identified as 'independent conservatives'.[86] They declared their opposition to all forms of provincial advance if their position was not safeguarded, and to the abolition of the nominated element and special constituencies. Their demands included separate electorates with weightages at every level of government, effective representation of Muslims on all autonomous institutions created by the legislatures, safeguards for Urdu and for the exercise of Muslim religious rights, and a share of the services according to their representative proportion in any given body.[87]

[85] Hailey to Simon, 28 August, 1928, Hailey Papers (13-B).

[86] Shafa'at was one of the Muslim politicians in Allahabad who opposed the boycott of the Simon Commission. Others were Maulana Wilayat Husain, Zahur Mehdi and Mohammed Husain. Jawaharlal wrote: 'I have been trying to pit myself against the bigoted and reactionary group of Muslims in Allahabad and, although I must confess that for the moment victory is theirs, I think their foundations have been shaken. I am not going to leave them in peace.' Jawaharlal to Syed Mahmud, 4 February 1928, *SWJ*, Vol. 3, p. 93.

[87] *Indian Statutory Commission*, Vol. 6, Part I, pp. 338-39.

Another volatile group which campaigned against the
Nehru Report was led by the Ali Brothers, though their reasons
for doing so were different from those of men like Shafa'at Ahmad,
Abdullah, and the Raja of Jahangirabad. It must be emphasised
that unlike other politicians, the Ali Brothers were not motivated by personal political considerations. They functioned as
politicians in order to champion what they considered to be
Muslim political interests. They did not think in terms of a
class or a region, because they were totally unaware of the
divisions amongst Muslims. They had a romantic concept of
the Muslim community, which took no account of political,
social, and economic differences that divided the community at
all levels. Whether it was in defence of the Kaaba or the Khilafat, they were the first to appear. As regards the Nehru Report,
their concern was not just UP Muslims but the Muslims of
India. They believed that if its recommendations were accepted
by the government, Muslims would find themselves in a subservient position everywhere. Their grievance was that after having
accepted the Delhi Proposals the Hindu Congressmen did not
adhere to their decision. Instead, they had succumbed to the
pressures of the Hindu Mahasabha and reversed their earlier
agreement. In May 1927, Shaukat Ali angrily protested that
the Congress had become an adjunct of the Mahasabha and
the Nehru Report bore the impress of Hindu influence. He
wrote:

I know the present Hindu mentality well. They do not want
our friendship; they want our allegiance and God willing,
they will never get that. For any honourable peace and
pact we are always ready but not for the slavery of the
Hindus; just as we do not want to remain slaves of the
English . . . . Non-cooperation was ruined by these [Hindus]
people, chances for Hindu-Muslim friendship throttled,
an understading between princes and people thwarted, the
Swaraj Party dismembered and now you yourself see what
is being done to kill the Congress, which has ceased to be
National now. It has become an adjunct of the Hindu
Mahasabha and will soon be a seeker of favours at the

door of the British. The Muslims trust in God and would
stand on their own legs.[88]

Shaukat Ali assailed the Congress leadership for rejecting the
Delhi Proposals after having accepted them at the Madras
Congress in December 1927. 'It is you who has changed', he
wrote to Ansari, 'while the Central Khilafat Committee and
I stand where we were, not in a spirit of obstinacy but because
we consider that Motilal and his Committee have intentionally or
unintentionally treated the Muslim point of view with undeserved
contempt . . . . It is so easy to play the generous liberal minded
patriot at the expense of one's people. For the time being it
pays and gains the applause and I congratulate Azad on the
part he played in the affair.'[89]

The attitude of the Ali Brothers towards the Nehru Report
was another indication of their growing estrangement from the
Congress. The communal tension in the mid-twenties had
already shaken their faith in the efficacy of Congress methods
to promote Hindu-Muslim unity. The Nehru Report was the
last straw. It widened the gulf between the Ali Brothers and
the Congress. The men who appeared as the erstwhile lieutenants
of Gandhi during the Khilafat movement and as staunch supporters of the Congress, now turned into relentless critics.[90]

ALL-PARTIES CONFERENCE TO NATIONAL CONVENTION

From August 1928 onwards, several leading Muslim politicians
in the UP endeavoured to mobilise opinion against the Nehru
Report throughout the country. Shaukat Ali, Hasrat

[88]Shaukat Ali to Ansari, 19 May 1929, Ansari Papers.
[89]Shaukat Ali to Ansari, 6 September 1928, AICC Papers (105).
Azad was deputed by Motilal to enlist the support of Muslims in Bengal,
where he wrote pamphlets and addressed public meetings as part of his
mission. He was instrumental in persuading the Bengal Provincial
League to pass a resolution in favour of the report. Azad to Motilal,
1 October 1928, in Urdu, AICC Papers (106).
[90]Gandhi reported to Motilal that the Ali Brothers 'had a fairly
heavy list of complaints against me. But I could make no impression
on them as they distrust the whole of my associates'. Gandhi to Motilal,
12 August 1928, Motilal Papers (G-1).

Mohani and Abdul Majid Daryabadi, editor of the Urdu news-paper, *Sach*, toured the Punjab and Bengal as part of their campaign.[91] They were joined by former Khilafat leaders such as Haji Abdullah Haroon of Sind who had submitted a memorandum to the Nehru Committee,[92] and Maulvi Shafi Daudi of Bihar. Their efforts were successful only in Bombay, where the Muslim League, consisting only of seventy-one members,[93] rejected the Nehru Report 'on account of sufficient provisions not having been made therein for the proper and efficient protection and safeguards of the interests of the Muslim community'.[94] In Bihar, they achieved no success because of the influence of Ali Imam and Syed Mahmud who prevailed upon the Provincial Muslim League to adopt the Nehru Report in November.[95] Even in the Punjab and Bengal, the UP Muslims met with stiff opposition. At the All-Parties Con-ference in September, the delegates from those provinces reached an important compromise over the question of reser-vation of seats for Muslim majorities. They agreed to abandon reservation of seats for ten years from the enforcement of the constitution but kept the option of raising the question thereafter.

To add to the [chagrin of the UP Muslims, Mohamed Ali was defeated by the Raja of Mahmudabad in the battle for the Muslim League Presidency. The Raja was a keen supporter of the Nehru Report and was a signatory to a manifesto issued by the

---

[97]In August 1928, Shaukat Ali, Daudi and Shuaib Qureshi attempted to organise an All-India Muslim Conference, but there is no evidence of its ever taking place. The only reference to this idea is to be found in the Abdul Majid Daryabadi Papers (5). Reports of Shaukat Ali's activities can be found in Azad's correspondence with Motilal in AICC Papers (106), and in Ansari to Motilal, 19 September 1928, AICC Papers (105/Supplementary Files).

[92]See, H.A. Haroon, *The Constitution of the Future Commonwealth and the Rights of the Muslim Minority: A Representation* (Karachi, 1928).

[93]'List of the Members of the Bombay Presidency Muslim League', Chagla Papers.

[94]Irwin to Peel, 12 December 1928, Irwin Papers (152-4). Chagla, Secretary of the League, resigned in protest against the decision to reject the Nehru Report. *Bombay Chronicle*, 10 October 1928.

[95]*Ibid.*, 6 & 17 November 1928.

Nationalist Muslims in its favour.[96] As president of the All-Parties Conference held in Qaiser Bagh, Lucknow, he urged all parties to extend their 'unqualified support' to the report. In September, he conceived the idea of launching a daily newspaper 'to educate the people and get the report ratified by all recognised institutions'.[97] His election, therefore, signalled the triumph of the pro-Report lobby and was a great shock to Mohamed Ali and his supporters. Their chances of using the Muslim League platform for articulating their grievances suffered a setback.

Towards the end of December, the UP Muslims made yet another attempt to turn the tables against their opponents. The opportunity arose at the Bengal Khilafat Committee meeting on 21 December, which met to elect delegates for the All-India Khilafat Conference. The Ali Brothers, in cooperation with Shafi Daudi, disrupted the meeting which was overwhelmingly in favour of the Nehru Report and had their own list of delegates adopted. They enacted a similar drama at the Central Khilafat Committee meeting. As a result, Mohamed Alam of the Punjab, T.A.K. Sherwani, and Mujibur Rahman resigned from its executive committee and along with forty-one other delegates, issued a statement condemning the 'methods of obstruction and procrastination adopted by the representatives of the other party'.[98] They met separately to accept the Nehru Report with certain modifications in the provision relating to communal representation, and agreed to boycott the All-India Khilafat Conference, which met under the presidentship of Mohamed Ali.

It was in the midst of such factional fighting that the All-Parties Convention was held on 28 December at Calcutta. The object of the Convention was 'to ascertain the opinion of the various political and other parties in the country on the princi-

[96]Other signatories of the manifesto were Ansari, Kitchlew, Zafar Ali, Yaqub Hasan of Madras, Chagla, Syed Abdullah Brelvi, Syed Mahmud, Arif Hasvi, Khaliquzzaman, and Maulvi Nasim of Lucknow. *Bombay Chronicle*, 26 October 1928.

[97]The Raja invited Brelvi of the *Bombay Chronicle* to join as editor on a starting salary of Rs 1,000 per month. Mahmudabad to Brelvi, 8 September 1928, Brelvi Papers.

[98]*Indian Quarterly Register*, 1928, Vol. 2, pp. 405-7.

ples underlying the report of the Nehru Committee and the draft constitution prepared by them'.[99] It had to resolve two basic questions. The first was the basis on which the future constitution was to be built. Should India except her political development in association with British claiming the same freedom and autonomy as the Dominions enjoyed? Or, did circumstances require that she should discard all British connections and claim the fullest independence in theory and in practice? The other question concerned the settlement of the communal question so that India might cease to be a house divided against itself and the demands embodied in the Nehru Report be regarded as representing the will of a united nation.

The Convention was attended by 1,200 delegates representing various political parties, trade unions, religious associations, commercial groups, landowners, princely states, and backward classes. Amongst them were 200 Muslims who, in their turn, represented the Central Khilafat Committee, the All-India Muslim League, the Shias, and the Ahmadiya community.[100] But many influential Muslims did not attend. They included Shaukat Ali, Shuaib Qureshi, Hasrat Mohani, M.H. Kidwai, leading *ulama* like Kifayatullah, and the Muslim members of the UP Legislative Council who rebelled against the Muslim League's decision to participate in the Convention and went over to the 'First All-India Muslim Conference' organised by Shafi and the Aga Khan.[101]

Amongst all the participants, the Congress leaders were particularly anxious to know the views of Jinnah who was nursing his ailing wife in Paris when the Nehru Report was published. When Motilal heard the news of his arrival in October, he was particularly excited. 'So much depends on

---

[99]*Proceedings of the All-Parties National Convention* (Allahabad, 1929), p. 5.

[100]There were also five Muslim delegates who represented the Punjab Congress Committee. They were Mohammad Alam, Rana Firoz Din, Mohammad Abdur Rahman, Afzalul Haq and Syed Mohammad Sadiq. AICC Papers (103).

[101]In Chapter four of his thesis, Dr Page has dealt with the All-Parties Muslim Conference in considerable detail. See 'Prelude to Partition', pp. 189-97.

Jinnah', he wrote, 'that I have a mind to go to Bombay to
receive him. If I have the necessary funds within the next few
days I hope to create a strong opinion amongst the Mussalmans
to greet Jinnah on his arrival. Therefore please lose no time to
raise as much money as you can for this great enterprise.'[102]
Motilal obviously presumed that Jinnah, 'the ambassador of
Hindu-Muslim unity', would not only support the Nehru Report
but would also help to secure the adherence of other
Muslims.[103] These hopes were not realised. At the All-Parties
Convention Jinnah proposed three amendments to the Nehru
Report: firstly, that one-third of the members of the central
legislature should be Muslims; secondly, in the event of adult
suffrage not being introduced, Punjabi and Bengali Muslims
should have reservation of seats for ten years; and finally, the
residuary powers should vest in the provinces.

These amendments were a restatement of what had already
been advocated in previous years. But the Hindu and Sikh
delegates at the Convention would have none of them and,
after a stormy meeting during which Jinnah argued in vain for
understanding and statemanship, the amendments were rejected
by an overwhelming majority. The Hindu Mahasabha and the

---

[102]Motilal to Thakurdas, 29 September 1928, Thakurdas Papers (71).
    [103]It is not without significance that many contemporaries referred
to Jinnah as the 'accredited spokesman of the Indian Muslims'. This
was, however, an exaggerated estimate of Jinnah's impact on Muslims.
He was certainly not as popular as Mohamed Ali, and his influence was
confined to small professional groups in large cities. Hindu politicians,
however, preferred to negotiate with Jinnah because of his reputation
as a nationalist as opposed to a communalist. As a member of the
Legislative Assembly and as leader of the Independent Party, he had
cooperated with Motilal Nehru's Swaraj Party. In February 1925, the
two parties agreed to work on the basis of a joint political programme.
Jinnah also joined Sapru, Sivaswamy Aiyer and Paranjpye in refusing
to sign the Majority Report of the Reforms Enquiry Committee, and
produced a Minority Report instead. In early 1928, Jinnah's departure
for Europe had a depressing effect on the All-Parties Conference held
in May 1928. According to Ansari, Jinnah was 'the only man to deliver
the goods on behalf of the Muslim League'. Motilal was also disappointed. 'Jinnah's absence from the country', he stated, 'is most unfortunate.
I can think of no other responsible Muslim to take his place.' Ansari to
Jawaharlal Nehru, 29 March 1928, AICC Papers (G-60); Motilal to
Thakurdas, 28 April 1928, Thakurdas Papers.

Sikh delegates, in particular, refused to accept 33 per cent
Muslim representation at the Centre, while the Liberals, in
cooperation with the Mahasabhites, stood firmly against the
proposal to vest residuary powers in the provinces. Jayakar,
who articulated their views, warned the delegates that, having
once restrained his supporters from rebelling against the Nehru
Report, it would be impossible for him to persuade them to
accept any further concessions.[104] The message was well taken.
Jinnah's amendments were rejected.

Jinnah's amendments were so finely balanced that they
temporarily helped to bridge the gulf that separated the UP
Muslims and their co-religionists in Bengal and the Punjab.[105]
He carefully linked the three proposals on which Muslim politicians had reached an agreement in March 1927 and presented
them as the 'united will of the Muslim community'. Moreover,
he took special care to emphasise the issue of reservation of
seats for Muslim majorities in order to warn the Bengali and
Punjabi Muslims that without reservation they would fail to
secure a majority in the council because their voting strength
was far below their proportion of the population. Jinnah
demanded that in the event of adult suffrage not being established the Convention should reserve seats for Muslim majorities
according to their population. This was a novel idea, for no
Muslim before Jinnah had sought such a guarantee. The
Punjabi and Bengali Muslims were impressed by this demand
because it seemed the surest means of ensuring their dominance
in the legislative council. And when the Convention rejected
Jinnah's amendment on this point, they performed a dramatic
volte face. As soon as the Convention was over, many of them
went over to the All-Parties Muslim Conference held in January

---

[104]*Proceedings of the All-Parties National Convention*, p. 91.

[105]According to the *Mussalman*, an enthusiastic supporter of the
Nehru Report before the All-Parties Convention, 'the amendments
moved by Mr Jinnah at the Convention reflected, generally speaking,
the opinion of the Muslim League as a whole .... The views which the
Muslim League delegation has expressed .... in the shape of the amendments may be correctly regarded as the views of Muslim India.'
Mussalman, 4 January 1929.

1929.[106] The appearance of various groups on the same platform was the most remarkable feature of the first meeting of this Conference. That Mohamed Ali should sit beside Mohammad Shafi whom he had so often derided as a government stooge, or that the Aga Khan should have been cheered by Azad Sobhani whose vitriolic speeches at Kanpur in 1913 had forced him to resign from the Muslim League, these were amongst 'the most delicious ironies of the Montagu-Chelmsford Reforms.'[107] Many Muslims who attended this Conference never returned to the Congress fold.

The intransigence of the Hindus at the Convention also disappointed many Nationalist Muslims. They believed that a generous attitude on the part of Hindus was not too high a price for winning Muslim support.[108] According to M.C. Chagla, secretary of the Bombay Muslim League and an enthusiastic supporter of the Nehru Report, if the Convention could not negotiate a settlement with the twenty-seven Muslim League delegates, it would not do so with a single Muslim in the whole of India.[109] Ansari, who presided over the Convention, was more bitter. He wrote to Gandhi:

[106] The objects of the Conference were 'to safeguard and promote the rights and interests of the Indian Musalmans at all stages of constitutional advance towards full responsible government', and 'to organise the Indian Musalmans and to coordinate the existing Muslim organisations having an All-India character for the purpose of giving expression to Muslim opinion on questions affecting the Musalmans of India'. Some of the leading Muslims present at the first conference were the Aga Khan, Mohamed Ali, Mohammed Shafi, A.K. Ghuznavi, Hasrat Mohani, Azad Sobhani, Firoz Khan Noon, Shafi Daudi, Syed Raza Ali, Shaukat Ali and Maulvi Mohammad Yaqub. The organisers of the Conference claimed that the majority of Muslim members of the Assembly and the Councils attended the first session. For details, see K.K. Aziz (ed.), *The All-India Muslim Conference 1928-1935, a documentary record* (Karachi, 1972).

[107] Page 'Prelude to Partition', p. 185.

[108] 'The heavens would not have fallen if a few amendments that were proposed had been generously accepted and the sad chapter of communal bickering and disharmony closed. The short-sightedness of Hindu politicians on this occasion could not be surpassed', declared Khaliquzaman from the vantage point of Pakistan. *Pathway to Pakistan*, p. 98; also, see Azad's reaction quoted in *Bombay Chronicle*, 29 December 1928.

[109] M.C. Chagla, 'Nationalism and the Muslim Question', Chagla

We wanted to be just and fair and in our effort to do justice and bring greater harmony and unity in the shape of the Nehru constitution, I am afraid we lost at Lucknow and Calcutta what we had gained at Madras. The Mussalmans were the first to revolt against the Nehru Report at Lucknow .... But, at the Calcutta Convention, it was the Hindu Mahasabha which completely did the work of destruction. I cannot help expressing that the speech made by Mr Jayakar and the subsequent attitude in the Committee taken by Pt. Malaviya, Dr Moonje and Hindu Mahasabha friends destroyed all chances of unity.[110]

The Nehru Report was the last straw for the Congress-Muslim relationship. After 1928, many Muslims who had earlier joined Congress became increasingly hostile to its activities. This was particularly evident during the civil disobedience movement. In marked contrast to the non-cooperation days, Muslims participated in very small numbers in civil disobedience.[111] In the Punjab, 'communal tension and preoccupation with communal affairs and controversies raised serious impediments in the path of the Congress'.[112] In Bombay, only a few Muslims were prepared to heed the Congress call and their contribution to civil disobedience was marginal.[113] Shaukat Ali, Gandhi's old Khilafat comrade, warned the Congress leaders that if picketting and boycott against Muslim merchants was

Papers; also, see Chagla's statement quoted in U. Kaura, *Muslims and Indian Nationalism: The Emergence of the demand for India's Partition* (Delhi, 1977), p. 40; and A. Hamid, *Muslim Separatism in India: A Brief Survey, 1858-1947* (Lahore, 1967), p. 201.

[110]Ansari to Gandhi, 13 February 1930, Ansari Papers.

[111]Irwin to Wedgwood Benn, 24 April 1931, Irwin Papers (152/6). For details, see J.M, Brown, *Gandhi and Civil Disobedience: The Mahatma in Indian Politics 1928-34* (Cambridge, 1977) pp. 124, 148-9, 291.

[112]AICC Papers (G/3), 1932.

[113]The *Anjuman-i-Islam*, a leading Muslim organisation in Bombay, declared its opposition to civil disobedience. In August 1930, the Governor of Bombay was satisfied that 'the Muhammadans are giving no trouble and show no inclination to join the Congress. Their leaders appear to be hoping to achieve a considerable proportion of their aims at the Round Table Conference'. Sykes to Irwin, 30 January 1930, 25 August 1930, Sykes Papers, MSS. EUR. F 150/2 (b), IOL.

started in Bombay, 'peace would become impossible and this would be the beginning of much greater strife then we have witnessed.'[114] In the UP, Muslim hostility was clear even in those areas which had generated wide support for non-cooperation in 1920-21. In Rae Bareilly, for instance, their opposition rested 'not so much on any inherent regard or affection for government, or upon absence of national feeling, as upon distrust and suspicion of the Hindu community, and the fear of being swamped by them.'[115] At the meeting of the All-India Muslim Conference in April 1930, Mohamed Ali, who had been Gandhi's closest colleague during the Khilafat and non-cooperation days, made a similar point in the course of a long and vigorous attack on the Mahatma and the Congress. 'We refuse to join Mr Gandhi', he said, 'because his movement [civil disobedience] is not a movement for complete independence of India but for making the seventy millions of Indian Mussalmans dependent on the Hindu Mahasabha'.[116] This was strong language, but this view of the Congress and Gandhi was shared by many Muslims.

It is clear from the debates over the Nehru Report that the Congress proceeded to solve the communal problem on a false premise. Its authors attempted to show that communal representation would not only postpone the introduction of democracy, but would also encourage people to

[114]AICC Papers (1/ Part II), 1932,
[115]A.P. Hume to G.K. Darling, 4 May 1932, Hume Papers (II-A), South Asian Archives, Centre of South Asian Studies, Cambridge.
[116]Quoted in Coupland, *The Indian Problem*, p. 111. Mohamed Ali and a strong body of *ulama* caused a split in the *Jamiat-ul-ulama*, a pro-Congress organisation dating from non-cooperation days, and decided to oppose civil disobedience. The Nawab of Bhopal, who tried to influence the *Jamiat* meeting at the suggestion of Irwin, reported that the Ali Brothers 'with a strong and influential body of *Ulemas* (*sic*) have definitely started a new *Jamiat-ul-ulama*. . . . They have decided to advise the Muslims to keep aloof from the present struggle and to disassociate themselves from the Congress . . . . The remnants of the old *Jamiat* who have been bought over by the Congress are divided amongst themselves and disruptive forces are already at work. But even the rump dropped the question of *fatawa* altogether and the resolution they finally adopted is too confused, halting and hesitating to do very much harm.' The Nawab of Bhopal to Irwin, 10 May 1930, Irwin Papers (152/24).

think communally instead of nationally. They believed that since communal representation kept up communal strife, its abolition would reduce Hindu-Muslim tension to the minimum. They concluded on the optimistic note that once the 'Third Party', as the Indian politicians called the British, withdrew from India people would start thinking in terms of larger political and economic problems. This would result in the formation of political parties chiefly on economic grounds. The report prophesied: 'We shall then find Hindus and Muslims and Sikhs in one party acting together and opposing another party which also consists of Hindus and Muslims and Sikhs'.[117] How unprophetic was this view is proved by the subsequent history of India!

The development of parties on non-communal lines did not take place for several complex reasons. One was that in mobilising support for their political campaigns, most Congress leaders hardly ever emphasised the common economic and political interests of the vast majority of the Indian people. Instead, they often sought a following by exploiting narrow sectarian and religious issues,' and by concluding agreements and pacts for short-term political gains. In relation to the Muslims they assumed, quite wrongly, that the community not only possessed common political and economic interests but was also distinct from the Hindus. The logic of negotiating the Lucknow Pact and many similar agreements lay in the recognition of the fact that the followers of Islam required special safeguards and concessions because their interests were different from those of the Hindus. In this way, the Congress accepted and prepetuated the communal categories created by the Raj. Not surprisingly, this encouraged certain vested interests amongst Muslims to assert their separatist claims, facilitated the growth of communal alignments, and made it easier for the government to justify the retention of communal representation in the Acts of 1919 and 1935.

In 1928, however, the Nehru Committee which was dominated by Congressmen suddenly realised the evils of communal representation and demanded their abolition. They probably imagined that, after having enjoyed certain constitutional pri-

---

[117] *All-Parties Conference*, p, 49.

vileges since 1909, Muslims would surrender them in the
interest of India's national unity. But such a proposition did
not even deserve consideration. On the contrary, soon after the
National Convention in December 1928, the organisers of the
Muslim Conference and their followers adopted an aggressive
communal policy. They spurned the Congress overtures for
reconciliation and appealed to their overlords in London and
Delhi to save them from the cheerless prospect of Hindu domination.[118] They regarded the settlement of the communal
problem as the *sine qua non* for India's participation in the
freedom struggle. And on this point men like Ansari, Jinnah
and Mohamed Ali were united.

'Hindu-Muslim unity is not only one of the basic items in
our programme', observed Ansari, 'but according to my firm
belief and conviction, the *one and only* basic thing.'[119] Jinnah
expressed the same idea and stressed that 'unless the majority
community and their leaders grasp that elementary principle
[namely, that the political demands of Muslims must be settled]
and deal with it in that spirit it will not be possible to get the
minority community into line with any national programme'.[120]
Not many Congress leaders took notice of this warning.

No doubt leaders like Motilal Nehru, Sapru, Gandhi, and
Jawaharlal Nehru endeavoured to allay Muslim fears and
apprehensions, but their attempts were thwarted by vocal and
powerful Hindu revivalist and communal elements in the
Congress. Leaders like Malaviya, Lajpat Rai, and Moonje, who
personified Hindu revivalism in its most aggressive form, only
paid lip-service to the Congress ideals of secularism and national
integration. After 1922, they did not hesitate to use a com-

[118]The Governor of Bombay reported that the Muslims 'do not
want to side with the Hindus, but before they will come out openly
on the side of the government they want some guarantee that they will
be backed up in their claims, such as that for special constituencies
under the next constitution'. He suggested that 'some such assurance
should if possible be given'. Sykes to Irwin, Sykes Papers (150/2/1).

[119]Ansari to Gandhi, 13 February 1930. The same idea was expressed
by Ansari's younger colleagues, including Khaliquzzaman, T.A.K.
Sherwani and Syed Mahmud. See Khaliquzzaman to Ansari, 1 March
1930, Sherwani to Ansari, 3 March 1930, Syed Mahmud to Ansari
(undated, marked 'Please destroy'), Ansari Papers.

[120]Jinnah to Chagla, 5 August 1929, Chagla Papers.

munal platform as a means of rallying public support and made concessions to communal feelings which were already running high.[121] Yet they were soon adorning the Swarajist benches in the legislature and were busy reaffirming their opposition to all forms of communalism from public platforms. The most communally-minded Hindu assumed the nationalist garb and freely sailed between the Hindu Mahasabha and the Congress. This is best illustrated by the career of Malaviya. He and many of his militant followers openly took up communal causes for short-term electoral or agitational purposes.[122] In 1931, he represented the Hindu communalist point of view at the Second Round Table Conference held in London, and then came back in 1932 to become the president-elect of the annual Congress session. Malaviya was only one of the several

[121]In July 1926, Sri Prakasa, a Swarajist candidate for the Benaras-Gorakhpur Assembly seat, urged Motilal Nehru not to put forward Saprus's suggestion (Sapru had suggested that the constituencies in which riots occurred should be disfranchised. Motilal agreed and went further in suggesting (a) that recipients of honours belonging to riot-ridden districts would have their names removed, and (b) exclusion from public service of anybody belonging to the area) regarding the Hindu-Muslim *entente* 'as a plank of our platform. It is too dreadful'. AICC Papers (13/1).

[122]Dr Page has attempted to establish a connection between political ambitions and the stimulation of communal antagonism. He has argued that the anti-Swarajist group wanted to drive a wedge between Hindu and Muslim Swarajists just before the provincial and local elections in 1926, and provides the example of Allahabad where Motilal and Malaviya confronted each other on their home ground. Malaviya's party exploited religious passions to displace the opponents. 'What created a permanent state of communal tension', suggests Page, 'in the province (UP) was not the evangelical zeal of Hindu and Muslim religious leaders but the political rivalries of the Swarajists and Liberals.' Page, 'Prelude to Partition,' pp. 59-60. There is much to be said in favour of this argument, but it cannot be denied that men like Malaviya were committed to an ideology which was bound to arouse religious passions. Their decision to turn to the exploitation of communal differences after 1922 may have been motivated by short-term political considerations but their adherence to the cause of cow-protection, *shuddhi* and *sangathan* was not a new development. Page has exaggerated the importance of the political argument and has ignored the ideological issues which meant a great deal to men like Malaviya.

leading Congress politicians who moved in and out of communal politics with remarkable ease.

Hindu communalists who masqueraded as nationalists could easily jeopardise the efforts of a Motilal or a Gandhi to come to terms with Muslims. This was because men like Malaviya and Lajpat Rai commanded considerable influence in the Congress, and also had strong links with religious and revivalist bodies throughtout the country. Congress relied on their support, and it could not ignore their views on various questions, including the communal problem. Even Motilal Nehru and Gandhi succumbed to their pressures. After the National Convention in December 1928, they were compelled to postpone their negotiations with Jinnah, Shafi, and Mohamed Ali. They were told to do so by the Hindu Mahasabha leaders. Lajpat Rai had warned Motilal not to make compromises with Jinnah.[123] Likewise, Moonje issued a stern warning to Gandhi. 'You should tell Mahatmaji', he wrote to Malaviya, 'that if he were to yield on these points [Jinnah's amendments], you would be painfully obliged to lead the opposition on behalf of the Hindus even against him, Jinnah and Motilal combined'.[124] He went on to add that Muslims must know that 'no compromise is possible for the purpose of tampering nationalism with communalism. It is in this sense that if the Muslims cannot trust and remain in the Congress and give up their separatist mentality, let us leave them alone to go to the Government for whatever it may grant them'.[125] Such statements only confirmed the suspicion of some Muslim groups that Swaraj in Congress terms meant Hindu domination.

[123]Lajpat Rai wrote: 'I will beg you not to place much faith in Jinnah's party. Jinnah has really no following'. He urged Motilal not to make any compromises with Jinnah about communal representation and warned him that 'I may frankly tell you that I won't accept any change'. Lajpat Rai to Motilal Nehru, n.d., AICC Papers (108/ Supplementary files).

[124]Moonje to Malaviya 31 July 1928, Jayakar Papers (437).

[125]Moonje to Gandhi, 5 August 1919; also see Jayakar to Gandhi, 23 August 1929, Jayakar Papers (437).

CONCLUSION

Were the Indian Muslims a monolithic community with common interests and aspirations? This study has shown that they were not. There is, however, one qualification needed. As a religious group, Indian Muslims (whatever the diversity in their beliefs) were a more homogeneous community than has usually been recognised. Common allegiance to Islam and its symbols—mosques, sufi shrines and *Hajj*—created amongst many Muslims a sentiment of belonging to a united and cohesive community. From time to time this sentiment proved more powerful than material interests and sectarian prejudices. Issues like the future of Khilafat and the Holy Places affected the religious beliefs and practices of Muslims; they proved capable of quickly arousing religious passions, which had been latent but not dead for many generations. It would not do to try and explain Muslim response to such issues simply in terms of the political machinations of certain leaders. Such a view ignores the importance of religious symbols in Indian Islam and underestimates the sense of religious unity amongst its followers—a sentiment by no means all-pervasive but extending, nevertheless, beyond the narrow coterie of 'professional politicians'.

Men such as Abul Kalam Azad, Mohamed Ali, Ansari, Ajmal Khan, and Zafar Ali were not only acutely aware of the religious and cultural heritage of Indian Islam, but also identified themselves with the fortunes of Islam in other parts of the world. The welfare of Turkey, the sole surviving symbol of 'Islam's temporal greatness', mattered to them. Above all, the Sultan of Turkey was the defender of the Holy Places, and when these places were threatened large sections of the Muslim community were stirred to action. Money and ornaments poured into the coffers of the Khilafat Fund, and thousands of Muslims from all walks of life flocked to the Khilafat meetings. Many left the fields and the factories to migrate to the *dar al-Islam*; students abandoned their studies and joined the non-cooperators; and many others gave up their jobs and titles. Their reasons for doing so cannot be understood unless we take into account the importance of the unifying powers of religious symbols in Indian Islam.

The role of the *ulama*, as we have seen, was of great importance in mobilising support for the Khilafat movement. They took the lead in voicing Muslim concern over Turkey and the Holy Places and, after 1918, they seized the initiative from the Muslim League leaders, thus unleashing forces of vast political consequence. Fired by religion and buoyed up by their romantic sympathy for the Turkish *Khalifa* they carried pan-Islamic ideology to town and countryside where, in mosque and *maktab*, Muslim artisans, weavers, and peasants were susceptible to their religious exhortations. They used the Quran and the *Hadith* as powerful weapons to gain adherence of the faithful who accepted them as infallible. They also forged an alliance with Muslim professional men and utilised their experience in agitational politics to further the cause of pan-Islamism. Their alliance proved successful, leading to a countrywide agitation which has few parallels in modern Indian history.

After 1922, however, when the Khilafat movement lost its momentum—largely because of developments in Turkey which were beyond the control of Indian Muslims—the *ulama* and their allies were left high and dry; their moment of glory when they seemed to carry all before them on the political stage was over. But their influence on the religious and educational life of Muslims did not come to an end. In fact, as Hindu-Muslim relations began to deteriorate, the services of the *ulama* were enlisted to whip up communal discontent. In Bengal, leaders like Fazlul Haq and Abdur Rahim effectively deployed the communal arguments against their Hindu opponents in the Swaraj Party. With the help of the politically conservative *ulama*, they incited their followers over the sensitive questions of cow-killing and music before mosques to exacerbate communal tension. The religious symbols of Islam cut across the dividing lines of class and caste and made it possible for Muslim leaders to rally a popular following. They were also assisted by the feeling that they possessed a trump card in that they could rally all Muslims to their side by the cry of 'Islam in danger'. Organisations like the *Tanzeem-ul-Islam* and the *Anjuman-i-Islam* raised such slogans to aoruse the religious passions of the newly enfranchised rural voters who were more susceptible to religious propaganda because of their grievance against zamindars and *mahajans* who, in the main, were Hindus.

However, the fact that Muslims had common religious experiences and were concerned to preserve their religious symbols was not enough to make their interests wholly separate and distinct from other communities. Even the zealotry of religious revivalists could not halt the continuous process of cultural and social integration in the countryside. Now and again differences between the communities flared up, but such cases were the exception, not the rule. In general, Hindus and Muslims continued to live together in harmony, as they had done in the past. The Governor of Bengal noted that the 'rank and file' of both the Hindu and Muslim communities cooperated with each other in all the 'daily business of life'. 'It is only at rare intervals,' he observed, 'when their religious feelings become inflamed, that they treat each other as enemies and clashes occur.'[1] Similarly, O.M. Martin, who served in several government departments in Bengal from 1915 to 1926, noticed the 'good feelings' between Hindus and Muslims. 'This was not a temporary occurrence', he recalled in his memoirs, 'but an old and cherished tradition.'[2]

The conventional view that Hindus and Muslims were as a matter of course antagonistic to each other is as misleading as the argument that Brahmins and non-Brahmins were separate

---

[1]Lytton, *Pundits and Elephants*, p. 172.

[2]'Memoirs of O.M. Martin' (Typescript), Martin Papers, Centre for South Asian Studies, Cambridge. In his autobiography, Rajendra Prasad referred to the 'perfect harmony' that prevailed in most parts of Bihar. 'Muslims would join Hindus in the boisterous festival of Holi [in Zeradei village] ... Hindus participated in Muharram by taking out *tazias*. The *tazias* of the well-to-do Hindus in Zeradei and Jampur were bigger and brighter than those of the poor Muslims.' R. Prasad, *Autobiography* (Asia Publishing House, 1957), pp. 13-14.

and rival categories in Madras Presidency.[3] Contrary to the argument of many historians in India and Pakistan, Muslims did not act as a monolithic bloc in Indian politics. Evidence of political divisions amongst them has been marshalled throughout this study. For instance, when the Lucknow Pact was concluded Muslims in Bengal, the UP, and the Punjab reacted differently to its terms. Their political differences also came to the surface in September 1918 when Montagu and Chelmsford were met by a cascade of not one, but forty-four deputations from Muslim bodies. Although each one of them claimed to represent all Muslims, their demands were by no means the same. Their claims to represent all-India Muslims were patently hollow; they were advocates of narrow sectional, regional, or local interests masquerading as the demands of Indian Muslims generally.

The response to the Nehru Report also shows how divided Indian Muslims were politically. The conventional view of the so-called 'Muslim rejection' of the Nehru Report is untenable. It is based on the assumption that the implications of the report were the same for Muslims all over India. It also presupposes that the political and economic standing of Muslims was the same all over India. We have, however, seen that the recommendations of the Nehru Report affected Muslims of each province differently and, naturally, they reacted to it in different ways. Dominant Muslim groups in the UP, Bengal, and the Punjab viewed the report from the point of view of their regional communal interests, and these also were by no means the same. So their reactions have to be studied not only in the provinces where, after 1920, the pickings lay, but against the background of their different socio-economic position.

So, it is hardly surprising that the response of Muslims towards the Congress showed a great variety. As a political organisation, the Congress meant different things to different Muslims. Men like Badruddin Tyabji, Mazharul Haque, Azad, Ajmal Khan, Asaf Ali, and Ansari saw it as a national body,

---

[3]Dr Washbrook argues that simply because a politician appeared as a non-Brahman, a Nadar, or a landlord it ought not to be supposed that all of his political contacts lay within those communities. If he were an important man, he was also vitally related to a cross-communal network. See Washbrook, *The Emergence of Provincial Politics*, p. 287.

speaking for all Indians. To groups like the aggrieved *wasi-qadars* of Oudh, the Shia zamindars of Daryabad and the pan-Islamist *ulama* in the early 1920s, the Congress provided the only all-India forum for voicing their particular grievances. Others, however, viewed the Congress demands as a threat to their material interests. The UP Muslims, for instance, feared that the introduction of representative institutions based on numerical representation would leave them at the mercy of the Hindu majority.

An obvious but important conclusion that has emerged from this analysis is that Muslim reactions to Congress varied from province to province and from city to city. Regional and local interests kept them apart, and their reactions to Congress demands, as indeed to British policies, rested mainly on 'local, special and temporary causes'. In 1919, men like Mohamed Ali emerged as lieutenants of Gandhi and staunch supporters of Congress. In 1928, however, they led an anti-Gandhi and anti-Congress crusade. Congress support was vital during the Khilafat movement, but it was an embarrassment during the hey-day of communalism in the late twenties. The champions of communal harmony and the architects of the Congress-Muslim League alliance of 1919-21 assumed a different role a few years later.

Divisions amongst Muslims did not, however, prevent the emergence of Muslim separatist politics. It was in part the logical consequence of British policies in India. Many officials of the Raj regarded Muslims, quite wrongly, as a separate, distinct, and monolithic community, and this notion contributed to the belief that they deserved special treatment.[4] Also, they

---

[4]Lord Ronaldshay, Governor of Bengal from 1917 to 1922 and later Secretary of State for India, observed: 'The Muslims have their internecine quarrels, but these apart, the solidarity of Islam is a hard fact against which it is futile to run one's head . . . . It was not always realized by the constitution makers even in India itself how fundamental and far-reaching is the cleavage between the two communities . . . . The divisions between Muslims and Hindus are not only those due to religious belief and practice, but to a profoundly different outlook on life resulting in social systems which are the very antithesis of one another.' *Essayez*, p. 119. T.W. Holderness thought the same. According to him, the Indian Muslims 'are for many purposes a nation. In administrative matters the British Government has constantly to consider

recognised their agitational potential after the 'Mutiny' and the revivalist movement of Syed Ahmad of Bareilly. So, they stressed the importance, as in the case of such powerful groups as the *taluqdars* of Oudh, of enlisting Muslim support in ruling the country.[5] In making the Morley-Minto Reforms, which translated these assumptions about Muslims into formal constitutional arrangements, the government offered a number of concessions to Muslims in recognition of their 'political and historical importance', and as part of its strategy of seeking allies in the unfamiliar surroundings of India.[6] This firmly established a Muslim identity in Indian politics.

Congress leaders did not successfully challenge the assumptions made by the British about Indian Muslims. On the contrary, they approved the principle of communal representation in December 1916 and thus perpetuated an artificial

Indian Muslims as a separate community, with interests distinct from and conflicting with those of the rest of the population.' T.W. Holderness, *Peoples and Problems of India* (London, 1911), p. 127.

[5] Alfred Lyall, Lieutenant Governor of the UP from 1882 to 1887, advocated the usual late-nineteenth century official line. He advised Morley, the Secretary of State for India, that Muslims 'embody a strong conservative element . . . (and) would be a substantial support to the Moderate Party in India (which) . . . our policy would be to enlist as allies and auxilaries on the side of the British Government against the extremists. It would be a grave mischance if the Mahomedans were alienated'. To Morley, 4 February 1909, quoted in Robinson, *Separatism*, p. 170. W.E. Curtis advocated the same line. 'From the political standpoint', he wrote, 'the Muslims are a very important factor in the situation in India. They are more independent than the Hindus; they occupy a more influential position than their numbers entitle them to; they have most profound pride in their religion and race, and in their social and intellectual superiority.' W.E. Curtis, *Modern India* (London, 1905), p. 113.

[6] This was of course a self-sustaining process. Once the principle of communal representation was accepted in 1909, it could not be easily abandoned by government. Notice, for example, Hardinge's opposition to separate electorates. 'I do not like it', he observed, 'but Minto gave definite pledges to the Muslims, and I do not see how we can possibly go back upon them . . . . We shall have to redeem our pledge to the Muslims . . . '. Hardinge to G.S. Clarke, 1/2 February 1912, Hardinge Papers (83).

political category created by the Raj.[7] After 1916, the Congress dwelt on the unity of Hindu-Muslim interests but it was then only of symbolic interest. Having once agreed to negotiate on the principle of communal representation, there was no wriggling out of it. In August 1928, the Nehru Committee Report attempted to abolish separate electorates and to discard reservation of seats for Muslim majorities in Bengal and the Punjab. But their recommendations evoked widespread opposition, particularly in the UP where Muslims were in no mood to give up the political concessions they had secured under the Reforms Act of 1919. It was convenient for Muslim government servants, landowners, professional men, and political agitators to assert their communal identity, which had the government's approval, in order to secure a strong position in the new power structure revolving around the legislative councils. Their plea for the protection of their community's interests was, in fact, a veiled plea for defending or improving their share of political power and patronage.

Muslim separatism gained considerable momentum but took a new turn after the Montagu-Chelmsford Reforms came into operation.[8] The implications of these reforms were not realised during the Khilafat and Non-cooperation movements when an anti-government spirit reigned supreme and many Indian politicians boycotted the 1920 provincial elections. By 1922, however, non-cooperation had spent its force and the Hindu-Muslim alliance began to crumble. This dramatic, if not surprising, development coincided with an intense struggle for power, influence, and patronage in the provinces. The reason for this is not difficult to explain. The devolution of power to Indians, the increase in the number of voters, and the extension of the scope and activities of self-governing institutions increased the competition for power at the provincial and local levels. This situation would not have arisen had the two major

[7]The authors of the Montagu-Chelmsford Reforms could thus justify their acceptance of separate electorates in the light of the Congress-League agreement.

[8]It is not without significance that separatist politics gained a new lease of life after each dose of reforms. The Acts of 1909, 1919, and 1935 can conveniently be treated as landmarks in the development of communal and separatist politics.

communities been evenly developed. But this was not the case. In Bengal, where Muslims were economically and politically weak, they were less well-represented within the council, and less capable for that reason of utilising the reforms for their own advantage. The Bengali Muslims naturally felt that they should have the full benefit of their majority position and, therefore, they clamoured for concessions and safeguards. The Hindu dominant groups, on the other hand, were willing to concede only a temporary reservation of seats for Muslims wherever they were in a minority, provided the Muslims agreed to joint electorates. The workings of the Bengal Legislative Council, the Calcutta Corporation, and the response to the Das Pact illustrate the nature of the communal struggle in the province. But this was only a beginning; the worst was still to come. After the initial burst of communal activity in the 1920s, Bengal could not extricate itself from the travail and trauma of communalism which affected large sections of the population. Until 1947, rioting between Hindus and Muslims took a great many lives and appeals for communal harmony fell on deaf ears.

The study of Punjab politics also illustrates how the Reforms Act of 1919 gave the Muslim majority the means of asserting its position in the new power structure, and made it necessary for the Hindus and Sikhs to defend their interests on the basis of their contribution to the province's revenue, their high level of literacy, and their overall dominance in public services and the professions. We have examined the impact of Fazl-i-Husain's policies as Education Minister and their polarising effect on communal relations. Many Muslims who benefitted from the extension of separate representation to public services, local bodies, and educational institutions rallied round Fazl-i-Husain who became a symbol of their aspirations. Being fully aware of the advantages they had secured, they had no interest in relinquishing them.[9] Hindus, on the other hand, saw Fazl-

[9] Hailey reported that 'every year the position of the Muslims here [Punjab] grows stronger. The great increase in the number of boys in our schools is largely from the Multan division; recent extensions of canal irrigation are benefitting mainly the Muslims of Western Punjab, and as a result of the Reforms the Muslim now occupies a far stronger position in the administration.' Hailey to Hirtzel, 15 December 1927, Hailey Papers (10-A).

i-Husain's policies as an assault on their social and economic position. 'The Hindu is beginning to find', observed Hailey, 'that the Muslim is using his power against him.'[10]

The inter-communal character of the Punjab Unionist Party was threatened by the communal bickerings in the province and its programme for benefitting its rural supporters was in jeopardy. It is not without significance that Fazl-i-Husain, the architect of the Unionist Party, supported the All-Parties Muslim Conference, an overtly communal body, and emerged as one of the self-styled champions of 'Muslim interests'.[11] This was another of the ironies of the Montagu-Chelmsford Reforms.

Communalism in the twenties, as we have seen, was not confined to elite groups jockeying for position but affected the common people as well. This was clearly reflected in the recrudescence of large sca'e communal rioting in Bengal, Punjab, and the UP. The timing of these riots was of crucial importance—they coincided with the disintegration of the Hindu-Muslim alliance in the Khilafat and Non-cooperation movements. In a sense, therefore, communal relations in the districts mirrored the national and provincial scenes. That this was so is also evident from the very different picture earlier during the honeymoon period of Hindu-Muslim relations from 1916 to 1922. Political accord at the national level, as is evident from the Lucknow Pact, helped the cause of communal amity at deeper levels of Indian society.[12] Political wranglings and squabbles between all-India leaders, on the other hand, encouraged local groups to exploit religious differences and to employ communal slogans to advance their vested interests.

[10]Hailey to James Wilson, 17 October 1924, *Ibid.* (6-C).

[11]This assessment is based on Fazl-i-Husain's correspondence with Hailey, Irwin, and some leading Muslim politicians. See Waheed Ahmad (ed.), *Letters of Mian Fazl-i-Husain* (Lahore, 1976).

[12]The Lucknow Pact, the Home Rule movement, the Rowlatt Satyagraha, and the Khilafat and Non-cooperation movements had created a climate of communal harmony in which disputes over cow-slaughter and music before mosques, which later sparked off violence, were amicably settled. For examples, see *Leader*, 7, 8, 10, 12 & 13 November 1917 *Tribune*, 20-23 October 1917. Other instances are given in Chatper four,

Thus after 1922, many of the proponents of Hindu-Muslim unity went along with the current of communalism and, in many instances, helped to revive communal and sectarian bodies. This did incalculable damage to the cause of communal harmony and destroyed any chance of keeping the localities free from communal rancour and bitterness.

This study has shown that the political relationship between all-India leaders at the national level certainly influenced, if not determined, communal relations in local areas. This generalisation applies to the nineteen-twenties as well as to the nineteen-thirties when the breakdown of Congress-Muslim League negotiations led to widespread communal rioting in many parts of the country. In the nineteen-forties, however, communalism gained its own momentum and developed independently of the activities of the all-India Congress and Muslim League leaders. At that stage it could not be checked by a Gandhi or a Jinnah. This paved the way for the division of the country in 1947.

GLOSSARY

alim (plural *ulama*)—scholars, learned men, particularly in the Islamic religious sciences.

amir al-mu'minin—generally translated as the Commander of the Faithful—the *Khalifa*.

anjuman—an association, usually of Muslims.

azan—the call or summons to public prayers.

bidah—literally, innovation; an accretion to pristine religious doctrine or practice.

dar al-harb—'the abode of war'; territory not under Islamic law and where Islam is under constraint.

dar al-Islam—'the abode of Islam'; territory where Islamic law prevails.

dar al-ulum—'the abode of sciences', a Muslim theological seminary such as Firangi Mahal or Deoband.

dargah—a term used in India for a Muslim shrine or tomb of a holy person and which is the object of pilgrimage.

dasehra—the Hindu festival commemorating Rama's victory over Ravana, the evil king of Sri Lanka.

fatwa (plural *fatawa*)—generally a written opinion on a point of Islamic law given by a *mufti* or an *alim* of standing.

fiqh—it is the name given to jurisprudence in Islam which covers all aspects of the Muslim collective and individual life. The laws that regulate the public and private life of the Muslims are based on religion; the science of these laws is known as *fiqh*.

hajj—the pilgrimage to Mecca performed in the last month of the Muslim lunar calendar. It is the fifth pillar of Islam, and an incumbent religious duty.

hijrat—act of migration from persecution to safety; especially of the Prophet Mohammad from Mecca to Medina in A.D. 622, the starting point of the Islamic era.

id al-fitr—festival at the close of a month's fast in Ramazan (see ramazan).

id al-azha—also called *id-i-Zuha,* or *Bakr Id,* 'The feast of sacrifice'.

ilm—'knowledge'. In Muslim theology, the word is always used for religious knowledge.

ilm'ul Hadith (*hadis*)—the science of the Tradition, i.e., the various canons which have been established for ascertaining the authenticity and genuineness of the *hadith* or Traditions.

imam—leader, especially prayer-leader in the mosque; used for Shia (see Shia) claimants; also honorifically for the founders of the four Sunni schools of jurisprudence.

jama'at—a body, a group, a congregation for prayers.

Jazirat-ul-Arab—'the island of Arabia', the area bounded by the Mediterranean, the Red Sea, the Indian Ocean, the Persian Gulf and the River Tigris and Euphrates.

jihad (*jehad*)—'an effort, or a striving', a religious war undertaken by Muslims against the non-Muslims.

Kaaba (*Ka'bah*)—the cube-like building in the centre of the mosque at Mecca, which contains the sacred black stone (Al-Hajaru'l-Aswad).

Khalifa—a successor; a lieutenant; a viceregent or deputy; the successor of the Prophet Mohammad as head of the Muslim community.

khatib—the preacher, or reader of the sermon in congregational prayers.

khutba—the sermon or oration delivered at the time of the congregational prayers on Friday, and on the two festivals in the morning after sunrise [*Id al-fitr, Id al-azha*].

madrasa (*madrasah*)—a secondary school or college for Muslims; a collegiate mosque.

mahatma—'a great soul'; applied to men who have transcended the limitations of the flesh and the world.

majlis—an assembly, an organisation, a body.

maktab—a school for teaching children the elements of reading, writing and Quranic recitation.

maulvi (*maulavi*) from *maula,* 'a lord of master'. A term generally used for a Muslim doctor of law; a professor; a learned man.

mufti—one qualified to give a *fatwa*.

muharram—the first month of the Muslim lunar calendar, the month in which Husain, the grandson of the Prophet Mohammad, was assassinated.

mulla—a theologian, a scholar. Usually denotes a person who is attached to a mosque.

namaz—the prescribed prayer in Islam.

qari—one who reads the Quran correctly, and is acquainted with the science of reading the Quran.

qiblah—the direction in which all Muslims must pray, whether in their public or private devotions, namely, towards Mecca.

rais—an Indian of respectable position.

ramazan—the ninth month of the Muslim calendar year, which is observed as a strict fast from dawn to sunset of each day in the month.

sahibzada—son of consequence.

saiyid (Syed)—descendants of Mohammad, (especially) a descendant of Husain, grandson of the Prophet.

sangathan—a movement which aimed at unity and the knowledge of self-defence among Hindus.

satyagraha—'possessed by the truth'; commonly used to denote the passive resistance movement launched by Gandhi.

sharia—the Islamic law, including both the teachings of the Quran and of the traditional sayings of the Prophet Mohammad.

Shia—'followers', the followers of Ali, the first cousin of the Prophet Mohammad and the husband of his daughter Fatima.

shuddhi—'purification', the reconversion to Hinduism of those who embraced other faiths.

silsilah—literally 'a chain', chain of spiritual descent, a sufi order.

Sunni—'one who follows the trodden path'. A term applied to the large sect of Muslims who acknowledge the first four *Khalifas* to have been the rightful successors of the Prophet Mohammad.

swaraj—rule over self, self-government, political independence (*purna swaraj*: complete independence).

tabligh—the Muslim conversion movement.

tanzim—'organisation'. A movement among Muslims which

aimed at securing better education and a closer approach to unity among Muslims.

tazia—lath and paper models of the tombs of Husain and his family, carried in procession at the Muharram.

ulama (sing. *alim*)—commonly applied to learned doctors in Muslim law and theology, who, by their *fatwa* or decision in questions touching private and public matters of importance, regulate the religious life of the Muslim community.

urs—'Wedding', term frequently used in India for the festival commemorating the death of a saint.

waqf (plural *auqaf*)—a term which generally signifies the appropriation or dedication of property to charitable uses and the service of God.

zamindar—'landholder'; the word was used during the Mughal period to denote the various holders of hereditary interests, ranging from independent and autonomous chieftains to petty intermediaries at the village level. In British India, a landholder who independently or joint'y engaged to pay rent to the government and had the right to collect rent and to regulate the occupancy of all other tenures on his estate.

BIOGRAPHICAL NOTES

AHMAD, RAFIUDDIN; educated at Deccan College, Poona, and University College, London; called to the Bar at the Middle Temple in 1892; member, Bengal Legislative Council, 1909; appointed Minister, Bombay Government, in June 1928, and re-appointed in November 1930. As a journalist was a regular contributor to the *Nineteenth Century*, *The Times* and the *Pall Mall Gazette*; received knighthood in 1932.

ALI, ASAF (1888-1953); educated at St. Stephens College, Delhi; called to the Bar in London, 1912; returned to India at the outbreak of War and joined the Home Rule League; participated in the Khilafat movement and gave up his practice during the Non-cooperation movement; General Secretary, Indian National Congress, 1927; member Congress Working Committee 1930; member, Legislative Assembly, 1934-46; arrested in August 1942, and released in May 1945; Minister of Transport and Railways in the Interim Government formed in August 1946; Governor of Orissa from June 1948 to Ma :952.

ALI, MOHAMED (1878-1931); educated at M.A.O. College, Aligarh, and Lincoln College, Oxford from 1898 to 1902, where he got a second in Modern History, 'missing a First, as I learnt subsequently from my tutor, by a very narrow margin'. On his return to India, Mohamed Ali joined the Rampur Education Department and later entered the Baroda Service, 1904-12. On 11 January 1911, he launched the *Comrade*, which was hailed as 'the new star in the firmament of Indian journalism'. From 1911 to May 1915, he was active in the Kanpur mosque agitation, the pan-Islamic movement and the Aligarh Muslim University movement; interned with Shaukat Ali, May 1915 to December 1919; led a Khilafat deputation to Europe, January-September, 1920; imprisoned for sedition, 1921-23; President, Indian National Congress, 1923; joined Shaukat Ali in the campaign against the Nehru Report, 1928; urged Muslims to remain aloof from the civil disobedience movement, 1930; attended the Round Table Conference, 1930-31.

ALI, SYED RAZA (b. 1882); educated at M.A.O. College, Aligarh; began practice at Moradabad in 1908, but soon moved to work at the High Court; took prominent part in the Kanpur mosque agitation; returned unopposed to the UP Legislative Council in 1916 and 1920; took active part in negotiating the Congress-League compact, 1916; same year settled at Allahabad; identified himself with the Khilafat movement but differed on non-cooperation; joined Muslim delegations to the Viceroy over Turkey in 1922 and 1923; President, All-India Muslim League, 1924.

ALI, SHAUKAT (1873-1938); born into a family associated with the court of Rampur. His father had a zamindari income of Rs 1,250 p.m., but died while Shaukat was seven years old. His mother, Begum Abadi Bano, later known as 'Bi Amma', sent Shaukat to Aligarh College in 1888; sub-deputy Opium Agent till 1912; organised Muslim University Fund collections; founded with Abdul Bari and M.H. Kidwai the *Anjuman-i-Khuddam-i-Kaaba*, 1913; interned with his younger brother, Mohamed Ali, May 1915 to December 1919; leading Khilafat agitator in 1920-21; Secretary, Central Khilafat Committee till interned with his brother in September 1921; President, All-India Khilafat Conference at Coconada, 1923; became increasingly estranged from Congress after 1923 and led the campaign against the Nehru Report, 1928; one of the organisers of the All-India Muslim Conference, 1929-31; attended the Round Table Conference, 1931; member, Legislative Assembly, 1935. Halide Edib described him as 'a very big man in every sense...He has a flowing beard, a shock of picturesque grey hair, and eyes which twinkle like those of a mischievous boy. His dress is suggestive of the vagueness of his politics. He wears a long shirt over tight Indian trousers and leggings; and a loose Arab *Mashlak* (mantle) with a Turkish *Kalpak* (fur cap) in the fashion of about sixteen years ago. His attire is reminiscent of a combination of Indian, Muslim, Arab and Turk; in a word, it is a reflection of Pan-Islamism...In carricatures he is represented as a big baby to whom the King gives a pretty doll so as to keep him quiet'.

ANSARI, MUKHTAR AHMAD (1880-1936); educated at Queen's College, Benaras, Muir Central College, Allahabad, Nizam's College, Hyderabad; B.A. Madras, 1900; went to England in 1901 where he was the first Indian house surgeon in the Charing Cross hospital, London; began his practice in Delhi in 1910; led the Indian Medical Mission to Turkey, 1912-13; received a special award from the Ottoman Consul-General in recognition of his services in Turkey, 1914. According to Meston, 'in Moslem circles he [Ansari] commands considerable respect...His work in the Medical Mission during the last Turkish War is a matter of pride to them...'; founded the Home Rule League at Delhi, 1917, and was elected its President; Chairman of the Reception Committee of the Muslim League, Delhi, 1918; played a leading part in the Khilafat movement; President, All-India Muslim League, Nagpur, 1920; President, All-India Khilafat Conference, Gaya, 1922; member, Congress Civil Disobedience Enquiry Committee, 1922, and opposed Council entry till mid-1923; Chairman, Reception Committee of the Special Congress at Delhi, September, 1923; drafted a National Pact with Lajpat Rai for improving Hindu-Muslim relations, 1923; President of the Congress in 1927; one of the founders of the All-India Muslim Nationalist Party, July 1929; member, Foreign Cloth Boycott Committee, 1929; opposed Gandhi's civil disobedience movement in 1930, but said or did nothing against the Congress policy and programme 'because of my loyalty and my deep attachment to the Congress and to those who have got its reins in their hands'; President of the Congress Parliamentary Board, 1934.

AZAD, ABUL KALAM (1888-1958); son of Maulana Khairuddin Ahmad (d. 1909), who worked in Calcutta under the patronage of a wealthy Surati merchant, Haji Zachariah;

travelled to Egypt and Turkey where Azad came into contact with Iranian revolutionaries and the Young Turks; launched the *Al-Hilal*, June 1912; interned in Ranchi, 1916-20; the most articulate supporter of non-cooperation among Muslims; President, Indian National Congress, 1923; in later life, he became a leading nationalist Muslim, acting as President of the Congress from 1938 to 1947 and as Education Minister after Independence.

BANERJEA, SURENDRANATH (1848-1925); educated at Doveton College, Calcutta; founder, Indian Association, 1876; proprietor, *Bengalee*, 1878; editor, 1879; member, Bengal Legislative Council, 1893-1901; President of the Indian National Congress, 1895, 1902; played a leading part in the agitation against the partition of Bengal in 1905 and the Swadeshi and Boycott movements which followed; left Congress in 1918 following differences over the Montagu-Chelmsford Reforms; Minister in Bengal government, 1921-23; defeated in the elections to the Bengal Legislative Council, 1923.

BARI, ABDUL (1876-1926); *alim* from Firangi Mahal, Lucknow, and the *pir* of the Ali Brothers, M.M. Chotani, Rani of Jahangirabad, and of the wife and sister of Abdul Majid Khwaja; one of the founders of the *Anjuman-i-Khuddam-i-Kaaba*; took a leading part in the Kanpur mosque agitation, and the Khilafat movement; President, *Jamiat-ul-ulama-i-Hind*, December 1919; after 1923 he was estranged from the Congress and complained that 'those who pretended to be our friends at one time and made a catspaw of the *ulama* now seem anxious to get rid of them'. In 1926, Maulvi Mohammad Yaqub described Abdul Bari as 'an interesting and an esteemable representative of the good old days, a distinguished figure out of the fast disappearing galaxy of that ancient culture which is still dear to us'.

BESANT, ANNIE (1847-1933); educated privately in England, Germany and France; worked in the Free Thought and Radical Movements led by Charles Bradlaugh, M.P.; joined the Theosophical Society in 1889, and was elected its President in 1907, 1914, 1921 and 1928; conducted a vigorous campaign for Home Rule for India, and formed the Home Rule League on 25

September 1915; interned by the Madras government; June 1917; released in September 1917 as a result of strong public agitation; campaigned for the release of the Ali Brothers, a move interpreted by the Governor of Bombay as an attempt to secure the support of Muslims 'who hitherto have been indifferent or hostile to her pretensions'; elected President of the Congress, 1917-18.

BHURGI, GHULAM MOHAMMAD (1878-1924); barrister and politician of a rich zamindar family settled in Sind from the Punjab; educated, Sind *madrasa*, Karachi, M.A.O. College, Aligarh, and London; called to the Bar, 1908; member, Bombay Legislative Council, 1910-19; General Secretary, Indian National Congress, 1917; member, All-India Muslim League Deputation to Britain regarding Reforms and Khilafat, 1919; President, Bombay session of the Khilafat Committee, 1920; President, Lucknow session of the Muslim League, 1923; member, Legislative Assembly, 1923-4.

BIRKENHEAD, FREDERICK EDWIN SMITH, 1st Marquess of (1879-1924); M.P., 1906; Attorney-General, 1915-19; Lord Chancellor, 1919-22; Secretary of State for India, 1924-28.

BRELVI, SYED ABDULLAH (1891-1949); educated at the *Anjuman-i-Islam* High School, Bombay, and then joined Elphinstone College from where he graduated in 1911; his Principal described him as 'a student of excellent character, hardworking, quiet in behaviour, courteous and respectful and is, I believe, a loyal subject'; joined the *Bombay Chronicle* in 1915 and was appointed its joint editor in 1920; took over as editor after the resignation of Marmaduke Pickthall in 1924; imprisoned in November 1930 in connection with the civil disobedience movement; released on 26 January 1931; member, Working Committee of the Nationalist Muslim Party; President of the All-India Newspaper Editor's Conference, 1943-45.

BUTLER, SPENCER HARCOURT (1869-1938); educated at Harrow and Balliol, Oxford; Assistant Magistrate and Collector, Allahabad and Roorkee, 1890-92; held several positions in the

UP revenue department, 1893-1906; Deputy Commissioner, Lucknow, 1906-07; Secretary, Foreign Department, Government of India, 1908-10; Lieutenant-Governor of Burma, 1915-18; Lieutenant-Governor and Governor of the UP, 1918-23; Governor of Burma, 1923-6; Chairman, Indian States Committee, 1928.

CHAGLA, MOHAMED CURRIM (b. 1900); educated at St. Xavier's High School and College, Bombay, and Lincoln College, Oxford; President of the Oxford Indian Majlis, 1922; Professor of Constitutional Law, Government Law College, Bombay, 1927-30; wrote articles and addressed public meetings in favour of the Nehru Report, August-December 1928; Secretary of the Bombay Muslim League, but resigned over the Nehru Report controversy; Vice-Chancellor of Bombay University, 1946-47; Judge of the Bombay High Court, 1941-47.

CHELMSFORD, 3rd Baron & 1st Viscount (1868-1933); called to the Bar, 1893; Governor of Queensland, 1905-09; Governor of New South Wales, 1909-13; Viceroy of India, 1916-21; First Lord of Admiralty, 1924.

CHINTAMANI, CHIRRAVOORI YAJNESWARA (1880-1941); Editor of the *Leader* (Allahabad), 1909-23 and 1926-1941; member, UP Legislative Council, 1916-23; General Secretary, National Liberal Federation of India, 1918-20 and 1923-29; Minister of Education and Industries, UP, 1921-23; member, UP Legislative Council, 1927-36.

CURRIMBHOY, FAZULBHOY (b. 1872); merchant and mill-owner of Bombay and a keen advocate of Muslim education; member of the *Anjuman-i-Islam*, Bombay; Trustee of Aligarh College and a member of the Muslim University Foundation Committee.

DARYABADI, ABDUL MAJID (1892-1976); educated at Canning College, Lucknow, M.A.O. College, Aligarh, and St. Stephens College, Delhi; member, Central Khilafat Committee until 1928; was associated with the *Hamdam* and Mohamed Ali's *Hamdard*; editor, *Siddique* (Lucknow) and *Sacch* (Lucknow).

DAS, CHITTA RANJAN (1870-1925); son of a reputed solicitor of the Calcutta High Court and pursued the same profession after his return to India in 1894; first came into prominence as counsel for defence in the trial of Aurobindo Ghose, editor of the *Bande Mataram*; joined the Congress as a delegate in 1906; came to the forefront of national politics in 1917 when he was invited to preside over the Bengal Provincial Conference; member, Non-Official Jallianwala Bagh Enquiry Committee; allied with Gandhi, 1920, and became leader of Non-cooperation in Bengal; President, Indian National Congress, 1922; organised the Swaraj Party with Motilal Nehru, and succeeded in having his policy of Council entry accepted by the Congress; elected to the Bengal Legislative Council, 1923; Mayor, Calcutta Corporation, 1924-25; chief architect of the 'Bengal Pact' with Muslim councillors in Bengal.

FAZL-I-HUSAIN (1877-1936); educated at Government College, Lahore, and Christ College, Cambridge; began practice in Sialkot, 1901-08 and later in the Punjab High Court, Lahore, 1905-20; elected to the Punjab Legislative Council, 1920; appointed Minister of Education, Punjab, 1921; re-elected unopposed to Punjab Legislative Council, 1923; re-appointed Minister of Education, 1924; appointed Revenue Member, Punjab, 1926.

HARDINGE, Baron Hardinge of Penshurst (1858-1944); joined Foreign Office, 1880; travelled extensively, holding diplomatic posts in Europe and Middle East; Permanent Under-Secretary of State for Foreign Affairs, 1906; Viceroy of India, 1910-16.

HAQ, FAZLUL (1873-1962); educated in Calcutta University; joined Goverment service as a Deputy-Registrar, 1906; resigned and joined the Bar, 1912; entered Bengal Legislative Council, 1913; Secretary, Bengal Presidency Muslim League, 1913-16 and from 1916-21 he was President of the All-India Muslim League; took a leading part in the Congress-League negotiations, 1916; Joint-Secretary, Congress, 1917; Secretary, Congress, 1918-19; resigned from the Congress after the acceptance of non-cooperation resolution; Minister of Education in Bengal government, 1924; represented Muslims at the Round Table Conferences, 1930-32;

founded the Krishak Proja Party in 1927; Mayor of Calcutta, 1935-36; Chief Minister of Bengal, 1 April 1937-38—March 1943.

HAQUE, MAZHARUL (1866-1930); educated in Patna and in England; called to the Bar, 1891; attended the Muslim Convention at Dacca in 1906 and was one of the founders of the All-India Muslim League; President, All-India Muslim League, Bombay, 1915; was instrumental in bringing about accord between Congress and the League at Lucknow in December 1916; supported Gandhi in Champaran, 1917; became a non-cooperator on Gandhi's call in 1920; launched the *Motherland*, an English weekly on 30 September 1921; opposed Council entry; elected first Indian Chairman of the Saran District Board, 1924-27; defeated in the election to the Bihar Legislative Council in 1926; retired from public life after 1927.

HASAN, MAHMUDUL (1851-1920); graduated from Deoband in 1873 and joined the staff there; Principal of the *Dar al-ulum*, 1890; launched an anti-British campaign in favour of Turkey, 1911; moved to the Hijaz with his associates to avoid arrest, 1915; arrested by the British, 1916, and interned at Malta, 1917-20; returned to India in June 1920 and joined the Khilafat movement.

HASAN, YAQUB (1875-1940); educated at M.A.O. College, Aligarh; founder member of the Madras Presidency League, 1908, and its secretary until 1921; member, Madras Legislative Council, 1916-20; member, Muslim delegation to Britain regarding Reforms and Khilafat, 1919; conducted Islamic Information Bureau and its journal, *Moslem Outlook* (London) along with M.H. Kidwai and the industrialist, Isphani; member, Madras Committee and Central Khilafat Committee, 1920-21.

HASAN, WAZIR (1874-1947); educated at Aligarh and Muir Central College, Allahabad; began legal practice in Jaunpur, moving later to Pratapgarh and then to Lucknow; one of the founder members of the All-India Muslim League, 1906; Assistant Secretary of the All-India Muslim League, 1910-12; Secretary, 1912-19; member of the All-India Congress Committee, 1919; dominated Muslim League politics, 1913-16, when he played an important role in Congress-League rapprochement; member, UP Legislative Council, 1916-19; resigned from the Muslim League in 1919; appointed Second Judical Commissioner, 1921; one of the Puisne Judges of the Chief Court after its inauguration in 1925; received knighthood in 1931.

IMAM, ALI (1869-1932); educated at Arrah Zilla school and Patna College; went to England in 1887 and was called to the Bar in 1890; practiced at Patna and became famous as a lawyer; member of Patna district and municipal boards, 1903; elected a trustee of Aligarh, 1909; President of the first session of the Bihar Provincial Conference, December, 1908; President of the Amritsar session of the All-India Muslim League and, in 1909, the leader in the League's negotiations with the Government of India; member of the Viceroy's Executive Council, 1910-15; Judge of the Patna High Court, 1917; President of the Nizam's Executive Council, 1919-22; represented India at the League of Nations; President of the All-India Nationalist Muslim Party, 1931, when he declared that separate electorate was 'not only the negation of Indian Nationalism but also positively harmful to the Muslims themselves'.

IMAM, HASAN (1871-1933); educated in Patna and in England; called to the Bar (Middle Temple), 1882; practiced at Patna and Calcutta until 1911: Judge of the Calcutta High Court, 1912-16; President of the Special Congress session held in September 1918; President, All-India Home Rule League; delegate to London Conference on Turkish Peace Treaty, 1921; participated in the agitation against the Simon Commission, 1927.

IQBAL, MOHAMMAD (1876-1938); educated at the Scotch Mission College at Sialkot, Government College, Lahore, Cambridge and Munich; returned from Europe in July 1908; associated with the *Anjuman-i-Himayat-i-Islam* of Lahore and with Punjab Muslim League; Secretary of the Punjab Khilafat Committee in 1919; resigned from both the Muslim League and the Khilafat Committee after the non-cooperation resolution was passed in September 1920; attended the Calcutta Unity

Conference, October 1927; one of the few Muslims in the Punjab who opposed the Nehru Committee Report in 1928; opposed the Sarda Marriage Bill and corresponded with Mohamed Ali on the subject; presided over the annual session of the All-India Muslim League in 1930 and called for the establishment of an autonomous state in the north-west of British India. Iqbal's fame, however, rests on his collections of Urdu and Persian poems and his *Six Lectures on the Reconstruction of the Religious Thought of Islam.* He is universally regarded as one of the greatest Urdu poets of the twentieth century.

JAYAKAR, MUKUND RAMRAO (1873-1959); educated at Elphinstone School and St. Xavier's College, Bombay; called to the Bar in London in 1905; practised as a barrister in Bombay High Court; member, Bombay Legislative Council, 1923, and was leader of the Swaraj Party in the Council, 1923-25; member, Legislative Assembly, 1926-30, and Deputy Leader of the Nationalist Party; attended the Round Table Conference in London and was member of the Federal Structure Committee; closely associated with the All-India Hindu Mahasabha and the *sangathan* movement organised by Moonje.

KHALIQUZZAMAN, CHOUDHRY (1889-1973); educated at M.A.O. College, Aligarh, 1907-16; joined Congress in 1916 acting as a member of the Lucknow Reception Committee; took a leading part in the Home Rule Movement, 1917-18; elected President of the Lucknow Congress Committee, March 1920; gave up practice during the Non-cooperation movement; joined the Swarajists, January 1923; Chairman, Lucknow Municipal Board, 1923; a leading Muslim politician in the 1930s and 1940s; after Independence, governor of East Pakistan.

KHAN, AGA (1875-1958); assumed spiritual headship of the Ismailis in August 1885; member of the Imperial Legislative Council, 1902-04; led the Simla Deputation to Minto, 1906; President, All-India Muslim League, 1907-13; resigned because he found it impossible to lead the Muslims 'for my advise will be loyalty of the kind that means trust and confidence and that trust and confidence the Muslims are not now giving to government'; President of the All-India All-Parties Muslim Conference at Delhi, December 1928; Chairman of the British Indian delegation to the Round Table Conference 1930, 1931; led the Indian delegation to the League of Nations, 1932, 1934-47; President of the League of Nations, 1937.

KHAN, HAKIM AJMAL (1863-1928); family came from Kashgar, Turkestan, and held important positions under the Mughal emperor, Babar; produced a long line of physicians of which the most famous was Hakim Sharif Khan, Ajmal's grandfather; educated in all the Islamic branches of learning and learned medicine from his father, Haji Mahmud Khan, and his brother; founder member of the All-India Muslim League, 1906; Board of Management of the *Nadwat al-ulama*; Chairman of the Reception Committee of the All-India Muslim League, 1910; Trustee of Aligarh, 1911; visited Europe in 1911; became involved in active politics on his return; President, All-India Muslim League, 1919; took part in the Khilafat agitation, and was the first man to renounce his title in April 1920; appointed Chancellor of the Jamia Millia Islamia, November 1920; President, Indian National Congress and All-India Khilafat Conference, Ahmedabad, December 1921; member, Congress Civil Disobedience Enquiry Committee and voted in favour of Council entry; joined the Swarajists, January 1923; retired from politics in 1925 because of ill-health. He was described by C.F. Andrews as 'quiet, humble, modest, with all the dignity of a man of character, learning and religious sincerity...'.

KHAN, NAWAB MOHAMMAD AHMAD SAID (1888-); prosperous landowner of Chhatari in Aligarh district; closely associated with the M.A.O. College, Aligarh; member UP Legislative Council, 1920-25, and leader of the Zamindar Party in the Council in the 1920s; Minister of Industries, UP, 1923-25; Home Member, UP, 1926-33; Acting Governor, 1928, 1933; attended the first and second Round Table Conferences; Prime Minister of Hyderabad, 1941.

KHAN, SARFARAZ HUSAIN (d. 1931); member, Bengal Legislative Council, 1909-12; Vice-President of the Home Rule

League started at Patna, 1916; Secretary, Bihar Provincial
Congress Committee, 1917; took prominent part in various
political meetings connected with the anti-Rowlatt Act agitation and the Khilafat and Non-cooperation movements,
1919-21; joined the Swaraj Party in 1922 and was elected to the
Central Legislative Assembly.

KHAN, SHAFA'AT AHMAD (1893-1948); educated in Government High School, Moradabad; Sidney Sussex College,
Cambridge; Trinity College, Dublin; and the University of
London; member, UP Legislative Council, 1924-30; President
of the Provincial Muhammadan Educational Conference, 1925,
1929; organised an agitation against the boycott of Simon
Commission; attended the Round Table Conferences, 1930-32.

KHWAJA, ABDUL MAJID (1885-1962); educated at M.A.O.
College, Aligarh, and Christ College, Cambridge; on his return
to India set up practice first at Aligarh and then at Patna;
elected Trustee of Aligarh, 1912; succeeded Shaukat Ali as
Secretary of the Aligarh Old Boys' Association, 1915; organised
the Home Rule League at Aligarh; gave up his practice during
the Non-cooperation movement, 1920-21; Principal, Jamia
Millia Islamia, 1922; Secretary, Congress Working Committee,
1923; Chairman, Aligarh municipal board, 1923; member of
the Muslim Nationalist Party founded by Ansari and Azad.

KIDWAI, MUSHIR HUSAIN (b. 1878); belonged to a petty
zamindar family of Gadia in Barabanki district; one of the
founders of the *Anjuman-i-Khuddam-i-Kaaba*; President, Oudh
Khilafat Conference, May 1920; joined the Swarajists, 1923;
President of the socialist group of legislative assembly members
formed in March 1924.

KHAN, ZAFAR ALI (1873-1956); educated at M.A.O. College,
Aligarh, from where he graduated in 1895; joined the service
of the Nizam of Hyderabad; took over as editor of the
Zamindar, formerly edited by his father, Sirajuddin Ahmad;
visited Turkey in 1912 to deliver the purse collected by the
Indian Muslims through the Indian Crescent Mission; one of
the leading figures in the Khilafat movement, and went to

England, Paris and the Middle East as a member of the
Khilafat delegation, 1925; joined the Ahrar Party in 1929;
member, Punjab Legislative Council, 1937-46.

KIFAYATULLAH (1875-1952); prominent *alim* of the Ahl-i-
Hadith school and head of the Aminiya Madrasa, Delhi;
first President of the *Jamiat-ul-Ulama-i-Hind*, 1919; took leading
part in the Khilafat movement and went to prison.

KITCHLEW, SAIFUDDIN (1884-1963); educated in India,
England and Germany; started legal practice at Rawalpindi,
1913; moved to Amritsar, 1915, where he took prominent part
in the Rowlatt Satyagraha; sentenced to life imprisonment but
was released under Amnesty, December 1919; took a leading
part in the Khilafat movement and gave up practice, 1920
member, Non-cooperation Committee of the Central Khilafat
Committee, 1920-21; interned for supporting the Karachi
resolutions, 1921-23; conducted the *tanzim* campaign, 1924-27.

LLOYD, GEORGE (1879-1941); educated at Eton and Trinity
College, Cambridge; Conservative M.P., 1910-18; Governor
of Bombay, 1918-23; M.P., 1924-25.

MADNI, HASAN AHMAD (1879-1957); educated at Deoband,
1892-99; joined its teaching staff on graduation and was Principal of the *Dar al-ulum* from 1926 to 1957; joined Mahmudul
Hasan in his pan-Islamic schemes, 1915-16; arrested along with
his leader and three other associates, 1916; interned at Malta
by the British, 1917-20; joined the Khilafat movement and
interned for supporting the Karachi resolutions, 1921-23.

MALAVIYA, MADAN MOHAN (1861-1946); educated in
Hindi and Sanskrit at the Dharmjyan Updeshak Pathshala, the
English District School and Muir Central College, Allahabad;
edited *The Hindustan*, 1887-89; *The Indian Union*, 1889-92; *The
Abhyudaya*, 1907-09; member, UP Legislative Council, 1902-12;
President, Indian National Congress, 1909 and 1918; member,
Imperial Legislative Council, 1910-19; founded Benaras Hindu
University, 1916; President, All-India Hindu Mahasabha,
1923-25.

MESTON, JAMES SCORGIE (1865-1943); educated at
Aberdeen Grammar School, Aberdeen University, Balliol
College, Oxford; entered ICS, 1885; assistant magistrate and
collector Saharanpur, Basti, Moradabad, Partapgarh, 1885-89;
served as assistant Commissioner and as settlement officer before becoming Third Secretary to UP government, 1899-1903;
Secretary to the Government of India, Finance Department,
1906-12; Lieutenant-Governor of the UP, 1912-18.

MOHAMMAD ALI MOHAMMAD, Raja of Mahmudabad
(1889-1931); descendant of Qazi Nasrullah, a Siddiqi Sheikh of
Baghdad, who came to India in the thirteenth century;
Mahmudabad's ancestors settled at Mahmudabad in the sixteenth century and greatly increased their estate in the eighteenth century; member, UP Legislative Council, 1908-09;
Governor-General's Council, 1907-20; played a leading role in
the Kanpur mosque agitation and the Muslim University movement; supported the Home Rule movement 'with a clique of
noisy and aggressive Muslims of the young party, who make
the Raja's house their headquarters and live and agitate at his
expense'; President, All-India Muslim League, 1915-19; Home
Member, UP government, 1920-25; President, British Indian
Association, 1917-21, 1930-31; Vice-Chancellor, Aligarh Muslim
University, 1920-23; encouraged the boycott of Simon Commission, 1927; supported the Nehru Report, 1928; President, All-
India Muslim League, 1928.

MOHANI, HASRAT (1877-1951); leading journalist, poet, and
politician; founded the *Urdu-e-Moalla* in 1903 which was published intermittently until the 1930s; attended the Surat
Congress in 1907 and joined the 'extremist' group of Tilak;
was in the forefront of the Kanpur mosque affair, the Silk Letter
Conspiracy, and the Khilafat movement; introduced the non-
cooperation resolution at the Khilafat Conference at Delhi,
November 1919; demanded complete independence for India
at the All-India Khilafat Conference and the Congress at
Ahmedabad, December 1921; President, All-India Muslim
League at Ahmedabad, 1921; imprisoned in 1922; joined
Shaukat Ali in the campaign against the Nehru Report; resign-
ed from the *Jamiat-ul-ulama*, 1929.

MONTAGU, EDWIN SAMUEL (1879-1924); educated at Clifton, City of London School and Trinity College, Cambridge; Liberal M.P., 1906-22; Parliamentary Under-Secretary of State for India, 1910-14; Secretary of State for India, 1917-22.

MOONJE, BALKRISHNA SHEORAM (1872-1948); educated in Hislop College, Nagpur, and Grant Medical College, Bombay, 1894-98; started practice as an eye specialist in Nagpur, 1901; attended the Congress session in 1904, and helped to organise the Central Provinces' Provincial Conference in 1905; joined the 'extremists' after the Surat split in 1907; took a leading part in the Home Rule League organised by Tilak after his release in 1914; member of the Swaraj Party, the Responsive Co-operation Party and the Hindu Mahasabha; President of the tenth session of the All-India Hindu Mahasabha, Patna, 16 April 1927; founder of the militant *sangathan* movement, and was accused by Muslims of fomenting communal trouble throughout India; closely associated with the *shuddhi* movement; bitterly opposed to the Delhi proposals and to any negotiations with Jinnah after the All-Parties National Convention, December 1928; represented the Mahasabha on the Joint Parliamentary Committee in 1933; formed the Hindu Military Education Society and launched its branch near Nasik.

NOON, FIROZ KHAN (b.1893) ; belonged to one of the important landowning families of the Punjab; graduated from Oxford, 1917; member, Punjab Legislative Council, 1920; Minister for Local Self-Government, 1927-31, and later Minister for Education, 1931-36; High Commissioner for India in Great Britain, 1936-41; Labour Member, Viceroy's Executive Council, July 1942-September 1945.

PHULWARI, SHAH MOHAMMAD SULAIMAN (1859-1935); leading Qadiriya *pir* and pan-Islamist *alim* from Phulwari and a close associate of Abdul Bari; educated at Firangi Mahal, Lucknow, and the Hijaz (1885-86); took a leading part in the Khilafat and Non-cooperation movements.

NADVI, SYED SULAIMAN (1884-1953); educated at Phulwari Sharif, Madrasa Imdadiyya, Darbhanga, and *Nadwat al-ulama*, Lucknow; edited *Al-Nadwa*, 1912; one of the founders of *Dar al-Musannifin*, Azamgarh, 1914, member, Khilafat delegation to Europe, 1920, and of delegation to the Hijaz, 1924-25.

NARENDRANATH, (Raja)(1864-1945); educated in Calcutta and Lahore; M.A., 1886; appointed Assistant Commissioner of Gurdaspur in 1887, Deputy Commissioner of Montgomery in 1895, and promoted to officiate as Commissioner for the Lahore division in 1911; represented the Landholder's constituency in the Punjab Legislative Council, 1921-37; President, All-India Hindu Mahasabha Conference, 1927, and for many years President of the Punjab Provincial Hindu Sabha; attended the Round Table Conference, 1930-31. After 1923, he emerged as a champion of the interests of Hindu commercial and professional classes. 'I for one', he wrote in June 1926, 'cannot whole-heartedly join any political party unless that party undertakes to protect the just and legitimate rights of the Hindus of the Punjab'.

RAHIM, ABDUR (1867-1947); called to the Bar (Middle Temple), 1890; practised as Advocate at the Calcutta Magistrate, 1900-03; member, Royal Commission on Public Services, 1913-15; officiated as Chief Justice, Madras, July-October 1916 and July-October 1919; member, Executive Council of the Governor of Bengal, 1920-25; elected to the Central Legislative Assembly, 1931; President, Central Legislative Assembly, 1935-45.

RAI, LALA LAJPAT (1865-1928); educated at the Lahore College, 1890; passed the Law examination in 1886; practised first at Hissar and later at Lahore; joined the Congress in 1888; seconded a resolution on the boycott of British cloth at the Benaras Congress in December 1905; deported to Burma in 1907; went to England in 1908 and delivered lectures on Indian political situation; established the Indian Home Rule in the United States on 15 October 1916; arrested in 1921 while presiding over the Punjab Provincial Political Conference; President of the Special Congress session, Calcutta, September 1920, and opposed Gandhi's non-cooperation resolution; supported non-cooperation at Nagpur, Dec. 1920; joined Swaraj Party; founded an Urdu daily, *Bande Mataram* and an English weekly, the *People*; President of the Agra Provincial Hindu Conference, Etawah, 27 October 1928, where he supported the Nehru Report; closely associated with the Hindu Sabha, the *shuddhi* and *sangathan* movements.

RAJAGOPALACHARI, CHAKRAVARTI (1879-1972); educated at Central College, Bangalore, Presidency College and Law College, Madras; joined the Bar in 1900 and practised at Salem; joined satyagraha campaign in 1919 and the Non-cooperation movement in 1920; General Secretary of the Indian National Congress, 1921-22; and member, Congress Working Committee throughout the non-cooperation campaign; member, Governor-General's Executive Council, 1946-47; Governor General, 1948-50; Chief Minister of Madras, 1952-54.

RAM, CHHOTU (1881-1945); born in a poor Jat family; served as Private Secretary to Raja Rampal Singh of Kalankar; President, District Congress Committee, Rohtak, 1917-20; editor of the *Jat Gazette*; resigned from Congress over non-cooperation; one of the founders of the Unionist Party and its leader in the Punjab Legislative Council, 1926-36; Minister in the Punjab government, 1924-45.

READING, RUFUS DANIEL ISAACS, 1st Marquess of (1860-1935); educated at University College, London, and Brussels and Hanover; M.P., 1904-13; Solicitor-General, 1910; Attorney-General, 1910-13; Lord Chief Justice of England, 1913-21; Viceroy of India, 1921-26.

SAPRU, TEJ BAHADUR (1875-1949); Advocate, Allahabad High Court, 1896-1926; member, UP Legislative Council, 1913-16; member, Imperial Legislative Council, 1916-20; member, All-India Congress Committee, 1906-1917; President, UP Liberal League, 1918-20; President, All-India Federation, 1923; member, Reforms Enquiry Committee, 1924; played a leading role in the making of the Nehru Committee Report, 1928; delegate to the Round Table Conferences, 1930-32; member, Joint Select Committee on Indian Reforms, 1933. 'It has been a very hum-drum sort of life', Sapru said on his 70th birthday, 'punctuated in private spheres by occasional moments of happiness and more by sorrow than anything else. In public life there has been nothing remarkable except that I have represented a school of thought which is on the wane'.

SASTRI, V.S. SRINIVASA (1869-1946); joined the Servants of India Society in 1907 and succeeded G.K. Gokhale in its Presidentship, 1915; member, Madras Legislative Council, 1913-16, and elected to the Legislative Assembly, 1916-20; member, Southborough Committee and gave evidence before the Joint Parliamentary Committee on Indian Reform Bill, 1919; member, Council of State, 1921-24.

SEN GUPTA, JATINDRA MOHAN (1885-1933); associated with various political movements in Bengal since 1919; Vice-President, Bengal Provincial Congress Committee; member, Congress Working Committee, 1922; elected Mayor of Calcutta Corporation for the first time in 1925 after the death of C.R. Das. At the same time, he was elected President of the Bengal Congress Committee and also the leader of the Congress Party in the Bengal Legislative Council.

SHAFI, MIAN MOHAMMAD (1869-1932); President, All-India Muslim League, 1913; President, All-India Muslim Educational Conference, 1916; member, Provincial and Imperial Legislative Councils, 1909-19; Education Member, Government of India, 1919-22; Law Member, Government of India, 1922-24; led the campaign in Punjab against the boycott of Simon Commission, 1927.

SHRADDHANAND (Swami) (1856-1926); educated at Queen's College, Benaras, and University College, Lahore; started legal practice at Jullundur in 1885; took an active interest in the Arya Samaj and emerged as the leader of its Gurukul section in 1893; founded the Gurukul at Hardwar in 1902; organised the Rowlatt Satyagraha in Delhi, and was invited by the Muslims to address them in Juma Masjid, Delhi; Chairman of the Reception Committee of Congress, Amritsar, December 1919; launched the *shuddhi* movement towards the end of 1922 and reconverted many Malkhana Rajputs to Hinduism; killed by a Muslim fanatic, Abdur Rashid.

SOBHANI, AZAD (b. 1873); rose to prominence during the pan-Islamic agitations of 1913-14; leading local agitator during the Kanpur mosque agitation; joined the *Anjuman-i-Khuddam-i-Kaaba*; President, All-India Khilafat Conference, September 1920; introduced resolution demanding complete independence at the All-India Muslim League session, January 1922. After the collapse of the Khilafat movement, he became associated with the labour movement in Kanpur.

SUHRAWARDY, HUSAIN SHAHEED (1893-1963); son of Sir Zahid Suhrawardy, Judge of the Calcutta High Court; educated at St. Xavier's College, Calcutta, and Oxford University; member, Bengal Legislative Council, 1921, and was Deputy Mayor of Calcutta for three successive years; Minister, Bengal Government, 1927-43; Chief Minister of Bengal, 1946.

TYABJI, BADRUDDIN (1844-1906); educated in England; called to the Bar (Middle Temple), 1867; leading Bombay barrister; member, Bombay Legislative Council; founder member, Bombay Presidency Association, 1885; President, Indian National Congress, 1887; Judge of the Bombay High Court.

TILAK, BAL GANGADHAR (1856-1920); born in an orthodox Chitpavan Brahmin family of petty landowners; studied Sanskrit, Law and Mathematics in Poona; one of the founders of the Deccan Education Society and the Fergusson College in 1885; imprisoned for 'sedition' on 14 September 1897, and in July 1908; released on 17 June 1914; launched the Home Rule agitation 1916, and rejoined the Congress in the same year; played a leading part in the Congress-Muslim League negotiations, 1916, and supported the Lucknow Pact. 'There is a feeling among the Hindus', he said, 'that too much has been given to the Muslims. As a Hindu I have no objection to making this concession....We cannot rise from our present intolerable condition without the aid of the Muslims. So in order to gain the desired end there is no objection to giving a percentage, a greater percentage, to the Muslims.'

WILLINGDON, FREEMAN-THOMAS, 1st Marquess of (1866-1941); educated at Eton and Trinity College, Cambridge; Liberal M.P., 1900-06; Governor of Bombay, 1913-19; Governor of Madras, 1919-24; Governor-General of Canada, 1926-31; Viceroy of India, 1931-36.

BIBLIOGRAPHY

UNPUBLISHED SOURCES

Private Papers

Aligarh Muslim University Archives, Aligarh [AMUA]
    Syed Ahmad Khan Papers.
    Papers relating to the Non-co-operation movement at M.A.O. College, Aligarh.

India Office Library, London [IOL]

Harcourt Butler Papers	MSS. EUR.	F.	116.
Indian Police Collection	MSS. EUR.	F.	164.
Chelmsford Papers	MSS. EUR.	E.	264.
Dunlop Smith Papers	MSS. EUR.	F.	166.
Hailey Papers	MSS. EUR.	E.	220.
Irwin Papers	MSS. EUR.	C.	152.
Lytton Papers	MSS. EUR.	F.	160.
Meston Papers	MSS. EUR.	F.	136.
Montagu Papers	MSS. EUR.	D.	523.
Reading Papers	MSS. EUR.	E.	238.
Ronaldshay Papers	MSS. EUR.	D.	609.
Sykes Papers	MSS. EUR.	F.	150.
Willingdon Papers	MSS. EUR.	F.	93.

National Archives of India, New Delhi [NAI]
    Jayakar Papers.
    Tyabji Papers.

National Library, Calcutta [NLC]
  Moonje Papers.
  Sapru Papers.

Nehru Memorial Museum and Library [JNML]
  All-India Congress Committee Papers.
  Brelvi Papers.
  Chagla Papers.
  Chhatari Papers.
  Daryabadi Papers.
  Khwaja Papers.
  Motilal Nehru Papers.
  Thakurdas Papers.

University Library, Cambridge [CUL]
  Crewe Papers.
  Hardinge Papers.

Firangi Mahal, Lucknow [FM]
  Abdul Bari Papers.

Jamia Millia Islamia, New Delhi [JMIL]
  Ansari Papers.
  Mohamed Ali Papers.
  Shaukat Ali Papers.

Centre of South Asian Studies, Cambridge [SAS]
  A.P. Hume Papers.
  J.C. Curry Papers.
  O.M. Martin Papers.

Government Records

National Archives of India, New Delhi [NAI]
  Records of the Home Department of the Government of India, filed as Home Political, Home Public, Home Education, Home Examinations, Home Judicial. Home Political files are divided into A, B and D (Deposit) categories.

The Uttar Pradesh State Archives, Lucknow [UPSA]
  Records of the UP government in the General Administration, Education and Police Departments.

PUBLISHED SOURCES

Official Publications

Bombay Legislative Council Debates, February-March, 1927 (Bombay, 1927).

Census of India, 1921, Vol. XV. *Punjab and Delhi*, part I. (Lahore, 1923).

Census of India, 1921, Vol. XVI. United Provinces of Agra and Oudh, part I. (Allahabad, 1923).

Census of India, 1921, Vol. XV. *Punjab and Delhi*, part II. (Lahore, 1923).

Census of India, 1921, Vol. V. *Bengal*, part I. (Calcutta, 1923).

Census of India, 1921, Vol. V. *Bengal*, part II. (Calcutta, 1923).

Census of India, 1931, Vol. V. *Bengal*, part II. (Calcutta, 1933).

District Gazetteer of the United Provinces of Agra and Oudh. Vol VI. *Aligarh*.

District Gazetteer of the United Provinces of Agra and Oudh. Vol. VIII. *Agra*.

District Gazetteer of the United Provinces of Agra and Oudh. Vol. XIII. *Bareilly*.

District Gazetteer of the United Provinces of Agra and Oudh. Vol. IX. *Farrukhabad*.

District Gazetteer of the United Provinces of Agra and Oudh. Vol. XXXVII. *Lucknow*.

District Gazetteer of the Bengal Presidency. Mymensingh. (Calcutta, 1917).

Government of India, *India in 1917-18* to *India in 1927-28*, reports prepared annually for presentation to Parliament.

Long, J. (ed.), *Adam's Reports on Vernacular Education in Bengal and Bihar* (Calcutta, 1868).

Nathan, R. *Progress of Education in India 1887-88 to 1891-92. Fourth Quinquennial Review* (Calcutta, 1893).

Proceedings of the North-West Frontier Enquiry Committee, 1922 (Simla, 1922).

Proceedings of the United Provinces Legislative Council, 1916 (Allahabad, 1917).

Proceedings of the United Provinces Legislative Council, 1923 (Allahabad, 1924).

Punjab Administration Report, 1922-23 (Lahore, 1924).

Punjab Administration Report, 1924-25 (Lahore, 1926).

Punjab Legislative Council Debates, 1923-26.

Report of the Working of the System of Government, United Provinces of Agra and Oudh (3 Vols., Allahabad, 1928).

Report on the Working of Municipalities in the Punjab, (Lahore, 1924).

Report on the Working of Municipal Politics in the Punjab, 1922-23 (Lahore, 1924).

Report on the Administration of Bengal, 1889-90 (Calcutta, 1890).

Report on the Administration of Bengal, 1918-19 (Calcutta, 1921).

Report on the Administration of Bengal, 1920-21 (Calcutta, 1923).

Report on the Administration of Bengal, 1921-23 (Calcutta, 1923).

Report of the Bengal Provincial Committee with minutes of evidence taken before the committee and memorial addressed to the Education Commission (Calcutta, 1884).

Report of the Punjab Provincial Committee with minutes of evidence taken before the committee and memorial addressed to the Education Commission (Calcutta, 1884).

Report of the North-Western Provinces and Oudh Provincial Committee: with minutes of evidence taken before the committee and memorials addressed to the Education Commission (Calcutta, 1884).

Report of the Municipality of the Suburbs of Calcutta, 1875-76 (Calcutta, 1876).

Resolution Reviewing the Reports of the working of Municipalities in East Bengal and Assam, 1906-07 (Shillong, 1908).

Resolution Reviewing the Reports on the working of Municipalities in Bengal, 1920-21 (Calcutta, 1922).

Resolution Reviewing the Reports on the working of Municipalities in Bengal, 1925-26 (Calcutta, 1927).

Resolution Reviewing the Reports on the working of Districts Boards in Bengal, 1923-24 (Calcutta, 1925).

Parliamentary Papers

Year	Command Number	Short Title
1888	5327	*Report of the Public Service Commission, 1886-7, with appendices (Calcutta, 1888).*
1914	8382	*Royal Commission on the Public Services in India.* Vol. I, Report.
1914	7293	*Royal Commission on the Public Services in India.* Vols. II to XI, Appendices to the Reports.
1918	9109	*Report on Indian Constitutional Reforms.*
1918	9178	*Addresses Presented to His Excellency the Viceroy and the Right Honourable the Secretary of State for India.*
1919	176	*Views of the Government of India upon the Report of Lord Southborough Committee.*
1919	141	*Report of the Committee appointed by the Secretary of State for India to enquire into questions connected with the Franchise and other matters related to Reforms.*
1921	1152	*Telegraphic information., etc., regarding Moplah Rebellion, 24th August to 6th December.*
1924	2360	*Report of the Reforms Enquiry Committee, 1924, and connected Papers, 1924-5.*
1925	2361	*Views of Local Governments on the Working of Reforms, 1923.*
1925	2362	*Views of Local Governments on the Working of Reforms, 1924.*
1930	3568	*Report of the Indian Statutory Commission,* Vol. I, *Survey.*
1930	3569	*Report of the Indian Statutory Commission,* Vol. II, *Recommendations*

1930   3572   *Indian Statutory Commission, Vol. III. Report of the Committees appointed by the Provincial Legislative Councils to cooperate with the Statutory Commission.*

Material Published by Indian Political Organisations

Annual Reports of the Indian National Congress.

All Parties Conference, 1928: Report of the Committee appointed by the Conference to determine the principles of the Constitution for India (Allahabad, 1928).

Aziz, K.K. (ed.) *All India Muslim Conference 1928-35: a documentary record* (Karachi, 1972).

Pirzada, S.S. (ed.) *Foundations of Pakistan: All India Muslim League Documents, 1906-47* (2 vols. Karachi, 1970).

Proceedings of the All Parties National Convention (Allahabad, 1929).

Representation of the Muslims of the UP (India) to the Indian Statutory Commission (Allahabad, 1928).

Newspapers and Journals

English

Aligarh Gazette (Aligarh), Maulana Azad Library.

Amrita Bazar Patrika, (Calcutta), National Library, Calcutta.

Bengalee (Calcutta), National Library, Calcutta.

Bombay Chronicle (Bombay) Microfilm, Centre of South Asian Studies, Cambridge.

Comrade (Calcutta and Delhi), Jamia Millia Islamia, New Delhi.

Hindoo Patriot (Calcutta), National Library, Calcutta.

Hindu (Madras), Microfilm, Centre of South Asian Studies, Cambridge.

Indian Annual Register, 1923-32 (Calcutta), published as the *Indian Quarterly Register*, 1924-29. Centre of South Asian Studies, Cambridge.

Leader (Allahabad), Microfilm, Centre of South Asian Studies, Cambridge.

Mahratta (Poona), Microfilm, Centre of South Asian Studies, Cambridge.

Mussalman (Calcutta), National Library, Calcutta.

Moslem Chronicle (Calcutta), National Library, Calcutta.

Moslem Outlook (Calcutta), National Library, Calcutta.

New Era (Lucknow), Jamia Millia Islamia, New Delhi.

Searchlight (Patna), Microfilm, Centre for South Asian Studies, Cambridge.

Tribune (Lahore), Nehru Memorial Museum and Library, New Delhi.

Urdu

Aligarh Magazine, Department of Urdu, Aligarh Muslim University, Aligarh.

Al-Hilal (Calcutta), Jamia Millia Islamia, New Delhi.

Hamdam (Lucknow), Jamia Millia Islamia, New Delhi.

Hamdard (Delhi), Jamia Millia Islamia, New Delhi.

Reports on the Native Newspapers of the Bombay Presidency, National Archives of India.

Reports on the Native Newspapers of Bengal, National Archives of India.

Reports on the Native Newspapers of the Punjab, National Archives of India.

Reports on the Native Newspapers of the North-West Provinces, North-West Provinces and Oudh, and the United Provinces, National Archives of India.

India Office Library Tracts

Language	Tract Number	Author and Title
English	1037	*All About Partition: Proceedings of the Town Hall Protest Meeting*, August 1905.
Urdu	640	B.B. Pant, *A Lecture on Nagree Versus Urdu*, 1869.
Urdu	640	D. Das, *Hindi versus Urdu* (Lahore, 1882).
Urdu	5	*Khwaja Kamaluddin's lecture, Anjuman-i-Himayat-i-Islam* (Lahore, 1894).

Urdu	3109	Mirza Hairat, *Khilafat-i-Usmani* (Delhi, 1901).
Urdu	1179	Mir Karamatullah (ed.), *Lectures of Maulvi Nazir Ahmad* (Lahore, 1890).
Urdu	1166	Nazir Ahmad, *Lecture at the Ninth Educational Conference* (Delhi, 1894).
English	1061	*R.M. Sayani: A sketch of his life and career* (Madras, 1912).
English	1084	*Submission About the Korbani Question* (Calcutta, 1911).

Proscribed Publications

Urdu	47	*Bulbalan-i-Hurriyat ke tarane* (Jaunpur, 1920).
Urdu	146	Ghulam Nabi, *Hind ka Sitara* (Budaun, 1922).
Urdu	154	*Suraj ki Devi.*
Urdu	123	Haji Ahmad, *Waqa-i-Punjab* (Delhi, n.d.).
Urdu	133	Maulana Sulaiman Ashraf, *Al-Bilagh* (Aligarh, n.d.).
Urdu	155	Mirza Fahim Beg Chughtai, *Sada-i-Baaz gusht* (Agra, n.d.).
Urdu	43	Misbahul Islam, *Tarana-i-Khilafat* (Deoband, 1914).
Urdu	108	Mohammad Haidar, *Qaumi Tarana: Azaadi ka Nuskha* (Pilibhit, 1921).
Urdu	10	Mohammad Jamal, *Angrezon ka zulm aur Iraqi maqtal.*
Urdu	153	Qazi Mohammad Jami, *Girya-i-Hind* (Pilibhit, 1921).
Urdu	109	Riyaz-ud Din, *Islami Jhunda* (Amroha, 1921).
Urdu	8	*Rasul Allah ke Roza-i-Mubarak pur gola bari aur Sada-i-intiqam.*
Urdu	44	Haji Ahmad, *Dard-i-Khilafat* (Aligarh, n.d.).

Published Works, Articles and Unpublished Theses

Ahmad, A. *Islamic Modernism in India and Pakistan 1857-1964* (London, 1967).

Ahmad, A. *Studies in Islamic Culture in the Indian Environment* (Oxford, 1964).

Ahmad, I. (ed.) *Caste and Social Stratification among the Muslims* (Delhi, 1973).

Ahmad, K. *The Sacred Journey: Being Pilgrimage to Mecca* (New York, 1961).

Ahmad. Q., Jha, J.S. *Mazharul Haque* (Delhi, 1976).

Ahmad, S. *Muslim Community in Bengal, 1884-1912* (Dacca, 1974).

Albiruni, A.H. *Makers of Pakistan and Muslim India* (Lahore, 1950).

Ali, M.H. *Observations on the Mussulmans of India*, 2nd edition (London, 1917).

Azad, A.K. *India Wins Freedom: An Autobiographical Narrative* (Bombay, 1959).

Aziz, K.K. *Ameer Ali: His Life and Work* (Lahore, 1968).

Aziz, K.K. *Britain and Muslim India* (London, 1963).

Baker, C. and Washbrook, D.A. *South India: Political Institutions and Political Change, 1880-1940* (Delhi, 1975).

Bamford, P.C. *Histories of the Khilafat and Non-Cooperation Movements.* Reprint (Delhi, 1975).

Banerjea, S. *Speeches and Writings of Surendranath Banerjea* (Madras, 1912).

Banerjea, S. *A Nation in Making.* Reprint of 1925 edn. (Calcutta, 1963).

Bapat, S.V. (ed.) *Reminiscences of Lokmanya Tilak* (Poona, n.d.).

Barrier, N.G. 'The Arya Samaj and Congress Politics in the Punjab, 1894-1908', *Journal of Asian Studies*, XXVI, May 1967.

Barrier, N.G. 'Muslim Politics in the Punjab 1810-1890', *The Punjab Past and Present*, April 1971.

Barrier, N.G. *The Punjab Alienation of Land Bill of 1901* (Duke University Monograph and Occasional Papers Series, 1965).

Basu, A. *The Growth of Education and Political Development in India, 1898-1920* (Delhi, 1974).

Bayly, C.A. *The Local Roots of Indian Politics—Allahabad, 1880-1920* (Oxford, 1975).

Bose, S.C. *The Indian Struggle 1920-1942* (London, 1964).

Brass, P. *Language, Religion and Politics in North India* (Cambridge, 1974).

Broomfield, J.H. *Elite Conflict in a Plural Society: Twentieth Century Bengal* (Berkeley and Los Angeles, 1968).

Broomfield, J.H. 'Four Lives: History as Biography', *South Asia*, August 1971.

Brown, E.C. *Har Dayal* (Tueson, 1975).

Brown, J.M. *Gandhi's Rise to Power: Indian Politics 1915-1922* (Cambridge, 1972).

Brown, J.M. *Gandhi and Civil Disobedience: The Mahatma in Indian Politics 1928-34* (Cambridge, 1977).

Chaudhuri, N.A. *Views on Present Political Situation in India* (Calcutta, 1921).

Chaudhuri, N.C. *The Autobiography of an Unknown Indian* (New York, 1951).

Cotton, H. 'India Old and New', *Asiatic Review*, July 1914.

Cotton, H. 'India Now and After', *Contemporary Review*, February 1915.

Coupland, R. *The Indian Problem 1833-1935* (Oxford, 1952).

Crawley, W.F. 'Kisan Sabhas and the Agrarian Revolt in the UP, 1920-21', *Modern Asian Studies*, Vol. 5, 1971.

Curtis, W.E. *Modern India* (London, 1905).

Desai, M. *Day-to-Day With Gandhi* (Varanasi, 1968).

Dwarkadas, K. *India's Fight for Freedom* (Bombay, 1966).

Edib, H. *Conflict of East and West in Turkey* (Delhi, 1935).

Farquhar, J.N. *Modern Religious Movements in India*, 1st Indian edn. (Delhi, 1967).

Faruqi, Z. *The Deoband School and the Demand for Pakistan* (London, 1963).

Frykenberg, R.E. (ed.) *Land Control and Social Structure in Indian History* (Wisconsin, 1969).

Gandhi, M.K. *The Collected Works of Mahatma Gandhi* (Delhi, in process of publication, 1958).

Gandhi, M.K. *An Autobiography on the Story of My Experiments with Truth.* Reprint (Ahmedabad, 1958).

Ghosh, P.C. *The Development of the Indian National Congress, 1892-1909* (Calcutta, 1960).

Gibb, H.A.R. *Studies in the Civilization of Islam* (London, 1962).

Gopal, R. *Indian Muslims: A Political History, 1858-1947* (Bombay, 1959).

Gordon, L. *Bengal: The Nationalist Movement 1876-1940* (Columbia University Press, 1974).

Gordon, R.A. 'Aspects in the history of the Indian National Congress, with special reference to the Swarajya Party, 1919-1927' (Unpublished D. Phil. thesis, 1970, Oxford).

Gordon, R.A. 'Non-co-operation and Council Entry 1919 to 1920', *Modern Asian Studies*, July 1973.

Gordon, R.A. The Hindu Mahasabha and the Indian National Congress 1915 to 1926', *Modern Asian Studies*, July 1975.

Gupta, S.L. *Pandit Madan Mohan Malaviya: A Socio-Political Study* (Allahabad, 1978).

Hamid, A. *Muslim Separatism in India: A Brief Survey 1858-1947* (Oxford, 1967).

Hardgrave, R.L. 'The Mapilla Rebellion, 1921: Peasant Revolt in Malabar', *Modern Asian Studies*, February 1977.

Hardy, P. *The Muslims of British India* (Cambridge, 1972).

Hardy, P. *Partners in Freedom—and True Muslims: The political thought of some Muslim scholars in British India, 1912-1947* (Scandinavian Institute of Asian Studies, 1971).

Haroon, H.A. *The Constitution of the Future Commonwealth and the Rights of the Muslim Minority: A Representation* (Karachi, 1928).

Hasan, Mohibbul. 'Mahatma Gandhi and the Indian Muslims', Biswas, S.C. (ed.), *Gandhi Theory and Practice: Social Impact and Contemporary Relevance* (Simla, 1969).

Hasan, Mohibbul. (ed.) *Waqai-i-Manazil-i Rum: diary of a journey to Constantinople* (Delhi, 1968).

Hill, J.L. 'Congress and Representative Institutions in the United Provinces, 1886-1901' (Unpublished Ph.D. thesis, 1966, Duke University).

Holderness, T.W. *Peoples and Problems of India* (London, 1911).

Hourani, A. *Arabic Thought in the Liberal Age, 1798-1939* (Oxford, 1970).

Husain, A. *Fazl-i-Husain: A Political Biography* (Bombay, 1936).

Ikram, S.M. *Modern Muslim India and the Birth of Pakistan, 1858-1951*, 2nd edn. (Lahore, 1965).

Iqbal, A. (ed.) *My Life a Fragment: An Autobiographical Sketch of Maulana Mohamed Ali.* Reprint of 1942 edn. (Lahore, 1966).

Iqbal, A. (ed.) *Selected Writings and Speeches of Maulana Mohamed Ali* (Lahore, 1946).

Jagdisan (ed.) *Letters of V.S. Srinivasa Sastri.* 2nd edn. (Asia Publishing House, 1963).

Jambunathan, M.R. (ed.) *Swami Shraddhanand* (Bombay, 1961).

Jayakar, M.R. *The Story of My Life, 1873-1922*, Vol. I. (Bombay, 1958).

Jha, J.S. 'An Unpublished Correspondence relating to the Bihar Hindu Sabha', *Journal of the Bihar Research Society*, January-December 1968.

Johnson, G. *Provincial Politics and Indian Nationalism: Bombay and the Indian National Congress, 1880-1915* (Cambridge, 1973).

Jones, K.W. 'Communalism in the Punjab. The Arya Samaj Contribution', *Journal of Asian Studies*, XXVIII, November 1968.

Jones, K.W. *Arya Dharm: Hindu Consciousness in 19th-Century Punjab* (California, 1976).

Joshi, V.C. (ed.) *Lala Lajpat Rai: Writings and Speeches*, Vols. I-II (Delhi, 1966).

Kaura, U. *Muslims and Indian Nationalism: The Emergence of the demand for India's Partition 1928-1940* (Delhi, 1977).

Khaliquzzaman, C. *Pathway to Pakistan* (Lahore, 1961).

Khan, S.A. *On the Present State of Indian Politics* (Allahabad, 1888).

Khan, Shafaat Ahmad. *What are the Rights of the Muslim Minority in India?* (Allahabad, 1928).

Kiernan, V.G. *Poems from Iqbal* (London, 1922).

Krishna, G. 'The Development of the Indian National Congress as a Mass Organisation, 1918-1923', *Journal of Asian Studies*, XXV, May 1966.

Krishna, K.B. *The Problem of Minorities* (London, 1939).

Kumar, R. (ed.) *Essays on Gandhian Politics: The Rowlatt Satyagraha of 1919* (Oxford, 1971).

Latif, S.A. *The Influence of English Literature on Urdu Literature* (London, 1925).

Lavan, S. *The Ahmadiyah Movement: A History and Perspective* (Delhi, 1975).

Lawrence, Second Marquess of Zetland. *Essayez* (London, 1956).

Low, D.A. (ed.) *Soundings in Modern South Asian History* (University of California Press, 1968).

Lelyveld, D. 'Three Aligarh Students: Aftab Ahmad Khan, Ziauddin Ahmad and Muhammad Ali', *Modern Asian Studies*, Vol. 8, 1974.

List of Taluqdars in Oudh: Corrected up to 31st March 1920 (Lucknow, 1924).

Lytton, Lord. *Pundits and Elephants: Being the Experiences of Five Years as Governor of an Indian Province* (London, 1942).

Mahmud, S. 'Looking Back', *1921 Movement: Reminiscences* (Delhi, 1971).

Majumdar, B.B. *Indian Political Associations and Reforms of Legislature, 1918-1927* (Calcutta, 1960).

Majumdar, B.B. *History of Political Thought from Rammohun to Dayananda, 1821-1884*, Vol. I (Calcutta, 1934).

Malik, I.A. *Punjab Muslim Press and the Muslim World, 1888-1907* (Lahore, 1974).

Mcpherson, K. *The Muslim Microcosm: Calcutta, 1918 to 1935* (Heidelberg, 1974).

Mcpherson, K. 'The Political Development of the Urdu- and Tamil-speaking Muslims of the Madras Presidency 1901 to 1937' (Unpublished M.A. thesis, W. Australia, 1968).

Minault, G. and Lelyveld, D. 'The Campaign for a Muslim University', *Modern Asian Studies*, Vol. 8, 1974.

Minault, G. 'The Khilafat Movement: A Study of Indian Muslim Leadership, 1919-24' (Unpublished Ph.D. thesis, Pennsylvania, 1972).

Mannheim, K. *Ideology and Utopia: An Introduction to the Sociology of Knowledge* (New York, 1953).

Muhammad, S. *Sir Syed Ahmad Khan: A Political Biography* (Meerut, 1969).

Mujeeb, M. *The Indian Muslims* (London, 1967).

Nagar, P. *Lala Lajpat Rai: The Man and his Ideas* (Delhi, 1977).

Narain, P. *Press and Politics in India, 1885-1905* (Delhi, 1970).

Nehru, J. *Selected Works of Jawaharlal Nehru* (Orient Longmans, in process of publication, 1972—).

Nehru, J. *A Bunch of Old Letters*. 2nd edn. (Bombay, 1966).

Nizami, K.A. *Some Aspects of Religion and Politics in India during the thirteenth Century* (Bombay, 1961).

Noer, Deliar. *The Modernist Muslim Movement in Indonesia 1900-1942* (Oxford, 1973).

O'Dwyer, M. *India As I Knew It, 1885-1925* (London, 1925).

Owen, H.F. 'Negotiating the Lucknow Pact', *Journal of Asian Studies*, XXXI, May 1972.

Page, D.J.H. 'Prelude to Partition: All India Muslim Politics 1909-32' (Unpublished D. Phil. thesis, Oxford, 1973).

Pandey, B.N. (ed.) *Leadership in South Asia* (Delhi, 1977).

Parel, A. 'Symbolism in Gandhian Politics', *Canadian Journal of Political Science*, December 1969.

Parel, A. 'The Political Symbolism of the Cow in India' (Unpublished Seminar paper, July 1968).

Parmanand, B. *Hindu Sangathan* (Lahore, 1936).

Philips, C.H. (ed.) *The Evolution of India and Pakistan 1858-1947: Select Documents* (London, 1962).

Philips, C.H. (ed.) *Politics and Society in India* (London, 1963).

Pirzada, S. (ed.) *Quaid-e-Azam Jinnah's Correspondence* (Karachi, 1966).

Prakash, I. *Hindu Mahasabha, Its Contribution to Indian Politics* (Delhi, 1966).

Qadir, Abdul. 'The Proposed Mohamedan University', *Muslim Review*, October 1910.

Qureshi, M.N. 'Pan-Islamism and Nationalism: Muslim Politics in British India, 1918-1924' (Unpublished Ph.D. thesis, London, 1973).

Rab, A.S.M. *A.K. Fazlul Haq: Life and Achievements* (Lahore, n.d.).

Rahman, F. *Islam* (London, 1966).

Rahman, M. *From Consultation to Confrontation: a study of the Muslim League in British Indian Politics 1906-1912* (London, 1970).

Rai, L. *A History of the Arya Samaj* (Bombay, 1967).

Rai, L. *Unhappy India* (Calcutta, 1928).

Raina, K.M. *Welding the Nation: Academic Addresses and Selected Writings* (Bombay, 1974).

Ray, R.K. 'Masses in Politics: The Non-Cooperation Movement in Bengal 1920-22', *IESHR*, XI, December 1974.

Reading, Rufus Isaacs, *First Marquess of Reading, by his son, 1914-1935* (London, 1945).

Reeves, P.D. 'The Landlords' Response to Political Change in the United Provinces of Agra and Oudh, India, 1921-37' (Unpublished Ph.D. thesis, Australia National University, 1963).

Reid, H.S. *Report on Indigenous Education and Vernacular Schools* (Agra, 1852).

Rizvi, J.D. 'Muslim Politics and Government Policy: Studies in the development of Muslim organisation and its social background in North India and Bengal, 1885-1917' (Unpublished Ph.D. thesis, Cambridge, 1969).

Robinson, F. 'Municipal Government and Muslim Separatism in the United Provinces, 1883 to 1916', *Modern Asian Studies*, Vol. VII, 3, 1973.

Robinson, F. 'The Politics of U.P. Muslims 1906-1922' (Unpublished Ph.D. thesis, Cambridge, 1970).

Robinson, F. *Separatism Among Indian Muslims. The Politics of the United Provinces' Muslims, 1860-1923* (Cambridge, 1974).

Rudolph, S.H. and L.I. Rudolph (eds.) *Education and Politics in India* (Delhi, 1972).

Saggi, P.D. (ed.) *Life and Works of Lal, Pal and Bal* (Delhi, 1962).

Saiyad, M.H. *Mohammad Ali Jinnah: A Political Study* (Lahore, 1953).

Sarkar, S. *The Swadeshi Movement in Bengal, 1903-1908* (Delhi, 1973).

Schimmel, A. *Gabriel's Wing. A Study of the Religious Ideas of Sir Muhammad Iqbal* (Leiden, 1963).

Siddiqi, M.H. 'The Peasant Movement in Pratapgarh, 1920', *IESHR*, X, September 1972.

Seal, A. *The Emergence of Indian Nationalism: Competition and Collaboration in the Later Nineteenth Century* (Cambridge, 1968).

Smith, W.C. *Modern Islam in India* (London, 1946).

Smith, W.R. *Nationalism and Reform in India*. Reprint of 1938 edn. (Kennikat Press, 1966).

Thapar, R. Mukhia, H. Chandra, B. *Communalism and the Writing of Indian History* (Delhi, 1969).

Thursby, G.R. *Hindu-Muslim Relations in British India* (Leiden, 1975).

Thurston, E. *Caste and Tribes of South India* (Madras, 1909), Vol. IV.

Tinker, H. *The Foundations of Local Self-Government in India, Pakistan and Burma* (London, 1968).

Tripathi, A. *The Extremist Challenge: India Between 1890 and 1910* (Orient Longmans, 1967).

Tripathi, R.P. *Some Aspects of Muslim Administration* (Allahabad, 1936).

Vahid, M. *Thoughts and Reflections of Iqbal* (Lahore, 1944).

Washbrook, D.A. *The Emergence of Provincial Politics. The Madras Presidency, 1870-1920* (Cambridge, 1976).

Wasti, S.R. *Lord Minto and the Indian Nationalist Movement 1905 to 1910* (Oxford, 1964).

Zakaria, R. *Rise of Muslims in Indian Politics: an Analysis of Developments from 1885 to 1906* (Bombay, 1970).

Urdu

Abdullah, S.M. *Mushahidat wa Ta'asurat* (Aligarh, 1969).

Adalat Gaushala Parastan (Jubbulpore, 1922).

Ahmad, B. *Tark-i-Mavalat* (Deoband, 1920).

Ahmad, T. *Mussalmanon ka Raushan Mustaqbil* (Delhi, 1945).

Askari, K.M. 'Aligarh ki siyasi zindagi', *Aligarh Magazine*, 1953-55.

Ashraf, I. 'Mohamed Ali: Ek Sada-i-Shikast Saaz', *Aligarh Magazine*, 1960-61.

Azad, A.K. *Masla-i-Khilafat wa Jazirat-ul-Arab* (Calcutta. 1920).

Azad, A.K. *Maqalat-i-Al-Hilal* (Lahore, 1960).

Azad, A.K. *Khutbat-i-Abul Kalam Azad* (Lahore, n.d.).

Azad, A.K. *Mazameen-i-Abul Kalam Azad* (Delhi, 1944).

Aziz A.M. *Arz-i-Haal* (Monghyr, 1915).

Butalvi, A.H. *Iqbal ke Akhri do Sa'al* (Karachi, 1961).

Daisnavi, A.Q. *Hasrat ki siyasi zindagi ki chand jhalkian* (Patna, n.d.).

Daryabadi, A.M. *Mohamed Ali: Diary ke chand warq* (Hyderabad, 1943).

Daryabadi, A.M. *Maqalat-i-Majid* (Bombay, n.d.).

Ghaffar, A. *Hayat-i-Ajmal* (Aligarh, 1950).

Ghani, N. *Mazahab al-Islam* (Lucknow. 1924).

Ghazi, A. 'Aligarh ki Tehrik aur Jamia Millia', *Aligarh Magazine*, 1953-55.

Hakim, A. *Mr. Gandhi Mussalmanon ke hargiz khair khwah nahin hain*, IOL. Urdu. D. 652.

Hasan, Mahmudul. *Tark-i-Mavalat* (Bijnor, 1919).

Husain, G. *Dastan-i-Hijrat* (Amritsar, 1921).

Ikram, S.M. *Mauj-i-Kausar* (Lahore, 1970).

Ikram, S.M. *Rud-i-Kausar* (Karachi, 1958).

Islahi, N. (ed.) *Maktubat-i-Shaikhul Hind* (Deoband, 1954).

Jafri, R.A. (ed.) *Nigarishat-i-Mohamed Ali* (Hyderabad, 1944).

Kashmiri, S. 'Zafar Ali Khan', *Naqqush*, January 1955.

Khairuddin, K. *Islam me koi firqa nahin hai* (Lahore, 1921).

Khan, M.H.A. *Safarnamah-i-Medina-i-Munnawarah* (Lucknow, 1914).

Khwaja, A.M. *Home Rule se kiya matlab hai* (Aligarh, 1917).

Majid, A. *Dars-i-Khilafat* (Budaun, 1921).

Malihabadi, A.S. *Allah ke ghar men* (Calcutta, 1972).

Maududi, A.A. *Islami Ibadat pur ek nazar* (Lahore, 1958).

Mian, M. *Ulama-i-Haqq aur unke mujahidana karname* (Delhi, 1946).

Mirza, A. *Jazbat-i-Qaumi wa Mahatma Gandhi* (Lucknow, 1921).

Mohiuddin, *Faryad-i-Muslim* (Amritsar, 1921).

Mussalman-i-Panipat ki Bipta wa afsana (Delhi, 1926).

Muttafaqah fatwa Ulama-i-Hind (Meerut, 1920).

Nadvi, A.H. *Hindustan ki qadim Islami darsgahen* (Amritsar, n.d.).

Nizami, K.H. *Kanpur ki khuni kahani* (Meerut, 1913).

Numani, S. *Makatib-i-Shibli* (Azamgarh, 1928).

Numani, S. *Maqalat-i-Shibli* (Azamgarh, 1938).

Numani, M.M. *Deoband aur Bareilly ke Ikhtilaf wa naza par faisla kun munazara* (Sambhal, 1966).

Rashid, H. *Urdu adab aur Islam* (Lahore, 1968).

Rudad-i-Anjuman-i-Himayat-i-Islam (Lahore, 1900).

Sadiq, A. *Majlis-i-Mausuma Indian National Congress ki Nisbat* (Amritsar, n.d.).

Sarwar, M. *Khutut-i-Mohamed Ali* (Delhi, 1940).

Sarwar, M. *Mazameen-i-Mohamed Ali* (Delhi, 1940).

Yaldaram, S.H. *Hikayat wa Ehsasat* (Aligarh, 1930).

Zafiruddin, M. *Islam kanizam-i-masjid* (Delhi, 1961).

Zuberi, M.A. *Zia-i-Hayat* (Karachi, n.d.).

INDEX

The appendage of letter 'n' in the pagination statement refers to the footnotes on the respective pages.